A POLITICIAN TURNED GENERAL

A POLITICIAN
TURNED GENERAL

The Civil War Career of
Stephen Augustus Hurlbut

Jeffrey N. Lash

THE KENT STATE UNIVERSITY PRESS
KENT & LONDON

© 2003 by The Kent State University Press, Kent, Ohio 44242

All rights reserved.

Library of Congress Catalog Card Number 2003008139

ISBN 0–87338–766-x

Manufactured in the United States of America

07   06   05   04   03   5   4   3   2   1

LIBRARY OF CONGRESS CATALOGING-IN-PUBLICATION DATA

Lash, Jeffrey N. (Jeffrey Norman), 1949–

A politician turned general : the Civil War career of

Stephen Augustus Hurlbut / Jeffrey N. Lash

p.   cm.

Includes bibiliographical references and index.

ISBN 0–87338–766-x

1. Hurlbut, Stephen Augustus, 1815–1882. 2. Generals—United States—Biography. 3. United
States. Army—Biography. 4. Southwest, Old—History—Civil War, 1861–1865—Campaigns.
5. United States—History—Civil War, 1861–1865—Campaigns. 6. Politicians—Illinois—
Biography. 7. Republican Party (Ill.)—Biography. 8. Illinois—Politics and government—19th
century. 9. Charleston (S.C.)—Biography. I. Title.

E467.1.H95L37 2003

973.7'3'092—dc21

2003008139

British Library Cataloging-in-Publication data are available.

CONTENTS

PREFACE

This study is a comprehensive narrative account and an intensive critical examination of both the turbulent early political career and the subsequent and controversial record of the military, political, and diplomatic service rendered by Stephen Augustus Hurlbut, an Illinois Whig and Republican politician, lawyer, and orator who rose to distinction as a prominent member of the Union high command in the West during the Civil War. Specifically, it is a biographical study of a "military politician" who also served in the Union army as a "political general" by an appointment from President Abraham Lincoln. This deliberately proposed distinction is significant, even crucial, because difficult conceptual and semantic problems otherwise complicate the historical treatment and assessment of the Northern (and the fewer Southern) "soldier-politicians" and "political generals" who exercised command in the Civil War. In logic, these terms are largely misnomers, yet scholars have used them interchangeably to describe two altogether different creatures of the Civil War period. Ulysses S. Grant in particular has accordingly been characterized as a "soldier-president" during his two terms as chief executive, but one of his political biographers has clearly and convincingly portrayed Grant as essentially a soldier who occupied the White House and nowise a politician.[1]

Many similar examples of this ambiguity abound in studies of Nathaniel P. Banks and Benjamin F. Butler. Their careful biographers have indisputably demonstrated, however, that even in wartime both Banks and Butler functioned basically as party politicians and not as army officers.[2] It should be equally well understood that many Northern political generals, such as Jacob D. Cox and John A. Logan, exhibited conspicuous military ability. Conversely, many professional soldiers, most notably George B. McClellan, who was the Democratic party's presidential candidate in 1864, and Isaac I. Stevens, who was the national campaign manager for the southern wing of the Democratic party in 1860, showed consummate political skill. This important qualification notwithstanding, for the purposes of this study I will call Hurlbut a "political general"— indeed, advisedly, because he did function in that practical capacity. But Hurlbut cannot be described, primarily or essentially, as a volunteer militia officer or as, later, a Union army general. Obviously, he cannot be classified as a soldier who happened to possess an inherently political nature and inclination, and who moreover harbored a vaulting partisan ambition. Rather, Hurlbut should be viewed and treated fundamentally as a militarily inclined party politician.

Beyond clarifying such admittedly arbitrary and yet conceptually and analytically useful interpretative terms, the present book proposes to chronicle and examine the remarkable Civil War career of one of Abraham Lincoln's political generals, as well as the antebellum and postbellum stages of that career. Lincoln, in bestowing military patronage upon the influential Republican Banks and the "War Democrat" Butler so as to mobilize increased support for the Northern war effort in the East, alike conferred high rank upon seemingly deserving Republican and War Democratic politicians hailing from his home state of Illinois. Yet until recently scholars have attached a comparatively smaller importance to the several prominent western political generals—that is, to such military figures as John A. McClernand, Benjamin M. Prentiss, John A. Logan, Richard J. Oglesby, William H. L. Wallace, and Stephen A. Hurlbut.[3] Overall, however, this study will necessarily concentrate on the unfavorable consequences of Lincoln's appointment of Hurlbut to high military rank.

As a matter related to my interpretative approach, I will emphasize and explore two comprehensive themes that, I believe, can explain why Hurlbut succeeded for so long and then, perhaps inevitably, finally failed as a volunteer officer. I shall also identify the motives that actuated his official misconduct as a corps commander at Memphis and as an acting departmental and army commander at New Orleans, and seek to evaluate his highly erratic and unstable personal behavior, particularly in the context of his chronic heavy drinking—if not alcoholism.

Regarding Hurlbut's abuse of alcohol, it should be strongly emphasized that numerous general officers in both the Union and Confederate armies imbibed as freely as did Hurlbut, perhaps even more immoderately. Stephen A. Hurlbut, Gordon Granger, Joseph Hooker, and Lorenzo Thomas within the Union army, and Earl Van Dorn, George Bibb Crittenden, and William Henry Carroll in the Confederate army, to identify but a few officers, earned reputations as heavy drinkers during the war. For instance, in October 1863 the Reverend Samuel W. Fiske, a captain in the 14th Connecticut Volunteers (who under the pseudonym of "Dunn Browne" contributed to the widely distributed *Springfield [Massachusetts] Republican*), explained this sorry situation, to his own satisfaction at least, in an article that his editor aptly titled, "Whisky in the Army."

The Union army's commissariat probably aggravated the problem of habitual intemperance among Northern general officers. The Union army's commissariat by explicit regulation (applying specifically to the Army of the Potomac, if not also to several Union armies in the West) permitted the issuance each week, along with regular rations, of three gallons of hard liquor to each brigadier general and proportionately larger or smaller quantities to officers holding higher or lower rank. Moreover, as Reverend Fiske observed, a newly promoted Union general officer, celebrating his elevation, naturally found it customary to quaff liquor with his comrades in arms, to "wet his commission."[4] In 1887 an Army of the Potomac veteran asserted that the Union commissariat seldom issued "whiskey rations" to rank and file soldiers and then only by special order from the army's medical department. Officers, in contrast, could easily exploit their exemption from this strict policy: "They had only to send to the commissary to obtain as much as they pleased, *whenever* they pleased, by paying for it." Mournfully recalling the numerous lives lost as a consequence of drunken Union officers exercising command and directing tactical maneuvers on bloody battlefields, the veteran sorrowfully recalled that ordinarily "there was nothing but his sense of honor, his self-respect, or his fear of exposure and punishment" to restrain a captain, a colonel, or a general from "being intoxicated at a moment when he should have been in the full possession of his senses leading his command on to battle."[5]

Nevertheless, whatever the contribution of the commissariat's policy to Hurlbut's heavy drinking, and however common among other Union generals, the effects of his imbibing—much of it on duty and even amid active campaigning in Missouri and West Tennessee—upon his capacity for command were adverse. Finally, it should be understood that most competent medical authorities agree that alcoholism, whatever its physical or psychological origins, is a disease. Thus, Hurlbut's drinking, at least to some extent, can be regarded as a self-destructive habit or pathological addiction and not willful overindulgence.

The paramount theme of this book is Hurlbut's loyal membership in what was to coalesce into an "Illinois Clique" of Republican politicians. Hurlbut's adherence to Lincoln, Grant, and other members of that group constituted the durable basis of his prolonged, albeit checkered, public career. The Illinois Clique, formed in the antebellum period, originally comprised erstwhile Whig and Democratic politicians (except for Grant, a soldier subsequently brought into the set's inner circle) turned Republicans. Their alliance was not founded on any absolute or uniform philosophical compatibility on such vexed sectional issues as slavery in the western territories or the constitutionality of a state's right to secede from the Union. Rather, these men joined together to assert a common political commitment to antislavery goals, demonstrate their partisan solidarity in the interests of state and national Republican victory over the Democratic "slave power," and gratify individual greed for party spoils across Illinois and in

Washington. Wracked by bitter and incessant dissension over the postwar questions of military reconstruction and urgently needed civil service reform, this group began to disintegrate after the Liberal Republican revolt against President Grant in 1872. While it lasted, this strongly unified and highly self-conscious phalanx of immigrants (mostly born in New England and the upper South) to Illinois attracted, besides Hurlbut, such prominent Illinois Republicans as Abraham Lincoln, Orville H. Browning, Lyman Trumbull, Elihu B. Washburne, Richard Yates, Richard J. Oglesby, Joseph Russell Jones, Joseph Medill, John M. Palmer, David Davis, John A. Logan, and ultimately Ulysses S. Grant.

The second comprehensive theme of this book is twofold. First, I assess the successes and failures of Hurlbut's military leadership, both as a field commander in Missouri in 1861 and as a division commander at the Battles of Shiloh and Hatchie Bridge in 1862. Second, I examine the record of his official conduct as an army commander in occupied Memphis and New Orleans, successively, from 1863 to 1865. Too long sustained in commands in the West by Lincoln and supported in those positions by Illinois governor Richard Yates and powerful congressional members of the Illinois Clique, in recognition of his faithfulness to the Republican party and usefulness to the Union cause, Hurlbut mixed martial law with pecuniary gain. He created and operated cotton "rings" that employed intimidation, coercion, bribery, and extortion. Moreover, his exercise of command in Memphis and New Orleans contributed only ineffectively to the process of liberal reconstruction, as then promoted by President Lincoln, in Arkansas and Tennessee, or blatantly obstructed it, as in the case of Lincoln's "Ten Percent Plan" in Union-held Louisiana. Hurlbut also advocated and executed a policy—as did other such racially conservative Union generals such as Butler, Banks, and Edward R. S. Canby—of forcibly relocating large numbers of blacks (mostly runaway slaves, or contrabands, seeking the protection of the Union army) from Memphis, New Orleans, and elsewhere to farmers, plantation owners, and even to a remote island colony on the Mississippi River, without express War Department authorization. These themes taken together support the characterization of Hurlbut as essentially a well-intentioned but weak-willed and insecure man whose admirable qualities and exceptional abilities could not overcome proclivities to greed, alcohol, and misuse, if not outright abuse, of power.

In preparing this present study (as was the case only for my doctoral dissertation, which also covered Hurlbut's Civil War career and more thoroughly his postwar career) I have incurred heavy debts to librarians, historians, and archivists in the East, South, and Midwest. I gladly and eagerly thank the courteous and skilled staffs of the Library of Congress, the National Archives, the South

Carolina Department of Archives and History, the South Carolina Historical Society, the South Caroliniana Library, the College of Charleston Library, the Bowdoin College Library, the Ohio Historical Center, the Chicago Historical Society, the Illinois State Historical Library, the Kent State University Library, the John Carroll University Library, the University of Illinois Library, the library of the University of Wisconsin at Madison, and of other distinguished institutions devoted to historical investigation and humane learning.

I especially wish to express my gratitude to one of my former mentors at Kent State University, Dr. Frank L. Byrne, now a professor emeritus of history, for his lively interest in and sustained encouragement of both my dissertation and this subsequent study. By affording me the benefits of his creative imagination, broad knowledge, trenchant analysis, and constructive suggestions in research and writing, he made the preparation and completion of this study both possible and successful. I also hasten to thank my other mentor, Dr. John T. Hubbell, full professor of history, former editor of *Civil War History,* and director emeritus of The Kent State University Press, for having given the doctoral thesis his meticulous and careful scholarly attention. He has freely furnished incisive editorial judgment and criticism, as well as the benefit of his wide knowledge of Civil War military history, in the preparation of the present study. Moreover, I wish to acknowledge and to extend my sincere appreciation to Dr. Sanford E. Marovitz, a repeatedly honored emeritus professor of English at Kent State University, for having read and criticized the earlier dissertation and for stimulating ideas and intriguing interpretations concerning its subject.

Any remaining errors are, naturally, solely my responsibility. Finally, I wish to dedicate this short work covering a Civil War general's career to my daughters, Kimberley and Charmayne, who can lay claim to a proud military heritage.

Yankee Heritage

The Southern-born-and-bred Stephen Augustus Hurlbut was scarcely in a position to boast of his New England pedigree, but in fact he had a proud Yankee heritage. His Scottish Puritan ancestor Thomas Hurlbut, a twenty-five-year-old blacksmith by trade, had sailed to New England from London, England, aboard the ship *Bachelor* on August 11, 1635, and finally settled at Wethersfield, Connecticut. Subsequently, Thomas Hurlbut helped to build and then commanded Fort Saybrook, a palisaded outpost near the mouth of the Connecticut River, during successive Indian wars, and he fought with conspicuous gallantry during the bloody Pequot War of 1637. In the years from 1647 until his death in September 1689, Thomas Hurlbut received grants of land from the Connecticut General Assembly for his Indian-fighting service; the largest cession comprised 120 acres, which the lawmakers conveyed on October 12, 1671. Moreover, he functioned as a deputy to the Connecticut General Court, served as a grand juror in 1645 and as a tax collector in 1647, and discharged a constable's duties in 1664.[1] His most notable immediate descendants, Stephen Hurlbut and Christopher Hurlbut, continued the tradition of heroism and fortitude, performing dangerous land-surveying work for Connecticut's Susquehanna Company in the Wyoming Valley of Pennsylvania during the Pennamite Indian Wars of the 1770s and elsewhere in the wilderness throughout the Revolutionary War.[2]

Following his service in Pennsylvania, Stephen Hurlbut returned to New England. On May 1, 1780, at Southampton, Massachusetts, his wife gave birth

Martin Luther Hurlbut, educator and Unitarian apologist. Cleveland Museum of Art.

to a son, Martin Luther Hurlbut, who in turn would in 1815 beget Stephen A. Hurlbut. Martin graduated with high scholastic honors from Williams College in 1804—having achieved an impressive mastery of the classics—and afterward studied Calvinistic theology under the Reverend Dr. Jesse Appleton at Portsmouth, New Hampshire. A slightly built man with austere features, including a strikingly prominent nose, Martin Hurlbut in 1807 began preaching as a newly ordained Congregational minister. Early in 1808, however, owing to the debilitating effects of a chronic pulmonary disease and to an acute and troubling throat disorder, he abandoned the ministry, leaving cold and snowbound Portland, Maine, to serve as a temporary assistant instructor at Andover Academy in his native Massachusetts. Thereafter, he set sail for Brazil to recover his failing health. In the fall of 1811, during his return voyage to New England, Hurlbut's ship stopped at the insular port of Beaufort, South Carolina. There he proposed himself as a candidate for the presidency of Beaufort College. In January 1812, Hurlbut, who by then had continued on to Portsmouth, New Hampshire, learned that the school's board of trustees had formally elected him as president. He promptly accepted its offer.[3]

Originally established as a college in 1795, Beaufort had not yet achieved fully accredited baccalaureate status. In 1812 it remained a preparatory school for aspiring young male scholars.[4] Convinced that he could bestow increased scholastic prestige on Beaufort College and impressed by the favorable reports about the town of Beaufort by the world-renowned New England geographer, the Reverend Dr. Jedidiah Morse, Hurlbut made the strenuous journey. In Charleston, recovering from seasickness before continuing to Beaufort, he enjoyed the hospitality of the Reverend Dr. Isaac S. Keith, one of several pastors of the Congregational church in Charleston and a mutual friend of Hurlbut and the Reverend Morse. Early in March 1812 Hurlbut sailed for Beaufort. Exposed on deck for the two nights of the voyage, he was nauseated and shivering when he finally completed his trip.[5]

The town of Beaufort, situated on Port Royal Island below Charleston, functioned as a coastal center of provincial southern culture. Notwithstanding its warm climate and scenic location on the Atlantic seaboard, Martin Hurlbut grew increasingly disenchanted with Beaufort, and his growing sense of cultural alienation would one day profoundly influence his son, Stephen Augustus. South Carolina's individualistic society compounded this unease, and he abhorred the South's quasi-feudal slave civilization. His dissatisfaction with the Southern setting sprang specifically, however, from his initially turbulent relationship with James Louis Petigru, Beaufort College's chief tutor.

Petigru, the brilliant but irascible scion of an old South Carolina family, had graduated with a baccalaureate degree and academic honors from South Carolina College in 1809. Although only twenty years old, early in 1810 he had eagerly accepted a teaching assistantship at Beaufort College. When the college's president died in the fall of 1811, Petigru became acting president, assuming responsibility for administering the school. But the trustees insisted on holding a regular election for a permanent institutional head in December 1811. He commanded all the trustees' support, but they nonetheless elected Hurlbut over Petigru as the new president on the recommendation of the Reverend Dr. Appleton.[6]

Almost immediately upon assuming office, Hurlbut clashed violently with
both Petigru and the board of trustees over what Hurlbut considered the school's
inferior academic standards, lax disciplinary procedures, and physical deterioration. Aggravating the situation, he had an altercation with Petigru over an
attempt to install a piece of Petigru's domestic furniture in Hurlbut's private
quarters.[7] Realizing the futility of further strife, however, they finally resolved
their differences and formed an enduring friendship. More significantly, in later
years, because of their professional association and personal relations and owing to his gratitude and obligation to Martin Hurlbut, Petigru would bestow
legal and political patronage on Hurlbut's son.[8]

Hurlbut's negative perceptions of slavery and of South Carolina's egalitarian
and chauvinistic social philosophy and politics, in addition to his quarreling with
Petigru, complicated his adaptation to the exotic Beaufort environment. He wist-
fully recalled the "green fields and quiet firesides of the *North*" and found himself
utterly estranged "in this land of storms, democracy, & negroes." In September
1813 Hurlbut vehemently denounced institutionalized Negro slavery (to his former
mentor, Jesse Appleton), although he also expressed his own racial prejudice. But
while Hurlbut privately objected to slavery on moral and religious grounds, he
recognized the necessity of owning slaves if he was to discharge properly his
academic duties and maintain his bachelor's household at Beaufort.

As the War of 1812 began, Hurlbut did not sympathize with the overzealous
"War Hawks" of Beaufort and Charleston; he was philosophically a strong
Anglophile. He was also a pragmatic, patriotic New Englander who held pro-
nounced Federalist convictions. He feared that the South Carolina Democratic-
Republican party's "degenerate offspring," particularly the ardent young patriot
John C. Calhoun, would miscalculate and risk a losing military struggle with
England, thereby precipitating the subversion, perhaps the surrender, of his
country's sovereignty.[9]

Convinced of the validity of his social and political views, Hurlbut would
later raise his son Stephen as a liberal opponent of Southern chattel slavery and
as a conservative Unionist. Another crucial factor in Stephen's future hybrid
upbringing as a New England child of Charleston would be his father's union
by marriage with the Bunce family of Beaufort. In 1813 Hurlbut courted and
married twenty-year-old Lydia Bunce, one of three status-conscious daughters
of Capt. Jared Bunce, who claimed descent from Oliver Cromwell. Originally
from Connecticut, the elder Bunce had failed as a merchant but then became a
shipowner, operating a merchant vessel, the *Georgia,* between Philadelphia and
Charleston.[10] Despite their northern roots, both Lydia Bunce's sisters had married South Carolina divines. Sarah had already borne two sons, Benjamin M.

Palmer Jr. and Edward P. Palmer—the youngest members of the socially and intellectually prominent Palmer family of Beaufort and Charleston. Hurlbut had thereby married a Yankee woman but, through Lydia's sisters, had assured his descendants of a close affiliation with the Palmers and similarly influential southern families. However, Stephen never tried to form strong family ties with his southern kindred before he left Charleston in 1845, and he was to have little association with them after the secession of South Carolina.[11]

Notwithstanding the bright promise of the Hurlbut and the Palmer connections, Hurlbut's marriage to the frail young Lydia Bunce was trying. The difficult birth of his first son, William Henry Hurlbut in 1813 and the untimely death of his second son, George Edward Hurlbut, late in 1814 struck Hurlbut as justifying, indeed necessitating, departure from Beaufort College. Anticipating bleak prospects for his pedagogical career at Beaufort—particularly in the absence of Petigru, who had left the academy late in 1812—and worried that William Henry would succumb to the malaria that frequently plagued Beaufort, Hurlbut resigned and removed his wife and son to Charleston in December 1814.[12] Establishing himself and his family in a modest residence at 237 Meeting Street, within a racially mixed section of Charleston's East Bay District, Hurlbut promptly assumed charge of a preparatory school previously operated by the Reverend Benjamin M. Palmer Sr. He formally opened the Academy for Boys on New Year's Day 1815 in the same building that housed his family.[13]

On November 29, 1815, after eleven months of professional and financial success as a schoolteacher and principal, Martin and Lydia welcomed the birth of their third child, a son. They named him Stephen Augustus.

CHAPTER ONE

The Making of a Carolina Yankee

Charleston, South Carolina, boasted in 1815 of its status as the South's second largest seaport, ranking closely behind New Orleans. Charleston offered tidewater plantation owners and independent backcountry crop farmers alike an accessible harbor through which to move their cotton to the textile manufacturing centers in New England, the British Isles, and maritime European countries. It was also a port into which funneled a heavy volume of highly valuable and sorely needed finished goods produced by many competitive American, British, and European industries.[1] Charleston ranked as the sixth most densely inhabited city within the United States, although the slave population accounted for the bulk of the total. Consequently, Charleston had feared a slave insurrection since the outbreak of Gabriel's Rebellion in Richmond, Virginia, in 1800, and since then the city's black community had multiplied rapidly. By 1820 Charleston had 10,653 whites, 1,475 free blacks, and 12,652 slaves. Given the widespread residential and economic mixing of the two races in Charleston, most of the urban slaves inhabited quarters with or belonging to their owners. Charleston's slaves outnumbered whites in three of the four wards of the city, including both the South End and East Bay Districts, where Stephen A. Hurlbut grew up into early manhood.

The slave population constituted the city's lowest and least mobile class, performing household tasks or laboring on the wharves. Not infrequently, urban slaveholders manumitted females and elderly bondservants, but this practice seldom elevated younger male slaves into the ranks of black freemen. Not far above this servile class stood the free blacks, whether emancipated or free-born; a few prospered, but most survived as independent but marginal artisans. A large working class of whites toiled in Charleston's flour mills, manufacturing establishments, and shipyards, while a highly educated and increasingly prominent professional class—professors, schoolmasters, and tutors, pastors and divines, lawyers, physicians, and entrepreneurs—also expanded and flourished. But the agrarian and mercantile aristocracies (socially and culturally compatible and economically interdependent groups) formed the highest and easily the most prestigious class in Charleston. The tidewater and Low Country cotton nabobs and merchant kings maintained opulent mansions in Charleston, wielding unchallenged political supremacy and financial influence.[2]

Within its class structure, the city exhibited a remarkable pattern of cultural pluralism and ethnic diversity, and it boasted a cosmopolitan range of artistic, educational, and religious activities. The young Hurlbut came to maturity in an exclusive and highly sophisticated world of neoclassical education. Indeed, owing to his father's success as a schoolmaster and his social prominence, Hurlbut grew up in affluent circumstances. After moving his wife Lydia and sons to several different addresses in Charleston, Martin Hurlbut had organized a flourishing boarding school within the academic buildings abandoned by the College of Charleston in 1818. He settled his family in a luxuriously furnished residence at 8 Montague Street, in the East Bay District, not far from the seacoast. Besides teaching eighty-five young scholars in his academy, Hurlbut also boarded eleven students at his spacious home.[3] His annual income of seven thousand dollars allowed him to participate in social and cultural pursuits that enriched his family's life.

But believing Northern social values and the peculiar philosophical and theological ideas of New England's intellectual class markedly superior to those of Southern slave society, Martin Hurlbut, along with other New England–born-and-educated clergymen, such as the Reverend Dr. Samuel A. Gilman, helped to found a separatist Unitarian congregation in Charleston in 1817. Renouncing his membership in Charleston's Congregational church in that year, Hurlbut resolved to rear his sons as Unitarians. Adherents of traditional Congregationalism affirmed the doctrine of the Holy Trinity, accepted the divinity of Jesus, and subscribed to the truth of his moral teachings and to the historicity of his miracles as described in the New Testament. Unitarians, however, denied the Trinity and rejected the deity of Jesus; they maintained instead that God existed, or subsisted, as one person or being, although they readily accepted the moral precepts as pronounced by Jesus and the historical authenticity of his miracles. The Unitarians strenuously denied the "monstrous" Calvinistic doctrine of total depravity and affirmed rather the perfectibility of man. Thus, when Martin Hurlbut, his wife Lydia, and their two children joined Charleston's Congregationalist Archdale Church in 1817 advocating this New England–rooted heterodoxy, he found himself subjected to ostracism and censure.[4] In 1822 Hurlbut edited eleven issues of *The Unitarian Defendant* and gained for Unitarians a secure place in Charleston's religious life and ecclesiastical structure.[5]

Hurlbut's affiliation with Charleston's nascent New England Society (NES), founded in January 1819 by Yankee immigrants to South Carolina, more definitely reflected his fundamental belief in northern cultural superiority. Initially composed of about forty-seven members (Hurlbut, who helped frame its constitution, gained formal membership in April 1819), the New England Society steadily added to its membership until it represented an influential and highly self-conscious Yankee minority in Charleston. Created to provide charity for transplanted northern families in Charleston and to preserve and perpetuate the northern cultural heritage, the New England Society served as a sanctuary, or cultural enclave, for alienated Yankee commercial folk and professional men.[6] The national appearance of the Democratic-Republican party (the precursor of the Democratic party) in the late 1820s intensified Hurlbut's growing incompatibility with Charleston society. An adherent of traditional Federalist principles (although the Federalist party itself had been defunct since 1816), Hurlbut avoided openly challenging the Democratic-Republican hegemony in Charleston. But he and fellow conservatives in the New England Society banded together to form the nucleus of what emerged as a more culturally and sectionally diverse Whig party—or at least political following—in Charleston.[7]

Significant elements, then, in Stephen's early years were the profound influences exerted by his father's classical learning and broad theological education, his Yankee cultural bias, his liberal Unitarian creed, and his northern brand of ardent, politically conservative nationalism. Martin, expressing a father's pride, assured Reverend Appleton in February 1819 that both his boys impressed him as "noble fine fellows" and that the district of Charleston could "show nothing like them" in intellectual precocity. He had already enrolled the boys in his boarding school, where his hired assistant instructed them in reading, writing, and grammar.[8]

However, the presence of black slaves in the Hurlbut household exercised an equally important influence on Stephen's development. Since 1812, the elder Hurlbut, a paternalistic and humane master, had owned nine slaves, including seven females. The bondservants both served as tangible symbols of bourgeois respectability in Charleston and cared for his wife Lydia and their two sons, as well as for the eleven young boarders. In November 1819 Martin felt compelled to sell five of these slaves. He had not managed his money prudently. He had spent excessively, continuing to do so even when the banking crisis associated with the Panic of 1819 paralyzed the national and the South Carolina econo-mies. The five slaves, members of a fatherless slave family, went to settle a nine-teen-hundred-dollar debt.[9]

Worse developments soon befell the Hurlbuts. In 1820 Martin and Lydia buried an infant son; in January of 1821 Lydia, only twenty-eight, died giving birth to a stillborn child. Two years later, in June 1823, Stephen's older brother, William Henry, succumbed to tubercular fever.[10] In 1822 they and other white inhabitants of Charleston had been unsettled to learn of a conspiracy in which a free black artisan, Denmark Vesey, had plotted a servile insurrection in Charles-ton.[11] This incident, combined with the deaths of four loved ones and his grow-ing financial problems, led to his decision in 1825 to remove his family from Charleston. Before leaving, however, he married Margaret Morford of Princeton, New Jersey, the daughter of a Revolutionary War officer. Selling his last four slaves in 1825 to a fellow Unitarian, Hurlbut moved his family to Philadelphia.[12]

But trouble followed. Martin Hurlbut experienced serious difficulty in com-mencing a new teaching career in Philadelphia, then buried yet another infant son. Finally, following the baptism of his wife by a Unitarian minister in Sep-tember 1826, Hurlbut returned, mortified but still hopeful, with his surviving family to Charleston.[13]

There he resumed his pedagogical career, obtaining in July 1827 a school-teacher's post under the auspices of the benevolent and philanthropic South Carolina Society, which had undertaken the task of educating the sons of its poorer members. Hurlbut did not accept this position in the society's Male Academy from a belated sense of cultural attachment to Charleston; rather, he did so because of financial necessity. He settled his family on Meeting Street in South Bay, where Stephen had been born twelve years earlier.[14]

Martin continued his active service in the New England Society, and he main-tained his ideological hostility toward South Carolina's states' rights advocates. Of particular significance for his son Stephen was his vehement opposition to the growing nullification movement, which now threatened disruption of the Union. Spearheaded by Vice President John C. Calhoun, the South Carolina Low Country planters protested what they detested as the Tariff of Abomina-tions of 1828. The cotton magnates and rice planters blamed their acute misfor-tunes on the national tariff alone, but they also sought to exploit their anti-protectionist and nullification argument to suppress the increasingly strident northern abolitionist attack on slavery. To help discredit the nullificationists,

Hurlbut published in 1828 at his own expense an anonymous brochure, *Review of a Late Pamphlet,* in which he expounded his interpretation of the Constitution and demonstrated the lack of logic in Calhoun's theory of nullification.[15] In this polemical manner Hurlbut had begun to instill into his precocious young son Stephen what he deemed the patriotic virtues of what before 1816 had been Federalist nationalism.

The nullification crisis intensified, but the Hurlbuts rejoiced in 1827 over Martin's renewed financial success and the birth of another son, William Henry Hurlbut II. By 1830 Martin had rented another spacious house, at 96 Church Street in South Bay, and had bought four other slaves, including a woman over a hundred years old.[16] But this rehabilitation of the family's fortunes only preceded a dreary repetition of earlier calamities. After losing another three infants to premature death and falling prey himself to a progressively severe case of tuberculosis, Martin sold his slaves and returned to Philadelphia in 1831. There he established a successful boarding school and rose to serve as a prominent member of the city's Unitarian society. He put his sons into his institution and other private academies, where Stephen in particular studied law, foreign languages, and classical literature until January 1837.[17] After completing his preparatory studies, Stephen agreed with his father that he should return to Charleston to pursue a career as a lawyer. Beckoned by bright prospects of professional success and distinction in South Carolina, especially if he should read law under the eminent lawyer and jurist (and Martin Hurlbut's old friend) James Louis Petigru, he sailed from Philadelphia for Charleston. Stephen kept no single address in Charleston, but in January 1837 he lived in Ward Two, on Meeting Street, close to Petigru's office.[18]

Then twenty-two, the young Hurlbut was supported by remittances sent by his father. In 1837 he passed his examinations and gained admittance to the Charleston bar, of which he remained an active member until 1845.[19] He lacked the means and experience necessary to open a private law office in Charleston; he hoped instead to study further with Petigru. The state's foremost Unionist Whig and opponent of Calhoun, Petigru had served as a professional reference for the elder Hurlbut when in 1838 he moved his Classical and English School in Philadelphia to a "large and convenient mansion" in that northern metropolis.[20]

Obliging Hurlbut again in 1840, Petigru employed Stephen as manager and chief clerk of his law office, at 12 St. Michael Alley; Hurlbut then resided at 20 Laurens Street. Petigru assigned to him a number of minor cases. In May 1842, for instance, Hurlbut assumed direction of the case of Ann Farmer, a Charleston widow. Lacking resources following her deeply indebted husband's death, Mrs. Farmer attempted to satisfy the creditor by disposing of one of her inher-

James Louis Petigru, South Carolina Whig and Unionist. Prints and Photographs Division, Library of Congress.

ited slaves. She met with Hurlbut, who drew up a contract stipulating that he would receive from her a note assigning him one hundred dollars and that he would sell her the eighteen-year-old "negro boy called Joseph" at auction. Hurlbut also obtained from Mrs. Farmer an agreement paying his expenses assigning him a standard 2.5 percent commission of the total proceeds from the sale of her slave; in all, he earned a substantial fee on the transaction.[21] The significant aspect of the Farmer case, insofar as it involved Hurlbut, concerned his attitude toward slavery. Although taught by his father to abhor the peculiar institution, Hurlbut found it professionally necessary to work within the institution of slavery. He eventually developed a deep racial prejudice against blacks. Later, as a Whig party legislator and Republican party campaigner in Illinois, he would claim that he had never participated in the domestic slave trade; his prompt disposal of Farmer's bondsman in 1842 belies that assertion.

A more significant and challenging action for Hurlbut occurred late in July 1843, when he advocated both in chambers and publicly the case of Capt. John Mullings. That plaintiff, the leader of twenty-seven steamboat pilots licensed by the Charleston City Council to operate in the Port of Charleston, had allegedly failed to fulfill his obligation to the owner of the brig *Stephen*. According to the council's Pilot Ordinance, a pilot could contract with a shipowner to take a merchant's vessel out to sea. By undertaking a second contract, he could sail, or arrange to sail, a second ship out of Charleston Harbor that same day and receive compensation in advance for both. Therefore, on April 28, 1843, Mullings had contracted with two merchants—the owners of the *Moses* and the *Stephen*—to guide the brigs to insular or coastal ports along South Carolina's seaboard. On April 29 Mullings piloted the *Moses* out of Charleston's harbor, but the pilot whom he had engaged to steer the *Stephen* out to sea failed to do so. Mullings bore the responsibility, and James Robertson, owner of the *Stephen*, lodged a complaint of "neglect of duty" against him. When summoned before the Board of Pilotage, Mullings denied the charge and moreover insulted Robertson. The city councilmen unanimously revoked Mullings's license. Chagrined and aggrieved, Mullings instituted a suit against the city council and the Board of Pilotage, complaining that both bodies had violated his constitutional right to a hearing and to the benefit of counsel.

Acting independently of Petigru (for in mid-October 1842 Hurlbut had announced the opening of his own law office at 25 Broad Street, there to practice law within the districts of Charleston and Georgetown), Hurlbut pressed Mullings's case. He gained the support of several lawyers, including Christopher G. Memminger, a prominent German-born lawyer and the future Confederate treasury secretary. Yielding to intense pressure from lawyers and residents, on August 24 both the city council and the Board of Pilotage restored Mullings's license. Hurlbut and his cohorts had previously called for a massive demonstration, and on the night of August 25 they assembled their followers in Temperance Hall, as they had planned. There Hurlbut proposed a series of specific resolutions condemning the earlier "arbitrary" revocation of Mullings's license—although he acknowledged the "tardy justice" that the municipal lawmakers had since rendered for Mullings. Hurlbut moreover demanded the modification or outright repeal of the Pilot Ordinance, thereafter sending to the city council and to Mayor John Schnierle memorials pleading for such action.[22] Hurlbut had properly invoked Mullings's constitutional rights, but his exceedingly zealous support of the suit also represented an attempt, as a Whig, to oust the Democratic aldermen who continued to dominate city council.

Indeed, Hurlbut's intrusion into municipal politics in the Mullings case co-incided with increasing participation in South Carolina politics. Imitating a pattern followed by many others, Hurlbut pursued three avenues to political distinction as a Whig politician in an overwhelmingly Democratic South Caro-lina: the law, the state militia, and civic organizations. Entertaining little expec-tation of substantial influence, Hurlbut strove to acquire not power or privilege but prestige and popularity. This pattern of ambitious public conduct began with his entrance to the Charleston bar in 1837 and continued with service in the Seminole War in Florida in 1840. Most of Hurlbut's legal colleagues and political friends—men such as John H. Honour, James H. Taylor, William Blanding, John Schnierle, and Francis Lance—could boast of Indian-fighting experience. Perhaps desiring to equal their military prowess and their impres-sive arts of command, Hurlbut might have sought service in Florida to enhance his reputation as a rising Whig politician.

Accordingly, when the recurrent Seminole War erupted once again in Florida in the winter of 1840, Hurlbut joined an elite company of the 17th South Caro-lina Militia Regiment, styled since 1807 the Washington Light Infantry. Seek-ing an eventual appointment as an officer, Hurlbut exercised his growing ability as an orator. Thus when on February 22, 1840, the Washington Light Infantry commemorated the birthday of Gen. George Washington by marching in a grand procession from its parade grounds to the sanctuary of the Unitarian Church on Archdale Street, Hurlbut "pronounced an elegant and tasteful ora-tion." For his oratorical ability and proficiency at close-order drill, he was quickly raised to the rank of sergeant. Hurlbut's comrades in arms recognized his intel-ligence and energy and later elevated him to commissioned rank in the position of regimental adjutant, under Col. Francis Lance. Hurlbut accompanied his crack unit to St. Augustine, where initially he did routine garrison duty on the Atlantic coast (besides gaining a knowledge of Spanish). Subsequently, he par-ticipated in reconnaissance operations across the Florida swamps, but he and his regiment failed to engage the Seminoles in a battle.[23]

Leaving service after the war as a first lieutenant, Hurlbut proudly returned to Charleston in September 1840 to celebrate the martial success of his com-pany. On February 4, 1841, along with his close friend William Blanding (also a Whig lawyer), Hurlbut served as a junior manager for the Annual Military Ball of the Washington Light Infantry, held at Charleston's Hibernian Hall on Meet-ing Street. He sold tickets to the gala affair and donned his resplendent dress uniform for the occasion. Together with Blanding and the senior managers of the ball, Petigru and General Schnierle, Hurlbut greeted over two hundred militiamen and their ladies, as well as upward of four hundred civilians and military and naval officers from the federal forts and garrisons in Charleston

Harbor. It was a festive and formal atmosphere of stirring martial music and "the whirling waltz and the crowded promenade."

Hurlbut had embarked on his career as a militarily minded politician. Hurlbut thereafter gained the rank of major in the 17th Regiment, which was part of the 4th Brigade of the South Carolina Militia. Finally, on March 4, 1845, Gov. William Aiken reviewed the exercises of the 16th and 17th Regiments at the Charleston Race Course. The *Charleston Mercury* reported admiringly that "several evolutions were performed, displaying much military skill and tactics and highly creditable to both officers and privates." Hurlbut and his fellow militiamen thereafter attended a grand "Military Ball of the Fourth Brigade" before participating in a 4th Brigade encampment at Camp Magnolia early in April 1845.[24] More significant for his career than his demonstrated mastery of infantry drill, however, was the fact that Hurlbut had earlier attracted the attention of a regular army officer at military functions.

Among the few Northern officers whom Hurlbut had chanced to meet and befriend in the early 1840s was the twenty-two-year-old 1st Lt. William Tecumseh Sherman. An Ohio native who had graduated from the U.S. Military Academy in 1840, Sherman had served in Florida during the Seminole War and as a quartermaster at Fort Moultrie in Charleston. Indeed, after June 1842 Sherman, who "formed many and most pleasant acquaintances in the city of Charleston," established a congenial friendship with Hurlbut, who in turn, as Sherman later recalled, "took a special interest in military matters."[25] Although the two men parted company in 1845, they would meet some sixteen years later in St. Louis, where Sherman's recollections of their friendship would contribute to his favorable estimation of Hurlbut's ability as a drillmaster of Union infantry at Benton Barracks.

If Hurlbut's service in the Washington Light Infantry had proceeded from determination to advance his political career, his cultivation of Sherman manifested an equally important ambition. Hurlbut aspired to prominence as a South Carolina militia officer (and later as the captain of a local military company in Illinois) because he sought to identify himself with younger members of the professional officer corps who had graduated from West Point. Indeed, as the status and prestige of regular officers like Sherman continued to grow, Hurlbut and many other Whig and Democratic politicians throughout the country sought to create and command volunteer militia units or military companies. Thus he acted not merely to reassert the old "citizen-soldier" tradition of patriotic service but to identify himself with West Point officers.

Hurlbut's participation in four civic organizations completed the groundwork for his rise as a southern Whig politician. Determined to secure his position in Charleston's society, Hurlbut joined the New England Society early in 1840. Still a proudly self-conscious, yet antiseparatist, minority group in South Carolina, the NES in 1840 included the sons of conservative Whig merchants, aspiring cotton and rice factors (brokers), and professional men.[26] Hurlbut's affiliation with the NES served three principal purposes: to preserve his Yankee cultural heritage, to assert his Whig political loyalty, and to gain legal business for his mentor, James Louis Petigru. Hurlbut began his service in the NES on a spectacular occasion. In April 1840 he paraded with William Blanding, William C. Breeze, Benjamin J. Howland, and other NES members in a grand procession of local civic organizations to celebrate the opening of the new Apprentices Library Society Building in Charleston. Hurlbut then served as a steward for the NES in December 1841, providing refreshments for the group's twenty-third annual anniversary dinner, at Stewart's Carolina Hotel on Broad Street. Hurlbut was elected as the society's treasurer and secretary for two consecutive terms, in 1843 and 1844.

However, he relinquished his offices to Blanding after June 1845 under a heavy cloud of suspicion.[27] In 1863, many years after this sudden resignation, a former NES member informed Col. Augustus O. Andrews (the wartime editor of the *Charleston Daily Courier*) that as the treasurer of the society in 1845, Hurlbut had agreed to serve as the sole assignee for the financially stricken group under the state's Bankruptcy Act. Hurlbut's erstwhile society associate accused him, without proof, of having defaulted as the NES's fiduciary. He further suggested that Hurlbut, actuated by greed and malice, had embezzled a portion of the organization's scanty funds.[28] Assuming the man's recollections to be accurate, this circumstance could have contributed to Hurlbut's departure from Charleston in 1845.

Hurlbut's service in the New England Society, however questionable the circumstances of that incident, coincided with his participation in the Charleston chapter of the International Independent Order of Odd Fellows, a secret fraternal and benevolent society founded in England in the eighteenth century. The Charleston chapter, established in 1840, lacked the social status of the local chapter of the competing Society of Freemasonry, an international secret society having comparable organizational goals. Composed largely of young, unmarried, and aspiring bourgeois professional men—such as slaveholder and insurance agency president John H. Honour and former Connecticut merchant and temperance advocate James H. Taylor—Charleston's Odd Fellows also drew members from the ranks of Seminole War veterans and lawyers, men like Francis Lance, John Schnierle, Peter D. Torre, and Hurlbut himself. The Masons attracted such men as Rev. Albert Case, who joined in December 1840 and boasted of the society's growing number of locally prominent Democratic and Whig party members.[29] The gregarious Hurlbut affiliated himself with Charleston's First Most Worthy Grand Lodge of the Independent Order of Odd Fellows in December 1841 and quickly rose to serve as the Noble Grand of the Howard Lodge of Odd Fellows, Number Three. As this group's chief presiding officer, Hurlbut superintended 158 officers and members, administered bylaws, guarded lodge property, and enforced the payment of dues.[30]

Known to his superiors as a conscientious and efficient lodge shepherd as well as a gifted orator, Hurlbut late in December 1841 agreed to speak at the first annual anniversary celebration of the Most Worthy Grand Lodge on New Year's Day, 1842. Peter D. Torre, the Grand Lodge's Right Worthy Deputy Grand Master, previously chosen to explain the principles and purposes of the Odd Fellows to the uninitiated general public of Charleston, had fallen ill; Hurlbut had succeeded him in office. Recognizing a propitious rhetorical opportunity, Hurlbut hurriedly prepared a suitable address. On January 1, 1842, clad in the full regalia of an Odd Fellow, he accompanied the order's colorful procession through the East Bay to the First Baptist Church, where he participated in ritual exercises before thousands of curious and baffled spectators. He then delivered a voluble oration, ostensibly to celebrate the founding of his society. In truth, Hurlbut sought to protect, consolidate, and expand his threatened order in its struggle against the political agitation then occurring in the North, in which seemingly fanatical opponents had attacked the followers of Freemasonry and, by association, Odd Fellowdom.

Fearing that such secret societies could subvert the American two-party system and undermine the tradition of open self-government, such northern politicians as Thaddeus Stevens of Pennsylvania strongly opposed the allegedly aristocratic organizations of Freemasonry and Odd Fellowship. Hurlbut specifically denounced those who were proscribing his society (and indirectly threatening his chances for professional success and political advancement). Indeed, "the rude jostling of the world, its petty struggles, its miserable heartburnings and jealousies," he declared, only "fall dead and blinded before the majesty of our order." He invited broadminded members of his audience to affiliate themselves with his society.[31] Hurlbut's call fell on responsive ears. Beginning with only thirty members in 1840 in its Howard Lodge in Charleston, the Odd Fellows grew by September 1843 to nearly twelve hundred initiates (belonging to one grand lodge and eight subordinate lodges, four within Charleston and the other four elsewhere across South Carolina), a massive increase largely attributable to Hurlbut's exceptional organizational skills and his oratorical forcefulness. The *Charleston Courier* recognized the quality of this, his earliest political declamation, characterizing it as "a chaste and eloquent oration" delivered before "a numerous and gratified audience of both sexes."[32] Indeed, Hurlbut's ringing Odd Fellows address, whatever the validity of his arguments, demonstrated his greatest asset—his powerful oratory. Moreover, his oration marked the formal beginning of the forensic, or polemic, aspect of his career as a politician.

In January 1843, after months initiating young novices into Howard Lodge, Hurlbut celebrated the second Odd Fellows anniversary in Charleston. But by this time he desired more than public notice. Possessed of a speculative spirit, he and other Odd Fellows concocted a quasi-philanthropic scheme to convert the society into a corporate enterprise. In league with Taylor, Lance, and Ker Boyce from the Bank of Charleston, Hurlbut and his associates advertised an intention to sell shares of stock to local investors to fund construction of an Odd Fellows Hall in Charleston. Their ambitious plan succeeded. By the fall of 1843, they had collected $11,489 in relief revenue and building funds. The organization, however, had spent only $1,341 to ameliorate the plight of needy families of Odd Fellows members and Charleston's indigent population. Neither did the lodge immediately raise its edifice in Charleston; however, it presumably contributed a substantial sum to help erect a national hall (worth sixty-thousand dollars) in Baltimore in 1843.[33] Thus, Charleston's Odd Fellows had diverted the bulk of the solicited assets into their private corporate account. Hurlbut traveled north to Baltimore in September 1843 as the secretary of the Right Worthy Grand Lodge of South Carolina. There, at the Grand Lodge of the United States, he received "repeated demonstrations of respect." In "an eloquent and powerful oration," he spoke for over an hour, essentially repeating his Charleston address of January 1842 but emphasizing the significance of the substantial growth of South Carolina's own Grand Lodge. He attended the third anniversary celebration of Odd Fellowship in January 1844—somewhat unnecessarily, perhaps, since he had effectively exploited the organization since 1841 and had already gained wide recognition as a benevolent Whig politician.[34]

Along with Hurlbut's association with Odd Fellowship came in particular an affiliation with the philanthropic South Carolina Society. One of the more prestigious and munificent of Charleston's numerous benevolent groups, the now venerable South Carolina Society had sprung from the Two-Bit Club that French-born residents had organized in 1737 for the relief of needy French Huguenot immigrants. Outwardly to demonstrate his public spirit but perhaps also to promote his political career, Hurlbut joined the society in February 1842; he was the 1,324th Carolinian to be admitted. Hurlbut occasionally attended the meetings, but his connection with this group was peripheral and could not produce a creditable record of benevolent or significant humanitarian accomplishment.

The society struck him from its rolls for failure to pay dues after 1845.[35] Hurlbut's slight association with the South Carolina Society was another clear demonstration of his lack of strong identification with southern society and culture. Having been raised as a New England child of Charleston by his father and imbued with the peculiar doctrines, theories, and principles of Unitarian theology and Federalist ideology, he developed no firm attachment to the land of his birth, education, and training.

Paralleling Hurlbut's participation in the New England Society, the Independent Order of Odd Fellows, and the South Carolina Society was an involvement with the American Republican Association of Charleston (ARA), beginning in June 1844. Organized as the South Carolina branch of the New York–based American Republican Party by Henry Gourdin, a highly conservative southern Unionist from Charleston, the ARA had effectively functioned as a Charleston nativist organization. Composed predominantly of Whig xenophobes, the ARA sought to use the national issues of divisive antiforeignism and anti-Catholicism—vexed questions vividly demonstrated by tumultuous riots pitting American Protestants against chiefly immigrant Irish Catholics in Philadelphia in 1844—to defeat the South Carolina proslavery and states' rights Democracy. Although Gourdin repudiated a growing following in the North and professed support of immigration into the United States, he attempted to stem the ever-mounting waves of Irish Catholic and German immigration by advocating changes in the naturalization laws. He demanded that Congress extend the period of probation for prospective foreign-born American citizens from five years to fifteen years and that authorities legislate against mass naturalizations conducted by municipal and state court justices on the eve of elections. In this respect, the embattled Charleston Whigs stood to lose crucial electoral support to the Calhoun Democrats, who generally won the foreign vote. The ARA's opposition to German immigration in particular sprang from both nativist cultural bias and a Whig political calculation. Late in the 1830s, increasingly massive waves of *Neudeutschen,* "New Germans," had begun arriving in Charleston. Although the newcomers practiced a Protestant Lutheran faith, as had previous groups of German immigrants (dating from the 1750s), the *Neudeutschen* hailed almost exclusively from the northern states of Germany, not from the western and southern districts of that country. Moreover, the New Germans spoke their own dialect of German, intermarried freely with Anglo Americans and other established ethnic groups in Charleston, and, unlike their predecessors, had begun rapidly assimilating into Charleston's society, a circumstance evidenced by their uniform residential distribution throughout the city (instead of dwelling within formerly isolated German enclaves).

Finally, the *Neudeutschen* had adopted a political philosophy or ideology similar to views of other large German populations in Richmond and New Orleans and had taken them even farther; they supported the prosecessionist and proslavery ideas of the South Carolina Democracy. Therefore, Hurlbut and his ARA cohorts saw these New Germans as a doubly formidable force within the Democratic party—a rapidly growing and tightly unified ethnic constituency in the party, and also an increasingly prominent, articulate, and intransigent ideological element explicitly committed to states' rights and the perpetuation of slavery.

Aside from the challenge of an alliance of the *Neudeutschen* with the already dominant Calhoun Democracy, the allegedly adverse effects of New German immigration on the social fabric of predominantly Anglo American and Irish and French institutions in Charleston antagonized and roused Hurlbut and his Whig associates. Thus, although only a recent convert to nativism, Hurlbut strongly subscribed to the ARA's exclusionist policies. He rose to the post of a corresponding secretary for the organization. Perhaps equally significant for the unfolding of his political career was his affiliation through the ARA with William Henry Trescot, who would become a leading South Carolina secessionist in 1861 and a special envoy to Peru and Chile in 1882.[36]

Obviously, the nativist agitation of Gourdin, Hurlbut, and Trescot failed to check the flow of New Germans and other immigrants. In fact, Hurlbut showed insincerity in his support of the ARA's proscriptive program. He counted among his circle of friends Ker Boyce and John Schnierle—men of Irish and German descent—and particularly Christopher G. Memminger, a German immigrant who had collaborated with him in the Mullings case.

Notwithstanding Hurlbut's demonstration of nativist prejudice in 1844, his involvement with fraternal and philanthropic civic organizations in Charleston set the stage for his emergence as a southern Whig politician. He first achieved a degree of political prominence in the wake of the celebrated Log Cabin Campaign of 1840. South Carolina had ranked as one of the strongest Democratic states in the Union before President Andrew Jackson defeated the state's nullification movement in 1832. But Jackson's action had alienated many South Carolina Democrats, who thereafter formed a radical Calhoun faction in the state. Other erstwhile Democratic-Republican party members in South Carolina who had opposed Jackson's economic policies in 1832 later banded with old-line National Republicans and conservative Unionists to organize a Whig grouping, chiefly in Charleston. No regular Whig party ever struck roots in South Carolina, although the state's large Whig following embraced a broad range of economic interest groups and social classes. Throughout the presidential campaign of 1840, the Whigs challenged the radical assertions of states' rights, their strict construction of the federal Constitution in defense of slavery and in perpetuation of the Southern political control of the national government. Whig ideologues and strategists like Petigru and George Bryan collaborated with Northern-born East Bay merchants, tidewater planters, and backcountry farmers to oppose the Calhoun Democracy and to promote an ideology of responsible political conservatism and a strong economic nationalism.[37]

South Carolina Whigs despaired of achieving significant electoral gains in their native state, but the Charleston wing, including Petigru and Bryan, sought at least to place conservative Charleston Democrats, such as Ker Boyce, into the state legislature. During the boisterous campaign of 1840, the twenty-five-year-old Hurlbut thrust himself into the arena of South Carolina's Whig politics. In a frenzied partisan atmosphere marked by greatly increased popular participation in electoral politics, Hurlbut became involved in a campaign of banners and torchlight parades, glowing bonfires and flag-waving rallies, enthusiastic political club meetings, and rousing stump speeches. He also drank the hard cider that was the Whig party's distinctive campaign beverage. Hurlbut strongly supported the Whig candidate, Gen. William Henry Harrison—the famous Indian fighter in the War of 1812—and after the election gloated over the defeat of the Democratic incumbent, Martin Van Buren. But he also applauded the narrow state senatorial victory of Ker Boyce, a candidate for whom he had served as secretary of a mass public meeting in mid-September 1840.[38] The president of the Bank of Charleston and a former member of the Hall of Representatives in Columbia, Boyce had gained a controversial triumph. The Democrats accused him of having indiscriminately purchased Democratic and Whig votes in a cynical bid to defeat his regular Democratic opponent. Angry Calhounites failed to prove their allegations, but in December 1840 Boyce relinquished his seat in the state senate, later procuring a new election scheduled for January 4, 1841.

Probably through Petigru's intervention, Hurlbut assumed late in December 1840 the key position of election manager for Charleston's Ward Two, with an office in the municipal courthouse. He had the important responsibility of determining the eligibility of several hundred voters who came to the polls at the courthouse on election day; he could exercise broad discretion in denying the ballot to anyone whom he deemed unqualified to vote. Perhaps not unexpectedly, given Hurlbut's almost fanatical partisanship and his partisan interpretation of the applicable law, Boyce won in January 1841—particularly in Ward Two—a more complete victory than in the election of 1840. After the election Hurlbut served as the secretary of a public meeting, where he acclaimed

Boyce's second electoral victory and loudly denounced radical Democrats for their slanderous charges.[39] Thus the Boyce affair demonstrated how effectively the Charleston Whigs had learned to implement a strategy of coalition with Charleston's Unionist Democrats to challenge vulnerable Calhoun Democrats.

Hurlbut's support of the reelection of Mayor Jacob F. Mintzing in the fall of 1841 similarly exemplified his contribution to a Whig alignment with Unionist Democrats. Hurlbut rebutted charges of fiscal extravagance and favoritism arising from Mintzing's previous administration. Though probably realizing that no Whig could gain the mayoralty of Charleston, he defended Mintzing, who advocated in principle a severe reduction of government expenses but the continuation of generous spending on existing public projects. Addressing a crowded public assembly at Charleston's city hall early in September 1841, Hurlbut made what amounted to the first frankly political speech of his career. In it he denied that Mintzing had spent excessively or that he had deliberately violated a city ordinance forbidding the municipal employment of a nonresident of Charleston, and he declared further that the German-born Mintzing had not brought an excessive number of German immigrants into his mayoral administration. Suppressing for the moment his growing animosity toward American citizens of foreign origin, Hurlbut adroitly avoided dealing with the technical merits of the case at issue and instead presented unassailable, if irrelevant, arguments invoking the constitutional rights of all American citizens and extolling the virtues and values of a diverse democratic society. He did so successfully; indeed, Hurlbut's support of Mintzing helped to defeat the Democratic "People's Ticket," headed by former Charleston mayor and Calhoun Democrat Henry Laurens Pinckney. When election officials finished tabulating the ballots early in September of 1841, the results demonstrated once again the remarkable success of the Whig and conservative Democratic coalition: Mintzing had overwhelmed Pinckney by a convincing margin of 1,053 to 513 votes.[40] Besides showing Hurlbut's flair for partisan oratory and his apparent familiarity with constitutional law, the Boyce and Mintzing affairs demonstrated his inclination to support candidates of any partisan stripe in order to achieve his own goal of electoral success—surely the mark of an already seasoned, if not astute, young party politician.

Despite Hurlbut's conspicuous involvement in Charleston politics, his participation in the presidential campaign of 1844 proved considerably more significant for his steadily growing career as a South Carolina Whig. Harrison had died shortly after assuming the duties of the presidency in 1841, and Vice President John Tyler of Virginia had succeeded him. Formerly a Jacksonian Democrat who had withdrawn from his party in 1832 owing to his opposition to Jackson's measures against nullification and who had since turned nominally

Stephen A. Hurlbut, rising Whig politician in the 1840s. From *Battles and Leaders of the Civil War* (vol. 10).

Whig, Tyler as president had subsequently opposed the whole Whig economic program, and angry Whigs had expelled him from their party. Whig senator Henry Clay of Kentucky, known as the "Great Pacificator" for his capacity for political compromise, sought to gain the Whig nomination for president in 1844. Clay, now sixty-seven, made his highly elaborated "American System" the foundation of his campaign. Specifically, he advocated creating a new national bank, raising the existing tariff higher so as to protect and promote American manufacturing in the face of strong European competition, and increasing federal spending on internal improvements, such as toll roads, railroads, and canals. Encouraged by Clay's prospects for victory, southern Whigs, many of whom had since 1824 distrusted his ambitious program of economic nationalism, now effusively praised him, in an effort to defeat the Calhoun Democracy. Consequently the American System served as the watchword of southern Whigs and as a partisan battle cry that Hurlbut, Petigru, and other South Carolina Whigs hoped would inspire their state's voters and ensure a Democratic defeat in the presidential election.[41]

To this end, Hurlbut helped to form the Charleston Clay Club in December 1843. Elected as secretary of the group's corresponding committee, Hurlbut prepared a number of campaign letters urging prominent Whigs in South Carolina, Georgia, and Virginia to promote a Clay victory in November 1844. In March 1844 he learned that Clay planned to make a grand tour of the South in order to mobilize the southern Whig state parties committed to his election. Equally importantly, Clay also sought to appease the many southern Whigs who quarreled with his equivocal stand on the proposed annexation of the Mexican province of Texas. Although Clay opposed immediate and outright annexation, to avoid precipitating a war with Mexico (as did the prospective Democratic nominee, Martin Van Buren), he hoped to conciliate southern Whigs by suggesting that he would support annexation later and on different terms, if the Texas question could be kept out of the present presidential campaign. Clay's hedging split the ranks of southern Whigs deeply; Hurlbut aligned himself firmly with Petigru, Bryan, and Blanding in repudiating annexation on both moral and political grounds.

Having publicly declared his position on the vexed issue of Texas, early in March 1844 Hurlbut moved, on his own initiative, a resolution that the Clay Club appoint a special Committee of Ten to meet Clay at the rail station in Columbia and escort him to Charleston. His motion adopted, Hurlbut traveled to Columbia with sixty Charleston Whigs, including Petigru and the Charleston physician and educator Dr. Samuel Henry Dickson. They gave Clay a rousing welcome. Back in Charleston, Clay rallied the tumultuously enthusiastic Whigs for the November election. Hurlbut himself served as one of numerous junior managers who sold tickets to the Citizens Ball for Clay on April 8, the day before Clay's departure.[42]

The second national Whig convention met in Baltimore on May 1, 1844, and Hurlbut traveled there as a member of the seventeen-man South Carolina Whig ratification convention delegation. He supported Clay's nomination by acclamation at Baltimore's Universalist Church, on North Calvert Street. On May 2, he served as the vice president of the "Whig Young Men's National Convention of Ratification," which confirmed the previous day's nomination of Clay. Thereupon, after leading the Charleston Clay Club in a showy procession through the streets of Baltimore to an orator's platform outside the city, Hurlbut vigorously waved a cumbersome party banner that bore the patriotic motto, "As in '76 so in '44, few but firm and faithful." Enduring a drizzling and freezing rain, he then marched his fellow Whigs to the convention grounds, where they heard the renowned sixty-two-year-old New England Unionist, Sen. Daniel Webster, deliver a spellbinding speech in support of Clay's candidacy. Flushed with pride over his participation in the Whig convention, Hurlbut returned to Charleston, where he addressed a special Clay Club rally held in Temperance Hall on May 28. There he "gave a glowing sketch of the proceedings of the Ratification Convention," and he urged his party cohorts, particularly Petigru and Dickson, to join him in campaigning more strenuously for Henry Clay.[43]

As the presidential election neared, however, Hurlbut despaired of a Clay victory in South Carolina, and the idea forcefully struck him that the Whig ticket in his state should have a plausible excuse for not making a stronger showing in the fall. Therefore, even before the balloting began, he denounced the traditional and constitutionally sanctioned system of choosing presidential electors in South Carolina. Accusing the oligarchical South Carolina legislature of having consistently created solidly Democratic electoral bodies to the total exclusion of the state's few Whigs, an indignant Hurlbut declared to a Whig gathering in Temperance Hall in August of 1844 that the unfair legislative method stood irreconcilably "at war with republican profession and practice." He denounced the procedure whereby such "packed bodies" of "hackneyed politicians and wire pullers" could repeatedly defeat Whig presidential candidates. Further, Hurlbut castigated the alleged pro-Calhoun Democratic disunionists in Charleston—partisans he described as the implacable opponents of "Union and Liberty." As Hurlbut had foreseen, Clay lost his bid for the presidency to the Democrat James K. Polk of Tennessee, who supported the immediate annexation of Texas.[44]

Hurlbut's conspicuous part in the presidential election campaign of 1844 in South Carolina contributed significantly to the development of his complex combination of abilities and made clear his deficiencies as a young partisan politician. His public record reflected many of the finest and the worst qualities associated with antebellum politicians. Thus Hurlbut revealed many facets of his personality and character: in supporting conservative Democratic candidates; in helping to establish, consolidate, and expand the groundwork of the Whig party's organizational structure in Charleston (for example, through the Clay Club); and in becoming the most influential and articulate spokesman of the Whig party's philosophy and goals in Calhoun's Charleston, especially on behalf of the more prominent, though more pragmatic and less ideological,

Whigs like Petigru and Dickson. Specifically, he demonstrated that he could be pompous, egotistical, cunning, overbearing, temperamental, impetuous, demagogical, intransigent, and contentious. On the more positive side, he was an efficient organizer, a gifted orator, a congenial and affable companion, a seasoned, energetic, and flamboyant campaigner, and an ambitious and loyal Whig partisan who displayed admirable courage in confronting the Democratic majority in Charleston.

Perhaps impressed by his own performance during the 1844 presidential campaign, Hurlbut prepared to challenge once again the dominant South Carolina Democracy in Charleston. His renewed battle with the Calhoun Democrats arose in consequence of the brief but tumultuous Hoar affair, which occurred in Charleston in December 1844. Samuel Hoar, a lawyer and congressman from Massachusetts, had severely condemned the harsh treatment of the northern free black sailors in Charleston. After the Denmark Vesey conspiracy in 1822, the South Carolina legislature had passed and thereafter had strictly enforced a series of oppressive Negro Seamen Acts that required all shipmasters in the port of Charleston to pay for the incarceration of black mariners for so long as their ships remained in the harbor.[45] Convinced that this discriminatory and unjust legislation violated the constitutional rights of both sea captains and their black sailors, Hoar proceeded to Charleston. That was rash indeed, for he had announced his intention to create a test case to bring before a federal or state court in South Carolina in order to procure an abrogation of the obnoxious black seamen acts.

Upon Hoar's arrival in Charleston, the South Carolina legislature demanded that Governor Aiken expel him from the state immediately; a formidable mob threatened to hang him should he refuse to leave. Alarmed, Petigru hastily organized a group of Whig supporters, including Hurlbut, to save Hoar if he should fall into the hands of the mob. An apprehensive Hurlbut prepared to march with George Cogdell, Henry King, and William Blanding to rescue Hoar, whom the mob had already forced to take refuge in the Charleston Hotel. But no riot or altercation occurred, for word reached Petigru's office that Hoar (whom the *Charleston Mercury* denounced as the "Agent" of the "Massachusetts Abolition Agency") had abandoned his mission and hurriedly evacuated Charleston.[46] As for Hurlbut, the Hoar episode clearly demonstrated once again his remarkable courage and his loyalty to Petigru. He had shown a willingness to confront mob violence and to defend free speech on the question of justice for blacks.

The subsiding of this uproar late in 1844 marked a break for Hurlbut after four years of almost incessant political activity. The interruption seemed only to increase his concern over his deteriorating personal circumstances, notwithstanding his occasional legal work with James Louis Petigru. His father had died in Philadelphia in January 1843. Hurlbut had seldom, if ever, seen his father since they had separated early in 1837 in Philadelphia, and he had scarcely known his young mother, Lydia, before she died in 1821. Appreciating his father's eminence among South Carolina's and Pennsylvania's Unitarians, Hurlbut had combined his oratorical and literary distinction in an expression of his regret at his father's death. After hearing a eulogy by the Reverend Dr. Samuel A. Gilman in Archdale Unitarian Church in January 1843, Hurlbut had begun preparing his own, which appeared in the Philadelphia *Christian Examiner*'s September 1843 issue. Hurlbut extolled his father's intellectual, moral, and social virtues and his significant contributions to the further development of Unitarian theology and Federalist ideology.[47]

But Hurlbut found considerable consolation in the coming to Charleston of his half-brother, William Henry Hurlbut II. Although only sixteen years old, the precocious William had already shown himself an apt student of rhetoric, foreign languages, and classical literature in his father's boarding school. But he had also exhibited a tendency to engage in reckless behavior with his boyhood companions in Philadelphia. On one occasion in 1838, for instance, a friend had pointed the muzzle of a supposedly unloaded pistol between William's eyes and pulled the trigger; providentially cheating death, William had jerked his head away but had still caught "one shot in the ear." This strikingly handsome and intellectually gifted but troubled youth meant not only to commiserate with his brother in Charleston but also to emulate him by entering a learned profession. He proposed to study to become a Unitarian clergyman under the Reverend Gilman.[48] Just as Martin had secured the patronage of Petigru to establish his oldest son Stephen in the practice of law, he had arranged to have Gilman initiate William into the ministry.

William's arrival in Charleston probably contributed to the early destruction of Stephen's career as both a lawyer and Whig politician; it precipitated his disgraceful departure, if not his forcible expulsion, from Charleston in the summer of 1845. William brought what should have been sufficient funds from Philadelphia to establish and maintain himself for a good while, but by the beginning of 1845 Stephen had incurred sole responsibility for his support. Wasteful spending otherwise increased his dire financial difficulty. In truth, since his return to Charleston in 1837, Stephen had shown a tendency toward extravagance. He had frequently attended convivial meetings of the Washington Light Infantry, the Independent Order of Odd Fellows, the South Carolina Society, and Whig politicians. He had not regularly attended services at Gilman's Archdale Church; he had eschewed association with Gilman and many of his New England Society colleagues in the newly formed Charleston Temperance

Society. Compounding his apparent indifference to religious observances and, worse yet, his heavy consumption of alcohol, Hurlbut also persistently gambled. An avid dealer and bluffer, Hurlbut nevertheless lacked skill and luck at cards, and so he lost repeatedly. By late in 1844 the expenses of his brother's theological education and his gambling losses had plunged him into poverty, despite his earnings as a lawyer (in partnership with John E. Carew, a magistrate and patriotic orator who had in January 1844 joined in firm of "Hurlbut & Carew"). Hurlbut's behavior began to reveal a disturbing dark side.

Initially he resorted to cheating at whist. Abandoning his playing partners whenever he folded his hand (as he frequently did), Hurlbut grew "notorious for being ever present at the settling when a winner, and ever missing when a loser." Finally, one of his indignant playing companions "most pointedly arraigned and exposed him" for his repeated failures to redeem "his swindling obligations." Hurlbut's accuser (who in 1863 would posthumously denounce him, through Colonel Andrews of the *Charleston Daily Courier,* for embezzling the New England Society's funds) further alleged that Hurlbut had blackmailed his own Charleston friends and that he had often obtained loans under false pretenses, "either leaving [his creditors] them in the lurch, or to pay the piper."[49] Hurlbut defiantly ignored the charges and resumed his playing of whist.

Whatever his manipulation of his card-playing companions, Hurlbut incurred an increasingly heavy burden of indebtedness. In mid-July 1845 he boarded a clipper ship in Charleston Harbor and sailed to Beaufort, where his father had met and married Lydia Bunce, apparently hoping to borrow funds from his deceased mother's two sisters or his surviving relatives still residing there. Hurlbut also besought financial assistance from Lt. Theodore Augustus Bell, a militia officer in the Beaufort Volunteer Artillery. Unsuccessful, Hurlbut returned to Charleston.

Shortly thereafter, a man who feared that calamity would arise from Hurlbut's financial embarrassments expressed his concern to Charleston authorities. Thomas B. Chaplin, the twenty-three-year-old proprietor of the Tombee Plantation, a 376-acre rice and cotton farm in the southwestern corner of St. Helena Island (east of Port Royal Island and within the Beaufort District of South Carolina), had once retained Hurlbut to assist him in drawing cash from his deceased wife's legacy. Chaplin, who owned between sixty and seventy male and female slaves, belonged, like Lieutenant Bell, to the Beaufort Volunteer Artillery, a permanent militia company, the duties of which included patrolling the Beaufort District in the pursuit of fugitive slaves and rebellious bondsmen. Hurlbut had apparently previously encountered both Bell and Chaplin as the adjutant of the Washington Light Infantry. On July 21, 1845, while visiting Beaufort, Chaplin dined with Bell and, "Heard that S. A. Hurlbut had stopped from Charleston very much in debt." The exceedingly anxious Chaplin then confided to his journal, "I hope he has not got me into any difficulty as he had some business of importance to transact for me." Chaplin requested William B. Fickling, a fellow militiaman and a Charleston magistrate, as well as his principal lawyer, to apprise James W. Gray, a mutual associate and the Master in Equity for Charleston, of Hurlbut's desperate situation.[50] Hurlbut, however, avoided disciplinary action by Gray and severed further association with Chaplin and Bell.

Hurlbut's increasing desperation for funds to cover his debts and his penchant for cheating finally drove him to swindle one of Petigru's closest Whig friends, Dr. Samuel Henry Dickson. Hurlbut had campaigned for Clay with Dickson in 1844 and had ingratiated himself with that influential medical scholar. Dickson, a forty-seven-year-old Yale graduate who had also earned a medical degree at the University of Pennsylvania (and had gained recognition besides as a lyric poet and essayist), had founded and served as the chairman of medicine at the South Carolina Medical College in Charleston.[51] Sometime early in August of 1845, Hurlbut obtained a check from Dickson, apparently a large personal loan. Hurlbut promptly cashed the draft at a Charleston bank. Traveling to Savannah, Georgia, on legal business, he forged another note from Dickson and cashed the counterfeit check there, leaving Dickson "to be paymaster of both" bills. Later apprised by Dickson of Hurlbut's "dirty trick" and fearing that Hurlbut's treachery, if publicized, would create a scandal that would embarrass or discredit the Charleston Whigs, a shocked Petigru urged Hurlbut to leave Charleston quickly; as Hurlbut had exhausted his resources, Petigru even "furnished him with funds to do so."[52] Concurrently, Hurlbut also fell under strong suspicion for his alleged defalcation of New England Society funds, for which he had responsibility under bankruptcy law.

Alarmed at the prospect of legal retribution by Dickson and of prosecution for forgery and embezzlement, Hurlbut and his brother hastily left South Carolina aboard a clipper ship bound for Philadelphia. From there, and after parting with William (who shortly thereafter gained admission to Harvard College and Divinity School), and surviving family members, Hurlbut, with resources supplied by his stepmother, headed west. He traveled by rail, stagecoach, and steamship to Chicago, then a small but rapidly growing city. Hurlbut continued westward, his apparent destination the thriving commercial center of Galena, on the Fever River, a tributary of the upper Mississippi. However, during a sojourn in rural Belvidere, Illinois, Hurlbut decided to settle there, establish a legal practice, and try to recoup his lost fortunes.[53]

Hurlbut's controversial and inconsistent public career in South Carolina probably reflected, in large measure, the contradictions and deep conflicts inherent in his dual identity as a Carolina Yankee. The anomalous product of a New England–centered slaveholding household in antebellum Charleston, Hurlbut underwent a confused and turbulent formative period. An early and rigorous intellectual and academic orientation and his highly competitive nature, in a southern society where formal education had generally less usefulness or distinction than in the North; repeated family bereavements and separations from his many siblings; ambivalence toward slavery and blacks and Southern urban culture, as opposed to the more liberal Yankee heritage; alternating domestic affluence and indigence; and scholastic training in classical literature and foreign languages, particularly in a society that more highly valued political rhetoric and stump oratory—all shaped his personality and character. Early in his career, beginning with his association with Petigru in 1840, Hurlbut developed a dependence on patronage to gain professional success in Charleston. By 1845, under Petigru's tutelage, he had grown into a skillful lawyer and politician. But Hurlbut had also demonstrated his own rhetorical eloquence, affability and sociability, organizational ability, and admirable ambition. He had also betrayed proclivities to cupidity, outright fraud, nativist intolerance, racial prejudice, and demagoguery. After establishing himself in the West, Hurlbut hurried to lay the foundations for his eventual success as an Illinois lawyer and Northern Whig politician.

CHAPTER TWO

Lawyer, Whig, and Republican

Belvidere, Illinois, where Hurlbut settled late in 1845, presented a sharp contrast to his former situation. Where Charleston could boast of a cosmopolitan Southern, commercial, coastal, populous, urban society, one that was racially mixed, ethnically diverse, and culturally sophisticated, Belvidere was Northern—or rather, western—rural, agricultural, inland, sparsely settled, predominantly white, socially backward, and physically crude.[1] Founded by emigrant settlers from New England and New York in 1835, Belvidere lay beside the pristine Kishwaukee River, which meandered through Boone County in far northern Illinois. Geographically, the small village occupied a remote, if promising, position between Chicago to the east and Galena near the upper Mississippi to the west. It lay also between Madison, Wisconsin, to the north and Springfield, now the Illinois state capital, to the south. Situated too near the main line of the new Galena & Chicago Union Railroad, Belvidere anticipated growth and prosperity when the railway should reach Galena and thereby connect Chicago and the East with Belvidere and the trans-Mississippi West.[2]

Into this frontier world came Stephen A. Hurlbut, a handsome, well-educated, and fashionable thirty-year-old Southern man.[3] Probably fearing disbarment in Illinois should he make any compromising disclosures, he carefully refrained from divulging the truth about his fraudulent misconduct in Charleston. After gaining admission to the Illinois bar and upon announcing his intention to practice law in the Twelfth Circuit Court District of Illinois, Hurlbut argued cases in Boone, McHenry, De Kalb, and Winnebago counties, which collectively formed part of the Seventh Congressional District of Illinois. He established both his personal address and his legal office in a building next to the American House hotel in Belvidere. In part because Belvidere was the seat of Boone County, he rapidly acquired an extensive practice.[4] In addition, only two other experienced lawyers, James L. Loop and Allen C. Fuller, presented Hurlbut with much competition for business.

Loop, a New Yorker who had come to Belvidere in 1838, had just completed a two-year term of office as the prosecuting attorney for the Twelfth Circuit Court. Fuller, a Connecticut native, had emigrated to Illinois by way of New York. (Before practicing in New York, he had studied law in Pennsylvania under David Wilmot, who would subsequently introduce in Congress the controversial antislavery Wilmot Proviso.)[5] Politically, Loop and Fuller supported the Democratic party, but they both held strong antislavery views. Both men would gravitate toward the Whig party—Loop in 1854 and Fuller in 1856—and they would join the Republican party by the fall elections of 1860. Hurlbut and a few lesser Whigs, meanwhile, strove to create a Whig party organization in Boone County. But because of their agreement on the question of Southern slavery and a growing personal association, by October 1851 Hurlbut and Loop had formed a law partnership. Long before, however, Hurlbut had compiled an eminently successful record as a lawyer in Illinois. He had pleaded cases and suits that involved disputed land boundaries, divorce, mortgage, and probate matters; he had collected annually about nine hundred dollars in fees.[6]

Meanwhile, Hurlbut began in 1846 to court Sophronia R. Stevens, the younger sister of Loop's wife. The Stevens family had moved from western New York to Belvidere late in the 1830s and by 1846 had become one of the village's socially prominent families.[7] Renouncing his bachelorhood at last, Hurlbut proposed to Sophronia, and on May 13, 1847, Prof. Seth S. Whitman, the former pastor of Belvidere's First Baptist Church and a substantial landowner in Belvidere, married the young couple. Stephen and Sophronia began attending First Baptist Church services in Belvidere, but privately Hurlbut continued to adhere to Unitarian beliefs. Later in 1847 Hurlbut purchased from Whitman a small parcel of land on the north side of Belvidere and thereafter paid for the construction of a two-story, red-brick house on his property. There he and Sophronia welcomed the birth in 1848 of their only child, George.[8]

Now a married man and an enterprising and successful lawyer who enjoyed increased recognition among his fellow residents in rural northern Illinois, Hurlbut confidently resumed the career he had earlier begun in Charleston as a Whig politician. In the spring of 1847, he ran as the lone Whig candidate for a seat in the second Illinois state constitutional convention from the preponderantly Democratic fifty-fourth Legislative District, comprising Boone and McHenry counties. Hurlbut competed with five other candidates, but on election day, April 19, he prevailed by the wide margin of 1,335 votes over his nearest Democratic contender. He won handily in part because of his growing popularity and his strong appeal as a forceful orator, but primarily because the rural voters of Boone and McHenry counties demanded, aside from substantive constitutional revisions, practical Whig-supported bank legislation to relieve the serious scarcity of currency in the district.[9]

By June 10 Hurlbut had proceeded to the statehouse in Springfield, where he took his seat at the convention along with seventy other Whig delegates and ninety-one Democrats. There he helped to formulate parliamentary strategy with hastily formed coalitions of Whigs and conservative Democrats. These bipartisan groups opposed factional minorities of "Locos," or radical "wolf democrats" (those who subscribed to the antibank and hard-currency philosophy associated with former president Martin Van Buren) in a wide range of issues involved in revision of the original Illinois constitution of 1818.[10]

Elected by coalition members to the powerful Judiciary Committee at the convention, Hurlbut gained a forum in which he could articulate his interpretation of orthodox Whig economic and social philosophy. First, true to his previous advocacy of Henry Clay's American System (a program for domestic economic growth based partly on the expansion of paper currency by the increased availability of bank credit and notes), he joined Whigs and conservative Democrats in supporting a successful proposal to establish a more uniform and liberalized system of bank laws. Opposing a Democratic resolution instructing the Committee on Incorporations to prohibit banks permanently within the "Prairie State," he recommended instead that the committee investigate the feasibility of a system patterned on the bank laws of New York. Liberal Democrats attacked Hurlbut's proposal, arguing that such a system would only remove the scarcity of credit and concomitant deflation only to create worse problems of numerous loosely regulated state banks and large quantities of inflated paper currency.

Finally, on August 5, by a margin of sixty-five to fifty-six ballots on the convention floor, Whigs and conservative Democrats succeeded in gaining approval of the report of the Committee on Incorporations, which was to be embodied in Article X of the proposed constitution. This clause prohibited the creation of state banks but authorized the legislature to enact laws that would permit corporations with banking powers to operate within the state. These laws could be approved or repealed by a popular vote.[11] Although this was scarcely a specifically

Whig victory, Hurlbut's vigorous advocacy of the New York State banking system as a model for Illinois had contributed to a decisive Democratic defeat.

Second, despite his earlier involvement with chattel slavery and his lack of sincere antislavery convictions, Hurlbut now considered it expedient, indeed necessary, to satisfy his abolitionist constituents. Therefore, he supported the adoption of Section 16 of Article XIII of the proposed constitution—a clause that, as had the constitution of 1818, prohibited slavery and involuntary servitude within Illinois except as a punishment for crime. On June 25, 1847, the convention held a fierce dispute over a Democratic resolution prohibiting free blacks from immigrating into Illinois and rendering it unlawful for migrating Southerners to emancipate their Negro slaves within the state. Amid the furious debate, in which delegates from both parties lost their ability to engage in rational argumentation or constructive discourse, Hurlbut expressed nativist as well as racist biases. Although he opposed the controversial Democratic resolution, he blurted out his opinion that he *regarded the foreigners in a less favorable light than the negroes.*[12]

Hurlbut's attempt to organize a Whig and Democratic coalition that could ensure the settlement and free status of blacks in Illinois failed because a preponderant alliance of Democratic—and Whig—delegates from central and southern Illinois overwhelmed his own bipartisan bloc, which was from the northern section of the state. By a margin of ninety-seven to fifty-six votes, the convention approved the Democratic resolution and a supplemental clause that left it to the people to authorize the first legislature convened under the new constitution to enact laws prohibiting free blacks from migrating to or settling in the state. Nonetheless, Hurlbut and his fellow Whigs achieved significant victories on other questions, particularly the citizenship qualification for the governorship and for the electoral franchise. Hurlbut and most other Whigs agreed to support a reduction (from thirty years to fourteen) of the period of citizenship required of a foreigner before he could hold office as the governor of Illinois. In return, the Whigs exacted from Democratic delegates support for Section 1 of Article VI, which established a residence requirement of a full year before an immigrant could vote in public elections in Illinois.

After the signal Whig victories gained upon two other vexed constitutional questions (an override of a governor's veto by a simple rather than by a two-thirds majority, and a poll tax to reduce the state's debt, to be paid both by citizens not owning land as well as by property holders), the convention adjourned on August 31, 1847. By a near-unanimous margin of 131 yeas to seven nays (with twenty-four delegates listed as absent), the delegates approved the constitution of 1847. On March 6, 1848, Illinois voters ratified the proposed constitution by a vote of 60,585 to 15,903; they approved of the controversial "prohibitory clause" regarding immigration of free blacks by the margin of 50,261 to 21,297 votes.[13] Notwithstanding his party's conspicuous defeat on the Negro question, Hurlbut had demonstrated his abilities as a politician. Moreover, he gained a wide reputation as a moderately conservative but racially enlightened, although decidedly nativistic, Whig who supported a looser system of bank credit, broader racial justice, and a stringent requirement for immigrants aspiring to vote. His contribution to the formation of several Whig and conservative Democratic coalitions had helped Whigs overcome opposition from economically and socially radical factions of Democrats.

Hurlbut's prominence at the constitutional convention stimulated his ambition to play a larger role in state, if not national, Whig politics. To achieve his goal, he flung himself into the 1848 presidential campaign, which pitted the Democratic candidate, Sen. Lewis Cass of Michigan, against the Whig hero of the late Mexican War, Gen. Zachary Taylor of Louisiana. Already the bitter sectional controversy between the free North and the slaveholding South over the proposed expansion of slavery into the trans-Mississippi territories had begun to convulse the country. The crisis had grown particularly severe in August 1846, when David Wilmot, now a Democratic congressman from Pennsylvania, introduced a controversial resolution, known thereafter as the Wilmot Proviso, that permanently excluded slavery from any territories taken from Mexico (the Senate would override the House to defeat it). Meanwhile, the former Democratic president, Martin Van Buren of New York, was boldly leading the Free Soil party in efforts to exclude Negro slavery from the prospective territories. For his part, Cass elaborated a populist principle of "squatter sovereignty." According to Cass, not Congress but only the people who inhabited a territory, acting through their legislature, could decide whether slavery should be established or prohibited there. The Democratic platform of 1848 equivocated in its endorsement of squatter sovereignty, while the Whigs avoided the slavery issue entirely by entering the presidential contest without a platform.[14]

It was not that the national Whig party lacked ideological principles, organizational structure, or supporters. Indeed, the party had as perhaps its most active campaign worker committed to the Taylor candidacy Congressman Abraham Lincoln from Springfield, Illinois. Lincoln, a thirty-nine-year-old Kentucky native, had moved to Illinois from Indiana in 1830, practicing law in New Salem, near Springfield, after 1831. He had then served in the Illinois state legislature, where he had acted as his party's floor leader, from 1834 to 1841. Distinguishing himself during his single term (1847–49) as the only Illinois Whig in the U.S. House of Representatives, he had in 1847 courageously ex-

Abraham Lincoln, future commander in chief, Union army. Illinois State
Historical Library.

pressed strong opposition to the prosecution of the Mexican War and had supported the Wilmot Proviso.

Thus in the volatile situation of mounting sectional controversy occurred
one of the most important events of Hurlbut's public career: he would meet a
future president of the United States who would for the next fifteen years repeatedly bestow on him generous, even often unmerited, patronage. Recognizing a potentially strong partisan ally, particularly in view of Hurlbut's growing
reputation as an eloquent orator and as a skillful campaigner, Lincoln in July
1848 sent a form letter and a piece of Whig campaign literature entitled *The
Battery* to his "Friend Hurlbut" at Belvidere.[15] Flattered and roused into even
more strenuous exertions for Taylor, in August Hurlbut organized a heavily

attended Whig rally near the Boone County courthouse in Belvidere. There, Hurlbut and two of his Whig party associates, Thomas B. Wakeman and Marcus White, publicly rededicated themselves to a Taylor victory and defied heckling Democrats who had unexpectedly appeared at the gathering. Both Belvidere's and Boone County's Whig party delegations declared their firm intention to cast unanimous votes for General Taylor, while Hurlbut personally gained the distinction of selection as a Whig presidential elector from Boone County in the event of a Taylor victory.[16]

In September, Lincoln, who had returned to Springfield, asked Hurlbut to join him in a Whig campaign swing through the northern sections of Illinois and Indiana. Hurlbut agreed and delivered stirring speeches before enthusiastic Whig rallies. Early in October he attended a massive Whig demonstration for Taylor that had gathered in Chicago's Public Square. There Lincoln "enchained" his spellbound audience with an impassioned—as well as rigorously logical— argument that advocated his Free Soil, but also moderately conservative Whig, doctrine prohibiting the establishment of slavery within the territories. Hurlbut, perhaps abashed at having met his superior as an orator, followed Lincoln on the platform and "spoke briefly, the lateness of the hour admonishing that an adjournment was in order."[17] Still, Hurlbut's appearance in Chicago with Lincoln proved highly beneficial politically. In the November election, Taylor defeated Cass for the presidency, and Lincoln gratefully remembered Hurlbut's canvassing efforts.

The elevation of Taylor to the White House not only flattered Hurlbut's pride but also afforded him the opportunity to seek a reward from the Taylor administration. Just after the Taylor victory, Schuyler Colfax, a delegate to the 1848 Whig national convention and the editor of the Whig newspaper in South Bend, Indiana, requested Hurlbut to speak to audiences in South Bend and LaPorte in support of the recent appointments to offices made there by Indiana Whig congressman Caleb B. Smith. Hurlbut obliged Colfax and afterward solicited his assistance in gaining an appointment as chargé d'affaires in some South American republic. Colfax appreciated Hurlbut's "eloquent speeches" but believed that Hurlbut should have addressed his request either to Lincoln himself or to Lincoln's and Hurlbut's mutual friend, Illinois congressman Edward D. Baker. Colfax manifested his gratitude to Hurlbut by recommending that Smith obtain a diplomatic appointment for him. He described Hurlbut as "talented, worthy, conversant with the Spanish language & of gentlemanly bearing," a man who would make "a good officer" to a Latin American country.

Unwilling to depend solely on Colfax, in February 1849 Hurlbut directly requested Congressman Smith to procure for him a diplomatic post; Hurlbut deemed it "my desert, politically speaking." He stressed his contributions to the Whig party since the presidential election campaign of 1844, particularly his recent success in gaining a seat at the constitutional convention for "two Demo. Counties." He described himself as "an undeniable Whig my life long & abhor Locofocoism & despise Long John [Wentworth] & take every opportunity of making it manifest." Hurlbut explained why he had sought Smith's, rather than Lincoln's, help in securing a diplomatic position. His explanation concerned Dr. Anson G. Henry of Springfield, Lincoln's physician and a vigorous Whig campaigner and organization worker. Hurlbut (mistakenly) asserted that Lincoln had tentatively pledged himself "to [nominate] Dr. Henry one of my Electoral Colleagues," while Congressman Baker found himself "too busy fishing for himself to do any thing for me without a quid pro quo." For that reason Hurlbut asked Smith to approach Lincoln, Baker, and other Illinois Whigs for him, as he could find "no time to logroll, nor to visit & propitiate cliques of politicians either at Springfield or Washington." If his "slight service" for Smith in Indiana afforded him a claim to a Latin American post, Hurlbut argued, Smith should dissuade Lincoln from recommending Henry. Finally, in elaborating on his preparation for a diplomatic appointment, Hurlbut briefly asserted, "As to qualification, I understand Spanish."

Not receiving a reply from Smith in February 1849, Hurlbut felt that Taylor's inauguration as president in March and thereafter the formation of his cabinet would improve his chances, despite Smith's lame-duck status. Thus in March 1849 Hurlbut again sought Smith's assistance in obtaining a diplomatic appointment. He confided to Smith on March 24 that he understood it to be but "poor business" to beg "Uncle Sam" for a post, but as "chapfallen Democrats here [in Illinois] say 'that we are to have an unmitigated Federal Administration'" at Washington, Hurlbut considered his application for foreign service as deserving of urgent deliberation. He admitted to Smith that "Sparta has many worthier sons than I," but he "cheerfully" assured him that none had rendered "more zealous" service. Nevertheless, Smith could not help Hurlbut; his term in Congress having expired on March 31, he lacked influence.[18]

In the end, besides showing Hurlbut's driving ambition and his continued heavy dependence on patronage, this episode reveals that he had not yet recognized Lincoln as a rising, ultimately towering, figure in the national or Illinois Whig party. Nor had he yet perceived of himself as a potential member of a nascent "Illinois Clique" of Whig, and subsequently Republican, politicians in Springfield and Washington. Entirely unwilling or unable to identify personally or professionally with Lincoln, Baker, Henry, or other Illinois Whigs, Hurlbut perhaps viewed an appointment to the diplomatic corps as a means of advancing his political career despite the fact that it would mean his temporary removal from political centers in the West.

Meanwhile Hurlbut continued his law practice with James L. Loop. From 1849 to 1854 he frequently appeared within the Twelfth District courts, his typical cases easily handled land-title disputes, mortgage foreclosures, and divorce suits. In August 1852 Hurlbut and Loop announced the dissolution of their legal partnership; Loop, besides his private practice, became solicitor-in-chancery to for Boone County.[19] Hurlbut, continuing on his own, became involved in a difficult and publicized criminal case in the spring of 1853 when he joined Allen C. Fuller to defend a De Kalb County resident, Perry Wiggins, against the charge of accessory to assault with intent to kill Wiggins's allegedly horse-stealing associate, Loren Heath. Perry's older brother, Ira, in a fit of anger over the ownership of the horses, had shot at, but missed, Heath. The De Kalb County authorities had apprehended Perry Wiggins, but Ira had escaped. In late April 1853, the first trial of Perry Wiggins (brought into the Boone County Circuit Court in Belvidere on a change of venue) resulted in a hung jury. On April 27 Hurlbut and Fuller, arguing Wiggins's case before a new jury, lost the case; Perry Wiggins had to serve a year of hard labor in the Illinois state penitentiary. The prosecuting and defense attorneys, the *Belvidere Standard* averred, had never "discharged their duties in a more able and energetic manner; this was the common remark." Yet a greater satisfaction for Hurlbut and Fuller came later, when authorities arrested Ira Wiggins in Ohio and returned him to Sycamore, in De Kalb County, for trial. In April 1854 the convicted older Wiggins received a sentence of ten years' labor in the state penitentiary.[20]

In another controversial and equally sensational criminal case, which also occurred during the spring of 1853, Hurlbut and Fuller succeeded in obtaining an acquittal for Capt. Allen Boomer, a Boone County resident accused of having induced his nephew, Giles Bennet, to cause a disastrous freight-train derailment on a Galena & Chicago Union trestle across the Kishwaukee River. A federal judge in Chicago had dismissed a U.S. marshal's charge against Boomer of obstructing a government mail route, but he nevertheless faced prosecution under the laws of Illinois. A jury in Boone County Circuit Court, however, decided that Bennet himself had likely planned the train wreck and accordingly declared Boomer not guilty.

Finally, early in October 1854, Hurlbut, Fuller, and Loop unsuccessfully defended Rufus Guild, indicted for shooting one Van Alstine of Caledonia, Boone County. Guild drew a sentence of seven years' confinement in the state prison for manslaughter. Again, a gratified *Belvidere Standard* commended prosecution and defense counsel, declaring that the lawyers had "put forth their utmost exertions."[21] Hurlbut had demonstrated significant growth in his ability to attract, if not always to win, difficult cases involving serious crimes, as well as his ability to dispose of less challenging civil actions.

Unfortunately, Hurlbut had not exhibited either the inclination or capacity to curb his extravagance. Though his residence was a modest one, on a small piece of land on Belvidere's residential north side, Hurlbut overspent on his house and family. Perhaps to his professional chagrin, in 1851 he had to mortgage or convey much of his open land to satisfy debts of $475.[22] Nonetheless, Hurlbut participated actively in Belvidere's civic affairs, as befitted a man of his gregarious nature. For instance, in November 1851 he served on the three-member building committee for a planned new Belvidere Union School, performing his delegated tasks "faithfully, *gratuitously,* and well." Later that November, while at the school's dedication ceremony, he delivered "an eloquent and effective speech, and presented to the Directors of the School the Deed and Key of the house."

But his conspicuous association with the Boone Rifles subsequently brought him more favorable public attention. Elected as the captain of this self-styled light infantry company in June 1855, Hurlbut, still military minded, methodically subjected his twenty-one militiamen—including Private Loop and Second Lieutenant Fuller—to rigorous close-order drill and marching exercises. Outfitting his men in gaudy, single-breasted blue frock coats with green collars and cuffs, green-striped azure pants, and regulation caps with streaming green pompoms, he paraded his elite company through Belvidere and other northern Illinois communities in the fall of 1855, earning lavish praise. His fellow militiamen expressed admiration for Hurlbut's marksmanship with a long musket. Firing at a bull's-eye three times from a distance of twenty-five rods (or nearly 138 yards), at a combined skirmishing exhibition and target-shooting contest south of Belvidere on December 3, 1855, "Hurlbut made the best shot." His comrades rewarded the winner with an oyster dinner at the American House—much to Hurlbut's delight. Later, in July 1858, Hurlbut and the thirty-two militiamen who then constituted his "beautiful company" participated in martial exercises at Freeport, in Stephenson County, with two other militia organizations to celebrate Independence Day. According to the *Freeport Bulletin,* the "soldierly bearing" of his militia company had well demonstrated that "Capt. Hulburt [sic] would be as much at home on the tented field as he now is on the rostrum, where he is acknowledged to have few superiors."[23] Clearly, Hurlbut understood that a continued cultivation of his interest in military service, which he had first shown in Charleston during his association there with the Washington Light Infantry, could improve his image and reputation as a patriotic politician and able lawyer in Illinois. Unlike numbers of other rising politicians in Illinois, he had not served in the

Mexican War. He might have intended the Boone Rifles to compensate, at least partially, for his lack of a distinguished military record.

Nonetheless, Hurlbut's primary preoccupation during the early 1850s remained Whig party politics. Indeed, by 1852 he had resolved to run for a seat in the U.S. House of Representatives from the newly formed First Congressional District of Illinois. In pursuit of this goal, Hurlbut expressed strong support of Gen. Winfield Scott of Virginia, the Whig candidate for president against the Democratic nominee, Franklin Pierce of New Hampshire.[24] Hurlbut hastened to attend the First District's Whig nominating convention, which met in Rockford, the seat of Winnebago County, on September 1, 1852.

There he encountered his principal political rival, later his influential patron, the eminent Galena lawyer Elihu B. Washburne, of Jo Daviess County. The thirty-six-year-old Washburne, a native of Maine and one of three brothers, had in 1840 moved to Galena, where he had established a successful practice. In 1844 (and again in 1852) he had served as an Illinois delegate to the Whig national convention. An unsuccessful candidate for a seat in Congress in 1848, he was now preparing to capture the Whig nomination for a second run. Washburne, although confident of victory, nonetheless apparently regarded Hurlbut and one other young Whig as potentially serious rivals and therefore determined to campaign vigorously against them. Hurlbut, effectively utilizing the powers of his self-appointed post as the "whip" of the Boone County Whig delegation at Rockford, surprisingly led Washburne during the preliminary balloting. However, to Hurlbut's dismay, in the succeeding five votes Washburne drew several counties' delegates away and finally defeated the disheartened Hurlbut by thirteen votes.[25]

Hurlbut refused to withdraw from the race for a congressional seat. Although nominated by sympathetic Boone County Whigs at Rockford to an approaching session of the Illinois General Assembly, he still hoped to win enough write-in votes to defeat Washburne at the polls. But in the voting in November, he lost heavily both to Washburne and the Democratic candidate for a seat in Congress, as well as to two Democratic rivals from Boone County, Henry C. Miller and Alexander H. Nixon, for the state legislature seat.[26] Washburne was to defeat his Democratic opponent and serve for nine consecutive terms in Congress as a Whig and, after 1854, as a Republican. Hurlbut, meanwhile, reluctantly conceded his resounding defeat in a letter to Washburne after the election. In it he declared that he perceived in the crushing defeat of Winfield Scott and the Whig party nationally "omens better for the future. The Democrats go in with such overwhelming power that they must fall to pieces." Dejectedly Hurlbut added, "I have retired forever from politics & shall never again make such exertion as I have done."[27]

Elihu B. Washburne, Republican U.S. congressman from Illinois.
Illinois State Historical Library.

As for the prospects of the national Whig party, Scott's devastating defeat led to the party's steady disbandment—and virtual disappearance—by the 1856 presidential election.

As it afterward developed, Hurlbut was right in predicting that severe controversy would divide the Democrats in Congress. But far more important for Hurlbut's career, the contest at Rockford had decisively shown Washburne's clear superiority to Hurlbut as a political tactician and party organization builder—twin advantages that Hurlbut could not overcome. Further, Hurlbut would for long thereafter fail to recognize Washburne's potential influence in the national and Illinois Whig party. Indeed, Hurlbut's avowed intention to end his political career in 1852 also showed that, having operated only locally and regionally as an independent Whig partisan, he had not yet perceived himself as a possible member of the increasingly influential inner circle of Illinois Whigs, and later Republicans, in Springfield and in Washington.

Hurlbut's prediction of a fateful split in the national Democratic party came true in 1854, during the presidential administration of Franklin Pierce. A profoundly wrenching and troubling division occurred within the Democratic ranks in consequence of a territorial measure introduced in Congress in January by Illinois Democratic senator Stephen A. Douglas. When finally passed in Congress, over strong Southern Democratic opposition, the Kansas-Nebraska Act created two new territories in the West, Kansas and Nebraska. Presumably Kansas would enter the federal Union as a slave state and Nebraska as a free state. The principle of squatter sovereignty (or as Douglas described it, "popular sovereignty") would be applied to both Kansas and Nebraska; Douglas's measure repealed the historic Missouri Compromise of 1820, which had barred slavery from this region. But this latter provision proved so controversial that by the summer of 1854 a fusion of Free Soilers, anti-Nebraska Whigs, and anti-Nebraska "Conscience" Democrats had laid the organizational groundwork for a new party, the Republican party, a sectional grouping dedicated to the repeal of the Kansas-Nebraska Act.[28]

For relatively unsuccessful and obscure western Whig politicians like Hurlbut and Lincoln, the furor over the Kansas-Nebraska Act proved highly beneficial, as it brought them back into public affairs. Indeed, the Kansas-Nebraska Act of 1854 formed the basis of Hurlbut's later prominence as an Illinois Republican, just as the Log Cabin Campaign and the election of William Henry Harrison in 1840 had established his earlier reputation in South Carolina.

Early in August 1854, a fusionist group of Winnebago County Whigs and Democrats invited Hurlbut and other anti-Nebraska men to attend a convention of protest in Rockford on August 30. Hurlbut, perhaps more desirous of gaining elective office for himself than of condemning the Kansas-Nebraska Act, promptly challenged Washburne for the convention's informal nomination as the Republican candidate for Congress from the First Congressional District. Prior to the selection of a nominee, a special Committee on Antislavery Resolutions assembled under the chairmanship of Hurlbut. Hurlbut deliberately framed radical antislavery statements in language designed to outrage and alienate the more conservative Washburne and thereby to win the nomination for himself should Washburne decide to withdraw. But to Hurlbut's surprise, Washburne—more from political expedience than ideological principle—heartily subscribed to Hurlbut's denunciations of the sinister and expansionist "Slave Power" in Washington and won renomination by acclamation. Washburne would gain the prize formally at the regular Whig nominating convention, also at Rockford, on September 6.[29]

Even then, Hurlbut strongly voiced objections to the nomination. On September 6, he explained to a fellow convention delegate, "when you say that E. B. Washburne is a good man, I agree with you. But when you say he is a wise man and a statesman, there is a chance for an argument." Hurlbut also attacked Washburne's reputation as "a man of learning," asserting that he "possesses frightful limitations." Shortly thereafter, a Washburne supporter informed the Whig nominee of Hurlbut's seeming lack of principle and deplorable lack of party unity amid the intensifying national crisis. He reported to Washburne that Hurlbut and another leading Boone County Whig, Charles M. Willard, had returned to Belvidere from the Rockford convention "threatening that they would give their influence to the loco Hunker [Democratic] candidate—I only hope they will carry their threat into execution," as "they will then go where they belong."[30] However, Washburne ignored Hurlbut and probably exacerbated Hurlbut's anger and chagrin by soundly defeating his Democratic opponent in November 1854, winning reelection for yet another two-year term. Hurlbut again temporarily withdrew from active politicking. He devoted himself to his practice of law, forming and dissolving a legal partnership, in 1855 and 1856, respectively, with A. F. Randall. Nonetheless, he served on the steering committee of the Boone County Agricultural Society, delivered lectures on the Constitution at the Belvidere Union School, and acted as the chief marshal for Boone County's Independence Day celebrations in Belvidere in 1855 and 1856, aided by the well-drilled Boone Rifles.[31]

But the course of events would again stir Hurlbut to political action. In 1856 widespread violence broke out in Kansas between proslavery settlers and free-state forces. The struggle intensified in consequence of John Brown's Pottawatomie Massacre and after the inflammatory "Crime against Kansas" speech delivered in May 1856 by Massachusetts Republican senator Charles Sumner.[32] Hurlbut expressed to anti-Nebraska Illinois senator Lyman Trumbull his strong views on the proper philosophical and political approaches to the resolution of the vexed question of slavery in Kansas and Nebraska.

Trumbull, a forty-three-year-old Connecticut native, had in 1837 moved from Georgia to Belleville, where he had practiced law. A Jacksonian Democrat, he had served as a member of the Illinois House of Representatives in 1840 and as Illinois secretary of state in 1841. Following tenure as a justice on the Illinois Supreme Court from 1848 to 1853, Trumbull had won election to Congress in 1854 as an anti-Nebraska Democrat; the state legislature had selected him for the U.S. Senate after Lincoln had adroitly withdrawn from consideration so as to prevent the election of a Douglas Democrat. Hurlbut advised Trumbull that he heartily approved of the "sound National Constitutional basis" on which the senator had rested his arguments against the expansion of slavery into the territories and that this reasonable approach had satisfied him and other moderate "old disbanded Whigs" in Illinois. Hurlbut praised Trumbull for judiciously avoiding the philosophical extremes of the "Radicalism & anarchy of fanatical Republicanism & the false heresy of Squatter sovereignty" and also for his criticism of the New York Republican senator William H. Seward's quasi-mystical and abstract application of a doctrine of "Higher Law" to the problem of slavery. He urged Trumbull to continue resisting the "pressure of Southern madness made rampant by political success."[33] Having encouraged Trumbull to maintain an ideologically and politically moderate position on the troublesome Kansas and Nebraska issues, Hurlbut prepared to attend the first Illinois Republican convention, which met in Bloomington late in May 1856.

There he helped to draft a party platform that, not coincidentally embodying his own moderately conservative constitutional views, also asserted firm opposition to the Democratic administration of Franklin Pierce, demanded the restoration of the Missouri Compromise of 1820, and proposed a constitutional amendment that would prohibit slavery in the territories. As a more immediately pressing practical matter, however, the Illinois Republicans advocated prompt recognition of Kansas and Nebraska as free states, specifically the early admission of Kansas into the Union under the previously framed free-state Topeka Constitution.[34] Not having been selected as a delegate to the approaching national Republican convention, Hurlbut thereupon returned to Belvidere. There he learned that John Charles Frémont, the famous "Pathfinder" and the hero of California's Bear Flag Revolution of 1846, had accepted nomination as the Republican party's first presidential candidate.

Even as Hurlbut pledged his support to Frémont, he prepared once again to challenge Washburne for his seat in the U.S. House of Representatives. He proceeded to the town of Woodstock, in Boone County, in mid-August to forge political strategy and tactics with his loyal supporters Charles M. Willard and Martin L. Sweet, two former Boone County Whigs. He sought this time to ensure, through more subtle and deliberate planning, Washburne's defeat at the First Congressional District's Republican convention, to be held at Rockford late in August. Learning of Hurlbut's designs, however, Enos W. Smith, a staunch Washburne man, warned the Galena congressman and expressed his confidence that "you will lay all that band of fellows straight out even if you have to do it by as handsome a *coup d' etat* as you made use of in '54."[35] Washburne immediately prepared to overwhelm Hurlbut at Rockford.

Meanwhile, Hurlbut organized the Belvidere Frémont Club and on August 21, 1856, personally assumed the group's chairmanship. Trying to show the con-

Lyman Trumbull, Republican U.S. senator from Illinois. Illinois State Historical Library.

vention delegates from Boone County that he supported Frémont more zeal-ously than did the self-aggrandizing Washburne, on August 23 he delivered the first of several addresses to the club members who met weekly at Belvidere's Christ Church to demonstrate their support for Frémont. Hurlbut then pro-ceeded to Rockford to challenge Washburne for the nomination. There Wash-burne, chiefly because of his superior organizational and tactical skills, wider professional reputation, and the power of his long incumbency, again soundly defeated him. Suppressing his disappointment, Hurlbut began stumping north-ern Illinois in support of Frémont. Notwithstanding, in November 1856 Frémont lost the election to Democrat James Buchanan of Pennsylvania.[36]

Despite Frémont's failure to win the White House, Hurlbut and other Republican politicians across the North continued to oppose the admission of Kansas into the Union as a slave state. In March 1857, Roger B. Taney, the chief justice of the U.S. Supreme Court, declared in a highly controversial ruling in the Dred Scott case that Congress lacked authority to exclude slavery from the territories. Later in 1857, a self-constituted proslavery territorial legislature, which seemingly had overridden the will of the majority of Kansas settlers, organized a constitutional convention that legalized slavery in the so-called Lecompton Constitution. Shortly thereafter, the legitimately constituted free-state legislature of Kansas submitted the proslavery constitution to the voters, who decisively rejected it in a territory-wide referendum. At this juncture, President Buchanan rashly urged Congress to ignore the free-state vote and instead to admit Kansas under the Lecompton Constitution. The doctrine of popular sovereignty having been thus perverted, Senator Douglas and other western Democrats broke with the Buchanan administration, supporting numerous "Conscience Democrats" who declared themselves firmly committed to the defeat of the Lecompton Constitution in Congress.[37]

Outraged at Buchanan's capitulation, Hurlbut impressed his opinion on Senator Trumbull in December 1857 that if Douglas supported even a semblance of the Lecompton Constitution in Kansas while campaigning for reelection in Illinois in 1858, he would surely suffer a crushing defeat at the hands of a powerful alignment of Republicans and anti-Nebraska Democrats. Hurlbut asserted, with reference to Southern Democratic power in Washington, that the "logic and the nerve are all on the Southern side of the Lecompton question" in Congress, but he assured Trumbull that "no amount of party discipline will hold over one third of the [Democratic] voters [in Illinois] if that Constitution is adopted." In such a case the Republicans would in 1858 sweep electoral contests in Illinois "like a whirlwind." Representing himself as a "conservative by instinct by education & profession," Hurlbut nevertheless promised Trumbull that if the Supreme Court under Chief Justice Taney "turned politician," he himself would espouse a more radical Republican position in retaliation. Finally, he indulged his penchant for political prophecy by predicting that the next national Democratic convention would endorse the late South Carolina senator John C. Calhoun's extremist belief that the Constitution specifically protected slavery within the territories. That, Hurlbut believed, would be an ominous development, one that would inevitably precipitate a bloody civil war between North and South.[38]

Although Hurlbut condemned Douglas's original sponsorship of the Kansas-Nebraska measure and his later interpretation of popular sovereignty, in a December 1857 letter, he praised the courageous stand Douglas had taken on the

Lecompton question. Adopting an equivocal position on popular sovereignty that would allow him, as a Republican, to criticize Douglas however the senator moved thereafter on Lecompton, Hurlbut frankly explained that even "admitting (which I do not) the cardinal principle of popular sovereignty," the doctrine could only inevitably lead to more anarchy and bloodshed in Kansas. But, he added, if popular sovereignty did "become the settled policy of the Country & we its opponents compelled to submit to it," then "in God's name let the founders of the Doctrine keep to the spirit of this creed & not falsify by pledges & betray trust on the first trial" for a "delusive triumph and a victory which leads to defeat." Hurlbut denounced the Lecompton Constitution and warned Douglas that "if the *Administration* party do force this miserable subterfuge upon the people—such an accounting as they will have to render has not been seen before" in the nation's history. Nevertheless, Hurlbut applauded Douglas's break with Buchanan over the Lecompton question and urged him to resist any attempted "Congressional or Presidential usurpation" on the overall Kansas question.[39] Hurlbut's overture to Douglas thus implied a coalition between Republicans and anti-Nebraska Democrats to defeat the Lecompton Constitution. Douglas expressed little interest in Hurlbut's suggestion, and the crisis in Kansas worsened.

Douglas's courageous repudiation of the Lecompton Constitution had encouraged many Democrats in the House to reject it. Late in April 1858, however, congressional Democrats passed a shrewd compromise measure, known as the English Bill, that provided for a third election in Kansas, in August. Three months before the vote, in May 1858, Hurlbut assured Senator Trumbull that the Republican party in his own district, at least, stood "firm [in its support for Trumbull], Douglas next & Buchanan nowhere." Hurlbut admitted that Douglas still commanded considerable support in the Second Congressional District and that many of the recent "converts from the Democratic party are disposed to go for him on the great compromise union saving principle," but he insisted that with vigorous Republican campaigning "[Douglas's] chances for Return to the Senate are desperate." He also suggested to Trumbull that even if Douglas should belatedly endorse the free-state Topeka Constitution, as he probably would do from political expedience, the continuing "desertion & cowardice" within the Illinois Democracy would ensure his defeat for reelection in 1858. Finally, Hurlbut asked Trumbull to apprise Sen. John J. Crittenden of Kentucky, "one of the old Whigs 1844," that Hurlbut had read the published version of Crittenden's speech on the Senate floor denouncing the Lecompton Constitution. Indeed, Crittenden's rigorously logical and yet impassioned speech had moved Hurlbut to "hearty cheers" and thanks to "God that there survived as yet one of the ancient standard-bearers" of conservative Unionism.[40]

Preoccupied with the burning questions of the day, Hurlbut neglected his law practice in Belvidere, although he continued to make appearances in Boone County courts.[41] He instead turned his attention to the coming Illinois senatorial election campaign, which pitted Abraham Lincoln, now the most prominent Republican in Illinois, against Douglas. Furnishing Lincoln with a detailed report on the political situation in northern Illinois as he viewed it late in May 1858, Hurlbut assured Lincoln that he would personally lead a ten-member and solidly pro-Lincoln Boone County delegation to the Illinois Republican convention at Springfield on June 16. "If it is desirable that any expression should be formally given of the feeling of the party, upon the Senatorial Question," Hurlbut asserted, "we at this end of the state are fully prepared to do so." Hurlbut denied rumors that appreciable "defection in our ranks in the 1st Dist." existed; he firmly believed that the "unanimous opinion of the party" there opposed Douglas and strongly supported Lincoln as his successor. He explained to Lincoln, however, that he and other formerly Whig northern Illinois Republicans were carefully avoiding casting "unnecessary abuse" on Douglas and other anti-Lecompton Democrats, fearing to alienate erstwhile anti-Nebraska Democrats who had recently turned Republican. Then, finally recognizing the potentially high national stature of Lincoln, Hurlbut eagerly sought to ingratiate himself with Lincoln, in the expectation of a reward in the event of victory over Douglas.[42]

Appreciating Hurlbut's incisive analysis but fundamentally disagreeing with his proposals and conclusions, Lincoln replied that Hurlbut need not promote his candidacy at the "county, or other local conventions and meetings"; the state Republican convention would itself settle the question. He also asserted that his own experience had not shown that "republicans from the old *democratic* ranks are more inclined to Douglas than those from the old whig ranks." Rather, the Douglas Democrats-turned-Republicans constantly declared, "'Take care of your old whigs, and have no fears for us.'"[43] The two men met later at the Springfield convention, where Lincoln accepted his party's nomination as a senatorial candidate. Hurlbut and Lincoln now finally formed an effective political relationship, amid the Kansas-Nebraska crisis and before the Illinois senatorial campaign of 1858.

Following the Springfield convention, Hurlbut returned to Belvidere to enter the 1858 congressional race against Washburne. Allen C. Fuller, now a judge, who had since 1856 supported Washburne, in July 1858 reported to Washburne Hurlbut's relentless ambition for a seat in Congress: "Our friend Hurlbut is in the field and is quite anxious to have this county go for him & I presume he will be gratified in this respect," although Fuller predicted certain victory for Washburne at Rockford.[44] From Marengo, in McHenry County, Sherman P. Flynn, another staunch Washburne supporter, apprised the Galena congressman of Hurlbut's boastful predictions of an imminent Washburne defeat, assuring Washburne that Hurlbut had merely reverted to "just playing his favorite game of 'bluff.'" Flynn also charged that Hurlbut, perhaps in sheer desperation, had in his campaign speeches falsely accused Washburne of having unfairly won the 1852 congressional nomination by appealing to voters with "the free use of money." Flynn concluded, "No reliance is to be placed upon him and my impression is that we will dispense with his services as a delegate."[45]

Nonetheless, at Rockford in August 1858 Hurlbut warned the convention members that Washburne's candidacy for a fourth term in Congress could discredit and weaken the Republican party in northern Illinois, a claim presumably arising from Hurlbut's accusations of corruption in 1852. When a motion unexpectedly arose from the convention floor calling for an informal ballot to identify a candidate for nomination, and was accepted, Hurlbut moved to reconsider it before such a ballot could be taken. Hurlbut contended that the delegates should not permit Jo Daviess County to maintain its "monopoly" on the congressional nomination, as he believed it had by supporting Washburne in his past three terms in office. Moreover, Hurlbut charged, during the Republican convention in 1856, Washburne had given "certain pledges" not to seek or accept renomination in 1858. Hurlbut's remarks generated "considerable acrimony" but failed to dissuade the Rockford delegates from proceeding to an informal ballot. Washburne gained the nomination for another congressional term, winning informal and then formal ballots by a margin of fifty-eight to thirty-one over his nearest contender. Compounding Hurlbut's disappointment, in November Douglas would defeat Lincoln for a Senate seat, although Washburne overcame his own Democratic challenger.[46] The foremost McHenry County Republican, Lawrence S. Church, reminded Washburne a week after the November election, "The *threat* made by Hurlbut in Rockford has not been realized, you will see, by the vote of 'Little Boone.'" Indeed, Hurlbut's native Boone County had given Washburne as large an electoral majority as Lincoln himself had gained from any heavily Republican district in Illinois.

Still, Hurlbut (as had Church) had won a minor prize at Rockford—nomination to the Illinois House of Representatives from the Fifty-fourth District. In November 1858 he would defeat a Democratic opponent to win a seat in the House at the state's Twenty-first General Assembly.[47] However, Hurlbut's first electoral victory did not offset the prohibitive price of his earlier, divisive political efforts. If he had by now earned Lincoln's gratitude, he had also thoroughly antagonized and alienated Washburne and many other prominent Republican leaders in northern Illinois. This hostility was to deprive him of their support when his Civil War career faltered late in the summer of 1861.

But in August 1858 all that, and Lincoln's eventual loss to Douglas, were in the future. Oblivious to his growing notoriety in the Washburne camp—or in the dominant faction of the Republican party in northern Illinois—Hurlbut turned his attention to the celebrated debates between Lincoln and Douglas.

Enthusiastic crowds had gathered at Ottawa, some eighty miles southwest of Chicago, on August 21 to hear the candidates engage in their first debate. Lincoln and Douglas there agreed to meet for a second debate on August 27 at Freeport, in Stephenson County, in northwest Illinois. To increase the number of Lincoln supporters present at the second debate and lend an air of militance, Hurlbut loaded the Boone Rifles on railroad cars and arranged for a special train to transport numerous Boone County Republicans to Freeport. There he listened intently as Douglas struggled to enunciate his vaguely defined Freeport Doctrine, which seemed to qualify his previous view on popular sovereignty. Hurlbut also heard Lincoln's persuasive reply. Hurlbut and his garishly uniformed militiamen paraded and drilled, with impressive martial pomp, to the accompaniment of fife and drums.

Later that day Hurlbut and his former associate James L. Loop subordinated national and state politics to their own partisan interests. In speeches at the Freeport courthouse, they charged Washburne with having unfairly gained renomination for Congress at the Rockford convention on August 19, and they decried his "perpetual" incumbency. Eagerly exploiting this open dissension within the Republican camp, the Democratic *Freeport Bulletin* urged "such men as Capt. Hulburt [*sic*] and Mr. Loop" to abandon the Republican party and instead "stand upon the Democratic platform for the sake of the Union, and against Abolition Sectionalism."[48] But Hurlbut returned to Belvidere, where he prepared for service in the Illinois House of Representatives.

Hurlbut sought first to locate suitable accommodations for himself and his family. With the assistance of Illinois secretary of state Ozias M. Hatch, he found and settled in a "pleasant place" near the capitol. Hurlbut participated in the first session of the Illinois General Assembly on January 3, 1859, and on January 5 the House speaker assigned him to serve concurrently on the standing committees of finance, internal improvements, and enrolled and engrossed bills. State legislatures in this period had constitutional authority to elect U.S. senators, regardless of the outcome of popular elections, and Hurlbut naturally voted for Lincoln. The legislature, though, the Democratic majority in which reflected what Hurlbut considered a gerrymandered system of districts, elected Douglas.[49] But Hurlbut gained a degree of revenge by leading other House Republicans in the defeat of a reapportionment bill that would have increased Democratic representation in the legislature. Cleverly linking the reapportionment measure to a sacrificial pork-barrel bill that he had introduced and that fiscally conservative Democrats strongly opposed, Hurlbut skillfully created a temporary coalition of Republicans and Democrats to defeat both bills with a decisive single vote. The *Belvidere Standard* gloated over these Democratic reverses, gleefully declaring, "They [Hurlbut and Lawrence S. Church] took the Democratic lion by the beard, and threshed him roundly in his own den."[50]

Following the conclusion of the first session of the General Assembly, Hurlbut and his wife and son returned to Belvidere. Proud of an impressive legislative performance, he informed Secretary of State Hatch in March 1859 that the "highly respectable body [of] my 'Constituents' are very remarkably well pleased with our session" and that the voters had drawn more pleasure from "what we did not do, than what we did." In particular, Hurlbut alluded here to his rural constituency's strong opposition to a proposed increase in the salary of state legislators, "supposing deluded mortals! That we had been guilty of more than Roman virtue of cutting off our own pay." In an implacably partisan vein, Hurlbut urged Hatch to press the state's attorney general promptly to indict the formerly Illinois Democratic governor Joel A. Matteson for "dabbling in public money." As governor from 1853 to 1856, Matteson had participated in a fraudulent scheme to reissue a large quantity of previously redeemed canal scrip worth over $224,000, an enormous sum (for those days) that the state treasurer had had finally to return to swindled certificate holders. Hurlbut expressed his hope that Matteson would be tried before the three-year statute of limitations lapsed. "Think it over coolly," Hurlbut advised Hatch. "If it were here [in Boone County] I would have him in the Penitentiary on that proof." Matteson notwithstanding avoided criminal prosecution, but the state of Illinois eventually recovered most of its funds by suing him.[51]

In June, Hurlbut returned to Springfield, where he served without special distinction in the second session of the General Assembly. He did, however, gain other favorable attention in Springfield the following October. In 1848, Hurlbut had joined the Belvidere Lodge of Masons, number sixty. He had participated in that benevolent society chiefly as a means of advancing his political career in Illinois, just as he had done in the Independent Order of Odd Fellows in South Carolina. In October 1859, in Springfield, Hurlbut won a special statewide election as the designated "grand orator" of Illinois Freemasons for 1860. Not less than five hundred Prairie State Masons, representing a majority of the members of 225 local lodges, voted for him. Gratified, he assumed his oratorical duties on October 6, following a colorful induction ritual in Springfield's First Presbyterian Church.[52]

Hurlbut then returned to Belvidere, where he resumed his bitter political feud with Washburne and the latter's supporters. Although he had anticipated a renewed challenge from Hurlbut, Washburne, who had just completed a campaign swing through the eastern section of the First Congressional District, learned from one of his supporters in November 1859 that "there has been some hard swearing done, S. A. Hurlbut and, Church, are of opinion that you have no right to travel across this district without their permission." Moreover, the Washburne man added, "Hurlbut says he will attend to your case in Boon [*sic*] & Winnebago [counties], and Church in McHenry (which he cannot do)." Church had abandoned Washburne in 1858 to join Hurlbut in a desperate effort to improve his own future congressional prospects, while Hurlbut was attempting to deter Washburne from seeking renomination for Congress in 1860. Besides threatening Washburne with political retaliation for "invading" his claimed political territory, Hurlbut denounced Elijah W. Blaisdell, the owner and editor of the *Rockford Republican* and one of Washburne's strongest supporters. In a letter to Secretary of State Hatch, he attacked Blaisdell's recommendation of William Holm, the Winnebago County clerk of courts, for Hatch's elective position. Blaisdell's "absurd course," Hurlbut asserted, had resulted from his having "exhausted his temporary popularity" as a possible candidate himself for executive political office in Springfield; Blaisdell also sought to avoid further embarrassment by attempting to "stir up the embers & put himself in the position of recognizing & cultivating local talent."[53] Hurlbut's warning failed to concern Hatch, who easily won another term of office in 1860.

Hurlbut resorted to whatever political strategy or tactic he could devise to defeat his perennial opponent Washburne. Hurlbut and his old Belvidere legal associate, now Judge James L. Loop of Rockford, as late as January 1860 unfailingly kept the "fires of their old animosity burning brighter than ever." As William Holm candidly informed Washburne, "It is said that the ferocity of H. knows no bounds, and that he is for any body any where who can effectually be set up to knock down Washburne." In all this, Hurlbut continued to show his lack of concern for party unity. Indeed, as Holm advised Washburne, Hurlbut would "patriotically surrender his own aspirations, and disinterestedly unite with his worst enemy to bring about this devoutly wished for consummation"—that is, Washburne's defeat. Hurlbut proceeded to the congressional nomination convention at Rockford late in July 1860 in this unappeasable frame of mind, where he made a bitterly abusive speech against Washburne. When two other rivals of Washburne had savagely "cut one another's throats" in the preliminary balloting, Hurlbut took their votes and made a final, determined bid for the nomination.[54] But his aggressive tactics failed again—Washburne gained fifty-three votes to his two remaining opponents' combined total of twenty-five. Hurlbut and Anson S. Miller, the humbled losers, nevertheless accepted the electoral result and, according to the *Rockford Republican,* in their speeches expressed "a spirit of hearty and generous concurrence" with Washburne's renomination.[55]

Reluctantly reconciled to his fifth consecutive defeat by the seemingly invincible Washburne, Hurlbut turned his attention to the approaching presidential campaign of 1860. He had advised Senator Trumbull in April 1860 that he and his fellow Boone County delegates feared that the Illinois Republican convention, to meet in Decatur early in May, would be torn asunder by factionalism and would deny Lincoln the nomination for president if Trumbull could not "bring positive strength to the Legislative Ticket." Trumbull's reelection, Hurlbut had shrewdly added, depended on the formation of a unified Republican majority within the Illinois state legislature. Having promised to support Trumbull at the convention, Hurlbut had traveled to Decatur and on May 9 sat among such notable Illinois Republicans as Richard J. Oglesby, Richard Yates, Joseph Medill, and a former Democrat turned Republican, the imposing "Long John" Wentworth.[56] The Illinois Republican convention nominated Lincoln as its "favorite son" for the presidency and elected a pro-Lincoln delegation to national convention in Chicago later in May. Helped by his own state's twenty-two votes, Lincoln had there won the Republican nomination for the White House.[57]

Though he did not attend the Chicago convention, Hurlbut remained eager to support the national Republican party. Creditably, he took fewer legal cases, willingly accepting the loss of fees, so that he could stump much of Illinois in support of Lincoln's candidacy.[58] After election as vice president of the Boone County delegation to a spirited Lincoln rally that met at Lincoln's residence in Springfield on August 8, 1860, Hurlbut entered on the hustings. He gave speeches in Springfield and canvassed communities across rural central and eastern Illinois. At Mattoon, on August 10, he and other orators addressed a "mammoth gathering" of twenty-thousand Republican party supporters. On August 11, boldly venturing into traditional Democratic territory, Hurlbut and his cohorts addressed six thousand Democratic and "Constitutional Union Party" voters at Olney. In a fiery, if vague, speech, he propounded his moderately conservative Republican view, confessing his South Carolina origins and contacts with slavery in the South but also repudiating as partisan extremes abolitionism and the now-discredited doctrine of popular sovereignty. In this way he gained "at least a dozen votes for old Abe" Lincoln. The *Belvidere Standard* later reported that "Mr. H. appeared a little fagged out" attacking "squatter sovereignty" and the Dred Scott decision at a meeting of the Belvidere Republican Club.[59]

Impressed by Hurlbut's oratorical performances and grateful for his effective, although predictably unproductive, electioneering in the Democratic strongholds south and east of Springfield, Lincoln requested him to speak to Republican and Democratic audiences in Indiana. Hurlbut obliged. Late in October 1860 a thankful Lincoln assured Hurlbut's wife, Sophronia, that "Your good husband, who is making speeches for us" in Illinois and Indiana, "is well" and "rendering us very efficient service."[60] As the election approached, Hurlbut returned to Belvidere and joined the rank and file of the "Wide Awakes," a partisan quasi-military unit that he and Allen C. Fuller had helped to organize late the previous September. Its 250 men, under Capt. Charles B. Loop, marched in torchlight parades and assembled at raucous party rallies across Illinois and in other Northern states in support of Lincoln's candidacy, quickly acquiring an enviable reputation for strict discipline and precision.[61]

As Hurlbut had foreseen, that November Lincoln defeated Douglas and two other candidates for the presidency, while Hurlbut himself won another term in the Illinois House of Representatives. In December 1860, before returning to Springfield, Hurlbut sought to effect a reconciliation between himself and Washburne in view of the sectional crisis that had arisen in the weeks following Lincoln's election—South Carolina and several other southern states had declared their intention to secede from the Union. Hurlbut wrote to Washburne, declaring that Illinois Republicans and Democrats, regardless of their philosophical differences or partisan rivalries, stood together in firm opposition to disunion and that nothing but the "baptism of blood through servile insurrection" into which the "seceding states are about to pass will restore any sympathy between the North & South." Any political concession or compromise effected in Washington to avert secession would amount to "simple folly," Hurlbut asserted; the Lincoln administration, which would take office in March 1861, and the newly elected Republican Congress should show the South a "calm confidence" springing from "conspicuous power" in resisting the forced dismemberment of the Union.

Hurlbut castigated President Buchanan—that "imbecile old man O.P.F. (Old Public Functionary)"—for his last annual message to Congress, in which he had "sinned away the day of Grace to the best of his miserable ability" and complicated matters for the new administration. In his message Buchanan had seemed prepared to repudiate, in theoretical terms at least, the constitutional right of a state to secede, and yet he had denied that the federal government had any authority to force a seceded state to return to the Union. Anticipating with pleasure Buchanan's departure from the White House, Hurlbut pointed out that numerous threats had been made against Lincoln's life by both Southerners and anti-Lincoln men in the North; Hurlbut assured Washburne that he and ten thousand other Wide Awakes stood prepared to march to Washington to ensure his safe and peaceful inauguration.[62]

Notwithstanding his belated affirmation of party unity, Hurlbut could not set aside his own ambition. He sought endorsement from David Davis, judge of the Eighth Illinois Circuit Court and Lincoln's campaign manager, as U.S. district attorney for northern Illinois. He also urgently warned Davis of a concerted and powerful movement in Illinois designed to procure a cabinet post for Norman B. Judd, chairman of the Republican State Central Committee at Chicago and a strong supporter of Lincoln. "Mr. Lincoln *must* consider himself at absolute liberty to use this State as best he can for the good of himself & the Republican party," Hurlbut argued—a discretion that extended to the prerogative, if not obligation, excluding Illinois associates from his cabinet, to avoid the appearance of favoritism.[63] Actually, Lincoln had already decided not to include any Illinois Republicans in his cabinet (though Lincoln was to give Judd another position in his administration). Still, Hurlbut's warning, however self-serving, had improved his own chances of obtaining Lincoln's patronage.

Meanwhile early in 1861 Hurlbut prepared to take his seat in the Twenty-second General Assembly of the Illinois state legislature. Now in his forty-fifth year, Hurlbut was outwardly a different man from the one who had settled in Belvidere in 1845. A newspaper reporter in Springfield described him as having a medium stature, a slight figure enhanced by an erect carriage, and "a roman nose, small mouth with firmly set lips, and an agreeable expression of countenance." But the years had taken their toll on Hurlbut's once handsome looks. Now partly balding, with grizzled, curly hair around large ears, he had grown paunchy; his formerly prominent chin was noticeably receding, and his once-sharp vision was now impaired. He showed unmistakable signs of advancing age. Notwithstanding his deteriorated physical appearance, Hurlbut struck one perceptive observer as decidedly "a man of genius" and "a creature of impulse," a man of strong will who spoke with a sarcastic tongue. Blunt, often outspoken, and "crusty," Hurlbut was a "dashing" debater with an "off-hand manner that is especially captivating." He impressed political associates as "a good parliamentarian and good tactician, probably the best in the House."[64]

Early in 1861 Hurlbut sought to ensure Republican control of the Illinois House by nominating the Republican jurist Shelby M. Cullom for the speakership. On the evening of January 5, two days before the beginning of the first session, Hurlbut and Lawrence S. Church pressed Cullom "so strongly" to permit them to advance his candidacy that he finally "consented, and became the nominee of my party associates." The Republican-dominated House then easily elected Cullom to the speaker's chair.[65] Hurlbut now proceeded to override Democratic opposition to liberal state bank legislation. A supporter of strong banks from his Whig days,

Hurlbut drew up a report recommending procedures and regulations that would, he anticipated, place Illinois's banking system on a sounder and more sophisticated fiscal basis. With Democratic opponents in the minority, Hurlbut's banking bill passed in both branches of the legislature in February 1861.[66] The first session of the General Assembly then adjourned.

Returning to Belvidere late in February, Hurlbut resumed his efforts to secure a position within the Lincoln administration, seeking Senator Trumbull's endorsement of his application to be the U.S. district attorney at Chicago. In the company of James L. Loop, he traveled by rail to Washington and (as he later described to Trumbull) in a "delighted" mood witnessed Lincoln's inauguration as the sixteenth president of the United States. After the solemn ceremony on Capitol Hill, Hurlbut advised Lincoln's private secretary, John G. Nicolay, that he intended to return to Belvidere for two weeks but would return to Washington about March 20, "when I hope to find the new order of things in successful operation"—and, by implication, such deserving candidates as himself might expect presidential appointments. He requested Nicolay to intervene with Lincoln to procure the office he sought.[67]

A disappointed Hurlbut learned that he had failed when he met with President Lincoln at the White House on March 21; Lincoln had awarded the district attorneyship to a Chicago supporter. Shortly thereafter, however, one "Belvidere" (a pseudonymous correspondent in Washington for the *Belvidere Standard*) announced, "It is rumored that S. A. Hurlbut can have the Consulship to Brazil (Rio de Janeiro), compensation $6,000," because "he stands high with the President." Moreover, Lincoln had instructed Hurlbut to convey dispatches and letters to the commandant of Fort Sumter, in Charleston Harbor; however, the *Standard*'s reporter added, "His mission is unknown."[68]

The Charleston assignment was important—indeed, urgent. Lincoln knew that Hurlbut had known several of the leading secessionists and Unionists of his native Charleston, particularly the Unionist jurist James Louis Petigru. Since February 1861, when the seceded states had formed what they called the Confederate States of America at Montgomery, Alabama, military forces had surrounded the isolated garrison at Fort Sumter. Lincoln now needed a trusted friend to obtain information as to the state of affairs in South Carolina. Flattered by Lincoln's expression of confidence—if daunted by the prospect of returning to Charleston, which he had fled sixteen years before in disgrace and where secessionists now ruled—Hurlbut agreed. Lincoln directed him to travel with Ward H. Lamon, a former law partner of Lincoln's and whom the president intended to appoint as U.S. marshal for the District of Columbia.[69] Though Lincoln may not have precisely informed Hurlbut of it, Lamon's mission was as important as his own; Lincoln had requested Lamon to make a diplomatic effort to avert hostilities over Fort Sumter. Lincoln also hoped that Hurlbut and Lamon could determine how much food and ammunition were left in the beleaguered fort.

Hurlbut left the White House after accepting his assignment with considerable trepidation. But he returned the following morning of March 22 and received from the president a short letter introducing him to Maj. Robert Anderson, in command at Fort Sumter. Drafted and signed by the infirm but brilliant Winfield Scott, the commanding general of the U.S. Army, the note simply read: "I take pleasure in presenting to you Hon. Stephen A. Hurlbut a native of Charleston where he has many friends," thereby assuring Anderson—a Kentuckian and a slave owner—of Hurlbut's staunch support of federal authority.[70] Lamon, who was to confer with the South Carolina governor, then at Charleston, would presumably obtain the governor's permission to visit Anderson himself, but Hurlbut would have only Scott's letter. Lincoln hoped that Confederate officers would defer to Scott's reputation and authority, irrespective of political considerations or formal diplomatic protocol.

Hurlbut and his wife entrusted their son to close friends in Washington and on Friday evening, March 22, departed with Lamon on their journey by rail to Charleston. They passed through Richmond, Virginia, where they observed the preparation of munitions for shipment south by rail, and reached Charleston at 8 A.M. on Sunday morning, the twenty-fourth. There they beheld eight newly arrived iron mortars at the railroad depot. After a carriage ride through the city's crowded, soldier-filled streets, Lamon took a room at the Charleston Hotel, while Hurlbut and his wife Sophronia proceeded to the home of Elizabeth Crocker Hurlbut Kerr, Hurlbut's sister.

By this time a succession of urgent messages from alert Southern correspondents in Washington announcing Lamon's peace mission had begun to reach the *Charleston Daily Courier*. Unaware of that and prudently attempting to conceal the true object of his journey, Lamon identified himself as a Virginian (he had been born in Virginia in 1828, settling in Illinois in 1847) in Charleston on postal business. Meanwhile, Hurlbut left his wife and sister and boldly "rode around the City, visiting especially the wharves and the Battery so as to view the shipping in port and the Harbour." Regretfully, he quickly discovered that not a "single vessel in port displayed American Colours"; the Stars and Stripes proudly floating over Fort Sumter was "the only evidence of jurisdiction and nationality." He attempted to arrange passage to Fort Sumter to meet with Major Anderson, but Confederate troops guarding the wharves barred him, despite General Scott's letter of introduction.[71]

After nightfall, Hurlbut rejoined Lamon, and the two men surreptitiously went to the home of James Louis Petigru and informed him of their secret mission. When Hurlbut and Lamon had departed, Petigru momentarily forgot the gravity of the crisis and guffawed, "Who would have thought that of all men Stephen Augustus would ever become an ambassador?"[72]

Early on March 25, Hurlbut obtained from Petigru information on what little Unionist sentiment there was in Charleston. He also conferred with many prominent South Carolina secessionists, including his old friend and former American Republican Association colleague William Henry Trescot, as well as numerous merchants and lawyers and bankers, as to the reasons underlying their disunionist attitude. Hurlbut eleven years afterward would recall that when he warned these overconfident men that the North would resort to war to prevent permanent disruption of the Union, "They laughed at me."[73]

Meanwhile, Lamon conferred at the Charleston Hotel with South Carolina's secessionist governor Francis W. Pickens and assured him of Lincoln's peaceful intentions. At one o'clock that afternoon, accompanied by the governor's principal military aide, Lamon boarded the steamer *Planter* and proceeded to Fort Sumter. Disembarked alone, for nearly an hour Lamon conferred with Major Anderson, walking the fort's ramparts and surveying its fortifications. During the short return trip, Lamon impressed on Pickens's military adviser the necessity of preserving the peace. In fact, Lamon had inadvertently exceeded Lincoln's instructions by conveying to Pickens and Anderson the impression that the president was willing to order the immediate evacuation of Fort Sumter.[74]

Lamon returned to the Charleston Hotel. Seated in the hotel's reading room before joining Hurlbut as arranged at the train station that evening, Lamon suddenly found himself accosted by several members of the Charleston Vigilance Committee. Whether mischievously or maliciously, the vigilantes "played off a joke upon him" and suddenly threw Lamon into "bodily terror." Pretending not to recognize him as "the Envoy from Washington" himself, one of the "boys" expressed his enmity toward the "cowardly messenger," "recommending a suit of tar and feathers for a sneaking attorney, named Lamon, reported to be in the city." Another vigilante, bitterly cursing Lincoln, brandished a thick rope with which he and his associates threatened to lynch Lamon. At this juncture, South Carolina congressman Lawrence Keitt (a friend of Lamon) opportunely intervened and guided Lamon out of the hotel and to the station, on the outskirts of Charleston. The party boarded separate cars on the outbound eight o'clock train of the Northeastern Railroad. Apparently unaware of the *Courier*'s reports and of Lamon's encounter with the vigilance committee, Hurlbut endeavored to keep his and Lamon's presence secret. Knowing the conductor, Hurlbut had him pass a hastily scribbled note to Lamon warning, "Don't you recognize us [that is, Hurlbut and his wife] until this train gets out of South Carolina. There is danger ahead, and a damned sight of it. Steve."[75]

Lamon carefully heeded Hurlbut's warning, and Lincoln's two peace envoys safely reached the North. But as early as March 25, the Charleston correspondent for the *New York Tribune* attributed the practical difficulties of their mission to Hurlbut's notoriety in Charleston. He informed his readers that although now a "presidential envoy" and, as he described him, a personal secretary to Lamon, a younger, rather disreputable Hurlbut had been "arrested for debt contracted some years ago." The following day, on the basis of information from vengeful local citizens, the correspondent elaborated that Hurlbut had been "driven from Charleston some time ago, on account of his heterodox views as to the Divine character of human Slavery." Consequently, the long-exiled Hurlbut "was yesterday exposed to numerous insults and annoyances from his enemies of bygone days."[76] Although neither the reporter nor his sources provided proof of the charges against Hurlbut, it is possible that in addition to his earlier alleged embezzlement and fraud, Hurlbut's unusually outspoken opposition to slavery might have further prompted his departure from Charleston in 1845.

Returning to Washington on March 27, Hurlbut reported his findings to Lincoln in a formal and confidential letter. As did Lamon in a separate report, Hurlbut dashed any hopes the president might have entertained of Unionist suppression of the secessionist movement in South Carolina. He bluntly advised Lincoln that in South Carolina "separate Nationality is a fixed fact, that there is an unanimity of sentiment which to my mind is astonishing—that there is no attachment to the Union." Any concession to, or conciliation of, the secessionists would inevitably prove futile; "National Patriotism, always feeble in Carolina, has been extinguished and overridden" by state loyalty. Furthermore, Charleston's merchant class saw a vested interest in an independent Confederate nation, expecting increased trade and prosperity in a golden "Southern Republic." Hurlbut also explained that although a substantial majority of Charleston's secessionists favored the peaceful separation, there existed and freely operated in South Carolina "a large minority indefatigably active and reckless," who sought to engulf the country in a bloody civil war over Fort Sumter and thereby win the strategic border states of Virginia, Maryland, Kentucky, and Missouri to the Confederacy. Concerning Fort Sumter itself, Hurlbut warned Lincoln not to attempt to reinforce or provision its besieged garrison—but neither should Lincoln abandon the fort. If hostilities should follow, Lincoln should allow the Confederates to make the first belligerent act. "If war comes," Hurlbut ominously declared, "let it come."[77]

Lincoln concurred, in part, with Hurlbut's views. Early in April 1861 he ordered a second relief expedition to Fort Sumter (in January 1861, President Buchanan had unsuccessfully attempted to resupply Anderson's garrison). The action precipitated a Confederate bombardment of the fort, which commenced on the morning of April 12. After bravely enduring an unrelenting barrage, to which he could return only ineffectual fire, Major Anderson on April 14 surrendered the shattered fort and its weary garrison to jubilant and boastful Confederate forces.[78] For Lincoln, for Hurlbut, and for the rest of the nation, the long-dreaded civil war had finally begun.

Hurlbut's courageous efforts to help Lincoln to avert the fall of Fort Sumter (or at least uphold the government's authority over that federal fortress) and his political involvement in the previous sectional crisis had at long last produced political prominence in Illinois. His path to such stature had been an uneven one. An able practicing lawyer in Boone County since his settlement in Belvidere late in 1845, he had achieved considerable distinction as a Whig and Republican state politician. However, his repeated and humiliating failures to defeat Elihu B. Washburne had resulted largely from Washburne's superior political astuteness and Hurlbut's unwillingness, or inability, to build a more effective and wider network of supporters. What commenced as a spirited political race for congressional office in 1852 had culminated in a bitter partisan feud by 1860, owing mainly to Hurlbut's determination to gain a reputation as the foremost Whig and Republican in northern Illinois. Still, Hurlbut was noted as a debater and an adroit coalition builder, antislavery rhetorician, and moderately conservative Republican (if with a nativist bias). He had shown unflagging energy in campaigning for Lincoln across Illinois and northern Indiana in 1860—accumulating in the process burdensome debts by neglecting his once successful and profitable legal practice. In the spring of 1861, roused to action by the attack on Fort Sumter, Hurlbut was poised to help quell the Southern rebellion while simultaneously advancing his career as a politician.

CHAPTER THREE

Suppressor of Rebellion:
General Hurlbut Invades the Confederacy

The Confederate seizure of Fort Sumter prompted an indignant Hurlbut to organize an infantry regiment of "Minute Men" in the northern counties of Illinois. He attended a war rally in Belvidere, a town then overflowing with patriotic men answering Lincoln's call for seventy-five thousand volunteers to serve for ninety days. Hurlbut, now commanding officer of the Boone Rifles, sought the captaincy of the newly formed Company B of what became the 15th Illinois Volunteer Infantry—one of the first regiments mustered into service for a period of three years. He was supported in his ambition by his former legal colleague Judge Allen C. Fuller. On April 20, Hurlbut's comrades in arms and other Boone County men unanimously elected him to be the captain of Company B. Fuller presented Hurlbut with "a beautiful sword" and scabbard. Hurlbut procured from Chicago crisp blue uniforms and black hats and then transported his men by rail to Camp Scott, near Freeport.[1]

At Camp Scott, Hurlbut drilled his company, composed principally of his former militia troops, and posted its men as guards at the "Camp of Instruction" (his company was the only one in the regiment with muskets) for three weeks before running for the colonelcy of the 15th Illinois. He had served as the regimental adjutant of the Washington Light Infantry in Florida during the Seminole War and had also acquired an enviable reputation as a militia company commander in the 1850s. However, most of the 15th Illinois's nine companies hailed from Stephenson, Winnebago, Lake, McHenry, Jo Daviess, and

Carroll counties, not from Boone. On May 14, the regiment elected another candidate, Thomas J. Turner of Freeport, as its colonel by a vote of 529 to 367. A forty-six-year-old, Ohio-born lawyer and erstwhile Stephenson County probate court judge, county paymaster, and state district attorney, Turner had also served as a Democratic member of the U.S. House of Representatives from 1847 to 1849. In 1854 he had become speaker of the Illinois House of Representatives and one year later the first mayor of Freeport. In 1847 he had founded the *Prairie Democrat,* Stephenson County's first newspaper. Though identifying himself after 1854 as an anti-Nebraska Democrat, Turner had served as the moderator for the Republican candidate (each candidate had a moderator) during the Lincoln-Douglas debate at Freeport in 1858. Finally, as a Republican delegate, he had attended the momentous Washington Peace Conference early in 1861, further enhancing his reputation in upstate Illinois.

Hurlbut, mortified, abruptly resigned his captaincy. Ostensibly, he relinquished his command because Turner (whom he derided as an "outsider") had not previously joined a regimental unit. Also, Turner quickly proved himself an incompetent drillmaster, in sharp contrast to Hurlbut.[2] For these reasons, Hurlbut explained, he sought a rank in the Union army commensurate with his supposedly superior military education and experience and consistent with his stature within the Illinois Republican party. But probably his action sprang from a combination of motives involving pride and humiliation. He harbored a deep envy of his political rivals, one of them Turner, who had seemingly surpassed him in their first efforts to win military laurels. Consequently, to equal his competitors by exploiting the patronage and patriotism of those Illinois Republicans who sought to increase the number of Illinois general officers, Hurlbut requested and obtained recommendations for appointment by President Lincoln as a brigadier general of U.S. Volunteers.

He quickly obtained these recommendations from Gov. Richard Yates, Congressman Elihu B. Washburne, and the wealthy Galena merchant Joseph Russell Jones. By 1856, with Lincoln's help, Yates had established himself as a leading Republican in Illinois and had won the gubernatorial election of 1860. Following the outbreak of war, he had insistently clamored for the nomination of a West Point graduate, Capt. John Pope of Illinois, to brigadier general in the regular army, besides the appointment of other men as colonels of the new Illinois volunteer regiments. Yates, who had collaborated effectively with Hurlbut in the General Assembly, could not immediately procure from President Lincoln a definite commitment; determined to ensure selection of four Illinois men as brigadier generals commanding the eighteen Illinois volunteer regiments, Yates hurried to Washington to pressure Lincoln. On May 29, Yates approached Lincoln at the

War Department and reminded him that he and other leading Prairie State politicians regarded Hurlbut "as one of the best military men in Ills." Lincoln thereupon replied, in characteristically humorous and self-deprecating terms, "I hadn't thought of him, but he is one of the best, and I'll be dirned if I don't believe he'll get it." Lincoln repeated this statement, and Yates relayed it to Hurlbut. Nevertheless, Lincoln still hedged.[3] Elihu Washburne's influence, however, proved decisive. He understood that Hurlbut's nomination would "gratify friends" of Lincoln from northern Illinois who desired to have at least one man from their section of the state appointed as a general officer. Early in June, therefore, Washburne urged the evidently reluctant Lincoln to make Hurlbut a brigadier general.[4]

However, Hurlbut's most vigorous supporter proved to be thirty-eight-year-old Joseph Russell Jones. The enterprising Jones had risen spectacularly as an entrepreneur in the upper Mississippi Valley by the 1850s. He was a partner in a mercantile firm and had managed the Galena and Minnesota Packet Line, a steamboat company that carried mail, cargo, and passengers between Galena, Dubuque, Iowa, St. Paul, Minnesota, St. Louis, Missouri, and other points. Jones had thereby accumulated substantial wealth, with which he had erected a magnificent mansion in Galena and from which he had contributed generously to the campaigns of Washburne and Lincoln. An aspiring politician himself, Jones had served with Hurlbut in the General Assembly early in 1861. In February 1861, President Lincoln had nominated Jones as U.S. marshal for the Northern District of Illinois, with his headquarters in Chicago. Thereafter, Jones had pressured Governor Yates to appoint a graduate of West Point, Yates's military aide, Capt. Ulysses S. Grant, also of Galena, as the colonel of a regiment of Illinois volunteer infantry.[5] Ironically, in hindsight, Jones now supported the appointment of Hurlbut, a fellow politician with scant militia experience, as a brigadier general, commanding over three or four Illinois regiments. Hurlbut himself had initially approached Jones only for assistance in obtaining a regimental commission from Yates. Jones had learned, however, that Hurlbut's close friends, especially Allen C. Fuller, had refused to intercede with Yates because of what they alleged to be Hurlbut's insobriety. Nonetheless, early in June 1861, Jones advised Hurlbut (who was in Belvidere, anxiously awaiting official word) that Washburne had urged Lincoln to give Hurlbut the rank of brigadier general of volunteers.[6]

Washburne's support of Hurlbut was probably an expression of gratitude to Jones for his financial support of his campaigns against Hurlbut. If so, it scarcely reflected a reconciliation of the rivalry that had divided the two men since 1852. Washburne and Hurlbut had since 1856 jockeyed for status within, and spoils through, the "Illinois Clique" of Prairie State Republicans, now headed by President Lincoln himself. Nevertheless, no inconsistency marked Washburne's strong

Richard Yates, Civil War governor of Illinois. Illinois State Historical Library.

endorsement of Hurlbut, or Hurlbut's solicitation and acceptance of that support. Washburne probably interceded to place a moderately conservative western Republican politician into the senior ranks of the Union army so as to
strengthen his state's influence in the national Republican party. He apparently
also sought to counterbalance Lincoln's previously announced appointments of
potentially prominent "War Democrats," such as Illinois congressman John A.
McClernand and a former liberal Democratic judge of the Massachusetts General Court, Benjamin F. Butler. Furthermore, Lincoln had also announced his
appointment of an unsuccessful aspirant for the Republican presidential nomination in 1860, the former governor Nathaniel P. Banks of Massachusetts.
Washburne could also have meant to use Hurlbut to cloak his own partisan
ambition, or even to destroy his political archrival. If Hurlbut succeeded, Wash-

burne could accept substantial credit for it, whereas if Hurlbut failed Washburne could justly censure him and perhaps ruin his political career.

Lincoln, in his efforts to build the "Union party" across the North—a broad bipartisan coalition to include Republicans and War Democrats alike—finally decided to nominate Hurlbut as a brigadier general. He announced the appointment on June 14, 1861, effective as of the previous May 17.[7] Clearly, Lincoln sought thereby to conciliate Governor Yates, having denied Pope (then a mustering officer in Chicago and Springfield) the requested regular brigadier generalship (although he did raise Pope to that rank in the volunteers, also effective May 17, 1861). Moreover, the nomination was a reward for Hurlbut's past political loyalty and the hazardous mission to Charleston before the fall of Fort Sumter. But ultimately Lincoln based his decision to appoint Hurlbut on the recommendations of Washburne and Jones.

Few Republican Illinois newspapers reported Hurlbut's appointment. The *Belvidere Standard* declared that "Mr. Hurlbut has had a regular military education," making him eminently qualified to "bear such a trust," inasmuch as "raw levies and raw officers are played out." The *Chicago Evening Journal*, in another typical Republican reaction, merely said that Hurlbut could boast of a reputation as a "man of military education—a thorough disciplinarian—[and moreover he] has seen service" in the Seminole War of 1840. But the *Rockford Republican*, knowing only of Hurlbut's militia background, mistakenly reported that "Mr. Hurlbut, we understand, is a graduate of West Point" and "a gentleman of extensive military knowledge and very decided military spirit." The *Republican* praised Lincoln's decision as a wise one: "A better selection for this responsible position could not have been made."

Still bitter at Hurlbut's blocking of Democratic gerrymandering and pork barrel legislation in 1859, besides his sponsoring of bank legislation that Democrats had opposed, the state's Democratic press perceived Hurlbut as vulnerable to attack and unanimously denounced the appointment. Thus the *Chicago Post*, eager to discredit Hurlbut, erroneously asserted that Hurlbut had run for the colonelcy of what later became the 21st Illinois Volunteer Infantry at Mattoon and that even the drunken and inefficient Capt. Simon S. Goode (whom one Union army veteran described as "reputed to be an English nobleman, but . . . a confirmed inebriate") had defeated him (Grant had superseded Goode in command earlier that June).[8] The *Chicago Times* reluctantly rebutted the *Post*'s report, but agreed with the *Post* and the *Illinois State Register* of Springfield that Hurlbut's commission constituted "a joke" and "an outrage." The *State Register* disputed the *Chicago Evening Journal*'s assertions regarding Hurlbut's military education and militia experience: "It is all pop-cock" and mere "trickery" whereby "an unmitigated, unscrupulous partisan" had obtained unmerited presidential patronage. "Mr. Lincoln had better find a more comfortable place for Mr. Hurlburt than in such prominent command of Illinois volunteers," the *Register* warned. The *Freeport Bulletin* reported that Hurlbut had resigned from the 15th Illinois Infantry in the expectation of a presidential appointment: "We think it was unkind in the President to tempt Mr. H. to forego the performance of 'paramount duties,' by the glitter of a General's epaulets." Finally, the *Ottawa (Illinois) Free Trader* asserted bluntly, "He is a one-horse lawyer, and a brawling precinct politician, and that's all." The "farce" of his appointment was an "insult" and "outrage" upon the experienced colonels and captains in the regiments to be "commanded by General! Hurlbut."[9]

Hurlbut in Belvidere learned of his appointment with mixed feelings ranging from gratification to trepidation. He congratulated himself for his special relationship with Lincoln, but he doubted his ability to lead a brigade into battle; his insecurity was betrayed by suddenly heavier drinking. Hurlbut's intemperance had begun during his command of Company B at Camp Scott. Separated unhappily from his family and unable to practice his legal profession; debilitated by the rigors of soldiering in open country; constantly exposed to the temptations of betting, gambling, and drinking among convivial comrades; and demoralized by the boredom and intense loneliness of life in an isolated camp, Hurlbut had indulged in excessive drinking for courage, consolation, and relief. But he also drank because he craved alcohol.

Knowledge of Hurlbut's increasing intemperance had theretofore remained confined to the inner circle of the Illinois Clique, particularly Trumbull and Washburne. Now, however, his dissipation attracted wider attention. On July 4 Maj. Gen. George B. McClellan, the commander of the Department of the Ohio with headquarters at Cincinnati, ordered Hurlbut to take command of Illinois troops at Quincy, Illinois, on the Mississippi, and protect the exposed tracks of the Hannibal & St. Joseph Railroad across northern Missouri.[10] Accordingly, early in July Hurlbut made three trips to Chicago to prepare the 19th Illinois Volunteers, a colorfully uniformed Zouave unit, for transport by rail to Quincy to join three other Illinois regiments. On each occasion, he engaged in wild binges. On July 11 Hurlbut, who had squandered his funds carousing, urged Joseph Russell Jones to meet him at the Briggs House early the next morning. Jones, who occupied a room in that hotel, "was promptly on hand," only to learn that Hurlbut "was in need of $200 until the Paymaster got around. *I had not the money.*" In reproachful terms, Jones informed Hurlbut that he had already advised Washburne of Hurlbut's intemperance and that Washburne anxiously "wished to know about his habits." An abashed Hurlbut assured Jones

Stephen Augustus Hurlbut (Brig. Gen., U.S. Volunteers). U.S. Army Military History Institute.

that "he had promised his wife not to drink anymore."[11] But instead of preparing the 19th Illinois, Hurlbut resumed his heavy drinking. On July 12 Jones composed a letter for Washburne in which he expressed his concern that "now if the Senate should cut off his head [that is, refuse to confirm his appointment as brigadier general] I shall be charged no doubt with having been the cause of it." He also expressed his hope that Hurlbut would keep "his promise to his spouse, but I very much fear he will not."

Finally, Jones informed Washburne that he had warned Judge Fuller, once the president of the Boone County Temperance Society in the 1850s (which Hurlbut had not joined, although he had addressed a "rousing" meeting in February 1858), about Hurlbut's drinking. Fuller had "said if I would write you that he was still getting tight he would write to Trumbull" and that Jones and Fuller would then exchange copies of their letters.[12] Thus Jones may have been positioning himself to repudiate Hurlbut. For, as with Washburne, if Hurlbut succeeded, Jones could claim credit, but if Hurlbut should fail, particularly because of intemperance, Jones could renounce him.

But Hurlbut thought he could depend on one sincere and selfless supporter in Chicago, a man who could personally attest to Hurlbut's avowed determination to conquer his insobriety. Henry S. Fitch was a shrewd young Chicago lawyer now on his staff. Fitch, who was in fact rather more solicitous of his own financial security than Hurlbut's welfare, late in June 1861 assured Senator Trumbull of Hurlbut's fitness and urged him to vote for his confirmation. More selfishly, on July 13 he warned Washburne of pecuniary calamity that would probably befall him if Hurlbut's confirmation failed. Fitch, looking ahead to a postwar political career, had dissolved a successful law partnership in Chicago in order to accept an unremunerative position on Hurlbut's staff: "To be disappointed now, as I should be if he is defeated, would *ruin me*." Fitch acknowledged that his chief's "habits may have been bad, but I am convinced from personal observation, that he is resolute in his reformation, and that *pride*, if nothing else, will entirely curb his indulgence."[13] Obviously, Fitch either knew nothing of Hurlbut's heavy drinking in Chicago or simply suppressed the truth.

Hurlbut's behavior in Chicago shocked and outraged Joseph Medill, the influential editor of the *Chicago Tribune*. Medill, who had vigorously supported his close friend Abraham Lincoln for the presidency in 1860, impressed upon Trumbull on July 13 that "an awful blunder has been committed in the appointment of Hurlbut Brig Gen." Hurlbut's "habits of intemperance wholly unfit him for so high a command. He has been in this city for a week past *drunk every day*." Medill also informed Trumbull that Hurlbut had just left Chicago with the 19th Illinois, amid excessive martial pomp and ceremony, "in a sad condition—scarcely able to walk at all, so drunk was he." Patriotic citizens of Chicago had felt "aggrieved and insulted" by Hurlbut's appointment, while Chicago parents had seen "some 1500 of their sons and relations [placed] under the command of this inebriate who may lead them to dishonorable graves." Medill indignantly asked Trumbull, "Will the Senate inflict this confirmed sot upon the army?" He had learned of a recent encounter in Chicago between Hurlbut and Judge Fuller, in which Fuller had recognized Hurlbut's insobriety and after which Fuller had "hung his head in grief and shame" and had promised Medill that he himself would urge Trumbull to oppose Hurlbut's confirmation. Medill declared that the "Senate must do its duty without fear or favor and weed out of the army the bad and incompetent officers." Finally, in exasperation and contempt, Medill inquired: "Why cannot the President give us for Generals, men who know something of the *trade of war* and at least *sober* men?"

Lincoln had already begun to suspect Hurlbut's intemperance, though he had not recognized the gravity of his condition.[14] A disturbing corroboration of the editor's accusations came from James Long, the Republican vice president of Chicago's Committee of Safety, a military preparedness organization. Long advised Trumbull on July 13 that Hurlbut's conduct in Chicago had produced widespread "distrust of ability, as it certainly does ridicule & disgust." For Hurlbut had rendered himself "so far intoxicated," Long complained, "as to bluster & boast" and to "make himself generally ridiculous both to officers & men. . . . [H]e certainly is an unsafe man to trust with the lives of our soldiers." Long urged Trumbull to vote against Hurlbut's confirmation in the Senate.[15]

Hurlbut reached Quincy and organized his brigade there on July 14. He wrote to Illinois senator Orville H. Browning solemnly promising that he would thereafter abstain from drinking in high commands in the Union army. Hurlbut rightly feared that Jones, Washburne, and probably Trumbull had brought Lincoln to consider dismissing him; he hoped that Browning, who had considerable influence with Lincoln, would restore the confidence that the president had once reposed in him, as well as support his confirmation. (Browning surely enjoyed Lincoln's confidence. He had served as a Whig in the Illinois Senate in 1836 and in the Illinois House in 1842, before playing important roles in the 1856 and 1860 national Republican conventions. Now fifty-five, he had accepted an appointment from Governor Yates in June 1861 to fill the U.S. Senate seat of the recently deceased Stephen A. Douglas.) On July 18 Browning replied to Hurlbut that he expected to "hear the very best possible accounts of you. I know the thing is in you, and it will be your own fault if you don't bring it out." Browning appreciated Hurlbut's "written pledge not to give occasion for scandal against you" and trusted that Hurlbut would not violate it. The entire Senate would consider his candidacy for a permanent military appointment on July 29; "I do not think there will be any trouble about your confirmation. I know of no reason for uneasiness or apprehension." He intended, he informed Hurlbut, to convey Hurlbut's abstinence pledge to Lincoln.[16]

Encouraged, Hurlbut addressed himself to the critical military situation prevailing in Missouri. Secessionist Missouri State Guard militia and guerrilla bands threatened to overturn the new state government, which Home Guard militia and other Unionist elements had established in St. Louis after the secessionist governor Claiborne F. Jackson had fled the city. Perceiving that the state was politically and strategically crucial and appreciating the necessity for an overall commander in the West, on July 3 Lincoln appointed John C. Frémont to the rank of major general in the regular army and named him commander (succeeding McClellan) of the newly created Western Department, a vast jurisdiction that embraced the whole of Illinois, the states and territories west of the Mississippi and east of the Rocky Mountains, and New Mexico, with headquarters at St. Louis. Frémont thus entered the Union army as one of the most prominent, and most promising, major generals.[17]

Meanwhile Hurlbut, obeying McClellan's earlier orders and anticipating their confirmation by Frémont, rapidly began putting his troops across the Mississippi River to protect the Hannibal & St. Joseph Railroad. He had under his command six well-organized infantry regiments: the 14th, 16th, 19th, and 21st Illinois Volunteers, and the 2d and 3d Iowa Volunteers, aggregating about six thousand men. Almost immediately, however, Hurlbut learned that contingents of his troops, particularly from the 16th and 19th Illinois, were vandalizing private property and stealing livestock in northeastern Missouri, under the guise of requisitioning supplies. Hurlbut, who had meant to exercise command from Quincy, issued peremptory orders to the commanders of the offending regiments to restrain their men or else they would suffer the penalty of severe punishment.[18] His orders stopped the offenses, at least temporarily.

Hurlbut had for the commanders of his four Illinois regiments two Republican politicians and two seasoned professional soldiers. One of the politicians was John M. Palmer, colonel of the 14th Illinois, who had served in the Illinois Senate in 1851 and had contributed significantly to the formation of the Republican party in Illinois; he had practiced law in central Illinois and served as a delegate to the Washington Peace Conference in 1861. The other was Robert F. Smith, colonel of the 16th Illinois, a Zouave unit. Smith had gained notoriety late in June 1844 for his association with the brutal murder of the controversial Mormon leader Joseph Smith at Carthage, Illinois. As the justice of the peace for his native Hancock County and captain of the Carthage Greys (a militia

Orville H. Browning, Republican U.S. senator from Illinois. Illinois State Historical Library.

company comparable to Hurlbut's Boone Rifles), Smith had arrested and incarcerated Joseph Smith in the county jail in Carthage on charges of inciting a riot, suppressing free speech, and committing acts of treason against the sovereign state of Illinois. He had failed, however, to use the Carthage Greys effectively to protect the Mormon leader, though Gov. Thomas Ford had specifically assigned to that company the duty of protecting Joseph Smith and his brother Hyrum from mob violence. In consequence of Smith's negligence (or conspiracy to commit murder—he had been the principal leader of the anti-Mormon movement in Hancock County), 150 vigilantes had stormed the jail and killed the Mormon prophet and his brother in cold blood, riddling their bodies with bullets. Smith had served with both Hurlbut and Palmer (then an independent Democrat) as a Whig delegate to the Illinois constitutional convention in 1847, but he had remained an otherwise obscure figure in the Illinois Republican party.[19]

The professional officers who led Hurlbut's two other regiments had impressive backgrounds. Ulysses S. Grant, the Ohio-born colonel of the 21st Illinois, an 1843 graduate of the U.S. Military Academy, a Mexican War veteran, and a former regular army officer, had obtained his commission from Governor Yates as the replacement of Colonel Goode through the timely intervention and patronage of Jones and Washburne. Grant, however, would serve under Hurlbut for only three weeks before reassignment. Col. John Basil Turchin commanded the 19th Illinois, the Zouave regiment that Hurlbut had led out of Chicago on July 13. Turchin (born Ivan Vasilevitch Turchininoff) was a Russian immigrant who in 1841 had graduated from the Imperial Military School in St. Petersburg and had served as a general staff officer in campaigns in Hungary and the Crimean War. He had settled in Chicago in 1856 to work for the Illinois Central Railroad. Besides his thick Russian accent, Turchin had brought to America his European notions of waging war against the civilian populations as well as the armies of the enemy. Indeed, following his service under Hurlbut in Missouri, he would earn a dubious sobriquet, the "Russian Thunderbolt," for his audacious but excessively forceful capture of Huntsville, Alabama. In May 1862 he would implicitly incite, if not expressly order, his troops to sack and burn the town of Athens, Alabama. Maj. Gen. Don Carlos Buell would court-martial and cashier him, but Lincoln, at the intercession of Turchin's wife, would reinstate him, with the rank of brigadier general, in July 1862.[20]

Thus Hurlbut's heavy drinking in Chicago had already produced destructive consequences for both secessionist and Unionist Missouri citizens; it was Turchin's 19th Illinois, as well as Smith's 16th, that had immediately preyed on homes and farms. Turchin (whom in April 1863 the *Richmond Daily Dispatch* would call a "Russo-Yankee dog" and "an inhuman wretch") had repeatedly observed Hurlbut's boisterous imbibing and recognized its incapacitating effects during the departure for Quincy. Perceiving weaknesses of character, leadership, and capacity to maintain discipline, both Turchin and Smith thereafter often failed to obey Hurlbut's strict orders against inflicting injuries on noncombatants in Missouri, despite their professed obedience to his regulations.[21]

The Civil War in Missouri, 1861. From John McElroy, *The Struggle for Missouri* (1903).

Having ordered his other regiments into northeast Missouri, on July 14 Hurlbut sent Grant's 21st Illinois to Monroe, a point on the railroad about fifteen miles west of Palmyra, Missouri. On July 19, having two days before received confirming orders from Frémont to move his entire brigade into Missouri, Hurlbut promulgated his plan for protecting the nearly 180-mile-long Hannibal & St. Joseph. He divided the railroad into two divisions of two sections each. The first division extended about ninety miles from St. Joseph on the Missouri River to Brookfield, a pivotal station and the site of a supply depot. He instructed Lt. Col. James M. Tuttle, commanding the 2d Iowa, to protect the road across section one, from St. Joseph to Hamilton, and Col. Nelson G. Williams, who led the 3d Iowa, to guard tracks in section two, from Hamilton to Brookfield. The second division of the railroad extended east another ninety miles from Brookfield to Hannibal and to Quincy on the Mississippi. Hurlbut directed Smith's 16th Illinois to protect section one, the stretch of track from Brookfield to Salt River, making his headquarters at Macon City. Colonel Palmer of the 14th Illinois was to defend the road in section two, from Salt River to Hannibal and Quincy, with his headquarters at Palmyra, the strategic junction of both the Hannibal & St. Joseph and the Quincy & Palmyra Railroads. Hurlbut kept Turchin's 19th Illinois in reserve in Marion County and sent Grant to the village of Mexico (about a hundred miles northwest of St. Louis) to protect the North Missouri Railroad pending the arrival of reinforcements from St. Louis. Despite these precautions, a band of secessionist guerrillas burned a logistically important railway trestle north of Mexico.

This loss notwithstanding, in order to establish a more effective control over the forces in his department, Frémont, who had reached St. Louis on July 25, formally named Brig. Gen. John Pope as the commander of the new District of North Missouri on July 29, with his headquarters at Mexico. Specifically, Frémont assigned Pope responsibility for strategic supervision of Hurlbut's operations in northeast Missouri and troop movements in the region of Jefferson City, the Missouri capital, about forty miles southwest of Mexico. Hurlbut retained tactical control over his brigade, with his headquarters at Macon City, formerly named Hudson, about fifty miles northwest of Mexico at the junction of the Hannibal & St. Joseph and the North Missouri Railroads.[22]

The appointment of Pope established a chain of command within which Pope, an 1842 graduate of the U.S. Military Academy, occupied an awkward, if not an anomalous, position of simultaneously serving one amateurish general, Frémont, and supervising another, Hurlbut. A thirty-nine-year-old Kentucky native, Pope had performed surveying duty in Florida and elsewhere as an army topographical engineer and had won two brevets with Gen. Zachary Taylor's army during the Mexican War. Following his appointment as a brigadier general of U.S. Volunteers, his first assignment had been at Alton, Illinois. On July 17 he became the provisional commander of the Northern District of Missouri. Thereafter, notwithstanding Frémont's assumption of departmental command, Pope adopted and executed an especially harsh occupation policy, particularly in his efforts to protect railroad tracks and trestles from guerrilla raiders. Pope issued proclamations demanding that the inhabitants, both secessionist and Unionist, of northern Missouri towns and counties create special committees of safety to guard railroads themselves; the committees and communities would be held responsible in the event of attacks. Specifically, Pope threatened to impose levies on—more precisely, exact tribute from—communities to pay for repairs to damaged railroad property. Pope's oppressive policy reflected his rec-

John Pope, commanding general, Union forces in North Missouri. Prints and Photographs Division, Library of Congress.

ognition that he could not protect the long exposed lines of two key, interconnecting railroads merely with Hurlbut's brigade and a few scattered regiments posted at strategic points between St. Louis, Mexico, and Macon City.[23]

In obedience to Pope, on July 15 Hurlbut, still at Quincy, had issued a proclamation to all the secessionist inhabitants of northeast Missouri denouncing them as traitors and for the "savagery" of their guerrilla warfare. He had also warned them that any interference with his troops would draw summary justice and death before a firing squad. On July 29, immediately following Pope's official appointment to command in northeast Missouri, Hurlbut, then at Hannibal, called on all "persons of property and influence" near the Hannibal & St. Joseph Railroad to form committees of safety to protect railroad tracks, trestles, depots, and telegraph wires from the ravaging attacks of "predatory bands" of guerrillas. Again he threatened to punish severely any found guilty of negligence or treason.[24]

No sooner had Hurlbut promulgated these proclamations than Pope changed his strategy for the protection of the northeast Missouri railroads. He decided to withdraw Hurlbut's regiments and other units nearer Mexico from guard duty along the railroads and to relocate them nearer the camps and railway stations. Having thus abandoned his attempts to use troops to protect the railroads, he adopted an even harsher policy toward the secessionist and—presumably inadvertently—the loyal Unionist inhabitants of northern Missouri. Pope now threatened to punish entire towns and counties for attacks on railroads. When, for instance, early in August, guerrilla raiders operating near Palmyra, the seat of Marion County, burned rolling stock on the Hannibal & St. Joseph, Pope quickly retaliated, ordering Hurlbut to occupy Palmyra. The Marion County authorities having refused to pay for the replacement of the destroyed locomotives and cars, Pope directed Hurlbut to impose burdensome requisitions on the entire citizenry of the town. Accordingly, Hurlbut required the residents of Palmyra to provide provisions and water for Colonel Smith's 16th Illinois and Marion County to bear the cost of occupation. This harsh policy was in effect only briefly; responding to angry "representations" from a committee of Palmyra citizens, Frémont soon countermanded Hurlbut's orders.[25]

In addition to his obvious inability to protect railroads with small, widely distributed forces, Pope's abrupt change of policy reflected a subtle and significant shift in his approach to the broader problem of suppressing pro-Confederate insurgency. Pope, who envied and detested Frémont and despised Hurlbut, consciously began to function as an essentially independent field commander. While outspokenly criticizing what he and other professional officers regarded as Frémont's extravagance in St. Louis, administrative ineptitude, and neglect of military affairs, Pope also perceived an opportunity, if not the necessity, to expand his immediate operational base and his command structure at Mexico. Since he could not openly question or challenge Frémont's authority, however, Pope determined to dominate, isolate, and (if circumstances warranted it) discipline Hurlbut, whose amateurism might frustrate his mission and ruin his reputation in Missouri.

Consequently on July 24, five days before his formal assignment to command, Pope had assigned Colonel Grant to assume command over all Union troops near Mexico. Grant, however, was promoted on July 31 by President Lincoln to the rank of brigadier general of volunteers (which the Senate confirmed on August 5), and on August 8 he reported for duty at Ironton, Missouri, the inland terminus of the St. Louis & Iron Mountain Railroad, which ran south and east from St. Louis. Pope nonetheless preferred Grant to Hurlbut and on August 10 requested Frémont to replace Hurlbut with Grant. But Frémont refused to reassign Grant or to remove Hurlbut from his brigade command. Pope deliberately proceeded to strip Hurlbut of troops, in part to build up his own small force at Mexico. On July 27 he ordered Hurlbut to send Turchin's 19th Illinois and the 2d Iowa to St. Louis and shortly thereafter moved Palmer's 14th Illinois nearer his headquarters at Mexico, leaving Hurlbut with only Smith's 16th Illinois, at Macon City, and the 3d Iowa, at Brookfield.

Thus Pope, as McClellan and Frémont had done before him, had assigned to Hurlbut a virtually impossible mission—guarding railroads and suppressing guerrillas without the necessary troops, particularly cavalry, ordnance, and ammunition. Moreover, Pope, perhaps preparing to sacrifice Hurlbut (and Frémont) as scapegoats in the event of failure to suppress the insurgency, consolidated an ever-larger force under his own immediate control. Ostensibly, he did so to protect some hundred miles of track on the North Missouri Railroad, which ran between St. Louis and Mexico. However, he was obliging Hurlbut, with a much smaller force, to protect nearly 180 miles of track. In any case, the Hannibal & St. Joseph—an "abolition road," as Hurlbut later termed it—remained vulnerable to disruption by guerrilla raiders.[26]

Increasingly frustrated, exasperated, and resentful, Hurlbut once again began to drink heavily. He was apparently quite oblivious to the unfavorable observations and reactions of his staff officers or soldiers. An appalled war correspondent for the *New York Times* subsequently recalled that in July and August 1861 he had often seen Hurlbut "so intoxicated as to be unable to walk"; "frequently" private soldiers had "picked him up from the ground where he had fallen in helpless drunkenness and assisted him to his quarters."[27] Hurlbut's intemperance impaired not only his ability to command his brigade but his control over the conduct of his troops. Colonels Smith and Turchin allowed, if not incited, their troops to commit depredations against both secessionist and Unionist residents. Officers and men arbitrarily arrested Missouri residents on faint suspicion of disloyalty, imposed heavy fines on some communities and exacted tribute from others, perpetrated thefts and robberies in private residences in which they had billeted themselves without authority, and raped slave women.

Hurlbut showed the malicious side of his own nature by his cruel, even brutal, treatment of John McAfee, the former speaker of the Missouri House of Representatives. McAfee was arrested about August 10 by a U.S. deputy marshal on the charge of aiding and abetting guerrillas and was brought to Hurlbut's headquarters at Macon City. Hurlbut personally ordered him to dig trenches and rifle pits under a blazing Missouri sun. He then ordered McAfee bound to the top of the cab of a locomotive preparing to transport him east to Palmyra. Fortunately for McAfee, the engineer and others got him aboard a passenger car before the train steamed away from the station; McAfee could easily have suffered an agonizing death by heat stroke, suffocation, or burns under a heavy shower of fumes and red-hot cinders from the smokestack. Pope expressed his concern over Hurlbut's detention of McAfee at Macon City but approved of remanding the former House speaker to St. Louis for further custody or trial. These outrages provoked a storm of protest among even the loyal inhabitants of northeast Missouri, who also complained to Frémont that "drunkenness is a great curse of officers and men" among both Pope's and Hurlbut's commands. This protest prompted Pope, belatedly, to exercise stricter discipline. In mid-September, as a token gesture, Pope finally arrested and sent to St. Louis for a summary court-martial three of his staff officers for "drunkenness, incapacity, and shameful neglect of duty." By then, however, neither he nor Hurlbut could have reversed the severe damage they had inflicted on Unionist morale, much less the strengthening of secessionist resistance that his and Hurlbut's gross dereliction of duty had caused.[28]

Ironically, Hurlbut learned with relief on August 5 of his confirmation in the rank of brigadier general. Senator Browning informed him, "You are confirmed—so are your staff officers—but I had to fight for you. I beg of you, my friend, to let your future conduct sustain me in all I have said of you." Hurlbut had stood "in great peril" of defeat on the Senate floor, but Browning had mobilized a majority, including the reluctant Trumbull, and had "saved" Hurlbut from dismissal. Browning reminded Hurlbut that his prospects for political prestige and military promotion depended on strict sobriety.[29] Browning recognized (as had both Washburne and Jones) that his standing with Lincoln and his position in the Illinois Republican party could suffer if Hurlbut betrayed his trust.

The organized force facing Hurlbut, the Missouri State Guard, was led by Col. Martin E. Green, a former judge of the Lewis County Court and a brother of U.S. senator James S. Green. The State Guard increasingly threatened Athens, Hannibal, and Palmyra. The *Keokuk (Iowa) Gate City* urged Hurlbut or some other "competent authority" to send a force to disperse the State Guard troops then approaching Athens (which lay northwest of Quincy and on the

Missouri side of the Des Moines River) and thus "squelch out secession manifestations on the border." The Republican *Illinois State Journal* of Springfield
bluntly asked, "Where is Gen. Hurlbut?" The Democratic *Quincy Herald,* which
had condemned the depredations of the 19th Illinois, now censured Hurlbut
for failure to act: "Where is Gen. Hurlbut, and what is he about, that he permits this gang of traitors and scoundrels to scour the country unmolested?"[30]

If perplexed observers could not perceive his campaign plan, the reason was
that Hurlbut had not devised any. When in mid-August Hurlbut learned that
Green, now commanding two thousand troops, threatened to attack a five-
hundred-man detachment of the 3d Iowa at Kirksville (about twenty-five miles
north of Macon City), Hurlbut acted promptly, but rashly. On August 16,
without informing Pope (who on August 9, by order of Frémont, had moved
his headquarters from Mexico to St. Louis), Hurlbut marched north to reinforce the isolated detachment with seven companies of the 16th Illinois, seven
hundred men and a two-pounder cannon whimsically dubbed "Old Abe." Reaching Kirksville on the eighteenth, Hurlbut received a three-gun salute from a 3d
Iowa battery. Green, overestimating the strength of Hurlbut's force, avoided a
direct engagement. Encouraged, Hurlbut sent by flag of truce a proclamation
that gave Green five days to disband and disperse his forces or be crushed. As a
3d Iowa soldier afterward reckoned, "Green doubtless chuckled over this, while
General Hurlbut's officers and men gnashed their teeth with rage." Instead of
obeying Hurlbut, whom he outnumbered two to one, Green on August 19
began boldly swinging his small army around Hurlbut, away from Kirksville,
and rapidly moved east and south toward Palmyra, his strategic objective. Green
sought to sever or at least disrupt rail communications between Illinois and
Missouri and points west; blocking the railroad at Palmyra would force Hurlbut
to abandon Kirksville in order to restore the line.[31]

Unaccountably, Hurlbut failed to act promptly. Only on August 21, two
days after learning of Green's movement southward, did Hurlbut finally report
to Pope that he would follow Green as soon as he could be reinforced at Kirksville
by the cavalry of Col. David Moore's First Northeast Missouri Home Guards.
Moore, an experienced soldier who had served as a captain of Ohio volunteers
during the Mexican War, had defeated, almost routed, Green on August 5 at
the Battle of Athens in far northeastern Missouri. Now, however, he procrasti-
nated, apparently assuming that his victory at Athens had effectively neutral-
ized Green's forces. Awaiting Moore's arrival, Hurlbut ordered troops to dig a
deep well for fresh water; he slaked his own thirst by resorting to the bottle. On
August 29, he was unfit for duty. Immobilized by his heavy drinking, Hurlbut
waited at Kirksville nine days.

On August 30, Moore still not having arrived, he decided to pursue Green with his combined force of about 1,350 infantry, cavalry, and three pieces of artillery. Pope had received Hurlbut's report of August 21 and learned that Green had cut the tracks at Palmyra. Accordingly, on August 31, while Hurlbut progressed slowly toward Palmyra, an enraged Pope directly ordered Colonel Williams, then at Brookfield, to transport the balance of his 3d Iowa regiment to Palmyra to reopen the railroad and to advise Hurlbut of his movement. Pope then sent a curt dispatch to Hurlbut in which he sharply rebuked his tardiness: "I cannot conceive how you could have remained ten days at Kirksville" and have allowed Green's forces to "interrupt travel and commit outrages unopposed all through Marion County." He informed Hurlbut of Frémont's "great surprise and dissatisfaction" over his "unexplained delay" at Kirksville. Not knowing that Hurlbut had finally evacuated Kirksville just the day before, Pope ordered him to march immediately to the support of Williams at Palmyra.[32]

Meanwhile, ignorant of Williams's movement, Hurlbut finally met Colonel Moore's cavalry regiment of 850 men and one gun on September 1 at Bethel in Shelby County. He directed Smith and Moore to move to Palmyra by way of Philadelphia, a town northwest of Palmyra and the suspected location of Green's army. Smith was to hold Palmyra and Moore was to pursue Green. Hurlbut himself, who had found it necessary to ride in a buggy during the march from Kirksville because of an injury sustained on August 19, led 120 sick men belonging to Smith's command and five hundred men of the 3d Iowa south to Shelbina, a station on the railroad about twenty-three miles east of his headquarters at Macon City and about thirty-five miles west of Palmyra.[33]

At Shelbina, on September 3 Hurlbut learned that Colonel Williams had restored the railroad at Palmyra and had continued on Pope's orders to Paris, about ten miles south of Shelbina, to carry out a punitive expedition. Erroneously informed that Williams had about 1,200 men, part of the 3d Iowa Infantry and the entire 2d Kansas Volunteers, Hurlbut believed that Shelbina had neither supplies nor military importance. Therefore, Hurlbut transported his immediate command by rail to Brookfield, apparently to protect commissary stores and other government property located there.[34]

Hurlbut had now committed two egregious blunders—he had divided his forces into three separate commands in the presence of the enemy and had not since August 21 reported either his location or movements to Pope. Instead of remaining at Shelbina in order to consolidate the two 3d Iowa detachments and concentrate his command before making a concerted movement against Green, Hurlbut created a situation that would cause the fall of Shelbina and precipitate his removal from command.

As Hurlbut continued to Brookfield on September 3, Williams and his combined force of about 620 men (not the 1,200 Hurlbut had supposed) left Paris
for Shelbina. Williams learned that Green had laid an ambush for him on the
main road south of Shelbina and that Green's army had grown to three or four
thousand men. Williams skillfully outflanked Green and reached Shelbina first;
the dust raised by Green's cavalry emerging from a tract of timber in rapid
pursuit was visible to his rear. Williams hastily barricaded the town's narrow
streets and withstood a siege by Green's superior forces. Green demanded an
immediate surrender, but with a defiant and insulting oath Williams refused.
On the morning of September 4 Hurlbut, unaware of Williams's situation, put
his command on trains for Brookfield. He then received a dispatch from Williams urgently requesting heavy reinforcements; Hurlbut replied that he would
take 350 men forthwith to Shelbina and help Williams hold the town. Informed
by Williams shortly thereafter that the enemy had begun directing a steady fire
of solid shot and shell on Shelbina from two pieces of light artillery, Hurlbut
instructed Williams to assault and capture the battery. Bravely and dutifully,
Williams undertook to lead his 620 men in an attack on Green's four thousand
infantry supported by artillery. But officers of the 2d Kansas objected, and
Williams himself recognized the obvious futility of such an assault. Green then
attempted to isolate Williams by destroying railroad tracks on either side of
Shelbina, but Williams's infantry repelled the raiding parties.

Finally, after about thirty well-aimed shots from Green's guns (a six-pounder
and a nine-pounder), the officers of the 2d Kansas prevailed upon Williams to
order a retreat. Reluctantly—only one soldier had been wounded—Williams agreed
to a withdrawal aboard railroad cars. The Kansas troops suddenly panicked, ran
headlong for the cars, and scrambled aboard a train moving west to safety. Narrowly avoiding the capture of his entire command, Williams and the 3d Iowa
troops, numbering about 280, accompanied by a hundred cavalry, boarded a second train and followed the Kansas volunteers west to Macon City—abandoning
coats, knapsacks, one transportation wagon, and four mules to the enemy.[35]

Williams's withdrawal from Shelbina, however hurried and disorderly, con-
trasted with Hurlbut's movement from Brookfield. Leaving 150 men of the 3d
Iowa at Brookfield to protect the government stores there, Hurlbut boarded a
train with 350 other 3d Iowa men on cars and moved east to reinforce Williams
at Shelbina. Hurlbut now compounded his poor judgment by yielding to an
impulse to drink. Apparently alarmed at the prospect of encountering Green in
battle, which he had carefully avoided since August 18, he drank heavily during
the movement toward Shelbina. Increasingly oblivious to the necessity for haste,
Hurlbut allowed the troop train to take eight hours to make the *"rapid run"*

from Brookfield to Macon City, some forty miles. At Macon City, according to the sarcastic description of a *St. Louis Missouri Democrat* reporter, Hurlbut "stopt the train and found some secession whisky, imbibed freely, as usual, and stayed till the boys [that is, Williams's] got in from Shelbina."[36] Arriving in Macon City on the afternoon of September 4, Hurlbut learned with dismay that Williams had abandoned Shelbina and had already reached Clarence, a station twelve miles east of Macon City. Instead of continuing on to meet Williams and proceeding to Shelbina to confront Green, Hurlbut decided to let Williams come all the way to Macon City. About eight o'clock in the evening, Williams finally reached the town with his two disorganized commands. By this time Hurlbut was cursing and shouting drunkenly in the town's streets, shocking officers and soldiers who observed him.

Anxious to blame Williams for his own blunder, Hurlbut confronted him and the officers of the 2d Kansas at his headquarters. But he misjudged the character and temperament of the thirty-eight-year-old Williams, a classmate of Grant's at West Point (he had left without graduating) and a strict disciplinarian. Williams refused to serve further under Hurlbut. Indeed, upon Hurlbut's "requiring the reason, it was given him in very plain terms." Furthermore, as the *St. Louis Missouri Republican* a few days later regretfully described the scene, "Gen. Hurlbut's condition *was such that he was unable to stand,* and Col. Williams ordered him under arrest."[37] Acting decisively, although with questionable authority, Williams hastily formed a detail of two soldiers who marched Hurlbut through the streets of Macon City before a crowd of astonished civilian and military spectators. Williams had Hurlbut confined in a railroad car for most of the night, until the general had recovered his sobriety and composure. The following morning, Williams reversed his decision and restored command to Hurlbut. Hurlbut ordered Williams and the Kansas officers to submit detailed reports on the Shelbina affair.

However, he hesitated to attack Green or even to notify Pope or Frémont of Green's victory. Hurlbut now knew that he would presently have to confront Green with 970 Union troops, not 1,550. Therefore, early on September 6, he called in 150 men of the 3d Iowa, then at Brookfield, to Macon City, but he also had to send two hundred men of the 2d Kansas west, because their terms of volunteer service had expired. Only on the morning of September 7, after repairing the railroad between Macon City and Shelbina, was Hurlbut finally prepared to take the entire 3d Iowa and two hundred men of the 16th Illinois, an aggregate of 1,120 infantry and cavalry, by rail to Shelbina.[38]

Meanwhile, Frémont and Pope had finally received reports from Hurlbut concerning the capture of Shelbina. Suddenly recognizing that Green did not, as he had supposed, lead a band of irregular guerrilla raiders but was a serious threat, Frémont on September 6 hastily devised an elaborate plan that had as its objective a "combined attack on Green's men and their total annihilation." He ordered Pope to move his reinforced command from St. Louis to Palmyra and then to advance westward across the Salt River toward Green's army at Shelbina. He also directed Brig. Gen. Samuel D. Sturgis, commanding the U.S. Arsenal at St. Louis, to transport his own command by rail to Macon City and cut off Green's probable line of retreat through Shelbyville, about ten miles north of Shelbina. Although Pope and Sturgis, both capable officers, skillfully executed Frémont's movement, the wily Green escaped by boldly marching his troops not north but southeast toward Florida, a town about twenty miles away. Despite Pope's urgent requests for additional troops, especially cavalry, Hurlbut failed to provide reinforcements before Green's forces had completely eluded Pope's grasp and escaped across the Missouri River northwest of Jefferson City.

On September 7 an enraged Pope proceeded by rail to Shelbina, where he met Hurlbut, who had finally reached the town. On learning of his intemperance at Kirksville and Macon City, Pope charged Hurlbut with dereliction of duty and incompetence and had him arrested. He also arrested Williams, asserting that Williams should not have evacuated Shelbina without the approval of higher authority. Specifically, Pope declared, Williams should have prevented the 2d Kansas Infantry from withdrawing. He ordered Lt. Col. Charles W. Blair of the 2d Kansas under arrest as well, for "mutinous conduct" at Shelbina. Pope explained to a *New York Times* correspondent that Williams "should have driven his sword through the officer who refused to stay longer" to defend Shelbina. Pope ordered both Hurlbut and Williams immediately to St. Louis, there to answer charges of misconduct.[39]

Pope's action represented less concern for military justice than personal and professional contempt for his two rivals, Hurlbut and Frémont. Although he had strong and, indeed, compelling grounds to arrest Hurlbut, Pope's measure and Hurlbut's misfortune in September 1861 presaged a wider series of conscious attempts later in the war by a West Point clique to dominate the Union high command in the West by forcing the resignation or dismissal of political generals like Hurlbut. Frémont could have pardoned Hurlbut, if only to spite Pope, an outspoken critic of his administration in St. Louis. Moreover, a pardon could placate, or at least avoid further antagonizing, Lincoln in a controversy over a recent confiscation order issued by Frémont that had generated a wave of protest among border state slaveholders. In the end, Frémont decided to furlough Hurlbut, who returned home to Belvidere to await disposition of his case. Williams, despite his courageous defense of Shelbina and Hurlbut's responsibility for its fall, was made a scapegoat for Pope's failure to capture or destroy Green's army. Green had completely outgeneraled and outmaneuvered Pope and Sturgis—both West Pointers and Mexican War veterans—and Pope could not admit it. He kept Williams under arrest in St. Louis until February 1862, when he assumed command of the Army of the Mississippi. Williams later returned to command the 3d Iowa, by then in western Tennessee.

Hurlbut's inept performance demonstrated clearly that he lacked capacity as a field commander. Hurlbut's fundamental blunder was blind maneuvering in the absence of accurate and reliable intelligence. Without timely and precise knowledge of the location, strength, dispositions, and intentions of Green's forces, Hurlbut should have communicated more fully with Pope at district headquarters and with his own subordinate commanders. However, considering that he was a stump politician and captain of a local militia unit suddenly elevated to the command of a brigade operating in an active theater of military operations, Hurlbut performed perhaps as well as he could have—or at least as capably as Lincoln, Frémont, or Pope could reasonably have expected. Indeed, many West Point officers in both the Union and Confederate armies performed rather poorly early in the war. Also, Hurlbut did exercise efficient and well-coordinated control over transportation on the Hannibal & St. Joseph Railroad. Further, and despite Pope's hostility and his deliberate efforts to hinder him, Hurlbut (unlike several clearly insubordinate political generals and even professional officers in the West) exhibited exemplary loyalty to his superior officers, Frémont and Pope—an attitude that he would creditably display, generally, for the rest of the war.

Before returning to Illinois Hurlbut stopped in Quincy to complain about accounts published in the September 12 edition of the *Quincy Daily Whig and Republican* concerning his conduct during the Kirksville campaign. In an indignant reply, he offered the journal's editor (through a mutual friend) an explanation of his apparent intoxication at Macon City—a defense upon which he would soon elaborate in the *Belvidere Standard.* He also stopped in Chicago and conferred with Joseph Russell Jones. He probably attempted there to rebut reports of drunkenness in Missouri, and he likely learned from Jones how sharply the Shelbina affair had reduced his standing in the Illinois Republican party. Jones reproved Hurlbut for his intemperance and showed him a copy of a letter that he had sent to President Lincoln recommending Hurlbut's dishonorable discharge from the Union army.[40] Realizing that he had now irretrievably estranged his patron, a humiliated Hurlbut proceeded to Belvidere.

Republican papers in Illinois and Missouri engaged in acrimonious and contentious debates over disturbing if unconfirmed reports of Hurlbut's drunkenness in Missouri. The *Belvidere Standard* reserved its judgment as to Hurlbut's misconduct. Noting that Hurlbut, then in Belvidere, was enjoying "a state of excellent health," the *Standard* blamed Pope's interference for Hurlbut's predicament: "We think it is time that the service was rid of such martinets as Pope." The *Chicago Tribune*, whose fiery editor, Joseph Medill, had denounced Hurlbut's appointment to high command in July, advised its readers to refrain from overly severe judgment against the general. A gratuitous "fling at Hurlbut's personal bravery" would be "undeserved and unjust, however liable he may be to censure for gratifying appetites unbecoming" a military commander. The *Tribune* made it unequivocally clear, however, that if the charges proved accurate, the "clamor" for his summary removal from command should "resound in every hall and chamber of the White House, whence his appointment came." The *Rockford Republican* also expressed unwillingness to censure Hurlbut, although it would condemn him if the charges preferred against him should be substantiated. But the *Republican* suspected that Hurlbut had indeed behaved improperly, on the basis of the "very fact" of Hurlbut's confinement aboard a cattle train for part of his journey to St. Louis, "as neither General Pope or any other man would dare to put such an indignity upon a sober, faithful, and capable officer of high rank."[41] The *Chicago Evening Journal* concurred with the *Tribune* and *Republican*. However, the *Journal* called the act of drinking when in command of troops a dastardly *"crime"* and urged the War Department to court-martial Hurlbut and to strip him of "his sword and epaulettes" should it succeed in proving the formal charges laid against him. Nevertheless, the *Illinois State Journal* of Springfield asserted that if Hurlbut had not recklessly put "an enemy into his mouth to steal away his brains," he was suffering unjustly and was "an awfully slandered man."

The less generous *Quincy Daily Whig and Republican* in its September 12 account of his Missouri campaign (to which Hurlbut had strenuously objected) concluded that "the General did not attend to his business; the Colonels maintained no concert of action, and the men took care of themselves." The paper charged Hurlbut with the "wretched mismanagement of our forces" in northeastern Missouri that had resulted in "raids, robberies, bridge-burnings, drunkenness, and insubordination." The *St. Louis Missouri Democrat* (in actuality a staunchly pro-Lincoln Republican organ) agreed that Hurlbut had acted irresponsibly, though its war correspondent informed his readers that they would be "laboring under a mistake" if they believed "the General is still entrenched behind a lot of beer barrels at Kirksville." Moreover, the *Hannibal Messenger* (which wondered whether Hurlbut had ordered the excavation of a well at Kirksville in order to find "whisky or water") declared, "We trust, if court-martialed, that this will be the last whisky appointment the President will make."[42]

Democratic journals in the West castigated Hurlbut unrelentingly, indeed gleefully. The *Illinois State Register* of Springfield demanded that "this fellow Hurlburt's spurs" be "hacked from his heels at the earliest moment." It recalled, "We expected little good of him when he was appointed" in June, "but we did not expect that our state would have to bear this much disgrace through his recreancy." Sharply critical of Frémont's failure to investigate the charges lodged against Hurlbut (whom it disparagingly described as the "Boone brigadier") before returning him to Belvidere, the *Register* declared that Hurlbut "should have been court-martialed and drummed out of the service." The *Quincy Herald,* closer to the scene of Hurlbut's Shelbina blunder, asserted that Hurlbut's appointment as a brigadier general sprang directly from Lincoln's "partisan bigotry"; it wished that the guerrillas had captured Hurlbut in Missouri.[43] The *Keokuk Gate City* excoriated Hurlbut for having stayed "dead drunk" and blamed him alone as a "drunken loafer" for Green's escape. The *Davenport Democrat and News* identified Hurlbut as one of that group of "self-elected political hacks, and ambitious place-seekers" whose record of mismanagement of military affairs had already proved consistent with "their excellent training on the stump and in the bar-room."[44]

Finally, in a more dispassionate assessment of Hurlbut's failures in Missouri, a correspondent (then stationed at Macon City) for the *New York Times* remarked on September 14 that Hurlbut had "done little or nothing except to tarnish as a soldier the brilliant reputation which he gained as a lawyer." The *Times* doubted whether Hurlbut in his "sober moments" possessed the attributes of a successful field general; Hurlbut "seems to have distinguished himself always by incapacity arising from his immoderate use of stimulants." A *New York Tribune* correspondent, then at St. Louis, reported that even before September 7 army headquarters had received "frequent reports" regarding Hurlbut's "irregular habits." Therefore, if Frémont should determine Hurlbut guilty of "wretched intoxication," Hurlbut should suffer exemplary punishment. But the reporter insinuated that Frémont had either tolerated—or ignored—misconduct of subordinate commanders. He concluded, "Intoxication has become so frequent among high officers in this vicinity that, unless a permanent check is placed upon it, the effect will be ruinous."[45]

More importantly, Hurlbut had alienated several of his Republican patrons in Illinois. Senator Browning complained on September 11 to Lincoln that "Genl Hurlbut is a failure. He has had his fame and his fortune in his own hands, and has thrown them both away." Browning assured Lincoln that the Democratic press had exaggerated Hurlbut's "mis-deeds" in Missouri but acknowledged that his recurrent drunkenness had at last flung him as a "worthless wreck, in the mud upon the beach." Hurlbut, having behaved so "badly" and broken his solemn promise not to drink again, had "deceived, and disappointed me, as he has you." Browning bluntly counseled the president to "let him go." Lincoln sympathized with Browning but refused to dismiss Hurlbut and doubted that the general would resign his commission or seek executive clemency, because Frémont had not yet preferred formal charges against him. Instead, on September 22, the president vaguely suggested, "Suppose you write to Hurlbut and get him to resign." On September 30 Browning inquired if the president had intended to ridicule him in view of his previous endorsement of Hurlbut and for accepting Hurlbut's earlier pledge that he would "resign if he drank a drop of liquor after going into the service."[46] But Browning refrained from seeking Hurlbut's resignation, and Hurlbut continued to protest his innocence.

Senator Trumbull also believed that Hurlbut lacked either the ability or willingness to reform. Colonel Palmer of the 14th Illinois, and a political rival, advised Trumbull that "poor Hurlbut has put a finish upon himself" through his drunkenness: "That's the end of him I suppose as a military man and probably as a business man and lawyer," because if a political figure "assailed as he was from the time of his appointment for drunkenness is unable to restrain himself he is beyond hope."[47] But unlike Jones, Browning, and presently Washburne himself, Trumbull declined to discredit Hurlbut further by complaining to Lincoln. He had neither supported Hurlbut's nomination for a brigadier general nor defended him and promoted his confirmation, as Browning had, on the Senate floor. Trumbull had voted for Hurlbut's confirmation, but he had shrewdly evaded the liability of identifying with him.

Congressman Elihu Washburne, like Senator Browning, experienced considerable chagrin because of his earlier support of Hurlbut and thereafter sought to maintain his political status in northern Illinois by privately repudiating him. In a letter to Lincoln he disparaged Hurlbut (and praised instead a fellow Illinois Republican and Mexican War veteran, Col. William H. L. Wallace). Washburne rated Hurlbut as one of the worst brigadier generals in the West.[48] Clearly, Washburne's original support of Hurlbut's nomination had sprung from a chiefly partisan (as well as cynical and self-serving) motive and not a patriotic one. However, his repudiation of Hurlbut probably arose from a perception of the man's recurrent intemperance and general unfitness for military command— misconduct and incompetence that had prevented neither Browning nor even Trumbull from voting for his confirmation in the Senate.

Meanwhile, Hurlbut hastened to defend his political reputation and military record with his version of the Shelbina affair and accusations he had devised in efforts to discredit his critics. He first attempted to refute what he characterized as libelous Democratic newspaper charges of his drunkenness. Indeed for the September 18 *Quincy Daily Whig and Republican* Hurlbut had presented an explanation for his alleged drunken behavior in Missouri. He declared that he had ingested large quantities of a potent drug to treat an intestinal disorder; the strong opiate had accounted for his physical imbalance and instability at Macon City. A highly elaborated version of this story appeared in the September 17 edition of the *Belvidere Standard*. In it Hurlbut asserted that he had not drunk excessively but had swallowed heavy doses of laudanum (a solution of opium in alcohol) to relieve severe dysentery. He had stumbled and staggered in front of his officers and soldiers at Macon City on September 4 because he had been injured in August when a staff officer's horse had crushed his foot.[49] Hurlbut apparently failed to recognize that he had thereby virtually admitted that he had imbibed alcohol during the Kirksville campaign, if only with doses of laudanum. Either strong drink or a highly narcotic drug had left him completely disabled at Macon City. Democratic newspaper editors quickly reprinted Hurlbut's explanations in a spirit of partisan derision. Recognizing his error, early in October Hurlbut pressed Frémont in St. Louis for a court of inquiry. There, he trusted, he could rebut the charges of a "calumnious press" and furthermore expose that "licentious extravagance" (of Democratic editors) that "recklessly ministers to the diseased excitability of the people & which spares no man and respects no position."[50]

Not receiving an acknowledgment from Frémont, Hurlbut on October 15 sought the intervention of William P. Dole of Indiana, now the superintendent of Indian affairs in the Interior Department. Hurlbut had never met Dole, but he could no longer ask for Lincoln's aid through Jones, Browning, or Washburne. Moreover, military regulations forbade officers from communicating directly with Lincoln or with War Department authorities outside of the proper army channels. In his letter to Dole Hurlbut denounced Congressman Francis P. Blair, Jr., the chairman of the House Committee on Military Affairs in Washington. A member of an influential Missouri family, Blair had organized the Union party in St. Louis during the secession crisis and had thereafter, as colonel of the 1st Missouri Volunteers and the 1st Missouri Artillery, prevented secessionist Missouri militia from seizing control of St. Louis. However, after Frémont's assumption of command of the Western Department, Blair had disagreed with him over military strategy and administration. When Blair returned to St. Louis from Washington early in September, Frémont had promptly arrested him for interfering with his management of military affairs in Missouri. In a letter to Lincoln on October 2, Blair in turn condemned Frémont for having allowed Martin E. Green, whom he scornfully described as the most notorious of the

"Guerrilla Chiefs of the enemy," to overrun northeast Missouri and to destroy the property of Unionists during Hurlbut's ill-fated Kirksville campaign. He particularly censured Frémont for having kept Hurlbut, whom he contemptuously termed a "common drunkard," in command even after Pope had presumably reported his intemperance and incompetence.[51]

Apparently informed of Blair's letter to Lincoln by Washburne or Browning, Hurlbut explained to Dole that he doubted that Pope—a West Point officer whom he had come to hate—had provided Blair a copy of an official report on his military conduct in Missouri. Should Pope indeed have furnished Blair with such information, he had thereby agreed to serve as the "willing instrument" of Senator Trumbull in a conspiracy to destroy his political and military career. Although he failed to produce proof of intrigue, an anguished Hurlbut harshly criticized both men, describing Trumbull in particular as a "wretched & most selfish politician" who harbored a "cold and fishblooded hostility" toward him. But Hurlbut also rendered a truthful, if somewhat exaggerated, account of Pope's calculated interference with his operations, including his own "peremptory & insulting" arrest by Pope on September 7 at Shelbina. The combined effects of Pope's opposition and Frémont's lack of "good sense" had prevented him from prosecuting the war in Missouri with "vigorous action" so as to "put down the *young rebellion* before it grew strong." Having described himself an object of malicious persecution, Hurlbut urgently requested Dole to persuade Lincoln to order his "sneaking adversaries" in the War Department to convene a hearing for him in Washington. He wished to have this hearing before reassignment to command.[52]

Dole, however, lacked influence with Lincoln, and on November 15 Hurlbut sought restoration to active military service through Governor Yates. Hurlbut described himself to Yates as "the best abused man in the State—but surviving" and urged him to convince Lincoln of his fitness for duty. In addition, and suppressing his distrust, Hurlbut complained to Senator Trumbull about his enforced absence from the army, although he defiantly declared that he could "afford to wait" indefinitely for vindication. Assuming that he would eventually be fully exonerated, however, Hurlbut entreated Trumbull to help him to obtain reassignment to the planned expedition against Charleston.[53]

Unfortunately for Hurlbut, no War Department court heard his case, and Lincoln wisely refrained from establishing a highly visible tribunal for an officer whose reputation for drunkenness and dereliction of duty could further hurt the Union cause in Missouri. Even so, Lincoln rescued Hurlbut's career. Disregarding the objections of Jones, Browning, Washburne, and perhaps Trumbull as well, in mid-December 1861 Lincoln yielded to Governor Yates who had, as requested, persistently asked for Hurlbut's restoration to active service. In doing so the president intended to exploit, for purposes of the ultimate reconstruction of the border-state West, the potential usefulness of a Republican general.

The War Department's announcement of Hurlbut's return to active duty late in December 1861 surprised and disappointed both Democratic and Republican editors in Illinois. Lincoln's action prompted the Democratic *Quincy Herald* to predict, "This will be unwelcome news" to the brigade assigned to his command because of "his incompetency and intemperate habits." But the *Belvidere Standard* perceived Hurlbut's reinstatement to be his belated vindication and expressed its regret that he had suffered "a measure of hasty condemnation and untimely public censure."

On January 1, 1862, Maj. Gen. Henry W. Halleck—a West Point graduate of 1839 who in November 1861 had succeeded Frémont as the supreme commander of the newly established Department of the Missouri—ordered Hurlbut to report to Benton Barracks, near St. Louis, where there was a camp of instruction.[54] Hurlbut's assignment created uneasiness among the raw Union recruits he began drilling on the parade grounds, because "rumors were flying about of his previous bad conduct, drunkenness and the like." However, "nothing to his discredit appeared at this time";[55] Hurlbut had to remain sober, not merely because of Halleck's observation of his behavior but because Halleck had placed him under the immediate command and close supervision of Brig. Gen. William T. Sherman.

Sherman, who had met Hurlbut in 1842 while on garrison duty at Fort Moultrie in Charleston, had resigned his commission in 1853. He had thereafter pursued unsuccessful careers in banking and law until 1859, when he had accepted a position as the superintendent of a military school in southern Louisiana. Appointed brigadier general of U.S. Volunteers in August 1861, Sherman had served in the Department of the Cumberland in Kentucky until November 13, when Brig. Gen. Don Carlos Buell had succeeded him. Certain Western editors had cruelly dubbed him "Crazy Sherman" for his controversial and outspoken views on the difficulty of defending Kentucky. The War Department had then assigned him to Halleck's staff in St. Louis, where he directed the training of new Union troops.

Hurlbut showed skill in exercising recruits for six consecutive weeks, marching and parading them with precision in both regimental and brigade formations at the training camp, and Sherman gave Halleck a favorable report on Hurlbut's efficiency as a drillmaster. Knowing that Hurlbut would refuse further duty under Pope (or several other officers), Halleck ordered Hurlbut to proceed to the newly created Military District of West Tennessee to serve under now major general Ulysses S. Grant, the acclaimed conqueror of Fort Donelson, as second in command of the occupied fort. Concurrently, on February 14 he named Sherman as the commander of the Military District of Cairo, with headquarters at Paducah, Kentucky. Halleck had thus accomplished his primary purpose with respect to both Sherman and Hurlbut—he had affirmed their fitness for renewed field duty, notwithstanding Sherman's reputation as a "lunatic" and Hurlbut's notoriety as a "drunkard."[56]

Hurlbut left St. Louis on February 15 aboard the steamer *Continental*, which crashed through thick sheets of ice down the Mississippi River to Cairo, Illinois. From there he proceeded by steamer up the Ohio River to the mouth of the Cumberland River, northeast of Paducah. He continued aboard another steamer up the Cumberland River to Grant's headquarters at Fort Donelson.[57] Hurlbut and Grant had not met since the now-famous officer had fallen briefly under Hurlbut's command in northeast Missouri in July 1861.

A West Point–educated veteran of the Mexican War, Grant had done garrison duty as a captain at forts in the East and on the Pacific coast from 1848 to 1854. Too long separated from his family (his wife and two sons had lived in St. Louis since 1852) and unable to obtain either a promotion or higher pay while stationed at Fort Humboldt, California, Grant had steadily engaged in heavy drinking and had increasingly neglected his duties. On April 11, 1854, Grant had resigned his commission, abruptly ending an otherwise successful career. Thereafter he had failed successively as a farmer and businessman; he was working as a clerk in his brothers' tannery in Galena, Illinois, when the war came. His fellow townsmen Joseph Russell Jones and Congressman Elihu Washburne rescued him. Appointed (as has been described) by Governor Yates as the colonel of the 21st Illinois Volunteer Infantry in June of 1861, Grant had thereafter served ably under Hurlbut, Pope, and Frémont in Missouri before and after his promotion to brigadier general in August 1861. Assigned to command at Cairo, a strategic point near the junction of the Ohio and Mississippi Rivers, Grant had occupied Paducah, Kentucky, after a Confederate violation of the neutrality of that crucial border state. Afterward he had engaged Confederate forces in the indecisive Battle of Belmont, Missouri, on November 7, 1861.

In February 1862, while Hurlbut drilled recruits at St. Louis, Grant assisted Union naval forces in a successful expedition to capture Fort Henry on the Tennessee River. Shortly thereafter, marching swiftly, he carried Fort Donelson, on the Cumberland River. It was clearly a brilliant campaign, and it gained the first important Union victory in the war. Grant's reduction of Fort Donelson effectively broke the seemingly impregnable Confederate defensive line across the upper trans-Appalachian South. Lincoln promoted Grant to the rank of major general of volunteers.[58]

Although he had not campaigned with Hurlbut since late July 1861, Grant had cherished a grateful regard for Hurlbut as his former commanding officer. Then too Grant might have wished to reciprocate the generosity of both Jones and Washburne—their mutual patrons—by showing favor to Hurlbut. Consequently, in orders assigning three Illinois politicians to division command, Grant named Hurlbut as the commander of the Fourth Division of the Army of the Tennessee, effective February 21, 1862.[59]

It was a remarkable achievement for a man whose military career had collapsed only a few months before.

Hurlbut participated in Grant's southward movement toward the strategic Confederate rail center and stronghold of Corinth, Mississippi. Hurlbut and Sherman—whom Halleck had recently reassigned from Paducah to serve under Grant, now commanding the Department of West Tennessee, and whom Grant had in turn appointed on March 1 as commander of his army's Fifth Division—marched west from Fort Donelson in March 1862 to embarkation points on the Tennessee River. From there, Union flotillas transported the troops up the river toward Corinth.[60] Disembarking their forces at Pittsburg Landing, a point twenty miles northeast of Corinth and 240 miles south of the mouth of the Tennessee, on March 17 and 19 respectively Hurlbut and Sherman assumed positions west of the Tennessee River and occupied ground near Shiloh Church, where they awaited the arrival of Grant and the rest of his army.

Though he was deep in enemy territory, Hurlbut apparently lulled himself into an unwarranted sense of security in the absence of an immediate threat and imprudently returned to the bottle. As the colonel of the 41st Illinois Volunteers (a regiment belonging to the First Brigade of Hurlbut's division) complained to his wife on March 22, "Genl Hurlbut is a drunkard & is drunk all the time when he can get any thing to get drunk on."[61] Hurlbut's relapse produced, or at least coincided with, rash attempts to advance farther southward, up the Tennessee.

Early in April, Confederate skirmishers began appearing in increasing strength on both Hurlbut's and Sherman's immediate fronts. Impatient of delay and anxious to redeem his reputation as a field commander, Hurlbut attempted to precipitate decisive engagements south of his most advanced lines. Sherman restrained him from reckless forward movements—an intervention that only convinced him that both Sherman and Grant lacked aggressiveness. Earlier, on the evening of March 27, Sherman had frustrated his ambitious proposal to launch a surprise attack on a body of Confederate infantry and two guns reported to be near the Purdy Road, below his division's position. Lt. Col. William Camm, whom Hurlbut had designated to lead four companies of the 14th Illinois Infantry into that battle, found Hurlbut alone and "sitting on a log in

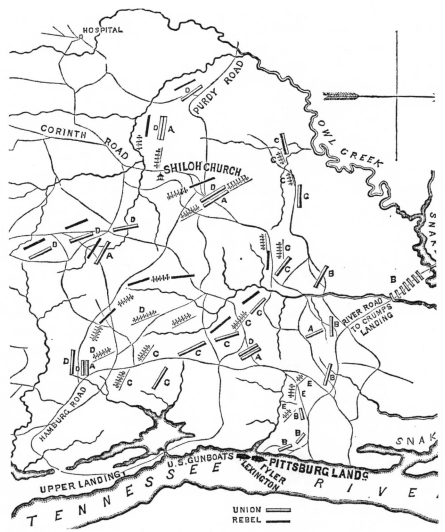

Map of Pittsburg Landing. From Horace Greeley, *The American Conflict* (1866).

his shirt sleeves" and heard him "saying they have no use for soldiers here"—
"Sherman would not let him go."

In the evening of April 4, Hurlbut learned of a sharp skirmish between Union
and Confederate cavalry in Sherman's front. Ordering the "long roll" of drums
and preparation for imminent combat, Hurlbut, who feared that Sherman would
shortly fall under attack, hurried infantry and artillery forward over a narrow
and muddy road to his support. After advancing for three-quarters of a mile,

Hurlbut received instructions from Sherman to return to camp. The sudden retrograde movement prompted derisive "jokes and retorts" among Hurlbut's weary and straggling troops: "The general himself did not escape being holloaed at ever and anon by some graceless wag."[62]

Thwarted in his efforts to attack Confederate skirmishers, Hurlbut concentrated on consolidating his Fourth Division, which consisted of three brigades totaling nearly fourteen thousand men under Col. James C. Veatch, Brig. Gen. Jacob G. Lauman, and his former Missouri subordinate, Col. Nelson G. Williams. The Union front faced south, and Hurlbut occupied its extreme left, with his own left flank resting upon the steep banks of the winding Tennessee River below Pittsburg Landing. Four other divisions—under Brig. Gen. Benjamin M. Prentiss, Sherman, Maj. Gen. John A. McClernand, and Brig. Gen. William H. L. Wallace—held ground to the south and west of Hurlbut's position. Ironically, Grant and Sherman both failed to perceive the massive Confederate attack that was in fact imminent, while Hurlbut, McClernand, and (though more slowly) even Prentiss himself—the three military politicians from Illinois—early recognized the impending danger.

Hurlbut as yet lacked precise knowledge of the Illinois War Democratic politician McClernand, the commander of the First Division, but he could have learned or else judged favorably of Prentiss. Having served as a captain in the 1st Illinois Volunteers during the Mexican War, Prentiss had returned to Illinois, studied law, and led an independent militia company originally called the Quincy Rifles (he later renamed it the Quincy Blues). He had joined the Republican party and had run unsuccessfully for Congress in 1860. Prentiss's political connections had secured for him an appointment as colonel of the 10th Illinois Volunteers in April 1861 and then as brigadier general of volunteers on May 17, 1861 (also the effective date of Hurlbut's and Pope's appointments). Following service in Missouri in the fall of 1861, he had assumed the command of the Sixth Division, Army of the Tennessee, late in March 1862. William Harvey Lamb Wallace, the forty-one-year-old, Ohio-born lawyer and Mexican War veteran then commanding the Second Division near Pittsburg Landing, had fought under Grant at Forts Henry and Donelson and had gained promotion to brigadier general of volunteers on March 21, 1862. Wallace, whom Congressman Washburne had praised by invidiously comparing him to the disgraced Hurlbut to Lincoln, had remained an obscure figure among Illinois Republicans.[63]

Grant himself had not yet arrived to assume command at Pittsburg Landing when, at daybreak on April 6, 1862, a Confederate army under Gen. Albert Sidney Johnston of Kentucky, numbering forty-four thousand men, attacked Grant's forty thousand troops and threatened to drive the Army of the Tennessee from its highly vulnerable position. After partially surrounding Prentiss in the "Peach Orchard" southwest of Hurlbut's position, the Confederates fell upon Sherman farther to the west. Hurlbut quickly put Veatch's Second Brigade into motion, hurrying the 2,800 men to support Sherman's collapsing left flank. He personally led Williams's First and Lauman's Third Brigades, with supporting cavalry and artillery, to reinforce the left and rear of Prentiss's isolated division. A veteran of the 61st Illinois Infantry (which had retreated to a high ridge about a half-mile to the rear of Prentiss's crumpled left flank) at this juncture "saw a seemingly endless column of men in blue, marching by the flank, who were filing off to the right through the woods." Hurlbut's prompt arrival encouraged the adjutant of the 61st Illinois, a German immigrant, to inspire his despairing commanding officer by shouting, "'Dose are de troops of Sheneral Hurlbut. He is forming a new line dere in de bush.'"[64]

While elements of Prentiss's division streamed in hasty retreat through Hurlbut's advancing formations, Hurlbut planted his artillery and bloodily repulsed repeated Confederate attacks, despite a disorderly flight of the 13th Ohio Battery. Indeed, the cannoneers of Capt. Charles Mann's Missouri Battery (a unit in the 1st Missouri Light Artillery, composed chiefly of Germans) showered so heavy a fire upon the attacking columns that "General Hurlbut twice rode up and complimented them, and his words moved the gallant Dutchmen to tears." Hurlbut boldly rode forward under a veritable storm of cannonballs and bullets to his most exposed lines, exhorting his hard-pressed men to shoot deliberately, in volleys.

Conspicuous in his resplendent general's uniform—complete with its yellow sash, epaulets, sword, and scabbard—Hurlbut ignored a shell that exploded within ten feet of his gray charger and a screaming rifle ball that struck a tree only a few feet from his head. A stern warning from one of his staff officers to avoid overexposing himself to enemy fire prompted an undaunted Hurlbut to reply, "Oh, well, we generals must take our chances with the boys." According to a *Cincinnati Gazette* correspondent's account, "Hurlbut himself displayed the most daring and brilliant gallantry," and his bravery inspired his men to inflict a "terrible slaughter" upon the attacking Confederates. The reporter added, Hurlbut "had a splendid force of choice troops, who fought like Turks." Seeing the "glimmer of bayonets" of a dense body of Texas infantry steadily advancing to attack Williams's brigade, Hurlbut ordered a deadly fusillade of musketry fire when it reached a point within three hundred yards of the Union lines. Thus the fierce bayonet charge failed, and frightful carnage ensued; Hurlbut's infantry killed or wounded upward of two hundred Rebel troops.[65]

But Hurlbut's division had suffered much heavier casualties. Veatch's Second Brigade, which Hurlbut had sent to the support of Sherman, had lost 630 men.

Williams's First Brigade and Lauman's Third Brigade had lost a total of 1,355 men killed, wounded, or missing and presumably captured. Also, Hurlbut had also quickly lost perhaps his finest subordinate commander. Colonel Williams, the hero of Shelbina acquitted himself heroically at Shiloh in the face of almost overwhelming numbers; early in the battle, as he was directing the fire of his 3d Iowa Infantry and other troops, a Confederate cannon ball struck his horse, killing the animal instantly and stunning Williams.

Brigadier General Lauman had also fought bravely. On the afternoon of April 6, Lauman's severely depleted brigade (less than three hundred infantry of the 44th Indiana Volunteers) found itself confronted near the Peach Orchard by fifteen fresh Confederate regiments, nearly ten thousand men. Hurlbut could not reinforce Lauman, who coolly recognized that he could neither hold his advanced position nor retreat without losing his remaining troops and batteries about a mile to his rear. Audaciously, and in desperation, Lauman ordered the 44th Indiana to attack. Rallying his battalion with a Mexican War battle cry ("Remember Buena Vista!"), Maj. Albert Heath led the charge; Hurlbut, who anticipated the annihilation of Lauman's whole command, exclaimed, "A gallant but rash movement!" But the Confederate forces, fearing that Lauman's assault only spearheaded a powerful Union counterattack, broke and fled. Lauman had thus narrowly prevented a Confederate breakthrough on Hurlbut's right flank, just as enemy forces prepared to penetrate and overrun the general's precariously anchored left.[66]

General Johnston had recognized the unexpectedly tenacious defense offered by Hurlbut's Fourth Division. Hurlbut's unyielding protection of the Union army's eastern flank threatened to defeat Johnston's strategy of cutting off Grant's army from its base, Pittsburg Landing. About two thirty in the afternoon on April 6, Johnston, together with Tennessee governor Isham G. Harris and Lt. John P. Broome, an officer of the Georgia Hussars assigned as a courier on his staff, rode to the rear of the thin Confederate lines immediately opposite Hurlbut's position. Suppressing growing anxiety over the outcome as "bullets flew thick about him," Johnston remarked to Governor Harris, "General Hurlburt is mighty stubborn." Leaving Harris and Broome, Johnston rode a short distance farther forward to rally his troops, shouting, "Boys, General Hurlburt seems to be mighty stubborn. We'll have to see what we can do with the bayonet." Valiantly, if rashly, Johnston led a bayonet charge against the weakened Union lines, and "Hurlburt's Brigade was broken into tatters." Tragically for the Confederate cause, however, Johnston fell mortally wounded by a bullet fired by one of Hurlbut's retreating troops and by a shell fragment.

His death was the more unfortunate for his army because he had not yet turned Grant's vulnerable left flank.[67] As Johnston lay bleeding to death, Confederate troops began to do so. Because the Confederates had now completely enveloped the Peach Orchard and had prepared to capture Prentiss and the 2,200 Union infantry still trapped in that deadly "Hornet's Nest," Hurlbut necessarily retired to Pittsburg Landing. Compounding the destruction of Prentiss's Sixth Division, Brigadier General Wallace fell severely wounded while trying to escape from "Hell's Hollow"; he would die on April 10. Wallace's Second Division had suffered heavy casualties, and a few disorganized survivors joined the Fourth Division near the river. There, under the cover of the concentrated fire of twenty-four-pounder Union navy siege guns, artillery, and field guns mounted on two Union gunboats, the *Lexington* and *Tyler* (a brilliant improvisation by Col. Joseph D. Webster, Grant's chief of artillery), Hurlbut consolidated his decimated units into a line opposite a densely wooded ridge to receive renewed Confederate assaults.

Meanwhile, Hurlbut had located and placed two twenty-four-pounders, six twenty-pounder Parrott rifled guns, and sixteen lighter pieces of field artillery, some of which ordnance had been supplied by Webster. Consequently, when the men of the 18th Louisiana charged down the slope against his hastily entrenched position, they "were cut to pieces" by Hurlbut's cannonade and "mowed down by hundreds" by the Union gunboats firing directly into their ranks.[68]

After a brief pause, Hurlbut again heard the shrill Rebel yell and beheld the tattered "Stars and Bars" raised defiantly aloft over the smoke-covered fields south and east of Shiloh Church. Grant, who had reached Pittsburg Landing from his field headquarters nine miles down river at Savannah, approved Hurlbut's dispositions on the Union left and encouraged him to hold before proceeding to the right flank. Hurlbut's combined force of infantry, field artillery, and naval gunnery repelled waves of Confederate attackers until darkness ended the first day of fighting.

During the night of the 6th, cold, heavy rain fell. Hurlbut, stoically ignoring hunger and fatigue, strengthened his lines further in expectation of another day's fighting. About ten o'clock in the morning, Hurlbut received orders from Grant to reinforce McClernand's division on the weakened right flank. Simultaneously, twenty thousand fresh troops arrived to reinforce both flanks. They were led by Maj. Gen. Lewis Wallace, commander of the Third Division (which had marched from Crump's Landing, four miles north of Savannah), and by Brig. Gen. Don Carlos Buell, commanding the Army of the Ohio (which had crossed the river).

Regretfully, Hurlbut found it necessary to hold the seriously depleted 15th Illinois (of which Company B was from Hurlbut's native Boone County) in reserve at Pittsburg Landing. As one member of Company D recollected, "As we filed along to our place in line, Gen. Hurlbut gazed on our decimated ranks with watery eyes." Several of the regiment's officers had died (though not Col. Thomas J. Turner, who had missed the battle), and "he mourned the loss of true and tried friends." His grief was mixed with anger at Grant's diversion of the few remaining and fragmented battalions of his division's First Brigade (the Second and Third Brigades having been deployed elsewhere) to the army's western flank; Hurlbut exclaimed, "Here is what I am ordered to march against the enemy."

Reluctantly but dutifully he led his infantry toward McClernand's sector, and Hurlbut early reached the Union right flank. There he pressed his weary troops forward against the stubbornly resisting Confederates, had a horse shot from under him and a bullet graze his right arm, and helped McClernand and Sherman drive the Confederates back toward Corinth. Hurlbut once again demonstrated imperturbability and courage under fire. For instance when a body of 3d Iowa infantrymen found themselves in the middle of an intense artillery duel between Union and Confederate batteries, guns "fired shot and shell" over their heads, and cannonballs "struck and burst" in their front and rear. A soldier anxiously wondered aloud if the battery behind them was Confederate, not Union. The Iowa soldiers heard a voice from behind them reassuringly reply, "It is ours, of course." As an Iowa veteran vividly recalled, "Looking around us we saw General Hurlbut, seated on his horse and smoking calmly." Thereafter, Hurlbut repeatedly encouraged his regiments to advance or to hold their lines, as need be. Union and Confederate charges and countercharges continued until Federal cavalrymen finally drove the Confederate infantry from the field. Wholly exhausted from lack of food and sleep, Hurlbut at length moved his depleted division back into camp near Pittsburg Landing, believing that he had played a necessary, indeed indispensable, part in the Battle of Shiloh.[69]

He had indeed. Given the important task of protecting the army's left flank, he had executed that duty skillfully and successfully, although his tactical movements had been necessarily limited to advancing and retreating in close formation. Hurlbut's experience in the Seminole War, leadership of a militia company, and mastery of close-order drill enabled him to perform brilliantly in a subordinate role, if not (as his campaign in Missouri had shown) for independent field command. Grant subsequently reported that Hurlbut, like the other division commanders, had acquitted themselves with "credit" at Shiloh.[70]

The battle, however, had reflected serious doubt on Grant himself; the Confederates had tactically surprised him (and Sherman) and had inflicted heavy losses. Moreover, it was not Hurlbut's valiant infantry but Webster's concentrated artillery and the two Union gunboats (which together had killed nearly four thousand Confederate soldiers) that had saved the Union left. Without Webster's initiative and the support of the navy, the Confederates would have overwhelmed and annihilated the Fourth Division, as they had already destroyed the Sixth Division and decimated the Second. Grasping these realities, Hurlbut, who envied Grant and begrudged his growing fame, believed that Grant had blundered egregiously at Shiloh, notwithstanding the Union victory.

Hurlbut expressed his opinion of Grant's generalship shortly after the close of the battle. On the morning of April 8 Hurlbut heard three heavy volleys of musketry just south of his position. Ordering his infantry to form line of battle, Hurlbut quickly dispatched a company of cavalry to ascertain the enemy's location and strength. But consternation and panic swept over some of his troops; hundreds of them fled toward the river "like frightened sheep," some of them clambering onto wildly bucking horses and mules, three skulkers attempting to mount a single balky mule. Hurlbut cried out furiously, "Shoot the infernal cowards; drive them into the river!" Hurlbut's officers, however, rallied the panicked infantry; no precipitate executions followed. Soon informed by his cavalry chief that it was not the enemy that had fired but Buell's troops, testing their weapons because the preceding night's rainfall had dampened their gunpowder, Hurlbut ordered his troops to stack arms and to eat breakfast.

Shortly thereafter, Grant and his aides approached Hurlbut's headquarters. Grant, who apparently had also heard the firing from Buell's troops, instructed one of his staff officers to apprise Hurlbut of a threatened Confederate attack and ordered Hurlbut to form his infantry into battle line. Reluctantly, Hurlbut obeyed Grant's peremptory order, notwithstanding Hurlbut's presumed explanation, but an officer heard him grumble irately to himself, "Humph! I know more about that than he does." As soon as Grant had departed, Hurlbut ordered his troops again to stack arms and return to their breakfast. Hurlbut asserted in a letter to his wife that "this battle was a blunder, one of the largest ever made" and that Grant was "an accident with few brains," a negligent commander who had inexcusably failed to give him coherent and explicit orders during the first day's fighting. Hurlbut was apparently not reminded, as he should have been, of his own blunder in northeast Missouri, when he had unfairly blamed Col. Nelson G. Williams for the evacuation of Shelbina (of which Hurlbut never absolved him, though he survived his injury at Shiloh and received a fitting commendation in Hurlbut's official report). Convinced that he had retrieved his honor and reputation, Hurlbut predicted the imminent collapse of the Confederacy.[71]

Hurlbut did in fact gain a substantial measure of respect from Republican and "War Democratic" editors. Shortly after the battle, the highly partisan Democratic *Chicago Times,* in its account of Hurlbut's gallant defense of the imperiled Union left on the first day, claimed that Hurlbut's troops had formed the "main prop" upon which a large part of the reeling Union army had rested. The

Republican *Illinois State Journal* of Springfield agreed, praising Hurlbut (as it did Grant, McClernand, and the slain Wallace—three other Illinois generals at Shiloh) as "a hero and a soldier." The *State Journal* denounced the "Democratic carpet knights" who in September 1861 had so "systematically and perseveringly vilified and abused" him and made him the "butt of squibs and calumnies." Indeed, the paper characterized Hurlbut as "a true knight" who had gained the favorable estimation of Major General Halleck (who had arrived at Pittsburg Landing from St. Louis) for his "gallant bearing, great coolness and soldier-like qualities." The *Belvidere Standard,* praising his "distinguished service" at Shiloh, particularly applauded Hurlbut's gallant defense of McClernand's imperiled left flank on the second day of the struggle. Hurlbut had personally directed the deployment of six Union regiments in a counterattack by which, although his troops suffered heavy casualties, he "saved the command of that officer from being absolutely cut to pieces." The War Democrat editor of the *Illinois State Register,* reflecting the sentiments of numerous journals in Illinois of its political stripe, grudgingly acknowledged, "We shall be glad, indeed, if the general has redeemed, or rather secured, a good name in the Pittsburg fight." However, the *Register* refrained from designating Hurlbut as the savior of Grant's left wing at Shiloh.[72]

The Army of the Tennessee continued its movement against Corinth, now under the direct command of Halleck, who had superseded Grant. Known as "Old Brains" for his reputation as a military scholar and legal theorist, Halleck feared to attack the Confederate army at Corinth directly and decided instead to lay formal siege to the strategic Confederate stronghold. Hurlbut drilled his troops, boasted of his leadership at Shiloh to war correspondents, and feasted on fresh mutton from an abandoned Confederate flock of sheep.[73] Late in May the Confederates suddenly evacuated Corinth, and Union forces occupied it. Halleck sent Hurlbut to LaGrange, Tennessee, a point on the Memphis & Charleston Railroad about forty-five miles east of Memphis, to protect that supply line. In July Grant resumed command of the Army of the Tennessee, confirming Hurlbut in the Fourth Division and naming him commander of the District of Memphis, with headquarters at LaGrange. Pursuant to revised orders, on July 15 Hurlbut marched his division to Memphis, where his command remained attached to Sherman's corps until September 5, when Hurlbut moved his division to Bolivar, Tennessee.[74]

Grant had recommended to Lincoln that Hurlbut should be promoted to the rank of major general of volunteers, largely for his meritorious performance at Shiloh. On September 17, 1862, Hurlbut received his appointment from Washington. However, he also received orders from the War Department assigning him to Cincinnati. Unwilling to be transferred, Hurlbut protested to

Grant that he could not accept his promotion if it meant relinquishing command of the Fourth Division. Grant intervened, obtaining revised orders that continued Hurlbut in his capacity as a field commander in Tennessee. On September 24, Grant named Hurlbut commander of the District of Jackson with headquarters at Jackson, Tennessee, eighty miles northeast of Memphis at the intersection of the Mobile & Ohio and Mississippi Central Railroads.[75]

Proud of his promotion but anxious to show Grant that he could perform as effectively as a field commander as he had as a tactician at Shiloh, Hurlbut quickly exploited an opportunity. When the Confederate armies of Major Generals Earl Van Dorn and Sterling Price attacked Corinth early in October 1862, Hurlbut obeyed orders and promptly marched his division southeast from Bolivar to support the Union forces defending Corinth. Defeated at Corinth, Van Dorn and Price hastily withdrew their forces to the north and west; Hurlbut (now under the command of Maj. Gen. Edward O. C. Ord, an 1839 graduate of West Point) moved rapidly to cut off their retreat. On October 5 the lead elements of his division intercepted a large Confederate force approaching the Big Hatchie River at Davis's Bridge, fifteen miles northwest of Corinth and two miles south of the Pocahontas rail station. Hurlbut's troops held the bridge against the Confederates, who fortified a commanding hill on their (eastern) side of the river. Hurlbut remained on the western side of the Big Hatchie.

Ord, having now arrived on the battlefield, personally directed Union forces to carry the bridge and secure a lodgment in front of the base of the steep hill. When Ord was incapacitated by a leg wound, command of his forces devolved upon Hurlbut. Hurlbut formed a simple plan to outflank the enemy by throwing the Fourth Division and two regiments of another Union division across the bridge and by steadily extending them around the right flank of the strongly entrenched Confederate lines. He expected his maneuver to effect either the capture or destruction of the enemy army. Dressed conspicuously in full uniform, Hurlbut intrepidly "rode across the bridge and into the thickest of the fire" with the 68th Ohio, 12th Michigan, and 46th Illinois Regiments. Having reached the east bank of the Big Hatchie unscathed, he ordered more regiments to the front. Hurlbut thereafter directed tactical movements on the eastern side of the river, demonstrating remarkable composure and bravery.

Perceiving disorganized bodies of the 53d Indiana clinging precariously to an exposed position upon his right flank downstream of Davis's Bridge, under a "murderous fire" from Confederate infantry and artillery, he took decisive action. "Seizing the colors of the regiment Hurlbut rode to the left, and advancing to the front" he dramatically "planted the colors firmly in the ground and ordered the regiment to form on them." Inspired, the 53d Indiana joined the

Union attack against the commanding heights of the hurriedly entrenched Confederate position. According to a subsequently captured Confederate army doctor, General Price exclaimed, "Who in the name of God are we fighting now? If it is not Hurlbut, it is some devil out of hell." Hurlbut personally planted a battery on the crest of the hill to hurl shells at the smoke of a concealed Confederate battery. Units of the two Union divisions, advancing valiantly through concentrated shelling and enfilading musket fire, turned the Confederate army's right flank, and Van Dorn's troops fled in disorder south into Mississippi. After seven hours of fierce fighting, Hurlbut's forces had killed or wounded almost five hundred Confederate soldiers, seized nearly three hundred prisoners, and captured two batteries. But the victory proved costly; Hurlbut's division had suffered equally heavy losses during the Battle of Hatchie Bridge, and Ord and other officers had been severely wounded.[76]

Although scarcely a grand strategic operation or a brilliant tactical maneuver, Hurlbut's interception and defeat of Van Dorn at Hatchie Bridge demonstrated increased ability as a field commander. However, because he and Maj. Gen. William S. Rosecrans, a West Point graduate who had driven Van Dorn out of Corinth, conducted a slow, halting pursuit of the defeated Confederates, Van Dorn's forces avoided capture or destruction, for which Hurlbut and Rosecrans blamed each other. Shortly thereafter Hurlbut prepared to return with a part of his division to Bolivar, leaving the rest under Rosecrans encamped about eight miles north of Holly Springs, Mississippi. He would have done better to stay with Rosecrans himself, for in his absence the officers and enlisted men at Holly Springs made themselves appear as "the very worst" of Federal soldiers, looting, pillaging, and plundering in the surrounding country. His subordinate commanders failed to restrain them. Whatever Rosecrans's direct responsibility at Holly Springs, Hurlbut now displayed unbecoming conduct of his own.[77]

Whether to celebrate his victory or suppress his anger with Rosecrans for Van Dorn's escape, Hurlbut, secluded in his tent near the Hatchie River west of Corinth, began drinking. In a state of near insensibility, forgetting his rank and responsibility, he mounted his horse and wandered aimlessly over the bloody battlefield, where he happened to see a teamster cruelly beating his braying mules with a whip. In his drunken temper, Hurlbut shouted, "You damned son of a bitch, stop that!" The burly muleskinner cursed and challenged him to a fistfight. Hurlbut, who "was game, and just full enough to be destitute of self-respect," tore from each shoulder the two stars signifying his rank, trampled them into the dirt, and proceeded to take what the robust wagon driver promised would be "the dam'dest licking a Major General ever had!"[78] His lips bleeding and his eyes blackened, a stunned Hurlbut painfully clambered back onto his horse and galloped back into camp.

The following day his staff accompanied Hurlbut to the "Academy Hospital" in Corinth, an institution managed by "Mother" Mary Ann Ball Bickerdyke, a matronly humanitarian of Galesburg, Illinois. Having studied nursing in Cincinnati, and a widow upon the outbreak of war in 1861, she had worked as a nurse in army hospitals in Cairo before founding the Academy Hospital. In her Hurlbut encountered a professional nurse who easily diagnosed his condition. However, she discreetly reported Hurlbut's obvious hangover and facial injuries as symptoms of a stubborn head cold. She ordered a warm bath and a steaming hot toddy to be prepared for him before having him put to bed.[79] But having grown inured to the effects of his habitual overindulgence, Hurlbut soon recovered. Hailed vociferously on October 8 by his veteran troops at Bolivar, Tennessee, he acknowledged them by graciously "doffing his hat" and showing "a pleasant smile."[80]

Despite Hurlbut's conspicuous success at Hatchie Bridge, Grant seemed altogether unimpressed. Rather than reassigning Hurlbut to a more active field command in his reorganization of the Army of the Tennessee promulgated on October 26, he kept him in the District of Jackson, though now as the commander of the newly formed Thirteenth Corps. Loath to serve in a rear area guarding railroads and administering trains, Hurlbut nevertheless exploited the opportunity to cultivate his Illinois troops, perhaps with an eye toward his political prospects following the war. Sometime late in October, for instance, at LaGrange on the Memphis & Charleston Railroad, he rode his sleek "trotting stallion" to an Illinois cavalry encampment, where he observed a young cavalryman grooming his horse. Apparently intoxicated once again and in the grip of his predilection for betting, he challenged the trooper to a race. Stripping off his coat and pantaloons and on binding a bright red silk handkerchief around his forehead, Hurlbut raced against the cavalryman; he lost and gave his thoroughbred to the winner, observing the terms of the contest, in a spirit of good sportsmanship.[81] One other incident illustrated the lengths to which Hurlbut would go to impress individual soldiers. During the furious Union attack across Davis's Bridge earlier in October, Hurlbut had promised an ill-clad Illinois infantryman that he would furnish him with fresh clothing should the Fourth Division defeat the Confederates. Following the Union victory, the soldier proudly proceeded to Hurlbut's tent and asked for pants and shoes, whereupon Hurlbut pointed to the bloody battlefield across the Hatchie River and with a wry grin said, "You go over that hill and in the ravine on the other side there are a lot of men who have more clothes than they need. You take what you want." Apprehending Hurlbut's meaning, the private looted the Confederate dead—a common act in the war.[82]

Hurlbut also courted the approval of whole regiments. During the battle at the Big Hatchie, Brigadier General Lauman had ordered Col. Isaac C. Pugh, who commanded the 41st Illinois, to guard the Fourth Division's wagon train and hold his regiment in reserve. Loudly complaining to his subordinate officers and "chafing under the noise of battle," the elderly Pugh (who had served as a volunteer captain in the Black Hawk War and during the Mexican War) angrily exclaimed, "They are having hell down there and the 41st can't get a smell." Hurlbut, learning of Pugh's reserve assignment, had Lauman's order countermanded and sent the 41st Illinois into battle.[83] A month later, on the parade ground at Jackson, Hurlbut assured the 95th Illinois that it was the finest regiment that the state had yet sent to the western theater. As a private soldier recalled the speech, "Gen Hurlburt says that this is too nice a reg to be put right into a fight & be cut all to the Devil without being thoroughly drilled." Hurlbut proceeded to LaGrange to confer with Grant. There an officer in the 103d Illinois Infantry remarked that "Hurlbut is the most popular man here as a division commander."[84]

Hurlbut's dissatisfaction over his rear-area assignment grew. Consequently he frequently complained to Grant of failing health and urged Congressman Washburne to procure Lincoln's permission for him to take a month's leave of absence. Expressing a desire to confer personally with the president at the White House, Hurlbut assured Washburne that he could persuade Lincoln to bestow commissions on numerous other Illinois Republicans, despite anticipated objections from eastern radical Republicans in Congress. By November 10 Washburne had obliged Hurlbut by obtaining a leave for him, but it would have to wait until January 1863. Hurlbut reconciled himself to the delay by flattering himself that presently he would triumphantly accompany Grant into the Confederate fortress of Vicksburg, a strategic bastion on the eastern bank of the Mississippi River about two hundred miles below Memphis.

Grant, however, had planned another assignment for Hurlbut. On November 25, 1862, he named him commander of District of Memphis, succeeding Sherman, with his Thirteenth Corps headquarters in that city.[85] Having in anticipation relinquished his command at Jackson on November 19, Hurlbut established temporary headquarters in Memphis while awaiting Grant's official announcement of his reassignment. There he encountered his foremost rival as an Illinois politician and another beneficiary of Lincoln's military patronage, Maj. Gen. John A. McClernand.

A fifty-year-old native of Kentucky, McClernand had emigrated to Illinois, where as a young man he had fought courageously in the Black Hawk War of 1832 and later studied and practiced law. He had held a colonelcy in the Illinois militia, sat in the Illinois legislature from 1836 to 1843, and had twice served, from 1843 to 1851 and 1859 to 1861, as a Democratic member of the U.S. House of Representatives. At the outbreak of war McClernand had left Congress to accept a commission as a brigadier general of U.S. Volunteers, effective May 17, 1861. He had then commanded infantry divisions under Grant at Belmont, Fort Henry, and Fort Donelson; his promotion to major general on March 21, 1862, made him junior in the West only to Halleck and Grant. But following Shiloh, McClernand had sought to operate independently of Grant, gaining the command of the Army of the Mississippi and obtaining Lincoln's and Halleck's approval in October 1862 for expeditions against Vicksburg. McClernand, like Hurlbut, envied and often disparaged Grant, Rosecrans, Charles S. Hamilton, and other members of the professional officer corps in the West. But Hurlbut (who genuinely admired Sherman and Ord) also criticized McClernand, declaring to Washburne early in December that "McClernand may as well show off his staff here as at Springfield & by my soul I don't know anything else he is fit for."[86] As of January 1, 1863, Hurlbut's mounting dislike of McClernand manifested itself, privately, in a letter to Sherman's wife. Sherman—promoted to major general of volunteers, effective on May 1, 1862—had on December 27 ordered a disastrous attack at Chickasaw Bayou, Mississippi. Sherman had then been placed, to his keen displeasure, under the command of McClernand in preparation for a riverine expedition against Arkansas Post. Hurlbut confided to Ellen Ewing Sherman, whom apparently he had met sometime before, that Lincoln's appointment of McClernand to command independent expeditions against Vicksburg and other strongholds was "an outrage so gross as to warrant every gentleman in throwing up his commission were it not for the serious condition of the struggle."[87] McClernand succeeded in reducing Arkansas Post, on January 11, 1863, and Sherman gained command of the Fifteenth Corps, which he thereafter ably directed in field and siege operations against Vicksburg.[88]

Hurlbut's fortunes in the first eighteen months of the Civil War coincided closely with the phenomenal rise of Ulysses S. Grant as the commander of the Army of the Tennessee. Almost cashiered in the fall of 1861 for intemperance and incompetence, Hurlbut had early forfeited the patronage of his Illinois Republican supporters and the full confidence of Lincoln, but he had earned Grant's gratitude in northeast Missouri and again in western Tennessee. Grant, himself recovering from criticism for rumored drinking in Tennessee and in Mississippi, revived Hurlbut's precarious prospects by having him promoted to major general after Shiloh and assigning him to posts where he could perform competently, if not conspicuously. Although Hurlbut had largely redeemed himself at Shiloh and at the Hatchie for his drunken blundering in Missouri,

Grant assumed considerable risk by assigning Hurlbut to Memphis, where he was unable to supervise him as closely as before. Preoccupied with his campaign against Vicksburg and with difficulties with other commanders—John A. McClernand in particular—Grant would abandon further efforts to control Hurlbut. Hurlbut, free to exploit his prominent position in the western command structure, would soon worsen the reputation Memphis already had as a cesspool of debauchery and corruption.

CHAPTER FOUR

Military Ruler of Memphis

Memphis, Tennessee, long proclaimed by its proud inhabitants and admiring observers as the rising "Charleston of the West," ranked as the South's sixth-largest city in 1861, with a population of twenty three thousand whites and five thousand blacks. It lay on the east bank of the Mississippi River about 250 miles south of St. Louis and nearly two hundred miles north of Vicksburg. Historically a busy commercial center, Memphis had fallen to Union naval and land forces early in June 1862. The strict occupation policy of William T. Sherman in the summer and fall of 1862 had driven thousands of Confederate supporters from the city but had also drawn large numbers of escaped slaves, Northern cotton speculators, liquor importers, gamblers, and prostitutes. Together with the Union troops holding the city, they had increased the population to over fifty thousand by December 1862. To replace the city's heavy prewar trade, cotton buyers and textile merchants developed a large and illicit exchange of Northern goods for cotton smuggled into Memphis from the surrounding region.[1] The city's commercial fortunes had substantially revived by early 1863, but its occupiers had converted once elegant mansions and hotels into army hospitals, prisons, and barracks.

Memphis had become a huge hospital for the Union army, with nearly eight thousand soldiers and sailors who suffered from battle wounds, chronic illnesses, and contagious diseases, particularly smallpox. The most notorious of the eleven army hospitals erected around Memphis formed one of three key elements of the newly constructed Fort Pickering, two miles south of the city on the Tennessee side of the Mississippi River. Besides a convalescent camp and a small stockade for mostly Confederate prisoners, the infamous "Small-pox Hospital" accommodated soldiers, both Union and Confederate, infected with potentially deadly disease.

Fortunately, in January 1863, Mary Ann Ball Bickerdyke, the former matron of the Academy Hospital at Corinth who had tended an inebriated Hurlbut, reported to the Union medical authorities in Memphis as the matron in charge of the civilian (chiefly female) nurses in army hospitals. Assuming additional duties as the nominal director of the smallpox hospital at Fort Pickering, she quickly discovered that this "loathsome place" had suffered "great neglect" and had grown "fouler and more noisome than an Augean stable." She and two leading Northern humanitarians then visiting Memphis had also found near the hospital (which a sanitation worker later described as "a charnel-house") nine corpses in advanced states of decomposition in the facility's hastily improvised morgue or "dead-house." For three weeks Bickerdyke cleansed, fumigated, and disinfected the hospital; she also directed the prompt burial of the dead. However, she still found it necessary to return weekly to the infirmary in order to maintain even tolerable sanitary conditions, because of the persistent negligence of assigned medical personnel. In Memphis she established the Gayoso Hospital of nine hundred beds in a commercial block of confiscated brick buildings near the once-elegant Gayoso House hotel on Main Street. There she and her assisting nurses, former slaves and Northern white women, offered their assistance in tending to the upward of six hundred Union soldiers wounded at the January 1863 Battle of Arkansas Post.[2]

If the smallpox hospital at Fort Pickering, two miles away, could not have marred the physical appearance of Memphis proper, the establishment of the Irving Block prison and the wholesale conversion of fine hotels into improvised barracks definitely did. Located on the west side of Court Square at the heart of the occupied city, the prison—previously a stately three-story commercial building and three brick warehouses that had once served as a makeshift Confederate army and navy hospital—confined both Confederate prisoners and civilians, both Northern and Southern, suspected of disloyalty to the Union. Theoretically, medical and military authorities exercised mutually exclusive jurisdiction over hospitals and prisons, respectively. The smallpox hospital at Fort Pickering and the ten other army hospitals in Memphis (including the Gayoso) fell under the western division of the Union army's medical department; however, the military commander of the District of Memphis could enforce orders concerning their administration. In sharp contrast, the medical authorities had no authority or means to enforce sanitary standards in prisons. Consequently, the prisons at Memphis quickly degenerated into pestholes, their squalor far exceeding even that of the hospitals. As the commander of the District of Memphis (and concurrently as the commander of Thirteenth Corps, Army of the Tennessee, with headquarters in that city), Hurlbut would effectively assume, whether he recognized it at first or not, responsibility for maintaining high sanitary standards and humane living conditions in both prisons and hospitals.

The proliferation of makeshift hospitals and the progressive deterioration of the Irving Block could not, however, have defaced the city's appearance or lowered its moral tone any worse than did other structures and enterprises. "Gambling halls, drinking saloons and houses of ill-fame, were to be met with on every corner" of Memphis, complained one Union private in 1863, who believed that such temptations "were the weapons used by Satan to rob the soldier of his money and drag his soul down to the black gulf of despair."[3] An English-born soldier, Cpl. George Hovey Cadman from Ohio, described the ubiquitous "Women, Whiskey, and dogs" as curses afflicting him and his comrades in arms in Memphis, complaining that the city by 1863 had turned into the "blessed abode of filthy Niggers, Dirty Irish, and Ugly women."[4] Moreover, the Gayoso House had become a notorious seat of sin. Mary A. Livermore, chief officer of the Northwestern Branch of the U.S. Sanitary Commission, stayed for several days there early in March 1863 during a tour of inspection of every military hospital on the Mississippi River from Cairo to Vicksburg. In Memphis, insolent Southern belles with "secession proclivities" insulted her on the city's streets, and she suffered almost unbearable "discomfort" at the Gayoso. "Nightly drunken rows and fights" involved boisterous officers and carousing soldiers and sailors, and the hotel resounded with the mingled "crash of glass, the ribald song, the fearful profanity, and the drunken mirth" of their debaucheries.[5]

Into this demoralizing and degrading environment came Stephen A. Hurlbut on November 26, 1862.[6] Now forty-seven years of age, Hurlbut failed to impress keen observers favorably despite his gaily-plumed hat. He was paunchy and balding, with a weak chin partially concealed under a shaggy mustachio and Vandyke beard; a fine aquiline nose formed his only distinguishing facial feature. Despite his eloquence as a political orator, Hurlbut struck perceptive observers as an arrogant, irascible, and frequently vindictive man. The Union *Memphis Bulletin* overlooked these defects, declaring that Hurlbut possessed legal and military abilities "of the highest order." In perhaps a guarded allusion to Sherman's early strict rule, the *Bulletin* expressed the hope that Hurlbut would rapidly prove himself "the right man in the right place," a commandant with "a clear head, a sound judgment and a kind and sympathizing heart."[7]

On December 22, 1862, obeying a presidential order that reorganized his army into four corps and designated four major generals to command them, Grant announced the appointment of Hurlbut to the command of the newly created Sixteenth Corps, instead of the Thirteenth, with his headquarters still at Memphis. However, Grant decided to deprive Hurlbut of the Memphis district command, assigning Brig. Gen. James C. Veatch of Indiana to that duty, effective on January 5, 1863. Veatch, who had commanded one of Hurlbut's brigades at Shiloh, had been promoted to brigadier general of volunteers on April 28, 1862. Thus, in effect, Grant created a combined operational and occupation command at Memphis, for Veatch also commanded the Fifth Division of Hurlbut's Sixteenth Corps. Veatch served in relative obscurity as a nominal post commander under Hurlbut's direct authority.[8]

Establishing his headquarters and personal residence at the Gayoso House, Hurlbut proceeded to select his staff. Unfortunately, he made patronage and favoritism—not ability—the criterion, auguring ill for the secessionist inhabitants of Memphis. To fill the position of assistant adjutant general Hurlbut chose Capt. Henry Binmore, formerly of the staff of Brig. Gen. Benjamin M. Prentiss. A twenty-nine-year-old English immigrant who had gained distinction as a political reporter and stenographer for the Democratic *Chicago Times* and the *St. Louis Missouri Republican* (a Democratic newspaper, despite its name), Binmore had also served as a private secretary to Sen. Stephen A. Douglas in Washington in 1860. At Shiloh, Binmore had narrowly escaped from the "Hornets' Nest" when the Confederates captured Prentiss and most of his division. Thereafter, Binmore had served as an aide-de-camp to Hurlbut, particularly during the latter's temporary attachment to Sherman's corps in Memphis in the summer of 1862. In August 1862, however, Binmore had nearly lost his position when a provost marshal had arrested him for drunkenness in public and again for threatening to kill Fleming Calvert, master of the steamer *Platte Valley.* Hurlbut had secured his release and, in November 1862, had brought him back to Memphis.[9]

Hurlbut also selected Capt. Asher R. Eddy, who had been until his dismissal in 1862 the chief quartermaster for the state of Illinois at Springfield, as his assistant quartermaster, later naming him as head of the "Abandoned Property Department." Hurlbut initially appointed Capt. William H. Thurston, a New Hampshire native and the former commander of the 52d Indiana Railroad Regiment, as his principal aide-de-camp. Thurston, a skillful civil engineer, had directed the reconstruction of trestlework bridges on the Memphis & Charleston Railroad in the fall of 1862 and had subsequently served as Hurlbut's provost marshal at Bolivar, Tennessee. Hurlbut later promoted him to the rank of lieutenant colonel and on February 28, 1863, named him as his assistant inspec-

Stephen A. Hurlbut, commander of the XVI Corps at Memphis. Prints and Photographs Division, Library of Congress.

tor general. To fill the office of provost marshal, Hurlbut appointed the noted Chicago lawyer Charles M. Willard, a former Boone County Republican and political ally and an erstwhile major in the 1st Illinois Light Artillery. He named

Capt. Edward Frank, also from Chicago, as chief of the special "Detective Department" within the provost marshal's office. Compounding the cronyism displayed in his staff appointments, Hurlbut brought, or welcomed the arrival of, his former law partner James L. Loop from Rockford, Illinois, to Memphis. He enabled Judge Loop to build up a lucrative law practice in Memphis and made him responsible besides for helping Captain Eddy administer the Abandoned Property Department.[10] Subsequently, Hurlbut would name another of his Illinois friends, Col. Edward McCarty, to his staff as well. Hurlbut had thus created an inner circle that would eventually coalesce into a well organized "cotton ring" at Memphis.

President Lincoln, Secretary of the Treasury Salmon P. Chase, and Major Generals Grant and Sherman had adopted stern measures to halt the traffic of proscribed Northern goods (such as food, salt, clothing, medical supplies, and valuable munitions) through Memphis, but the steady flow of contraband into the Confederacy in exchange for smuggled cotton continued largely unchecked. Grant in particular had endeavored to stop the illicit trade, not least by naming Sherman, in June 1862, as the commandant of the District of Memphis. As Grant had clearly intended, Sherman stringently curbed smuggling. Moreover, he had severely punished, or threatened to punish, the secessionist civilian population of Memphis and western Tennessee for supporting guerrilla raiders. Like General Pope in northeast Missouri in 1861, Sherman acquired a reputation as a strict, even harsh, occupation commander.[11] Grant expressly directed Hurlbut to continue Sherman's strict policy, and Hurlbut probably did seek to restrain the prohibited trade in cotton. But Hurlbut would abuse Grant's confidence by building an extortionate cotton ring within Memphis, merely pretending to enforce Treasury Department regulations and War Department orders (as transmitted to him through Grant) prohibiting smuggling.

Sherman had been unable to halt or even substantially reduce the volume of smuggling in West Tennessee. Before Hurlbut's arrival at Memphis, Grant decided to adopt a drastic measure—a serious error of judgment that reflected a deplorable and prejudicial view of Jewish civilians as a class selfishly profiting from the war. On November 9, 1862, Grant ordered Hurlbut to grant no travel permits, denying them particularly to suspected cotton traders and above all to "the Israelites." Grant provoked a firestorm of protest against his "Jew Order," but Hurlbut proceeded to Memphis personally convinced that Jewish traders were contributing substantially to the rampant cotton speculation throughout the lower Mississippi Valley. But Memphis had a total Jewish population of only a thousand in 1863, and although a few Jewish merchants (among a disproportionately larger group of non-Jewish speculators) had reaped enormous profits

Ulysses S. Grant, commanding general, Army of the Tennessee. Prints and Photographs Division, Library of Congress.

from black marketing, the majority of Memphis Jews obeyed the law that forbade the practice.[12]

If Grant had thus put Hurlbut into an almost impossible situation, Hurlbut himself thoroughly underestimated the complexity of the contraband trade.

Consequently, instead of attempting to identify and destroy the well-organized—and chiefly Northern-financed—cotton rings, he imposed arbitrary and harsh sanctions upon individual southern Jews, isolated punitive acts calculated to impress his superiors with his rigor. A flagrant example occurred in the last days of 1862, when Hurlbut ordered the arrest of Abraham Ephraim Frankland, a prosperous British-born Jewish merchant and an active synagogue member in Memphis. Frankland's prominence probably increased his vulnerability to false accusations. In January 1858, he and associates had organized the fraternal, religious, and benevolent Euphrates Lodge No. 35 of B'nai B'rith in Memphis (the first lodge in the southern states) and had served as its treasurer. Frankland also participated in the synagogue of Congregation B'Nai Israel. Before the war Frankland and Abraham S. Levy, also a Euphrates Lodge member, had joined in partnership to auction and trade slaves (although only about one in twelve Jewish traders in Memphis had dealt in the profitable slave trading).

Frankland had antagonized Hurlbut, chiefly because he had refused to swear loyalty to the U.S. government, but also because he had harbored a Jewish Alabama-based merchant strongly suspected of smuggling in Memphis, although Frankland himself had not dealt directly in the trader's illicit transactions. Hurlbut—who shared anti-Semitic prejudice with Grant and other Union generals in the West—had Frankland seized and brought to the Gayoso House. In Hurlbut's temporary absence, Captain Thurston threatened to throw Frankland into the Irving Block prison unless he disclosed the secret location of "the other old Jew." When Hurlbut arrived, he personally directed the interrogation, denouncing him for espionage. Ironically it developed that he especially resented Frankland's having declared in 1862 to a man Frankland claimed was Hurlbut's Jewish friend, Abraham Strauss, in Cincinnati that "if the war had not been carried on to give the military a chance to steal everything in the South but the land, it could have been brought to a close long ago." Hurlbut clapped him into the Irving Block prison. Several prominent Memphis citizens demanded that Hurlbut parole him, and Hurlbut promised to release Frankland on the following day, provided he "give bonds for twenty thousand dollars for good behaviour and appearance when required." Frankland paid this exorbitant bail to Provost Marshal Willard. He never stood trial in a military court, and he never recovered his twenty thousand dollars.[13]

Emboldened by his successful fleecing of Frankland, Hurlbut followed a similar procedure to deprive another Jewish merchant in Memphis of nearly all his property. Isaac A. Meyer had obtained the necessary permits to conduct a mercantile business in Memphis. Arriving there early in December 1862 with a plentiful supply of clothing and dry goods, three weeks later his partner (allegedly) robbed his most valuable clothing stock. Shortly thereafter, a Union soldier had assaulted Meyer and attempted to snatch his expensive gold watch and chain. Meyer had lodged a complaint, but neither Hurlbut nor Veatch had ordered an investigation.[14] On March 15, 1863, Hurlbut had Meyer arrested. His new provost marshal, Lt. Col. Melanchthon Smith (an erstwhile Republican party rival of Hurlbut), who had replaced Willard in February, hauled him into the Irving Block prison. Meyer remained incarcerated for sixteen hours in that "very filthy and sickly place, not fit for a good dog," before gaining his release upon payment by his friends of two ten-thousand-dollar bonds and forfeiture of all his personal property—including his gold watch and chain, and other items worth $670. For the next three months, Meyer was required to report twice a day, in person, to Smith to render exact accounts of his business transactions.

In June, Meyer learned that shortly after his release from prison Hurlbut had directed Smith to convene a provost court to try his case. But Smith had not summoned Meyer, nevertheless finding him guilty of aiding deserters and (though Smith could invoke no military order forbidding it) selling fourteen dollars' worth of civilian clothing—a paper collar, a silk necktie, a colored shirt, and a pair of blue denim pants—to a Union soldier. On March 25 Hurlbut ordered the entire stock of Meyer's goods confiscated and sold at auction. He further ordered Meyer to leave his jurisdiction in Memphis and the District of West Tennessee (the commander of which was one of his subordinates). Meyer bribed one of Smith's clerks for a written copy of the sentence and courageously Meyer confronted Hurlbut at his headquarters, but not before an army detective had threatened to banish him from Memphis "by the first gunboat or to shoot me." Having "astonished" Hurlbut by producing tangible proof of his loss of personal property, although not his already-confiscated inventory, Meyer demanded a written order for the immediate restoration of his gold watch and chain. After two weeks of meeting alternately with Hurlbut and Smith, Meyer at last recovered his personal property, despite a detective's earlier boastful taunt that Meyer "would never get back my watch and chain, and I [Meyer] would see him [the detective] wear it." Meyer thereafter asserted that Hurlbut had entrapped him by sending a detective, posing as a private soldier, to buy articles of clothing supposedly prohibited for sale to troops in Memphis. Furthermore, Meyer alleged that Hurlbut personally had "robbed me of my nine years' and six months' hard earnings by false play" whereby the general had fraudulently "appropriated three-fourths of the porceeds [sic] of the sale of my stock of goods for his own use."[15]

In a more subtle but equally arbitrary manner Hurlbut wrested funds from another Jewish trader shortly before his command in Memphis ended. On March

24, 1864, Hurlbut's provost marshal general, now Capt. George A. Williams, arrested Martin Kenosskey, a resident of Grenada, Mississippi. Williams had intercepted Kenosskey in the act of removing a large quantity of gold bullion (later appraised at $8,861) south across the Union lines at Memphis. Having prohibited purchases of Southern goods with specie, Hurlbut imprisoned Kenosskey in the Irving Block after trying and convicting him on charges of smuggling. Kenosskey remained incarcerated for the rest of the war. After his release, on May 27, 1865, he demanded that Secretary of War Edwin M. Stanton return to him his commandeered gold bullion. Stanton promptly demanded an explanation from Hurlbut, who by then was the acting commander of the Army (and Department) of the Gulf at New Orleans. On June 25 Hurlbut replied to Stanton that Kenosskey, whom he termed "a Jew, Cotton & Gold Dealer and Smuggler," had forfeited his gold, which his provost had converted into currency. Hurlbut had spent $3,860 of it on Secret Service work in Memphis. Upon leaving the Sixteenth Corps on April 16, 1864, Hurlbut claimed, he had returned the remaining $5,001 to Thurston. However, in the absence of the immediate successor to the Sixteenth Corps command, Thurston had returned the funds to Hurlbut. (In truth, Maj. Gen. Cadwallader C. Washburn had assumed on April 17, 1864, command of the newly established Department of West Tennessee, which replaced the District of West Tennessee; the field elements of the Sixteenth Corps had been assigned to Brig. Gen. Grenville M. Dodge). Hurlbut had spent most of the money, he assured Stanton, on Secret Service activities in New Orleans late in 1864 and early in 1865. Finally, on October 15, 1865, Hurlbut furnished a dossier of vouchers and accounts showing the disposition of most of the remaining currency.[16]

The Frankland, Meyer, and Kenosskey cases clearly demonstrate not only Hurlbut's anti-Semitism but also his proclivity for the arbitrary abuse of power. They also reveal the malicious and vindictive sides to his nature—qualities manifested in 1861 when he had mistreated John McAfee. These affairs paralleled calculated extortions of money from wealthy but desperate relatives of Confederate prisoners in Memphis.

Ironically, though, these sordid episodes emphasize the sporadic nature of Hurlbut's attempts to enforce prohibitions against smuggling across the lower Mississippi Valley. Worse yet, Hurlbut proved unable or unwilling to withstand the temptation to drink. Hurlbut's intemperance in Memphis had begun in August 1862 when his Fourth Division was attached to Sherman's corps command. Hurlbut had been chairman of a special court implementing a law of July 17, 1862, that authorized the discharge of any volunteer officer whom the president deemed incompetent or otherwise unsuitable. On one remarkable occasion, Col. Thomas Worthington (former commander of the 46th Ohio Infantry, son of an Ohio governor, and an 1827 West Point graduate) had attended one of its sessions. Worthington subsequently complained to Lincoln that Hurlbut, "a General officer scarcely ever clear of liquor[,] staggered into his court room to decide on the cases of men better and abler than himself to suppress the rebellion." Hurlbut had delegated the judicial proceedings to his assistant adjutant general, whereupon the "sycophantic and ignorant" Binmore had arbitrarily recommended the dismissal of certain battle-tested veterans—but men unpopular with Hurlbut—so as to "curry favor" with Hurlbut and gain his recommendation for promotion to brigadier general. In exchange, Hurlbut had (allegedly) induced Binmore, a noted journalist and reporter, "to cover up the blunder, incapacity, and falsehood, of a prominent commander [Hurlbut] in late campaigns in Missouri and Tennessee." Worthington's charges and insinuations, regardless of the merit or truth, were self-serving since he had been cashiered.

Nevertheless, Hurlbut's dissipation was soon observable by others as well. Junius Henri Browne, the Western correspondent for the *New York Tribune* and also a frequent contributor to the *Cincinnati Times,* criticized Hurlbut's excessive drinking as highly detrimental to the efficient administration of the District of Memphis. On January 26 Browne wrote, "It is to be hoped Memphis will be better governed by General Veatch" than by Hurlbut, who "for weeks" before leaving Memphis on January 13, 1863, for Belvidere on leave had rendered himself "a daily spectacle of disgusting drunkenness." On February 6, Browne reported to his Cincinnati office that Veatch had dutifully and expeditiously begun to improve the management of Memphis, whereas Hurlbut had only "distinguished himself by the most supreme neglect of the best interests of the city" and "seemed to have little ambition beyond his daily habit of intoxication." Late in February, Alfred H. Bodman, the foremost Western correspondent for the *Chicago Tribune,* found Hurlbut at his headquarters "so grossly intoxicated that he was not able to exhibit the ordinary amenities of conversation prevailing among gentlemen."[17] Undoubtedly, Hurlbut occupied a difficult position, but his drinking aggravated his situation. Worse still, it diverted his attention from Confederate cavalry raids into western Tennessee and the rampant smuggling through Memphis, and it progressively destroyed his sense of justice in dealing with the civilian population.

Hurlbut's excessive drinking in Memphis probably contributed to an indiscretion that developed into a flagrant act of insubordination. According to informed "official sources" in the Confederate *Vicksburg Citizen,* Hurlbut outspokenly expressed strong disagreement with Grant's strategy for opening up the Mississippi River below Memphis by the reduction of Vicksburg and strongholds between there and New Orleans. Hurlbut considered Grant's policy as a "bad one," because even if successful it would leave the rebellion in "full strength" in other parts of the deep South. Shortly thereafter, the *Citizen* reported, Hurlbut and Grant had "enacted a pretty little scene" at Memphis. Hurlbut had refused to execute an order from Grant, because, "he said[,] he came South to protect, and not to destroy it." Grant "intimated that Hurlburt was a traitor," whereupon Hurlbut had replied that "he would take his men over to the d—d secesh rather than obey Grant."[18] If the *Citizen*'s reports were substantially accurate, Hurlbut had not only breached military security but had disobeyed a direct order. Given his previous dutiful obedience to superior officers, these quarrels with Grant probably reflected a breakdown of moral inhibition and judgment. For his part, Grant had apparently failed to enforce secrecy among his corps commanders; according to the *Citizen*'s report, Sherman and others had publicly expressed their opinions of Grant's plans. In any case, Grant did not report Hurlbut's insubordination to the War Department, and tension apparently subsided upon Grant's departure from Memphis.

To his great relief, Hurlbut finally obtained Lincoln's permission to take a leave of absence. He departed from Memphis on January 13 to spend three weeks with his family in Belvidere. During his absence, Brig. Gen. Charles S. Hamilton, a former division commander in the Left Wing of the Sixteenth Corps (and effective January 16, the commander of the District of West Tennessee) assumed temporary command. On January 26, Brigadier General Veatch also left on leave, and Hamilton also became acting commander of the District of Memphis.[19] A native of New York and an 1843 graduate of West Point who had served in the Mexican War with distinction, Hamilton had performed poorly as a division commander in the Army of the Potomac. Transferred to William S. Rosecrans command in the West, he had led troops more skillfully in the Battles of Iuka and Corinth. He had gained thereby Grant's recommendation for promotion to major general, despite Grant's persistent doubts about his competence. Nominated by Lincoln on January 22, Hamilton would win the confirmation of the Senate on March 9, four days before confirmation of Hurlbut as a major general as well.[20]

At Memphis, Hamilton eagerly anticipated Senate action, but he awaited with less pleasure Hurlbut's return from Illinois, which would terminate his brief tenure as a corps commander. Hurlbut's promotion to major general would be effective September 17, 1862, whereas his own would be backdated to September 19, making him junior. Hamilton moved quickly to perpetuate himself in his position and to undermine Hurlbut. He condemned Hurlbut's excessive drinking in letters to Sen. James R. Doolittle of Wisconsin, Hamilton's adopted home state. On January 30 he advised Doolittle that "Hurlbut drinks like a fish." Upon Hurlbut's return to Memphis, he "by virtue of his two days' rank— will supercede me & have me out of place or command," just when Hamilton had almost succeeded in "getting things all straight here"—matters of military administration had been "in terrible confusion when Hurlbut went off" on leave. When Hurlbut resumed command of the Sixteenth Corps on February 5, he kept Hamilton temporarily in command of the District of Memphis, Veatch being still absent, but on February 12, he recommended that Grant immediately assign the meddlesome Hamilton elsewhere.[21]

But Hamilton secretly continued to promote himself as a prospective corps commander by hurting the reputations of Grant and Hurlbut. Around January 20, Grant had returned to Memphis for a week and while in the city drank excessively, prompting Hamilton on February 11 regretfully to inform Senator Doolittle that *"Grant is a drunkard."* Hamilton reported that he and Brig. Gen. Isaac F. Quinby had finally found it imperative to take Grant "in charge, watch-ing with him day & night, & keeping liquor away from him." The two officers had also telegraphed Julia Dent Grant, left by Grant at LaGrange, to hasten to Memphis "to take care of him"; Grant had stayed "beastly drunk," "utterly incapable of doing anything" for several days. Hamilton also apprised Doolittle of Hurlbut's return to Memphis (a severe "blow" to his own ambition for ad-vancement) and of Hurlbut's renewed drinking. Although he had thus far "seen little of Hurlbut"—Hamilton indeed admitted that he had never personally seen Hurlbut drunk—the "stories of his drunkenness are rife through the city, and he is known oftentimes by the soubriquet of 'drunken Hurlbut.'" His own occasional observations of Hurlbut's rubicund "face & manner give evidence of much intemperance." As we have seen, none of this had its desired effect. Hamilton would hold command of the District of West Tennessee until April 1, 1863, and on April 18 would resign his commission.[22]

Nevertheless, Hamilton's criticism of Grant's and Hurlbut's imbibing in Memphis had emphasized important similarities and differences between the intemperance of both men, particularly with respect to their continued capac-ity for exercising effective command. Obviously, both Grant and Hurlbut quali-fied as binge drinkers. When they drank, they drank excessively and frequently without self-restraint. But where Grant, as a matter of preference or tempera-ment, habitually drank without company, the more gregarious Hurlbut pre-ferred to drink with comrades. And where Grant apparently drank with some suppressed sense of regret or embarrassment, Hurlbut drank freely in public, almost defiantly and scornful of criticism. Moreover, Grant had the advantage of having trusted subordinates and his wife who sought to control his binge drinking and at least to conceal his intemperance from the scrutiny of civilians. Hurlbut's staff officers, however, cared nothing that their commander drank freely in public and scarcely attempted to restrain him, even if he would have permitted them to do so. Hurlbut's wife, Sophronia, had not accompanied him to Memphis, so that he lacked her influence in helping him fulfill his previous pledge to her to stop or else curb his drinking. Finally, Grant apparently carried his liquor less noticeably than did Hurlbut. For, where Grant usually drank himself into a generally subdued, although a thoroughly befuddling, stupor, Hurlbut drank boisterously, and he blustered on growing intoxicated, as he had so offensively bragged in Chicago in July 1861. And where Grant's drinking apparently did not significantly affect his making of crucial military policy or decisions, Hurlbut's imbibing invariably impaired his judgment and produced uniformly unfavorable consequences for him, both on and off duty. As an illustration of this comparison, in March 1863, the U.S. Sanitary Commission officer, Mary A. Livermore, traveled to the Vicksburg theater to inspect the army's field hospitals. Arriving in Mississippi, she there anticipated meeting a much dissipated and inebriated Grant, having previously learned of his reputation as a drunkard. Yet, when she beheld his "clear eye" and robust look she gladly pronounced him a sober man. Conversely, she still regretfully remembered her encounters with drunken army of occupation commanders during her prolonged journey down the Mississippi from Cairo to Memphis. She and her associates recollected those officers in whom they had recognized the indications of "intemperance" since their "eyes had become practiced in reading the diagnosis of drunkenness."[23]

Grant's superior tolerance for liquor notwithstanding, he never expressed objections to Hurlbut's heavy drinking. Nor did he oppose a doubtful plan of Hurlbut's to permit an increased quantity of bottled alcohol to be imported into the District of Memphis, despite the probably detrimental effects of such a proposal on the efficiency and morale, and the moral character, of Hurlbut's troops. In the summer of 1863 many disappointed Treasury Department agents and disgruntled liquor dealers had loudly complained to Grant of Hurlbut's strict policy, which had banned the importation of all distilled and malt liquors into Memphis. Ironically, and perhaps even hypocritically, Hurlbut, who had himself maintained a plentiful supply of commissariat-issued or other black-marketed Northern whiskey, enforced stringently his impractical "non-importation" policy. Highly sensitive and responsive, however, to the commercial interests of both government agents and liquor dealers and perhaps suspecting that the prohibition on the importation of alcohol cleverly served as a blind for Hurlbut's heavy consumption of liquor, Grant demanded an explanation for this policy. Accordingly, on August 26 Hurlbut explained his nonimportation policy but went on to say that he had reconsidered. He now expressed his opinion that he should be permitted by Grant to allow the controlled importation of certain "Wines & Malt Liquors" into Memphis, but that he should continue to prohibit the importation of spirituous liquors such as whiskey, brandy, rum, and gin. Grant concurred with Hurlbut's proposal and authorized him to exercise his discretion concerning which classes of liquors should be brought into Memphis. Hurlbut's plan, however, revoked or at least effectively nullified an order that Brigadier General Veatch had issued shortly after assuming command of the District of Memphis early in January 1863, prohibiting the sale of all intoxicating liquors within his administrative district. Presumably, his sweeping order had also forbade the sale of malt liquors, including beers, in order to render his policy consistent with Hurlbut's concurrent policy of prohibiting the importation of all kinds of bottled alcohol. Consequently, by either relaxing or by partially reversing his earlier policy late in the summer of 1863, Hurlbut, as Sixteenth Corps commander, had gained popularity and approval among thirsty soldiers and sailors stationed at or near Memphis. But he thereby also overrode or undercut Veatch's authority and only further increased the already-superabundant supply of wines, ales, and beers available for purchase on Memphis's black market. Not until April 1864 did Hurlbut reestablish his originally conceived nonimportation policy, thereafter implemented by Brig. Gen. Ralph P. Buckland, Veatch's successor to the Memphis district command, and by Treasury Department agents.[24]

Whatever the controversy and criticism surrounding Hurlbut's and Grant's immoderate drinking in Memphis over the winter of 1863, Hurlbut returned to Belvidere in mid-January to rejoin his family after a year's separation. But while his fellow townsmen at an enthusiastic reception had hailed him as "the hero of Hatchie," Hurlbut succumbed suddenly to what he described as "an attack of erysipelas." Afflicted by a severe inflammation of his facial skin, perhaps occasioned by heavy drinking, he regretfully informed Congressman Washburne that although he could not early resume active duty around Memphis, he could nonetheless travel to Washington to confer with Lincoln about bestowing military patronage on other deserving Illinois Republicans. Specifically, Hurlbut requested Washburne to obtain executive orders from Lincoln for him to report to Washington and for an extension of his leave of absence until late in February. He promised, however, to return to duty in any event, because "I have no desire to remain still & I know Grant wants me back before he leaves Memphis for Vicksburgh & the South." But Lincoln refused Hurlbut's bold request, explaining that he could not grant him an extension of his leave without the concurrence of Secretary of War Stanton and Halleck.[25]

Thwarted in his plan to see Lincoln, Hurlbut reconciled himself to bragging to Belvidere townsmen about his prowess at Shiloh while he also bitterly denounced the Northern Peace Democratic "copperhead politicians," who sought vigorously to "embarrass the government and prevent the prosecution of the war" against the Confederacy. And in assuring local citizens of an early end to the war in the West, Hurlbut predicted the fall of Vicksburg to Grant and the opening of the Mississippi to navigation south to New Orleans by March 1, 1863. Then on January 31, while on his return trip to Memphis, Hurlbut stopped in Springfield, Illinois, and delivered a harangue to a mass Union party rally held in the Illinois House of Representatives. He particularly decried the sabotage of the Northern war effort by Peace Democrats. But here the conservative Democratic *Chicago Times* (a journal that still supported the war effort but bitterly opposed many of the Lincoln administration's policies for conducting the war) declared that Hurlbut's tirade had "menaced with military violence" the legislature and the citizenry of Illinois, while the *Illinois State Register* characterized Hurlbut's speech as a body of "bombast, fustian, and falsehood" in its seemingly demagogical excoriation of the much-misunderstood Northern Peace Democracy. Powerless to punish his critics in Illinois, Hurlbut headed south and arrived in Memphis by February 5 exhibiting "his usual good health and spirits," despite his disappointment that Grant had previously departed and had not reassigned him to active field duty near Vicksburg.[26]

Although Hurlbut had expressed resentment over the *Chicago Times'* condemnation of his Springfield speech, he also determined to stop the newspaper's harsh and unceasing criticism of Lincoln's war policies and military measures, particularly the Emancipation Proclamation. Angered by the *Times'* "false and calumnious attacks" on Lincoln, Hurlbut prepared to suppress that journal in Memphis and all across western Tennessee. He did so partly because the *Times* had vilified the president, although primarily to satisfy his desire for political revenge.[27] Essentially, however, such a contemplated policy amounted to an attempt by Hurlbut and by Illinois Governor Yates to protect each other against further attacks upon them by the *Times.* For his own part, Hurlbut bitterly resented the *Times'* earlier deprecation of his military administration in Memphis and moreover he had gratefully supported Yates's past efforts to discredit the paper. "Drunken Dick" Yates had not only helped to put Hurlbut into the Union army in 1861, but he had continued to defend him—despite the *Times'* well-founded charges of drunkenness against Hurlbut. And for his part, Yates, who had grown thoroughly incensed during 1862 over the *Times'* outspoken opposition to his administration at Springfield, urged Hurlbut to prohibit circulation of the Chicago paper precisely when its almost seditious defamation of Lincoln seemingly justified its suppression.[28] Having planned with Yates to gag the *Times,* Hurlbut returned to Memphis and, on February 8, ordered the suppression of the journal. But Grant intervened, rescinding Hurlbut's order on February 13. He assured Hurlbut that although he too considered the *Times* to constitute a disloyal paper, he could not sustain Hurlbut's regional and discriminatory ban because the paper circulated freely elsewhere in the Mississippi valley.[29]

Notwithstanding Grant's sympathy with Hurlbut, Hurlbut himself came under violent denunciation in Illinois for his order. Generally Republican editors across the Prairie State refrained from castigating Hurlbut and instead profusely praised Grant's prudence and justice, although the *Belvidere Standard* expressed strong reservations about Grant's loyalty to the Union cause. And in explaining that Brig. Gen. Jeremiah C. Sullivan, commanding officer of the District of Jackson, Tennessee, had with justification expelled the *Times* from his own jurisdiction, the *Standard* therefore asserted that "military commanders are warranted in kicking it out of their lines." Moreover, the *Chicago Tribune* approved of what it termed Hurlbut's "stringent and wholesome order," while the *Illinois State Journal* called his ban "a just and necessary rebuke" to the secessionists of Memphis. Not surprisingly, the Democratic *Chicago Times* unsparingly chastised him, charging that the "abolitionist" partners, Hurlbut and Yates, had conspired to suppress the *Times* throughout West Tennessee and even in Illinois, while as "boon companions" they "get drunk together, and have the *delirium tremens* together" in Springfield. Characterizing Hurlbut as a brazen "ass" and the "wretched instrument" of an intriguing Governor Yates, the *Times* also alleged that the two men, in their "drunken carousals and in the phrensy of their delirious excesses" at Springfield and Memphis, had irresponsibly but deliberately attempted to violate the constitutional right of free speech in West Tennessee. And, in censuring Lincoln for his support of Hurlbut's confirmation as a major general in March 1863, the *Times* declared that only Lincoln's "wickedness" could account for both his establishing and sustaining Hurlbut in command at Memphis. For Lincoln recognized, the *Times* charged, that Hurlbut had remained "notoriously addicted to drunkenness." But in disagreeing with the assessment of the *Chicago Times* the Democratic *Quincy Herald* expressed its opinion that Hurlbut and Yates had not frequently succumbed to intoxication together, but rather that they had scarcely recovered their mutual sobriety. "It's the same old drunk, with both of them," the *Herald* sarcastically quipped.[30] The Democratic *Illinois State Register* of Springfield declared, however, that Hurlbut's arbitrary decision to ban the *Times* had sprung from "a very large head" swollen with vainglory and from "a bottle of similar dimensions," but it commended Grant for his timely revocation of the "imperial order" of the rabidly "demagogue abolition General Hurlbut." And, in referring to Hurlbut's denunciations of the Northern Peace Democracy on January 31 before a large gathering of Republican "abolition leaders" in the Illinois capitol, the *Register* deplored that inflammatory "kind of fustian" that "has become so fashionable in the army since drunken Steve Hurlbut first indulged in it here at Springfield." But, determined to win the war of words, the *Illinois State Journal* of Springfield vigorously denounced the *Times'* "characteristically foul and infamous assault upon Gen. Hurlbut and Gov. Yates," further declaring that the "judgment of loyal men will sustain General Hurlbut."[31]

Overruled by Grant and condemned by Democratic editors in Illinois for his suppression of the *Times,* Hurlbut quickly moved to regain Grant's confidence in his judgment as an administrator. Thus in February and March 1863 he announced his intention to enforce more stringently Grant's orders against clandestine cotton-buying in the lower Mississippi valley. But although he frequently warned of stern measures to be taken against military corruption and civilian profiteering in Memphis, he actually made only feeble attempts to eliminate or reduce the illicit cotton trade.[32] Ironically Hurlbut's inaction at this time sprang, in part, clearly from his unwillingness to interfere with the continuing speculative operations of Grant's own enterprising patron and friend, Joseph Russell Jones. For, as Grant had penetrated farther into Confederate Mississippi in late 1862 and early 1863, Jones and his brother and another Galena merchandiser, John Corwith, had followed the Union army. The three men had often obtained special passes and permits from Grant to trade for Confederate cotton beyond the Union lines, and had created a special arrangement with Grant whereby they could expeditiously ship their cotton north for sale in Memphis, St. Louis, and Chicago. On his first trip into Mississippi (December 14, 1862, to January 6, 1863), Jones had purchased and had later sold profitably for five thousand dollars a large quantity of Southern cotton. But after his second trip (January 20 to February 4, 1863), he had turned over only $2,500 because he had sold his cotton bales at lower prices of twenty-five to forty cents a pound rather than the higher price of sixty-five cents a pound that prevailed in mid-February. Their premature cotton transactions at the reduced prices, Jones explained to Washburne, had alone prevented the three Galena businessmen from potentially realizing "an eternal, hell-roaring fortune" to the amount of thirty-five thousand dollars because of Grant's indulgences. But Jones himself had not returned to Illinois before he had shrewdly left his fellow trader, Corwith, in Memphis (having also there tantalized Hurlbut with references to his strikes in Mississippi) to conclude their "little worldly matters" of commerce. Jones then returned to Chicago and, remarkably, in consideration

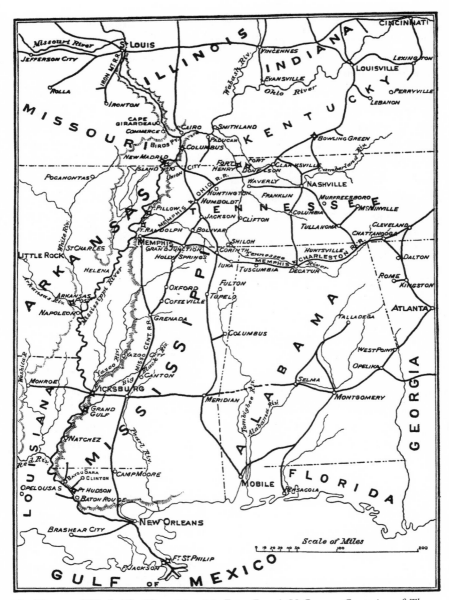

The Theatre of War In The West, 1862–1863. From Francis V. Greene, *Campaigns of The Civil War*, vol. 8: *The Mississippi* (1882).

of his knowledge of Hurlbut's continued excessive drinking, assured Washburne that Hurlbut, if placed under the command of "first rate, *live* men" and generals such as Grant, Sherman, and James B. McPherson, could help "whip hell out of

that Virginia Army" of Confederate General Robert E. Lee. However, a disappointed Jones added that Hurlbut as a commandant on the Mississippi lacked
"snap" and did not "seem to care a d———n" about winning the war in the West.[33]

Whatever Jones's pejorative judgment, Hurlbut carefully avoided antagonizing Grant and did not attempt to dissolve or even impede Jones's speculative
enterprises. He anxiously sought, however, to convince Grant that with impar-
tiality he systematically and regularly confiscated the ill-gotten cotton of other
active Northern traders. Thus Hurlbut demonstrated his seemingly unbiased
rigor late in April 1863 by seizing and then impounding in a Treasury Department warehouse in Memphis the Arkansas-grown cotton of Nathaniel W. Dean.
The speculating Dean complained to Washburne, then at Grant's headquarters
near Vicksburg, that Hurlbut's decision to commandeer the cotton struck him
as "arbitrary and exceedingly unjust, and he *assumes* what is very wide of the
mark" as to the whole truth concerning his alleged smuggling. Further, he urged
Washburne to intercede with Grant toward the restoration of his merchandise,
and asked Washburne in exasperation: "Why is it that H. is kept in command
here? Nothing will be done to a dead certainty so long as it is the case." Dean
added, "There is no difference of opinion about it, *any* change will be an im-
provement."[34] But Washburne wisely refused to attempt to persuade Grant to
replace Hurlbut at Memphis and moreover refrained from obtaining an order
from Grant for the return of Dean's valuable cotton. Obviously, Washburne
recognized that Grant had appreciated Hurlbut's cooperation in not interfering
with Jones's cotton smuggling operations in Mississippi, about which Jones had
already privately informed Washburne. Though Washburne might have agreed
with Dean that Hurlbut posed an obstacle to the speculative enterprises of
larger Northern traders, he nevertheless clearly understood that Dean did not
figure significantly among an inner circle of Illinois Republican politicians, as
did Jones and Hurlbut themselves, and he therefore shrewdly refused to intercede with Grant for him. More important, the Dean episode demonstrated the
highly erratic and inconsistent pattern of Hurlbut's only sporadic and selective
enforcement of cotton smuggling regulations. Generally, he hunted down and
punished small operators like Dean but avoided interfering with larger operators such as Jones, although Jones—unlike most other traders, large or small—
had at least obtained permission from Grant to trade.

Hurlbut's personal involvement in the procurement of proscribed cotton for
pecuniary gain further weakened his theretofore generally lax enforcement of
orders against smuggling at Memphis.[35] In March and April 1863, while Grant
remained preoccupied with his attempts to capture Vicksburg, Hurlbut secretly

established a clandestine relationship with a former captain in the Confederate 1st Missouri Volunteers, David Hirsch, and Hirsch's speculating young associate, Samuel Beman of Memphis. He also employed Judge Loop and Colonel McCarty in an effort to circumvent Grant's orders against cotton smuggling. Emboldened by Grant's absence, Hurlbut accepted payments from Hirsch and Beman (through Loop and McCarty) to allow the speculators to operate unmolested. This profitable arrangement ended abruptly in the summer of 1863 when Beman took his fortune to New York where, safe from reprisal, he betrayed Hurlbut by denouncing his complicity at Memphis. Stunned by Beman's treachery, Hurlbut first sent Loop back to Illinois with his and Loop's illicit loot and then separated himself from his cotton trading partners in Memphis to avoid exposure. He retaliated against Beman by forcing his partner, David Hirsch, to pay a five-hundred-dollar fine for smuggling and by banishing him permanently from Memphis. The exiled Hirsch then traveled to Washington where on December 23, 1863, he complained to Lincoln about his mistreatment at Hurlbut's hands. Having proceeded to New York to rejoin Beman, late in January 1864 Hirsch swore an oath of loyalty to the federal government. Subsequently, he also importuned Grant to seek justice and exoneration for him. But Grant referred Hirsch's case to Secretary of War Stanton who upheld Hurlbut's action in July 1864. Stanton denied Hirsch's demands for financial restitution and for permission to return to Memphis.[36]

Even before Stanton could investigate the validity of Hirsch's charges against Hurlbut, Hurlbut attempted to forestall the possible convening of a special court-martial as to his misconduct by discrediting Hirsch. In March 1864 he assured Stanton that he could prove Hirsch's allegations as totally "false, the coinage of a disappointed traitor" to the Union.[37] Then, in April, he sent a number of scarcely disinterested affidavits of Loop, McCarty, and others to the War Department, testifying to his innocence of cotton profiteering. In his own statement, Hurlbut sought to exonerate himself by attacking the credibility and integrity of his accusers, advising Stanton that he knew Hirsch to be an unscrupulous seducer and adulterer who had earlier brazenly cohabited with Beman's married sister in New York. He also denied Hirsch's allegations regarding his drinking, weakly asserting, "This has become a very old story" revived by Hirsch and Beman, whom he termed two "scoundrels" and "quick witted rascals." Finally, Hurlbut, evidently temporizing in order to prepare a stronger and a more elaborate defense of his official conduct, requested Stanton to establish a special court of inquiry in Memphis to investigate the charges against him.[38] But Stanton, motivated primarily by an interest in protecting Lincoln from embarrassment and criticism arising from an official recommendation to convene a court-martial of Hurlbut, denied Hurlbut's request for a court of inquiry and instead proceeded to suppress all evidence relating to the affair.

Dissatisfied with Stanton's disposition of his case, and pending the secretary of war's anticipated action on Hirsch's outstanding complaints, Hurlbut nevertheless anxiously sought to secure public vindication through Senator Trumbull and other leading Republicans in Congress. In writing to Trumbull from Belvidere in May 1864, shortly after his removal from command in Memphis, Hurlbut flatly denied personal "collusion & participation in speculations" and described the charges made against him as "utterly false." Swearing besides that "My hands are clean & I am comfortably poor today," he assured Trumbull that the "infinite corruptions in Office & Elsewhere on the Mississippi know me as their national enemy and hide from me while they sting." Candidly, Hurlbut urged Trumbull to extend to him "not friendship but *justice*," and to obtain for him an early appearance before the Joint Congressional Committee on the Conduct of the War, from which forum he would discredit Hirsch and Beman and also declare what he knew of "the effect of 'Trade' as they call it" in Memphis.[39] But Trumbull, as had Stanton, prudently recognized that a body of self-contradictory, perjurious, and equivocal testimony given by Hurlbut before the Joint Congressional Committee could only politically embarrass Lincoln and therefore he too refused to gratify Hurlbut.

Although preoccupied with efforts to exonerate himself, Hurlbut had not entirely ignored his military duties and responsibilities while commander of the Sixteenth Corps at Memphis. He attempted, however unsuccessfully, to relieve western Tennessee of the operations of Confederate Maj. Gen. Earl Van Dorn and of the massive and destructive cavalry raids of Brig. Gen. Nathan Bedford Forrest. But after the fall of Vicksburg on July 4, 1863, Hurlbut obeyed Grant's orders to mobilize and execute heavy cavalry raids into northern Mississippi. Indeed, the troopers succeeded in destroying much of the Southern railroad system in that part of the state, including a devastating raid on Grenada, a strategic rail junction, which led to the destruction of scores of locomotives and hundreds of railroad cars. By the fall of 1863, however, Hurlbut had shown to both Grant and Sherman that he lacked the ability or will to defeat or disperse either Van Dorn or Forrest. Recognizing Hurlbut's inability, Grant thereafter left him in command at Memphis, although he continued to detach large units from his command for service elsewhere.[40]

Convinced of Grant's growing lack of confidence in his military ability and also apparently anxious to resume his practice of law and political career in Illinois, Hurlbut perceived the fall of Vicksburg as the time for him to submit his resignation as a Union army officer. However, his decision to resign could also have arisen in connection with Beman's sudden departure from Memphis and subsequent denunciation of Hurlbut's complicity in cotton smuggling in Memphis. Indeed, even before Hurlbut had tendered his resignation in letters to Grant and Lincoln, Maj. Gen. Cadwallader C. Washburn, Elihu B. Washburne's younger brother, had learned of Hurlbut's proposed resignation. Cynically, but probably also accurately, he informed his brother, "I suppose the scamp has made money enough to do this."[41] For his part, Hurlbut explained to Grant on July 7 that he urgently needed to return to his law practice, especially because he believed that Grant's victory at Vicksburg had sealed the doom of the Confederacy in the West and had thus effectively rendered unnecessary his continued service in Memphis. Disingenuously and rather vaguely, he assured Grant that he had "no ambition to subserve, and seek the politician if ever I was one in the officer." Naturally, Hurlbut failed to apprise Grant of the repeated instances of his having sought the intervention of numerous Illinois Republicans to further his military career. Grant endorsed Hurlbut's letter to Lincoln and moreover informed the president that Hurlbut had his "entire confidence" and that he had gained "great credit" for himself as an officer. On August 14, Grant expressed his gratitude to Hurlbut for his loyal service in the Army of the Tennessee, while he admitted that he had warmly admired Hurlbut "as a military man, from the time I fell under your command in North Mo. to the present." Meanwhile, on July 10, 1863, Hurlbut had tendered his resignation to Lincoln, complaining to the president about his assignment to an obscure command at Memphis near the "Border Region," the lapse in his legal endeavors, and his poverty amid the temptations to profit in the contraband trade at Memphis. But Lincoln refused Hurlbut's resignation, preferring instead to use him to promote his plan for gradual emancipation in Arkansas.[42]

He directed Hurlbut to meet with the former Democratic U.S. senator from Arkansas, William K. Sebastian, in Memphis. Sebastian, a planter and lawyer from Helena, had served in the Senate from 1848 to 1861 when his colleagues had expelled him for disloyalty. Now Hurlbut was to assure him that Lincoln would support his bid for a return to the Senate if Sebastian would reciprocate by supporting the emancipation program in Arkansas. Hurlbut questioned the sincerity of Sebastian's commitment to securing the freedom of the slaves, but he dutifully conferred with him at Memphis early in August 1863. On August 11, Hurlbut sent two letters to Lincoln. In one, he formally withdrew his resignation from the army. In the second, he reported that Sebastian had impressed him as politically timid and excessively conservative on the slavery question. "I doubt if Sebastian has nerve enough to accept the necessities of the times and to begin philosophically by heating the caldron from the bottom," Hurlbut advised the president, while he suspected Sebastian would "waste his time by trying to heat it from the top." In this respect, and somewhat exceeding Lincoln's ideas on reconstruction, Hurlbut believed that only a violent popular revolution in southern Arkansas could destroy slavery throughout the state, short of a Union military conquest. Sebastian, however, apparently still entertained the notion that slaveholders in Arkansas would voluntarily free blacks if presented with the proper incentives— or else with coercion.[43] Whatever Lincoln's opinions of Hurlbut's views on recon- struction in the West, his secretary, John Hay, described Hurlbut's "splendid let- ter" of August 11 as "full of the old arrogant and incisive energy of the man." Hay accredited Hurlbut's bold prediction that the rebellion in the West would con- tinue to crumble rapidly, particularly among cotton planters in Mississippi where the "horrors of rebellion" had "broken their spirits." Finally, Hay concluded that the blunt tone of Hurlbut's missive "is very like the old Hurlbut we used to know in Illinois the reliant arrogant brilliant leader in a political war."[44]

Convinced also that both Tennessee and Mississippi would presently submit to a scheme of gradual emancipation, Hurlbut repeatedly urged Lincoln in the fall of 1863 to adopt a lenient policy to hasten the restoration of the seceded states back into the Union. Similarly counseled by other Union generals in the West that the time had arrived to offer defeated Southerners a fair program of political reconstruction, Lincoln proposed his famous "Ten Per Cent Plan" in December 1863. His program contained liberal provisions for the pardon and restoration of rights to former Confederates who would swear an oath of fu- ture loyalty to the United States (excepting high-ranking civil and military offi- cials of the Confederacy) and for gradual emancipation and broader political participation in the slave states. However, many radical Republicans in Con- gress immediately offered and inflexibly maintained strong opposition to the plan throughout 1864.[45] Although a seemingly insignificant incident in Hurlbut's public career, the Sebastian affair actually emphasized the chief reason why Lincoln had purposely long maintained Hurlbut in high military command. For Hurlbut, who shared Lincoln's constitutional views on the vexed questions of emancipation and reconstruction, held the promise of helping him to achieve the ultimate restoration of seceded states in the West. Thus, Lincoln sought to use Hurlbut to counterbalance the influence of more radical—or perhaps more conservative—political generals serving in the trans-Appalachian South. As well, Hurlbut could help prevent the West Point–dominated officer corps from as- suming exclusive control not only over the direction of the Union war effort but over the process of reconstruction in the western Confederacy.

While Hurlbut continued to ponder the complicated and controversial prob- lems of reconstruction, in September 1863 he returned his attention to his duties as the commander of the Sixteenth Corps at Memphis. However, Lincoln's refusal of his resignation and Hurlbut's inability to expedite, or even significantly to affect, the slow process of presidential reconstruction in Arkansas apparently demoralized him and led him largely to neglect his assigned duties. His increasing negligence provoked the expression of strong criticism from the assistant inspector general of the Department and Army of the Tennessee and an erstwhile member of Grant's staff throughout the Vicksburg campaign. As a twenty-six-year-old native of Illinois, Lt. Colonel James H. Wilson had graduated from West Point in June 1860 (ranking sixth in his class) and had thereafter served with the U.S. Army Corps of Topographical Engineers. After completing a stint of volunteer service on Maj. Gen. George B. McClellan's staff during the Maryland campaign in 1862, Wilson had accepted a reassignment to Grant's staff. Having inspected Union forces, forts, and fortifications at posts, districts, and cities located along the Mississippi, Wilson also reviewed Hurlbut's Sixteenth Corps at Fort Pickering and Memphis on September 16, 1863. There, Wilson deplored Hurlbut's apparent unwillingness to forward several cavalry regiments to Grant at Vicksburg, although both the infantry and cavalry in Hurlbut's mixed command lacked active duty. Consequently, in a letter to Brig. Gen. John A. Rawlins, Grant's assistant adjutant general, Wilson explained Hurlbut's determination to withhold the cavalry by asserting that Hurlbut ("who, by the way, between me and you, is small enough to be envious and jealous of General Grant") feared an excessive depletion of his corps command. Wilson also censured Hurlbut, and his subordinate generals, for failing to exercise closer control over their troops. Indeed, Wilson spent the entire day of September 16 reviewing the Sixteenth Corps and returned to Hurlbut's headquarters "pointing out how it could be still further improved in drill, discipline, and administration." Attributing Hurlbut's negligence to his preoccupation with matters of "cotton, Confederates, and corruption," Wilson expressed his disgust for the "whole system" of permitting high military commanders to occupy "undisputed territory," and he complained that "We want soldiers, not traders; generals, not governors and civil agents."[46]

But Hurlbut apparently ignored Wilson's prudent recommendations. And his inattention contributed to the increasingly rapid and alarming degradation of the physical surroundings within Memphis, the station he had made his official headquarters since November 1862. Although the body of Memphis aldermen and the Memphis post commander, Brigadier General Veatch, rightly bore heavy blame for the ensuing deterioration, and near breakdown, of sanitary conditions in the city, Hurlbut himself yet had primary responsibility for maintaining the health of the District, a command remaining under his jurisdiction. Thus late in September 1863 a correspondent for the *New York Times* acidly remarked, "All the pestilences, vices and corruptions of the continent seem to have congregated in this unfortunate place." In particular, he complained that over Memphis the "air is filled with the stench of putrid carcasses of horses and mules" lying dead on the city's streets and spreading disease to its inhabitants. And, in compounding the pervasive fetor with offensive squalor, doctors and nurses in military hospitals had continued to "eject their filthy offal at their very doors." The *Times'* correspondent, in alluding to Hurlbut, asked: "Would it not be well for our military ruler, who displays so much energy in hunting hidden abuses, to direct a part of his attention to this reeking and heaven-offending nuisance?"[47] Hurlbut, however, continued to relegate the problem of sanitation in Memphis to Veatch and the Memphis aldermen. Besides, he faced more immediate and compelling problems: namely, the reorganization of his staff and prostitution.

The arrival of Sophronia and son George in Memphis in November 1863 unexpectedly resulted in a dramatic and highly significant change on Hurlbut's staff. Previously, on January 16, 1863, Maj. Charles Willard, Hurlbut's provost marshal, had resigned his post allegedly because of failing health. Subsequently on February 25 Grant himself had ordered Hurlbut to banish Willard from Memphis, or else imprison him in the Irving Block if he would not leave the city. For Willard, a former Republican who later proved a "perfect Copperhead" Peace Democrat in Chicago, had come vehemently to oppose the war and publicly had uttered controversial political statements in Memphis.[48] Having exiled Willard, Hurlbut named Lt. Col. Melanchthon Smith to Willard's office, but he kept Binmore, Thurston, Eddy, and Frank. However, in November 1863 Assistant Adjutant General Binmore also lost his high staff position. His unceremonious dismissal occurred within the framework of rampant prostitution in Memphis. Since his assumption of district and corps command in Memphis in November 1862, Hurlbut had made ineffectual and sporadic attempts to break up the prostitution rings in Memphis. By contrast, early in 1863 Brigadier General Veatch had peremptorily ordered the expulsion from Memphis of women of known ill repute. Veatch's decisive action, however, had only temporarily reduced the number of these women plying their trade. Indeed in the spring of 1863 more prostitutes had settled in Memphis than in any other period under Union occupation rule. Prompted by necessity, in May 1863 Hurlbut decided to close all bawdyhouses in Memphis, and he threatened to penalize those steamboat captains who transported suspected prostitutes from Cincinnati, Louisville, and St. Louis.[49]

Nonetheless, by the fall of 1863 Hurlbut had allowed his subalterns or "favored officials" to establish and run a "license-system" of brothels "for a consideration." In truth his subordinate officers flagrantly abused even this system or practice of bribery and extortion. For example, in making further mockery of Hurlbut's "fierce pronounciamento" of May 1863 against prostitution, one major after "shutting up" a brothel had "quartered himself in the house for two weeks, keeping a guard at the door, and living in cohabitation with his mistress, who was kept a close prisoner." Thus in this situation many other Union officers such as the slight, irascible Binmore (whom one Northern army correspondent scornfully described as "a little red-headed English dude or Cockney") never ceased patronizing houses of ill fame. Then early in November 1863, apparently acting in a moment of drunken bravado, he introduced "an abandoned woman" from Chicago as his spouse to Sophronia R. Hurlbut. Shocked, Sophronia exposed Binmore's coarse hoax. Her husband promptly arrested Binmore, having initially restrained a strong impulse to kill his offending adjutant, and replaced him with Lt. Col. Thomas H. Harris. At Hurlbut's request, President Lincoln then issued an order, which summarily and dishonorably discharged Binmore from the Union army. The removal of Binmore particularly gratified the staunchly Republican editor of the *Daily State Register* in Des Moines, Iowa. Expressing an opinion widely shared among other newspaper editors in the West, he explained that the "Goodly Arrest" of Binmore had resulted from "his dissolute habits" and the "tyrannical and abusive manner" with which he had treated those who had transacted business with him. Referring to Binmore, "He went up like a rocket, and now he is coming down," the *State Register*'s editor concluded.[50] The Binmore incident, although trivial, had nonetheless demonstrated how Hurlbut had consistently tolerated a pattern of behavior marked by such alcohol-induced antics among the officers and soldiers at the Gayoso House—a policy or practice that U.S. Sanitary Commissioner Mary A. Livermore had not overlooked the previous March. The incident not only displayed Hurlbut's quick temper but also showed his ambivalence toward unregulated prostitution: he arrested Binmore but released his paramour.

Following the removal of Binmore and the assignment of Sherman to Memphis in mid-January 1864, Hurlbut introduced his family (after November 1863 he had moved Sophronia and his son, George, to a "fine mansion" along Union Street) to Sherman at the Gayoso House. Hurlbut's wife, whom one army correspondent in Memphis had previously described as "a lady of commanding height" and a woman of a "pleasing countenance and manners," had desired to meet Sherman before returning with George to Belvidere.[51] Grant and Sherman, having gained the signal victory at Vicksburg, had thereafter performed different assignments. In November 1863 Grant had defeated a Confederate army at Chattanooga, while Sherman had led his infantry command to the rescue of besieged Union troops at Chattanooga and also at Knoxville. Returning to the Mississippi valley, Sherman proceeded first to Memphis to prepare for an expedition into eastern Mississippi. At Memphis, Hurlbut accompanied Sherman to stage plays and to Union party rallies where Sherman found himself greeted by loyal Memphis residents with "a storm of applause" although "Hurlbut did not mingle with them and was difficult of access." Preferring that Major General McPherson, rather than Hurlbut, lead the planned expedition against Meridian, Mississippi, Sherman had hoped to enjoy a respite after Chattanooga. But he finally decided to take command of the operation himself, recognizing that Hurlbut outranked McPherson (appointed major general, U.S. Volunteers, on October 8, 1862, three weeks after Hurlbut's promotion) and neither Grant nor Sherman had "confidence enough" in Hurlbut's "steadiness to put him in charge on this expedition." Hurlbut "is too easily stampeded by rumors," Sherman confided to his wife, Ellen, on January 28, while "I have a better sense of chances." But Sherman nonetheless took Hurlbut to Mississippi because "it was politic to break up the force at Memphis which was too large to lie idle, and Hurlbut would not reduce it. I had to bring him away and make a radical change," Sherman explained to his wife.[52] Because Hurlbut had lost to Grant and Sherman in 1863 thousands of men from his Sixteenth Corps, he thereafter contended that he needed the entire balance of his corps to defend Memphis and West Tennessee from possible Confederate incursions. Ultimately, however, Hurlbut's opinion that he had essentially like status and stature as Grant and Sherman in the Union high command accounted for his resistance to further depletions of his dwindling command. He could not tolerate the anomalous position of holding high rank without having a large force under his immediate command. Simultaneously, he could not endure the humiliation of remaining subservient to those he viewed as belonging to a clique of West Point officers.

Despite his pretensions, Hurlbut sent his wife and son up the Mississippi to Cairo, Illinois, while he himself sailed down river with Sherman to Vicksburg. On February 10 Hurlbut, under Sherman's command, led twenty thousand men of the Sixteenth Corps on a devastating raid across central Mississippi to capture the pivotal railroad center at Meridian. Hurlbut's troops destroyed abandoned Confederate rolling stock and wrecked upward of sixty miles of strategic Mobile & Ohio, Southern of Mississippi, and Selma & Meridian Railroad tracks and trestles before returning to Vicksburg in triumph. Sherman reported to Grant that, largely as a result of Hurlbut's "experience and skill" as a field and tactical commander, the Meridian expedition had partaken "more of the character of a pleasant excursion than of hard military service."[53] Undoubtedly, Hurlbut had shown some ability for field command, as he previously had exhibited at the

William T. Sherman, first commander of the District of Memphis. Prints and Photographs Division, Library of Congress.

Battle of Hatchie Bridge in October 1862. But Hurlbut at Hatchie Bridge had really faced an already defeated and demoralized force, while during the Meridian expedition he had encountered little organized resistance.

Returning to Memphis late in February 1864 Hurlbut resumed his command of the severely attenuated Sixteenth Corps. He reestablished communication with

Brigadier General Buckland, commanding officer of the District of Memphis (Brigadier General Veatch having been transferred east the previous month to northwest Georgia). But almost immediately he continued his participation in clandestine practices at the Memphis post. Having risked incurring a special court-martial or else a summary dismissal from the army for his reported acceptance of payments to help Hirsch and Beman purchase proscribed cotton, Hurlbut thereafter increasingly turned from profiteering to extortion. In truth, early in January 1863, less than two months into his administrative tenure at Memphis, Hurlbut had allowed the heads of abandoned property and the detective departments to plunder Memphis, thereby instituting a veritable "reign" of terror, which an Indiana infantryman characterized as "Hell-Under-Hurlbut." Besides arbitrarily confiscating the property of expelled Confederate sympathizers and suspected smugglers, Captains Eddy and Frank had in 1863 systematically looted luxurious Memphis homes, not refraining from soiling pages of classic books for use as "waste paper" and wantonly beating exquisitely wrought heirloom pianos "to pieces with axes." In a report that branded Hurlbut as "The Federal Tyrant at Memphis," an appalled correspondent for the *Charleston Daily Courier* asserted that in March 1863 treasured literature and the fine arts perilously stood "about the same chance for preservation as did the Alexandrian library in the hands of the followers of Mahomet." In expressing its similarly provoked outrage, the *Richmond Sentinel* angrily declared that the "Renegade" General Hurlbut, "who is now tyrannizing over the people of Memphis, is a degenerate South Carolinian," formerly a regimental militia adjutant and a man who, although the offspring of "Puritan parents," had departed from the Palmetto State in 1845 while "leaving no good reputation behind him."[54] By the fall of 1863 Memphis struck a Northern reporter as the "El Dorado of officials" under Hurlbut's command. This correspondent for the *New York Times* asserted that the "immense amount of confiscated property of every description that falls into their hands" had enriched the "whole set" of Union army quartermasters, commissaries, and provost marshals. Moreover, besides "living sumptuously in the palatial mansions of the banished secesh," the reporter complained that detectives ostentatiously proceeded through Memphis in "splendid equipages" from the profits of their "malversations in office."[55]

Hurlbut's newly appointed provost marshal, Capt. George A. Williams, who had succeeded Lieutenant Colonel Smith, proved even more rapacious than Captains Eddy and Frank. A native of New York State and an 1852 graduate of the U.S. Military Academy, Williams had served before the war in Texas as an instructor in tactics and as the commandant of the corps of cadets at West Point. After the outbreak of war Williams had shown conspicuous bravery while serving as a captain in the 1st U.S. Infantry during operations in the Corinth and earliest Vicksburg campaigns, even gaining Grant's repeated recommendations that Lincoln promote him to brigadier general. Apparently disappointed in seeking expected promotion, late in June 1863 Williams sought and obtained his position as chief provost marshal on Hurlbut's staff, following the transfer and reassignment of Smith, who had been mortally wounded at Vicksburg on June 25. He evidently thereafter exchanged his honor and integrity for the pursuit of power and wealth. Williams struck admiring observers as a courteous and gracious officer and a man who moreover exhibited a "fine countenance and cultured demeanor." Strangely then, he had surrounded himself with subordinates whom one baffled Northern army correspondent described as the "rudest set of fellows" in Memphis, and subalterns whose insolent, accusatory, and "ruffianly style" presumably came from their previous training in "hog driving." In the summer of 1863, under Hurlbut's active but carefully concealed direction, Williams expanded an extortion ring to involve the commanding officers of the stockade at Fort Pickering and of the Irving Block prison. Thus, a censorious correspondent for the *Mobile Advertiser And Register* (one who had sojourned in Memphis in October 1863 and who had observed the regulated importation and exportation of Tennessee-grown cotton through the lines around Memphis) discovered that "all cotton that is not submitted to the Provost Marshal for him to slice his per centage from is confiscated." The Confederate reporter asserted that "Government detectives" deprived loyal Tennessee planters of purchasable cotton by claiming that they had imported their cotton from northern Mississippi. He implied that Williams shared this loot with Hurlbut, whom the reporter termed the "chief commander and head thief" of Memphis. Consequently in exploiting these opportunities, "the goose that lays the golden egg is set upon the well feathered nest of the Yankee commander."[56]

Apparently acting on Hurlbut's authority, Williams also demanded ransoms from wealthy residents of Memphis who sought to effect the release of Confederate soldiers or Southern sympathizers and secessionists. John Hallum, an ambitious thirty-year-old lawyer in Memphis and a former infantry lieutenant for two years in the Army of Tennessee who had served on the staff of Confederate Brig. Gen. Gideon J. Pillow, also served as perhaps the most active and influential of those middlemen who sought to liberate the inmates of the stockade. In the summer of 1863 Hallum collected money from relatives and friends of prisoners. Through Hallum they paid more than $65,000 in cash to Williams and to the two prison commandants (with Hurlbut presumably appropriating the lion's share of the loot) to free more than two hundred men from Fort Pickering and Irving Block, the latter prison known to Southern soldiers and residents alike as the dreaded "Bastille" of Memphis. Previously, late in May 1863, Hallum had accused Hurlbut's "ruffian guard or the hateful detectives" as eager to arrest and to cast unsuspecting Southern men into "these lousy, filthy bastiles," while asserting that the "black holes of Calcutta furnish no parallel for these prisons."[57]

Furthermore, Hallum had long hated Hurlbut. Seeking to discredit Hurlbut across the South, Hallum (cryptically employing the pseudonym "Fath" to avoid military reprisal) late in May 1863 had denounced him in a letter that he had sent to the editor of the *Memphis Daily Appeal* in Atlanta. Hallum had called Hurlbut "a beastly old sot" and had declared that words could not "portray the depths of his depravity." He had further reviled "old Gen." Hurlbut, describing him as "gross, he is insulting, uncouth and belongs to the lowest order of humanity." And Hallum had thanked God that "John Barley Corn will soon consign him to that dept. for which he is so well fitted where he will meet many of his comrades in rascality and brutality." Moreover, based on personal knowledge, Hallum had accused Hurlbut of having used "his official position in speculating upon the Government he claims to serve." He had also charged Hurlbut with having accepted bribes from cotton speculators and for ordering "scouts" into the surrounding countryside to steal valuable horses and mules. He had concluded by declaring that Hurlbut's "soul (if he has one) can be bought and bartered."[58] Unfortunately for John Hallum, his letter was widely reprinted in the South and this eventually brought Hallum's denunciations to Hurlbut's attention in March 1864. Besides infuriating Hurlbut with his invective, Hallum angered him by assaulting and injuring Col. John McDonald in an explosive fit of violence.

McDonald was an erstwhile major in the 8th Missouri (Union) Infantry—the regiment whose officers, according to a *Charleston Mercury* account, early in December 1862 had contributed to rampant "incendiarism" in Memphis by failing to control that regiment's "roughs" who maliciously had repeatedly pierced, with their bayonets, the municipal fire department's water hoses. McDonald had left the army in disgrace in the fall of 1863 following his court-martial on charges of cowardice in a battle with enemy troops. Thereafter, he had engaged in the "mercantile business" of illicit cotton buying in Memphis when Hurlbut, altogether unaccountably, appointed him to a staff position. McDonald then obeyed Hurlbut's orders in January 1864 to organize an enrolled militia brigade in Memphis, a unit composed of men whom even Hurlbut's hometown paper, the *Belvidere Standard,* had previously characterized as the wretched "crowd of gamblers, thieves, speculators, secesh spies, and other human vermin" that infested Memphis.[59]

Actually, Hurlbut had long entertained an almost obsessive preoccupation with an ambitious—if not also a highly impractical and plainly unnecessary—

plan to create, mobilize, and deploy a Memphis Home Guards regiment. However, he doubted that Lincoln or Stanton would uphold his authority to order the formation of a militia unit composed of disaffected Southern draftees. He revealed as much in a surprisingly frank conference he held with James B. Bingham, the Unionist editor of the *Memphis Bulletin* and a trusted confidant of Unionist Gov. Andrew Johnson. Earlier, however, in August 1863 Bingham had complained to Johnson about Hurlbut's weak support of the legislature's plan to mobilize loyal men to perform military and police duty in Memphis and western Tennessee. Bingham attributed Hurlbut's lack of cooperation—or "indifference," as another Memphis Unionist described it—to the general's opinion that the governor "did not care for that part of Tennessee this side of Tennessee river." Bingham thereafter criticized Hurlbut's (and Veatch's) conduct that discouraged the growth of loyal Unionist sentiment in Memphis by granting special favors and trade privileges to wealthy secessionists, a policy that "has weighed like an incubus upon the Union Cause." Nevertheless he determined to organize his own militia force. At length, Bingham had approached Hurlbut in January 1864 to obtain permission to raise a volunteer regiment of loyal Unionist militia in Memphis. As a result, on January 2 Bingham had informed Johnson that, unexpectedly, he had found Hurlbut "*apparently* sober" while he had received prompt although reluctant authorization to form a rival volunteer Home Guards unit. But he felt compelled to advise the governor of disturbing statements made by Hurlbut. Accordingly, Bingham apprised Johnson of a conversation held earlier between Maj. Basil Norris, an officer who had served in the Union army's medical department in the East, and Hurlbut at Memphis. For, as Norris had described their encounter to Bingham, "while *beastly* intoxicated," Hurlbut had threatened to resign his commission in the army if Stanton revoked his Home Guards order. Bingham recalled that, during their conference at army headquarters on January 2, Hurlbut had declared that he bore a "grudge" against Memphis. Furthermore, Bingham informed Johnson, Hurlbut had pejoratively termed Memphis "only a military post, and a d——d small one at that." And Hurlbut had vengefully assured him that "if he had his way he would destroy all of it except the fort [Pickering]." Despite this threat and Hurlbut's "active opposition," Bingham succeeded in forming a militia regiment.[60]

Meanwhile, whatever Bingham's continuing dismay over Hurlbut's evidently increasing unsteadiness, Colonel McDonald dutifully completed his execution of Hurlbut's orders by impressing three thousand men to form the militia brigade. Apparently unknown to Hurlbut, however, in March 1864 McDonald also accepted $7,500 in payments from the enrollees (through Hallum, who acted as their intermediary) to secure their early discharge from further militia

duty. Nevertheless, McDonald then accused Hallum of having forged the re-
leases and of having disbanded the whole brigade. In revenge, an enraged Hallum
burst into McDonald's office at the Gayoso House, broke his jaw with his fist,
and then revealed to local newspapers his version of the Home Guards scandal.[61] In mixing Confederate patriotism with pecuniary gain, Hallum had also
forged and distributed passes to other Memphis residents to procure an exemption for them from militia service and had charged each of his clients a fifty-
dollar fee for his intervention. Hallum's chicanery struck Hurlbut as treason-
ous. At this juncture, Hurlbut moved to punish Hallum for his earlier charges
of drunkenness and corruption, for his pummeling of McDonald, and for his
responsibility for the dissolution of the enrolled militia. More urgent and important, however, Hurlbut also sought to silence Hallum so as to protect himself and other members of the extortion ring. He arrested Hallum on March 31
for "surreptitiously procuring passes and exemptions, and disposing of the same
for large sums of money," and ordered him to pay a fine of one thousand
dollars. He also permanently banned Hallum (who did plead guilty to the charge
of procuring militia exemptions for private citizens, but who also denied the
related charge of his conspiracy to disband McDonald's militia brigade), from
practicing law in the military courts of Memphis and required him to serve
sixty days in the stockade at Fort Pickering.[62]

On April 3, two days after his confinement with the three hundred other
prisoners who occupied the narrow wooden blockhouse within Fort Pickering,
Hallum obtained permission from the fort commandant to communicate in
writing with Hurlbut. Hallum asked Hurlbut to modify his punitive order by
allowing him to pay the one-thousand-dollar fine and by permitting him to
resume his legal practice in Memphis so that he could support his sick wife and
his small children. But Hurlbut refused to release him. Subsequently Hallum's
suffering intensified as the conditions in the blockhouse dangerously deteriorated: a contagion of smallpox among his fellow prisoners occurred, a severe
infestation of lice and other vermin developed, the latrines grew increasingly
foul, a single kettle served as both a cooking and washing vessel, visitors could
not see the prisoners, and on one occasion the prisoners did without food for
four consecutive days. Consequently, on April 10 Hallum again implored Hurlbut
to release him, declaring that his sufferings had grown "excruciating in the extreme being confined as I am with negroes and criminals," while barely subsist-
ing on coffee and bread. Hurlbut refused to show mercy and returned Hallum's
letter to the commanding officer of Fort Pickering with the endorsement that
prison guards should report any attempted bribe from Hallum so that he would
have occasion to "give Mr. Hm a lesson that he will remember." On April 18

Hallum again asked Hurlbut to order his conditional release. He informed Hurlbut that he had previously complained to the commandant of Fort Pickering about the alarming outbreak of smallpox within the blockhouse. However, that officer had dismissed Hallum's complaint as a "gross lie" or else the "culpable neglect" of the post's surgeon.[63]

Hurlbut had already forgotten Hallum, particularly in view of his sudden removal from command at Memphis by Sherman two days earlier on April 16. But even if Hurlbut had relented and had finally agreed to release Hallum, he had nonetheless demonstrated that as the supreme commander at Memphis he could, although he never did, order the medical officers under his authority to maintain proper sanitary practices and healthful surroundings within army hospitals. Simultaneously, however, neither the medical officials at Memphis nor the chief surgeon at Fort Pickering held any authority to direct Hurlbut to maintain even a habitable environment within military prisons. In the end, however, Hallum had to complete his sixty-day term. He did so although, on May 12, he promised to give Hurlbut's successor, Major General Washburn (who had assumed command of the newly created Department of West Tennessee), information on the operations of a local mercantile firm secretly in cotton smuggling in Memphis if Washburn would release him. Washburn returned Hallum's letter to the commandant of Fort Pickering with the endorsement that Hallum should be released if he gave "really valuable" intelligence regarding the firm's illicit contraband trade. But his information deemed insignificant, Hallum continued to languish and he barely survived his horrible and sickening ordeal in the infested blockhouse.[64]

Hurlbut had finally overreached himself. The notoriety surrounding Hallum's arrest and excessively harsh punishment as a scapegoat for the military's corruption in Memphis, as well as the general clamor raised by Northern and Southern merchants alike over Hurlbut's extortionate practices, brought about a War Department inspection of the Irving Block prison. Late in April 1864, after Hurlbut had returned to Belvidere, an officer reported to Secretary of War Stanton that he had observed shockingly inhumane conditions in the Irving Block. For example, in one befouled dungeonlike cellblock, he had found twenty-eight prisoners cruelly "chained to a wet floor, where they had been constantly confined" for months and never "released, even to relieve the calls of nature." It was an accurate account: one Confederate veteran later asserted that, for upward of two weeks in November 1863, he and eighteen other prisoners had remained fettered to the cellar floor with iron balls and three-feet-long chains. And "my daily fare," the former prisoner recalled, "consisted of two stale crackers and a piece of rotten bacon and some water, or coffee made of beans and dried Cherokee rose leaves." Although he verged on "starvation" within the Irving Block, a provost marshal, presumably Capt. George A. Williams, transferred him to the pestilential and rat-infested U.S. Military Prison at Alton, Illinois, for further detention and for sentencing. Peremptorily, Stanton then removed Provost Marshal Williams from his position as the prison commandant, pending a further investigation of his apparent misconduct. On May 7 Hurlbut remonstrated against Stanton's action, affirming and defending Williams's "incorruptible integrity." Informed of developments, Grant himself lodged a testimonial with the secretary of war in behalf of Williams, citing Williams's meritorious service in the West. Grant's timely intervention, though not Hurlbut's, proved decisive and Stanton subsequently reinstated Williams. The latter then returned to Memphis, cleaned up Irving Block prison, and dissolved the remnants of the extortion ring. But only then, and only after being harshly criticized by Judge Advocate General Joseph Holt for his primary responsibility for the "gross mal-administration" of Irving Block prison, did Williams belatedly apprise the War Department's commissary general of prisoners of the "utter inadequacy" of Irving Block as a military prison. In July 1864 the War Department officially designated the Irving Block as a U.S. Military Prison.[65] Indeed, as Major General Washburn had described the situation in Memphis to his congressman-brother Elihu one week after Hurlbut's removal from command on April 16, "Persons here report to me the existence of a very bad state of things, and my arrival has been greeted with a good deal of satisfaction."[66] Despite belated efforts of the War Department to ameliorate conditions in Irving Block prison, neither Stanton, Grant, nor Washburn sought to improve the situation at the military stockade or the "Smallpox Hospital" at Fort Pickering, as Washburn's callous neglect of Hallum clearly showed.

While Hurlbut's harsh administration in Memphis came under increased official scrutiny in the spring of 1864, Hurlbut meanwhile also consistently failed to rid West Tennessee of destructive cavalry raids executed by Forrest. Charged reproachfully with "marked timidity" by Sherman for his procrastination, vacillation, and inefficiency in ordering vigorous pursuits of Forrest's marauding cavalry, Hurlbut subsequently bore much heavier blame on April 12 when Forrest captured Fort Pillow about thirty-five miles north of Memphis, and allowed the massacre of its black and white garrison of 557 defenders. Shocked and outraged by the carnage at Fort Pillow, on April 16 the *New York Times,* expressing the anger and exasperation felt in the North, asked indignantly, "Who commands in West Tennessee?" The *Times* further wondered, in view of the "idle army of such magnitude" as the Sixteenth Corps around Memphis, how the western Tennessee country could have been "ceaselessly traversed, trampled upon, and its inhabitants butchered by rebel bands?" The *Times,* in censuring the "local military authorities" for the capture of Fort Pillow and now anticipating an attack upon Memphis, demanded that Grant discipline or replace his "responsible subordinates."[67]

Even earlier, amid the gravely deteriorating military situation in West Tennessee, Sherman, then commanding the Division of the Mississippi, had also informed Grant (then with the Army of the Potomac and the general in chief of all Union armies) on April 2 that "Hurlbut will not resign and I know no better disposition of him than to leave him at Memphis." However, there had then commenced a confused, but hurried and urgent, effort among Grant, Sherman, and Halleck to reassign Hurlbut, as Sherman declared that he needed a "bolder man" at Memphis. Finally, in the wake of the uproar over Fort Pillow, Grant ordered Sherman to relieve Hurlbut of his command of the Sixteenth Corps at Memphis. And, in exasperation, on April 15 Grant also sarcastically inquired of Sherman: "Does Hurlbut think if he moves a part of his force after the only enemy within two hundred miles of him that the [Memphis] post will run off with the balance of his force?" Sherman shared Grant's frustration and indignation over the Fort Pillow massacre, attributing the disaster to Hurlbut's timidity, as he was one of the "inferior officers on the river." He therefore explained to Grant that "Hurlbut has full ten thousand (10,000) men at Memphis but if he had a million he would be on the defense." Consequently on April 16 Sherman advised Hurlbut that Grant himself had relieved him of duty and had ordered him to return to Belvidere by way of Cairo, Illinois, to await further orders. But since he recognized the "general gritting of teeth" and overheard the muttering of curses among incensed Sixteenth Corps officers and men who evidently blamed him for the carnage at Fort Pillow, Hurlbut had to content himself by delivering a farewell address to a militia unit and by reviewing a new regiment of "negro soldiers," an organization of U.S. Colored Infantry, before he immediately left Memphis aboard a steamer bound for Cairo.[68]

Hurlbut's departure and Sherman's action, which had effected it, finally gratified James B. Bingham, the editor of the *Memphis Bulletin.* Late in November 1862 Bingham had welcomed, however hesitantly, Hurlbut's arrival in Memphis. On January 2, 1864, however, he had assured Tennessee Governor Johnson that the reported replacement of Hurlbut in command at Memphis by Brig. Gen. David Hunter (a West Point officer closely associated with Lincoln) "would be hailed with universal joy by all loyal people." Then, on April 23, a week after Hurlbut's dismissal, he expressed to Johnson his view of the matter (an opinion only belatedly held by Grant and Sherman) by observing, "Hurlbut—thank the Lord,—has left Memphis, and I hope never to return again. He was permitted to remain too long for our good."[69] The *Belvidere Standard,* however, deplored Hurlbut's removal from command. In rejecting accounts of Hurlbut's previous "mismanagement" of Memphis, as alleged in reports from the Memphis correspondent of the *Chicago Tribune,* the *Standard* denounced Hurlbut's accuser as "some professional lickspittle" while blaming Sherman, or Grant, for having depleted Hurlbut's command and for stripping his department of the troops required for the effective defense of Memphis and Fort Pillow. Unlike Hurlbut, an officer of "no military merit" could defend Memphis, the *Standard* asserted, and it recommended Hurlbut for a field command.[70]

His military career seemingly ended, Hurlbut renewed his efforts to clear his reputation by further attempting to refute the charges of David Hirsch and Samuel Beman, two erstwhile members of a now-disbanded cotton ring. Early in August 1864, however, President Lincoln (who on June 6, 1864, had received a visit from Hurlbut—an Illinois delegate to the National Republican Party Convention, which would nominate Lincoln as the party's 1864 presidential candidate) again revived his faltering career. He assigned Hurlbut to serve temporarily under Maj. Gen. Edward R. S. Canby, a West Point–educated career army officer who commanded the Military Division of West Mississippi (known informally as the "Trans-Mississippi Division"), with headquarters at New Orleans. On his steamboat trip south to New Orleans in mid-August, Hurlbut stopped briefly at Memphis so as to organize and assemble a new staff composed primarily of members of his former associates. Avoiding the Gayoso House, on the night of August 20 Hurlbut stayed instead at the Shelby Street quarters of Captain Eddy. But Hurlbut had scarcely even retired when units of Forrest's cavalry suddenly came thundering into Memphis. Forrest, a resident of Memphis before the war, boldly dashed for the Gayoso with the intention of capturing both Hurlbut and Washburn. The Confederate cavalry chief especially desired to seize Hurlbut personally. In December 1863 Forrest had remonstrated against Hurlbut's threats to execute captured Rebel cavalry as spies or saboteurs. Forrest had then assured Hurlbut that he would retaliate for wrongful executions of Southern soldiers or mounted infantry. And, in ominously alluding to Hurlbut's reported vandalizing of secessionist mansions in Memphis, he had further warned Hurlbut that he would "hang every man detected in burning the residences and property of noncombatants." Moreover, Forrest (who himself at Fort Pillow failed to show quarter to black garrison troops) demanded that Hurlbut "conduct the war on principles of civilization and humanity." Finally in the spring of 1864 Hurlbut had refused to deliver Col. Fielding Hurst, the Southern-born commanding officer of the Sixth Tennessee Cavalry, to Forrest for trial and punishment. Forrest had alleged that Hurst and

Union cavalry troops had murdered and then mutilated a captured Confederate soldier—besides killing six other prisoners. Then in June 1864 Major General Washburn had himself rejected Forrest's still unsubstantiated allegations regarding Hurst's atrocities.[71]

His demands for justice spurned by both Hurlbut and Washburn, Forrest attacked Union headquarters in Memphis. At the Gayoso House, however, Washburn narrowly eluded Forrest (as had Buckland at another location) albeit by hastily escaping under fire to Fort Pickering and fleeing, though scantily clad, in light undergarments. Nevertheless, the Confederate troops stormed the Gayoso and then quickly killed numerous drunken and cursing Union soldiers who died in a hail of bullets while desperately attempting to defend themselves. Forrest's men shot up the hotel's hastily evacuated barroom before resuming their search for Hurlbut and Washburn and by entering and ransacking rooms on upper floors of the Gayoso. Disappointed, they captured other officers and fled with them into northern Mississippi.[72]

Hurlbut's avoidance of seizure in Memphis, however, had demonstrated the larger significance of Forrest's otherwise successful raid. Since the beginning of his commands at Memphis late in November 1862, Hurlbut had entertained a persistent and exceedingly imprudent preoccupation with improving the defenses of Fort Pickering. As Frémont in St. Louis in 1861 had devoted excessive resources and effort to the construction and fortification of Benton Barracks, or Camp Benton, so also Hurlbut in Memphis from 1862 to 1864 had given an abundance of resources and labor on erecting extended earthworks and fortifications at Fort Pickering. Worse still, he had based his increasing absorption with these projects on a false strategic assumption. Neglecting the direction of his forces in efforts to repel Confederate cavalry raids into western Tennessee or finally against Fort Pillow itself, Hurlbut had rather concentrated his attention and energies on procuring more ordnance (chiefly heavy siege guns) for emplacement at Fort Pickering and on removing into the fort theretofore scattered munitions, stores, and other supplies. Accordingly, as the Memphis correspondent for the *Cincinnati Daily Commercial* in July 1863 approvingly concluded, "General Hurlbut has prepared matters here to meet any emergency." Referring to a possible Confederate cavalry attack against Memphis, the reporter declared that the fort's guns commanded all the eastern and southern approaches to the city, while Hurlbut had remedied the past neglect of both Major General Sherman and Brig. Gen. Alvin P. Hovey, each of whom had in turn previously commanded at Memphis. Thus, the correspondent explained that Hurlbut had consolidated and concentrated all the government's valuable armaments and stores, ensuring that they "are in the fort and *perfectly protected.*"[73] However,

Hurlbut had assumed that he could eliminate or reduce the vulnerability of Memphis to assault by removing its munitions and supplies into Fort Pickering and simultaneously by strengthening the fort itself. Forrest's raid showed that the fort's heavy guns could not protect Memphis from attack. Forrest had neither contemplated nor attempted a seizure of armaments, but had planned to capture the entire Union high command.

Relieved over his escape, Hurlbut thereupon proceeded southward to New Orleans where he reported to Canby. On September 23 he assumed temporary command of the Army of the Gulf (established February 23, 1862) and also of the Department of the Gulf. Though technically these commands had been merged into Canby's Military Division of West Mississippi (effective with Canby's promotion to major general of U.S. Volunteers and assignment to the trans-Mississippi command on May 7, 1864), the Department of the Gulf and the Army of the Gulf had both continued to function as essentially autonomous administrative and military entities. Moreover, Hurlbut had assumed temporary command of these organizations in the absence of the Massachusetts Republican political general Nathaniel P. Banks. Therefore, in view of the loosely defined jurisdictions over which he held charge within Canby's larger divisional jurisdiction, and given the political instability in wartime New Orleans, Hurlbut would compound the confusion of many overlapping authorities and competing economic interests in an effort to revive his career as the commander of a former Confederate stronghold.[74]

After seventeen months of command in Memphis, Hurlbut had shown himself to be a harsh and arbitrary military ruler. Grant's decision to assign Hurlbut to the Memphis post command had reflected a serious error of judgment; however, practically or realistically, he could not have entrusted Hurlbut with an important field command. Hurlbut drew criticism mainly for his perceived corruption in the control of the cotton trade at Memphis—charges associated with reported instances of bribery and even extortion from vulnerable traders. Although he carefully concealed his participation in the cotton and extortion rings he himself had created, Hurlbut's tolerance of the practices of his subordinates allowed them to employ those rings to plunder Memphis, further complicating the problem of illicit cotton trading on the Mississippi. Moreover, Hurlbut incurred censure for the inconsistent and capricious practices—as traders and treasury agents complained of them—by which he regulated the movement of cotton through Memphis. Hurlbut's erratic and sporadic enforcement of orders and regulations banning the illicit smuggling of cotton and contraband, occurring within the framework of his frequently heavy drinking, diverted his attention from addressing more urgent problems: suppressing of

Confederate military penetration of western Tennessee; pacifying the large and hostile population of Memphis; and the proper and humane management of a complex system of army hospitals and military prisons within his administrative jurisdictions. Ultimately, Hurlbut's venality, intemperance, and his inattention to his pressing military duties as Sixteenth Corps commander justified his removal from command at Memphis.

CHAPTER FIVE

Army Commander at New Orleans

The fall of New Orleans on April 26, 1862, to combined Union naval and land forces had dealt the Confederacy a particularly devastating blow. Largely owing to its strategic position on the Mississippi River, its capture had led to a succession of other successful joint operations against Confederate strongholds farther north, including Baton Rouge, Port Hudson, Natchez, and ultimately, Vicksburg. The Union seizure of the South's largest seaport had severely reduced the quantity of European munitions flowing into the embattled Confederacy. But, as around Memphis, the Confederates had partially recouped their losses by trading in cotton with Northern speculators and contraband runners who had swarmed into the occupied Crescent City. Furthermore, the surrender of the city to Union forces had significantly increased its population. Like Memphis, New Orleans had lost thousands of its secessionist inhabitants during the war, including those serving in the Confederate forces. But by 1864 its population had grown to more than 140,000, which included about nineteen-thousand slaves (whom Lincoln had specifically exempted from the terms of the Emancipation Proclamation of 1863), eleven-thousand free blacks, about fifty-five-thousand naturalized citizens of Irish, German, French, and Spanish descent, and thousands of Union soldiers and sailors, Northern traders, draft dodgers, liquor importers, and prostitutes. Moreover, again as in Memphis, smuggling had compounded the city's problems with crime and vice, thus increasing its wide reputation as the "Wickedest City in America." Indeed, in a speech late in January

1863 Hurlbut himself had referred to New Orleans as the "Sodom and Gomorrah of the West." The incidence of gambling and prostitution and the consumption of liquor, regulated or unlicensed, had reached staggering proportions by 1864. Simultaneously, political instability arising from the secession of Louisiana and the subsequent Union establishment of martial law had further complicated the occupation of New Orleans and the reconstruction of Louisiana. Citizens swearing loyalty to the federal government had voted on February 22, 1864, to establish what became known as a "free state" legislature in New Orleans under a moderate Unionist governor, Georg Michael D. Hahn, but the Hahn administration had not consolidated its position in New Orleans or within occupied Louisiana before Hurlbut reached the city early in the fall of 1864.[1]

Though his decision to establish his Memphis headquarters at the Gayoso House had proved highly imprudent, Hurlbut's taste for lavish Southern living had scarcely changed. In New Orleans he made both his departmental headquarters and his domestic residence within the St. Charles Hotel, a luxurious establishment near Jackson Square in the center of the city. As the newly appointed temporary commander of the Army of the Gulf and the Department of the Gulf, Hurlbut followed the example of his predecessors, Benjamin F. Butler and Nathaniel P. Banks (the actual commander, for whom Hurlbut was acting), who had also made their headquarters at the St. Charles. Welcoming Hurlbut to the Crescent City and praising his accomplishments, the *New Orleans Bee* observed, "As a true patriot and faithful soldier no man in the country can show a better record."[2] Significantly Hurlbut brought Sophronia and George to New Orleans, early in November; their presence probably explained the absence of reports of drinking in public on his part during his brief command in southern Louisiana.

Organizing his staff, he chose Lieutenant Colonel Harris as his adjutant general and Lieutenant Colonel Thurston as his inspector general; both had served him in Memphis. His other staff officers had previously served Banks, particularly Lt. Col. Harai Robinson, whom Hurlbut maintained as the provost marshal general of the Army and Department of the Gulf. Lincoln had in late July 1864 apprised Major General Canby (the commander of the Trans-Mississippi Division, who also made his headquarters at New Orleans) of complaints he had received from Northern cotton traders whom U.S. district attorneys, marshals, and provost marshals at New Orleans, presumably including Robinson in particular, had allegedly victimized by means of "blackmail, and spoils." Accordingly, Lincoln had ordered Canby to identify and disband Union army cotton rings found operating in New Orleans.[3] Showing procrastination bordering on insubordination, however, Canby had hesitated or failed to direct Banks to investigate the charges. Hurlbut made Robinson his principal assistant, with Canby's tacit approval. Nonetheless, Hurlbut was prepared to cooperate with Governor Hahn and establish harmonious relations between his administration and Hahn's free state government.

The first commanding general of the Union Army and Department, Maj. Gen. B. F. Butler, had established his headquarters in New Orleans on May 1, 1862, only five days after the fall of the city to Union naval forces led by Flag Officer David G. Farragut. "Beast" Butler, as Southerners later called him, had instituted an especially harsh military rule over the city. He had publicly hanged William B. Mumford, a gambler who had torn down an American flag, and he had threatened to punish women of New Orleans as common prostitutes for affronts or insults to his troops. Recalling Butler in December 1862, President Lincoln had named Major General Banks, another of his prominent Massachusetts political generals, to succeed him. Banks, dubbed the "Bobbin Boy" of Waltham, Massachusetts (a city famous for its cotton and wool mills), had exercised a more conciliatory policy toward the inhabitants of New Orleans, and early in 1864 he had supported the moderate wing of the Free State party in occupied Louisiana, to ensure the election of Michael Hahn as governor.

The thirty-three-year-old Hahn had emigrated to New York as a six-year-old from Bavaria. He and his widowed mother and four young sisters had settled briefly in Texas and finally in New Orleans about 1840. A lawyer, school-board president, and Douglas Democrat before the war, in 1861 Hahn had sharply criticized slavery and strongly opposed the secession of Louisiana, courageously refusing to support the Confederacy. Following the fall of New Orleans, he had sworn loyalty to the U.S. government; on December 3, 1862, he was elected (as was moderate Republican Benjamin F. Flanders) to serve as a Republican member of the Thirty-seventh Congress from the First Congressional District of Louisiana (their brief terms of office expired on March 3, 1863). He had also purchased the *New Orleans Daily True Delta* late in February 1864. Subsequently, a constitutional convention had assembled in New Orleans and, complying with the terms of Lincoln's "Ten Per Cent" plan of reconstruction, the delegates had framed a free state constitution that abolished slavery in Louisiana and, as Lincoln wished, had indicated that the legislature would eventually enfranchise a few of the state's blacks.[4]

The free state legislature would convene in New Orleans on October 3, 1864, to prepare a petition for the early return of the state to the Union under the liberal terms of presidential reconstruction. As the name "Ten Per Cent Plan" implied, Lincoln's policy encouraged the establishment of legitimate governments in former seceded states; if pardoned ex-Confederates totaling at least 10

percent of the votes cast in a state's 1860 elections—a small minority, indeed—
swore allegiance to the United States and accepted the end of slavery, the state
could hold special elections to establish state legislatures and seat a governor.
The state could then apply to Congress for readmission to the Union. Presumably to this end, Hurlbut met with Hahn at the statehouse at New Orleans on
September 25, 1864. That conference, in which the free state government's accomplishments and present difficulties were frankly discussed, fully satisfied
Hahn regarding Hurlbut's pledge to continue Banks's support of his administration. The meeting further reassured Hahn as to Hurlbut's concern for the
efficient management of municipal finances and public services, as well as for
the welfare of the city's nineteen thousand newly emancipated blacks.[5]

Hahn did not know, however, that while Hurlbut recognized emancipation,
he scarcely entertained genuine interest, as a practical matter, in promoting the
welfare, or protecting the recently gained freedom, of the former slaves. A seemingly insignificant affair that occurred shortly after his assumption of command
in New Orleans clearly demonstrated his lack of commitment. This episode
also showed that he sought to continue a policy he had pursued at Memphis,
forcibly to return blacks to farms and plantations in western Tennessee and
northern Mississippi—as had Butler, Banks, and Canby in New Orleans. The
American Missionary Association (AMA), originally founded as an antislavery
organization in 1846, had from the beginning of the war effectively engaged in
the work of educating slaves and freedmen in certain occupied Southern cities.
Substantially expanding its program in New Orleans, by December 1863 the
AMA had commissioned two agents to administer its schools for slaves. Its
representatives—the principal AMA school commissioner, Dr. Isaac G. Hubbs
of New York, and his colleague—had arrived in New Orleans in January 1864.

On March 22, 1864, Banks had named three men to a military Board of
Education for Freedmen; Banks had created the board to establish a more coordinated system of education for New Orleans's emancipated blacks. (He had
simultaneously expanded Butler's repressive system of hiring out slaves to planters
and farmers in the delta region.) Two of Banks's staff officers, Maj. Benjamin
Rush Plumly and the Reverend Lt. Edwin M. Wheelock, were appointed as the
board's chairman and secretary, respectively; he had offered the third position
to Hubbs. Hubbs, who continued as principal director of AMA schools in New
Orleans, quickly antagonized both Plumly and Wheelock (erstwhile abolition-
ists who had socially and economically conservative views on the welfare of
freed blacks) by promoting an ambitious and seemingly politically motivated
and radical plan for a system of publicly supported schools for blacks in New
Orleans. He even sought to confiscate schools attended by white students for

the exclusive use of blacks and to create a statewide system of plantation schools for former slaves. Banks, however, had adopted a conciliatory policy toward Louisiana planters and farmers, who vehemently opposed efforts to increase the independence of emancipated blacks, especially their former plantation hands. Consequently, Banks increased military authority over the eight AMA "colored schools" and their 1,800 black students.[6]

Hubbs, for his part, scarcely reversed the AMA's steadily declining influence in New Orleans. An independent AMA investigation had revealed that in the summer of 1864 Hubbs had embezzled board-of-education funds and extorted payments from the twenty-five AMA teachers and their assistants. Furthermore, Plumly and Wheelock accused Hubbs (apparently with doubtful justification— Seymour Straight, a prominent Baptist layman and a strong AMA supporter, later pronounced Hubbs innocent) of having seduced and ruined Miss Frances Bartlett, a young AMA teacher in New Orleans. Hubbs abruptly resigned his position on the Board of Education in September 1864, following Banks's departure from New Orleans, although he had continued, with seeming impunity, to exercise his functions as the chief AMA commissioner as well as the AMA's principal administrator of black schools.[7]

At this point Hurlbut addressed the Hubbs case, apparently on the instigation of AMA headquarters officials in New York or field agents in New Orleans, and urged to take drastic action by Plumly and Wheelock. On the basis of unproven allegations and doubtful evidence, on October 16, 1864, in General Orders No. 280, Hurlbut pronounced Hubbs guilty of embezzlement, extortion, and seduction and ordered him to leave New Orleans and the Department of the Gulf within ten days. Hubbs proceeded to New York, where AMA headquarters officials thoroughly repudiated him.[8] The AMA had established Hubbs's guilt as to embezzlement and extortion (not seduction), but Hurlbut had not expelled him for defalcation of governmental funds, wrongful appropriation of AMA teachers' and agents' pay, or ravishment of the young AMA teacher. Rather, these charges were a transparent pretext for Hurlbut's real purpose: Hubbs had to be banished because he had become a threat to Canby's, Banks's, and Hurlbut's plans for the forcible relocation of former slaves to plantation owners and farmers.

The Hubbs affair marked Hurlbut's first clearly arbitrary exercise of power at New Orleans. He had not required Hubbs to answer charges in a provost court— the procedure he had previously employed in Memphis to try, convict, and sentence suspected cotton smugglers. (Hurlbut could have invoked martial law as justification, however, and cited precedents by Sherman and himself in Memphis and by Butler in New Orleans.) More important, the incident demonstrated Hurlbut's willing support of the repressive and perhaps racist policies of his two predecessors.

Even as the commander of the Sixteenth Corps at Memphis in March 1863, Hurlbut had advocated a policy of forcibly returning slaves, or "contrabands," to Unionist planters and farmers in western Tennessee and northern Mississippi, if only to relieve himself of the responsibility for their welfare. Nearly twelve thousand contrabands had dwelt in poverty and squalor in Memphis; hundreds died weekly from epidemics of smallpox, despite the army medical department's efforts. As the planting season approached, Hurlbut had recognized an opportunity to remove from his charge at least two thousand blacks by hiring them out to local planters and farmers. In March 1863 Hurlbut had explained to Lincoln that he then had almost five thousand black women and children alone, barely surviving on spare government rations, besides other men assigned as auxiliaries to military units. Hurlbut had recommended specifically to the president that he should be allowed to hire out two thousand men, a plan also recommended to Lincoln and Stanton by John Eaton, Grant's general superintendent of contrabands for the Department of the Tennessee.[9]

Having received no reply from Lincoln on the subject, on March 26 Hurlbut had requested Grant's authority to enroll some of the contrabands in auxiliary military service in Memphis and to hire out the remaining slaves to planters and farmers. He had admitted to Grant that he could not determine how to deal with the "vast number of worthless negroes" in Memphis who survived by "stealing & vice"; he sought authority to "seize the horde of pilferers" and compel them to perform agricultural labor. Authorized by Grant on March 29 to exercise his own discretion, Hurlbut had thereafter returned numerous contrabands to the plantations and farms from which many of them doubtless had originally fled. Moreover, on March 30, he had issued an order to disband forthwith the congested "negro camps" at Cairo, Illinois, and Columbus, Kentucky. With the exception of the blacks then serving in the Union army, Hurlbut had directed the removal of all other black men, women, and children some thirty miles farther south to Island No. 10 in the Mississippi River, where, according to a *St. Louis Missouri Republican* reporter, "they are to be put to work tilling the soil." Aside from Eaton's civilian agents, who included a few white teachers and nurses, the transplanted contrabands populating this isolated colony numbered 894—of whom 249 were men, 415 women, and 230 children under twelve. A cynical correspondent for the *Mobile Advertiser & Register* ridiculed the "Yankee philanthropy" and especially the "Abolition Societies," which, he asserted, had compelled upward of seven hundred contrabands to inhabit 150 tents scattered over a desolate "negro colony" planted on a "barren sandbar."[10]

However, in New Orleans in the fall of 1864 Hurlbut dutifully enforced Banks's policy of prompt payment of black plantation hands. In January 1864, Banks had issued an order, effective until February 1, 1865, that placed liens on planters' cotton and other staple crops to assure full compensation of black workers, because the planters often defaulted. Recognizing his responsibility for the fourteen thousand freedmen employed or supported by the Union army within New Orleans alone and also for the thirty-five thousand blacks toiling under contract on some 1,073 plantations in Union Louisiana, Hurlbut necessarily relied on the Reverend Thomas W. Conway, the superintendent of the army's Bureau of Free Labor, to exact payment from defaulting planters. Thus, for instance, when in mid-November 1864 one planter sold his crop for two thousand dollars and tried to abscond with his "fine, clean greenbacks," Hurlbut directed Conway to use a military detail to detain the planter. The planter "tried to get away," but Conway informed him, "Gen. Hurlbut had ordered him to be kept fast till the money was paid." Under a threat of imprisonment, the planter returned the funds to Conway.[11]

Hurlbut's careful enforcement of compensation of blacks represented no departure from his previous policy, much less a change in his attitude toward the freedmen in New Orleans. On the contrary, Hurlbut sought to expand and perpetuate the "free labor" system temporarily instituted by Butler and Banks. Numerous Northern profiteers who had appropriated confiscated plantations to exploit the black workforce had begun to leave the Department of the Gulf; Southerners had begun to return to the Mississippi Delta to reclaim their abandoned plantations. On March 11, 1865, as the spring planting season approached, Hurlbut issued General Orders No. 23—without the War Department's or Banks's concurrence—which promulgated a new program for the disposition of the freedmen. Section 5 of his orders established the wage rates for black men, women, and small children of both sexes and requirements for food, clothing, shelter, medical care, and educational instruction for juveniles. Section 9, the cardinal provision of Hurlbut's orders, established a highly efficient (albeit hastily devised) contract labor system. Although it granted to freedmen the right to choose their employers, section 9 stipulated that a black worker would have to remain on a plantation for a full year. A worker who left a place of employment and returned later would forfeit all wages earned before leaving. Since planters paid their hands but four times a year (on May 1, August 1, November 1, and on or before January 31), a laborer thus stood to forfeit a great deal of money.[12] Not an unreasonable requirement in itself, this section failed to account for unforeseen circumstances in the lives of workers; greater allowance for mobility would have proved less demoralizing than the commitment demanded by the section.

However, Hurlbut's General Orders No. 23 succeeded in integrating elements of the previous contract labor systems of Butler and Banks and in establishing comprehensive and coherent regulations for a closely coordinated and systematic labor program. He also rendered the earlier systems more efficient, by ensuring clearer communication and closer cooperation between Superintendent Conway's Bureau of Free Labor, the plantation owners or masters, and the freedmen themselves. Nonetheless, Hurlbut's labor system had serious defects and potential abuses. It deprived black plantation workers of their freedom of work, freedom of contract, and freedom to negotiate wages and of regular payments. Generals Butler and Banks had granted the freedmen a measure of discretion to choose certain kinds of nonagricultural work or at least to labor under different planters; Hurlbut determined to restrict their freedom and bound them more firmly to the soil. Butler and Banks had attempted to establish a relatively uniform wage rate, regardless of the worker's gender or age; Hurlbut created a highly differentiated wage structure of "first," "second," and "third-class"—male, female, and juvenile (under fourteen) hands. These three classes corresponded to good, average, and poor laborers, as arbitrarily assigned by the planter; women and children were considerably less. Hurlbut had given to planters the right to determine a worker's productive value. Thus, theoretically at least, a planter could arbitrarily deny the efficiency or usefulness of even his most productive black hand and simply by invoking Section 5 of Hurlbut's labor orders deprive that worker of fair compensation. Moreover, the trimonthly schedule of payments, besides the risk of the forfeiture of pay, discouraged workers from escaping oppressive masters, a circumstance that established a thinly disguised peonage throughout occupied Louisiana. Hurlbut's general orders also produced abuses of military power and authority, as if his only purposes were to repress freedmen and conciliate plantation owners. In the weeks following the promulgation of General Orders No. 23, hundreds of planters sought to convince their hands that the Union army had revived chattel slavery. Strangers impersonating Union army officers declared that the free state legislature had reestablished the institution of slavery in Union-held Louisiana.

Recognizing the difficulty of distinguishing men and women of the free black professional and artisan classes within the city from the plantation workers whom he had virtually confined to the rural districts, Hurlbut required free urban blacks to obtain "circulation cards," with which they were to be allowed to travel freely and unmolested within his jurisdiction. However, numerous free blacks who had not yet acquired the necessary passes found themselves subject to a strict travel restriction, far exceeding in severity a similar limitation previously imposed by the Louisiana *Code Noir* (Black Code), which French rulers had established in

1724. On March 21, 1865, an assembly of "colored Citizens of New Orleans" presented Hurlbut with a resolution condemning his (and Banks's) labor policy and denouncing his restriction on travel as "unconstitutional." Hurlbut denied these charges and refused to reorganize his plantation program.[13]

Hurlbut's contract-labor system produced a wave of protest from the antislavery press in occupied New Orleans and in the North, particularly from the *New Orleans Tribune,* which in October 1864 had gained distinction as the first black daily newspaper in America. The *Tribune*'s managing editor, forty-four-year-old Belgian native Mons Jean-Charles Houzeau (christened, in full, Jean-Charles-Hippolyte-Joseph Houzeau de Lehaie), had emigrated to America from England in October 1857, settling briefly in New Orleans before removing to Texas. A distinguished journalist and an amateur astronomer, Houzeau had participated conspicuously in literary and intellectual circles in Belgium, France, and England. A zealous antislavery crusader in Texas, he had opposed chattel slavery and the secessionist movement in the Lone Star State. Indeed, for the next four years he had courageously abetted fugitive black slaves. In February 1862 Houzeau had boldly aided Charles Anderson (the brother of Maj. Robert Anderson, of Fort Sumter fame) in reaching the North—after which Houzeau was forced to flee to Mexico. Returning only briefly to Union-occupied New Orleans in January 1863, Houzeau had thereafter plied his journalistic trade in Philadelphia. In October 1864, pressed by the free black proprietors of the *New Orleans Tribune* to accept a lucrative offer to become its managing editor, Houzeau accepted.[14]

Shortly thereafter, as his black employers had rather anticipated he would, Houzeau began attacking the glaring inequities and abuses that he perceived as inherent in the "free labor" systems instituted by Generals Banks and Hurlbut. Attributing Hurlbut's new contract-labor policy to motives of "prejudice" and "discrimination," Houzeau bitterly criticized sections 5 and 9 of General Orders No. 23. In a series of editorials (of March 14, 16, 18, 22, and, particularly, March 28, 29, and 30), Houzeau condemned Hurlbut. As Houzeau afterward recalled, "The system was so wrong that even the general himself felt implicated." Hurlbut had cravenly "surrendered to the enemy, and it was thoroughly disagreeable for him to have this fact proven" irrefutably, "and this in the pages of a black newspaper to boot!" A sharp clash between Hurlbut and Houzeau quickly followed. Hurlbut sought to ascertain who had composed the articles for the *Tribune* and, on learning of Houzeau's identity as a Belgian immigrant, Hurlbut had menacingly spoken of "'chasing me out of the country.'" Hurlbut could not fulfill this threat because Houzeau's editorials had generated a storm in Northern antislavery newspapers—agitation that ultimately compelled the returning Major General Banks and his own successor, Maj. Gen. Absalom

Baird, to reform Hurlbut's labor system.[15] Evidently, Hurlbut's Negrophobic and xenophobic biases, first manifested in antebellum South Carolina, continued to shape his views regarding blacks and foreign immigrants.

All this foreshadowed opposition by Hurlbut and Canby to Hahn's free state government. Hahn, like Hubbs, challenged the absolute supremacy of military authority they sought to exercise over the reconstruction process in Louisiana. Canby and Hurlbut proceeded from a false perception of a struggle between the military authority and the civilian political structure. These generals would also come to oppose the Hahn regime on secondary grounds, regarding it as frankly liberal in its approach to fiscal policy and excessively supportive of the rights and welfare of the freedmen. Hurlbut's opposition to the Hahn regime probably also sprang from a more selfish motive. Grant now served in Virginia and Sherman in Georgia, and Canby was preoccupied with military matters in his larger jurisdiction. Hurlbut recognized that the weak and overlapping patchwork of state and municipal authority in New Orleans could facilitate the formation of cotton and extortion rings potentially even more profitable than those in Memphis. The appointment of his former Memphis officers and Harai Robinson, Banks's controversial provost marshal, to his staff seemingly confirmed his intentions.

Hurlbut wasted little time in what became an active extortion ring in New Orleans around Lieutenant Colonel Robinson. Evidently Hurlbut could inspire an almost blind loyalty and devotion in his subordinates. For example, in Missouri Hurlbut's unbecoming conduct had led to the arrest and prolonged detention of Col. Nelson G. Williams, who nevertheless had later bravely fought under him at Shiloh. In Tennessee, Capt. George A. Williams, who could have become an outstanding infantry officer in the regular army, apparently sacrificed honor and integrity to become the ringleader of Hurlbut's cotton and extortion rings. In Colonel Robinson, Hurlbut found another admirable soldier who underwent a similarly radical transformation to execute Hurlbut's wishes. In 1861 Robinson had gained the colonelcy of the 1st Louisiana Cavalry Volunteers and had fought gallantly against numerically superior forces across southern Louisiana. Intelligent, patriotic, and an inspiring leader (who spoke French and Spanish fluently), on August 30, 1863, Robinson had ordered the execution of two ringleaders of a mutiny in the 2d Rhode Island Cavalry—a depleted unit designated for consolidation with the 1st Louisiana. His decisive action had outraged the governor of Rhode Island, but both Secretary of War Stanton and Major General Banks had upheld it. As a volunteer aide to Banks at New Orleans, Robinson had rendered distinguished service at Baton Rouge in 1862 and during the Port Hudson campaign of 1863. At Baton Rouge Robinson had even expressed a genuine sympathy for blacks. According to a correspondent for the *New York Tribune,* Robinson had related to him stories of runaway slaves who had made daring escapes in western Louisiana to reach freedom across the river at Baton Rouge. The blacks had been "hunted with bloodhounds to compel their return" to bondage. This inhumanity had prompted Robinson to consider a punitive cavalry raid across the river for the purpose of "extirpating these quadrupedal adjuncts to Louisiana civilization." Robinson "would have no such brutes or doings as those, he said, in *his* vicinity." Thereafter, Robinson had commanded the 1st Louisiana in the Military District of New Orleans until an appreciative Banks had appointed him his provost marshal in 1864.[16]

Hurlbut quickly demonstrated his intent to extort tribute from the civilians in his district. In the fall of 1862, Major General Butler had peremptorily ordered more than a hundred affluent subscribers to the secessionist "Committee of Safety," a voluntary citizen's organization created to support the Confederate defense of New Orleans, to answer for their treason by making three large payments in gold bullion or federal currency to the U.S. Treasury. Noting the huge sum of $1,036,865, the committee members had contributed to the Confederates, Butler had announced his intention to employ the money to establish a special fund for the relief of contrabands in the Gulf Department; he and Banks had then wrung two payments, aggregating $260,000, from the nearly ruined subscribers. But both Butler and Banks had then left New Orleans; consequently, early in October 1864, Hurlbut demanded the final installment of $250,000. He gave the subscribers only one day in which to deliver their payment or find themselves summarily "subjected to imprisonment, and seizure of their property!" The committee members made the payment, but neither Hurlbut nor Robinson ever accounted for the money, nor could they have diverted it into Butler's defunct contrabands' fund.[17] Neither the provost marshal at New Orleans nor the War or Treasury Departments in Washington ever made restitution. As he had done so effectively in Memphis, Hurlbut had used the threat of incarceration and confiscation to coerce obedience. Nevertheless, a gratified *New York Times* reporter declared that Hurlbut, in his pursuit of the "same laudable object" that Generals Butler and Banks had striven to achieve, "deals with the disaffected with just as little tenderness as Butler was apt to exercise." In contrast, the *Richmond Whig* sarcastically remarked, "the new Yankee commander at New Orleans is operating under the Butler creed."[18]

The suspicious conclusion to the Committee of Safety affair coincided with efforts to subordinate the free state government in Louisiana to military authority. Clearly, Lincoln had appointed Hurlbut to the Department of the Gulf

Edward R. S. Canby, commanding general in Union Louisiana. Prints and Photographs Division, Library of Congress.

command, in part at least, to counterbalance manifestations of local political interference from Canby, whom he had appointed as commander of the Trans-Mississippi Division. Canby's record had theretofore given the president no reason for complaint or disappointment. Canby had graduated from West Point in 1839, fought in the Second Seminole War and in the Mexican War, and campaigned against the Navajo Indians in New Mexico immediately before the present war. As a colonel in command of Fort Defiance, New Mexico, in 1862 Canby had captured bodies of Confederate troops in his department. Named a brigadier general on March 31, 1862, and promoted to major general, U.S. Volunteers, on May 7, 1864, Canby had proceeded to New Orleans with Lincoln's confidence. By July 1864, however, Lincoln suspected that Canby harbored hostility toward the Hahn government. Hurlbut, instead of counterbalancing Canby, supported his efforts to impose military control over reconstruction. Accordingly, when Hurlbut late in October 1864 learned that the state legislature had decided to abolish Butler's military Bureaus of Finance and of Streets and Landings, thus reviving civic institutions and depriving the Union military of patronage appointments, he denounced the lawmakers. In letters to Mayor Stephen Hoyt of New Orleans, Hurlbut declared that only he and neither Hahn nor Hoyt had the authority to make such appointments; the legislature's action, he charged, represented a political challenge to his jurisdiction.[19]

Hurlbut also determined to prevent Hoyt or the state legislature from substantially increasing the city's or the state's public indebtedness and, he alleged, plunge Louisiana ever more deeply into fiscal crisis—although he had doubted his power to annul a series of legislative measures having that effect. Hurlbut inquired of Canby—who was one West Point officer whom he respected—"to what extent am I compelled" to "recognize the acts and proceedings of the State of Louisiana in its several branches" with regard to its "reckless" fiscal and monetary policies. Canby on October 29 expressed his approval of Hurlbut's bold assertion of military control over all municipal appointments: "It is scarcely necessary for me to say" that "all attempts at civil government within the territory declared to be in insurrection, are the creation of military power" and are therefore subject to martial law. Canby further assured Hurlbut that his action would receive prompt War Department ratification.[20]

Manifestly, Canby either seriously misunderstood the legitimacy of the Hahn government or erroneously perceived that territory to be a part of the trans-Mississippi Confederacy and thus in his own sector. In any case, Canby and Hurlbut overestimated their ability to compel Hahn's and Hoyt's submission. Hahn complained to Lincoln on October 29 that Hurlbut and Canby had made the "most barefaced and *unnecessary* attempts" to "crush out a state government" established under the terms of presidential reconstruction. He urged Lincoln to return Banks to his command in New Orleans; otherwise "we must break down in our efforts to build up a loyal State government here." The governor also suspected that "copperheadism is well represented among the highest military officials now in command" of occupied Louisiana. Apprised of Hahn's complaint, Hurlbut quickly retaliated by ordering Provost Marshal Robinson to search the governor's mansion, in Hahn's absence, for an active Confederate sympathizer whom he claimed Hahn harbored. The outraged governor remonstrated, but his protest was ignored by Hurlbut and Robinson.[21]

Although not yet informed of Hurlbut's raid on Hahn's official residence in New Orleans, Lincoln recognized that Hurlbut was betraying his trust and cooperating with Canby. In the evening of November 14, he had regretfully confided to Orville H. Browning, who since leaving the Senate in 1863 had practiced law and worked as a lobbyist in Washington, that "Genl Canby and Genl Hurlburt [sic], in Louisiana, were doing all they could to break down the state government." Canby and Hurlbut had sought to "deprive the negroes of all benefit" the emancipated blacks had expected to obtain under the liberal free state constitution.[22] On the same day, Lincoln composed a private letter for Hurlbut in which he expressed his displeasure at Hurlbut's and Canby's interference with the Hahn government and their mistreatment of the freedmen. He informed Hurlbut that since the summer of 1864 he had "painfully" perceived a "bitter military opposition" to the government of Louisiana, whose free state constitution had proved more beneficial for Louisiana freedmen than did the Illinois constitution for blacks in that state. Lincoln assured Hurlbut that his authority exceeded that of Hahn in wartime Louisiana, but he nevertheless reprimanded Hurlbut for having deliberately and unduly interfered with the state legislature. The president bluntly warned Hurlbut in particular, and through him Canby, that "a purpose, obvious, and scarcely unavowed, to transcend all military necessity, in order to crush out the civil government, will not be overlooked."[23]

Surprised by Lincoln's reprimand but convinced that the president misunderstood the relationship between civilian and military authorities in New Orleans, Hurlbut defended his treatment of freedmen. On November 29 he replied to Lincoln that he fully appreciated the benefits of the free state constitution and that it was the state legislature that was neglecting the economic welfare of freedmen. He assured Lincoln that he would "do everything in my power to advance the condition of the Colored Race," both as "a measure of humanity and justice" and to ensure the "eventual safety and unity of the American nation." To that end, he would have to continue opposing the liberal pretensions of Louisiana legislators and the demagoguery of Hahn and Hoyt.[24]

In fact, Hurlbut immediately resumed his efforts to subordinate the political authority of the Hahn government to military oversight. Late in November 1864, Hurlbut overrode Hahn by appointing John A. Roberts as drainage commissioner of New Orleans. Hahn protested to Hurlbut, defending the free state legislature's record, which included legislation for the economic, social, and physical betterment of freedmen; the establishment of a free school charter to increase the accessibility of public secondary education for blacks and whites; and creation of a state militia to ensure the safety of loyal Louisiana citizens. Finally, in January 1865 a discouraged and disgusted Hahn won election by the Louisiana legislature to the U.S. Senate.[25] On March 4 a conservative Unionist, James Madison Wells, was inaugurated as governor.

The Louisiana-born Wells had been a prosperous slaveholder but an opponent of secession. Hurlbut, perceiving in Wells a willingness to be dominated by the Union high command at New Orleans, delivered the keynote address to a joint session of the Louisiana legislature upon his accession. In a forceful oration that one gratified Northern journalist gleefully described as having taken "the whole city by surprise," Hurlbut called for fiscal retrenchment, the elimination of wasteful spending by state and municipal governments. He also gratuitously insulted the free state lawmakers. According to David L. Phillips (the principal editor of the Republican *Illinois State Journal* in Springfield, who had journeyed to New Orleans to report on Canby's and Hurlbut's operations in the Gulf states), Louisiana politicians had regarded Hurlbut as "a small Illinois lawyer, an inferior interloper in Gen. Banks's command." Hurlbut publicly declared his superiority to these southern politicians as a general in the Union army and as "an orator, lawyer, and Statesman."[26]

Hurlbut's extortion and profiteering now assumed new forms and proportions. Having wrested funds from the disbanded Committee of Safety, Hurlbut turned his attention to another vulnerable civic institution, the Christ Church of New Orleans. Like the Committee of Safety affair, the Christ Church episode had begun during the rule of Major General Butler. Butler had closed the church because of its allegedly disloyal services, and the Reverend Frederick E. R. Chubbock, Butler's post chaplain, wanted to conduct services for Union troops in the vacant building. In October 1862 Chubbock had obtained from Butler a direct order compelling the deacons of Christ Church to deliver the keys. The church's principal deacon, Charles L. Harrod, had reluctantly complied and allowed Chubbock to borrow the golden communion plate for use in worship services. But Chubbock had decided to keep the plate in his own possession. In July 1864 Chubbock had persuaded Banks to force the delivery of Christ Church's deeds and assets to him, including "a massive elegantly carved oak pulpit, that cost in New York $1500 to $1800." Chubbock had resigned his position as post chaplain and returned to Massachusetts with Banks in September 1864, taking with him tangible assets of Christ Church. In October 1864, Hurlbut ordered his provost marshal secretly to confiscate the church's remaining "books, papers, records, titles and money." Apparently to conceal the appropriation of this property, in December 1864 Hurlbut published special orders for the prompt restoration of all sequestered Christ Church property to the deacons—but by that time, no assets remained. In February and March 1865 Hurlbut refused to hear complaints from Harrod and the other church deacons, and he finally left New Orleans in June 1865 without making restitution; nor did he ever account for his disposition of the church's funds or assets.[27]

Meanwhile, Hurlbut had found another and perhaps more advantageous reason for opposition to the free state government, a reason that led him in March 1865 to support Governor Wells, practically his and Canby's puppet, in an effort arbitrarily to remove Mayor Hoyt of New Orleans. Hoyt was a Massachusetts native whom President James K. Polk had appointed in 1847 as a captain and commissary officer and who had served in the Mexican War; later he became mayor of St. Louis. Banks had appointed him the mayor of New Orleans early in 1864. Hurlbut censured Hoyt for allegedly loose administration of municipal finances in October 1864. But Hurlbut had not understood how the replacement of Hoyt by Wells could benefit him until March 1865, when he learned of a New Orleans banking controversy that conspicuously involved Hoyt.

The issue had arisen before the war. The antebellum Free Banking Law of Louisiana had governed the distribution and redemption of New Orleans municipal and Louisiana state bonds. To implement the statute, twelve local banks had been organized by 1860 in New Orleans; bonds of Louisiana, and particularly the certificates of New Orleans, had been deposited by the banks with the state auditor for public sale in 1861. Before the fall of New Orleans in 1862, the state auditor had absconded with the bonds and sold them for cash to support the Confederate war effort. The unknown bondholders had not yet presented their bonds to the banks for payment, and the banks were liable only when the bonds were redeemed. However, in March 1865, upon Wells's inauguration as governor, the local banks demanded that the city of New Orleans pay them the outstanding balance. In addition, the banks demanded the coupon-specified interest on the bonds (that is, to cover in advance their anticipated losses), although they could not produce coupons, bonds, or even bond numbers to substantiate their claims. In January 1864 a reporter for the *New York Times* sarcastically noted that the banks had kept up "a mock appearance of business, based upon their old *State bonds*—no longer worth the material on which they were printed."[28]

Obviously anticipating an enormous profit, the banks arranged the self-aggrandizing intervention of Governor Wells in their bid for restitution in advance, and they also accepted Hurlbut's intercession. Early in March 1865 Hurlbut ordered the First National Bank, an institution established on January 18, 1864, by the Treasury Department as the occupied city's fiscal agent, to pay a million dollars in federal currency to the banks. The First National Bank flatly refused. Clearly it recognized that the banks sought to obtain U.S. currency with the intention of later reimbursing the First National with valueless Confederate paper money. To avoid further confrontation, Hurlbut rescinded his order. Recognizing that he could not lay hands on the funds of the First National Bank, which had the support of politically radical Treasury Department officials and Free State Party members, Hurlbut directed that the case be tried before the conservative Judge Charles A. Peabody of the U.S. Provisional Court for the State of Louisiana. Peabody, a New York lawyer whom Lincoln in 1862 had appointed as the administrator of a provisional system of federal courts in Union-held Louisiana, served concurrently as the chief justice of the state's supreme court. Though he was himself a sitting federal judicial official, Judge Peabody decided in favor of the banks, declared that the First National should pay the banks to cover their anticipated losses, and he overruled the city's motion for an appeal to the state supreme court.[29]

Mayor Hoyt "bitterly" opposed the enormous payment; he "regarded it as corrupt, unjust and destructive, of the credit of the city of New Orleans." Accordingly, Hoyt refused to order the First National Bank to pay the million dollars to the banks. In prompt retaliation, on March 21 Hurlbut urged and then supported Wells's peremptory removal of Hoyt from office. As George S. Denison, a radical Republican Treasury Department official in New Orleans, explained to Salmon P. Chase, the chief justice of the U.S. Supreme Court and the former secretary of the treasury, "I think this has been done with the approval of Gen. Hurlburt [sic], who is glad to put out of the way any of Banks's friends." Wells thereupon appointed Dr. Hugh Kennedy, the conservative editor of the New Orleans Daily True Delta and the former president of one of the local banks, mayor of New Orleans. New Orleans–based radical Republicans like Denison particularly feared that Hurlbut and Wells would not only plunder the First National Bank but weaken the radical wing of the Free State Party by putting Kennedy into power. Denison confessed to Chase, "Perhaps I judge harshly of these proceedings, but I cannot help regarding with suspicion everything done by Hurlburt." But Hurlbut's intrigue with Wells ended abruptly late in April, when Banks returned to New Orleans. Banks ordered the reversal of Peabody's decision.[30]

Clearly Hurlbut's involvement in the scandal sprang partly from a political motive, because he had expressed determination to undermine or destroy the radical wing of the Free State Party. It had aligned itself with the directorate of the First National Bank, a creation of the Treasury Department in New Orleans; it had strongly opposed Canby's and his policies of returning freed New Orleans blacks to planters and farmers, and of denying contrabands education; and it had advocated, more than had the moderate Unionists Hahn and Hoyt, increased government spending on the freedmen, on public works and services, and particularly on popular education. The First National Bank incident, however, also demonstrated Hurlbut's increasing political and fiscal conservatism. Although originally a moderate conservative, in Louisiana Hurlbut adopted an extremely conservative attitude, particularly on the questions of the sovereignty, even the legitimacy, of the free state legislature. Concurrently, he criticized Hahn's and Hoyt's fiscal irresponsibility, suggesting a sinister association with radicals like Denison who advocated considerably greater expenditures. However, in the First National Bank affair Hurlbut had in theory and practice supported a plan that could have severely damaged the credit of New Orleans. Simultaneously, Hurlbut had assumed with Canby a regressive policy with respect to the freedmen at a time when Lincoln and Hahn had sought to extend the franchise to a few blacks, for which he had publicly professed support in the summer of 1863.

Hurlbut continued to complain to Lincoln of corruption and extravagance by the free-state legislature. He did this when the War Department directed him to publish stern orders prohibiting his staff officers from accepting cash bribes in exchange for illicit cotton speculating privileges. Moreover, in October 1864 he had prohibited officers and enlisted men from patronizing theaters, billiard rooms, drinking saloons, brothels, and gambling houses on Sundays in New Orleans, obeying a similar order promulgated by President Lincoln on November 16, 1862. These pious actions sprang from a personal motive, to assert once again the supremacy of his military power over civilian political authority; the free-state legislature was considering the formal licensing of gambling houses in New Orleans. The fact was that since the departure of Butler from New Orleans late in 1862, gambling houses in New Orleans had grown even more numerous. Hurlbut also recognized an opportunity to draft numerous Southern gamblers into the Home Guards militia. As a *New York Times* correspondent observed, by his "bold step" of closing the gambling houses on Sundays, a move that had "astonished the military world," Hurlbut had also perceived "a weak spot when he fixed the penalty of delinquents to service in the army as cooks and teamsters." Highly gratified, the *Times* reporter concluded that Hurlbut had thus ushered in "a new era for New Orleans," where "the Sabbath has always been the grand pleasure day."

But in Illinois, the Democratic *Quincy Herald* expressed skepticism about Hurlbut's prohibition of "theatres and billiard saloons" in New Orleans on Sundays. The *Herald* derisively asserted: "There is one institution the General will never order to be closed. That is the place where he takes his toddies."[31] His enrollment order, however, enabled him to put not only secessionists but also Northern draft dodgers or their hired substitutes into the Union army in Louisiana—in itself a commendable action. In a letter to the editor of the *Richmond Daily Dispatch* early in March 1865, a Southern sympathizer declared that "so numerously had the draft-skulkers congregated here from other points, that General Hurlbut determined to make a descent upon them." The strict enforcement of his order, the writer observed, had deprived them of a refuge from conscription and "the business in substitutes has become brisk accordingly."[32]

Ironically, and perhaps more significantly, Hurlbut's interest in operating another cotton ring sprang, in part, from Lincoln's ambivalence about, even seeming encouragement of, smuggling at New Orleans. As in Memphis, a large and illicit exchange of contraband goods for cotton had developed in New Orleans; the trade had flourished even under the guns of the Union warships blockading New Orleans and other ports along the Gulf coast. In September 1864 Canby issued General Orders No. 51, which called for the confiscation of all cotton that speculators thereafter imported into occupied Louisiana from surrounding Confederate regions. His action resulted in the seizure of much cotton that had been exchanged for contraband to support the Confederate war effort but did not significantly reduce the volume of cotton flowing, or rather pouring, into New Orleans. Lincoln had long understood the broader economic and military implications of the contraband trade. In December 1864 the president explained to Canby that at least one-sixth of the South's annual yield of field cotton regularly passed through the Union blockade and reached Europe, where it brought, even at low wholesale prices, fully six times the number of gold dollars, or its equivalent in munitions, than an entire year's crop had realized overseas before the war. An excessive amount of Northern bullion flowed to Europe to pay for the unusually expensive cotton abroad, particularly since the inception of commercial nonintercourse with the South. The Union blockade of Southern seaports, coupled with the Confederacy's cotton embargo of the North, the president explained, had seriously impeded the importation of much-desired Southern cotton into the North. Lincoln contemplated an attempt to halt the European armaments entering the South and at the same time to stop the gold drain, which continued to deplete the Treasury, by shrewdly exploiting what he described as the "pecuniary greed" of Northern speculators at New Orleans.

Lincoln therefore urged Canby to exercise leniency toward Northern traders at New Orleans, making it possible for Northern food and clothing to be exchanged for Confederate cotton, thus simultaneously diverting Southern cotton from Europe, depriving the Confederates of foreign ordnance, and relieving the scarcity of cotton and gold across the North.[33] Canby firmly opposed Lincoln's plan. In January 1865 he replied to Lincoln that the Confederates would still seek European munitions in preference to Northern foodstuffs and clothing, while unchecked smuggling in New Orleans would only increase the Union military's suspected collusion. Disingenuously, in view of his concurrent efforts to undermine the free state government and without offering an explanation, Canby warned Lincoln that his plan, if implemented, would also hinder presidential reconstruction in Union Louisiana.[34]

Hurlbut had viewed Canby's earlier stringent orders against smuggling as a most propitious opportunity for a cotton ring in New Orleans. Believing that strict enforcement of Canby's orders could enable him to demand bribes from cotton speculators who wanted to do business with Southern cotton factors (brokers) around New Orleans, Hurlbut assured Lincoln of the necessity and prudence of Canby's orders. He warned Lincoln that General Orders No. 51 as promulgated by "Genl Canby will bring the whole force of the Cotton speculating interest to Washington with the most powerful & combined effort" either to urge Canby's removal from command or to agitate for the repeal or modification of his orders. Hurlbut pressed upon Lincoln his opinion that "rigid non intercourse should be kept" in effect at New Orleans and that the president should jealously guard against "influence of any kind" that "may be allowed to interfere with its execution" for at least three months within southern Louisiana and Mississippi. Further, Hurlbut had expressed his view that no patriotic Union man could "deal in purchases of cotton without violating his allegiance to the Country" and without committing treason by exchanging contraband for cotton with the "Confederate Military authorities," as the "enormous gains made by these adventurers are the evidence of the illegality and risk of the traffic."[35] As previously indicated, however, in December 1864 Lincoln suggested that Canby modify his orders, though the president would not revoke them. Lincoln apparently understood that a limited relaxation of Canby's ban on smuggling could actually support the Union war effort, whereas Canby's orders had neither eliminated nor significantly reduced rampant cotton smuggling or the military's contribution to it.

Recognizing the clear advantages to himself of inflated prices for Southern cotton on the New Orleans black market, Hurlbut exploited Lincoln's and Canby's preoccupation with more pressing matters to effect a series of cotton transactions, in association with Colonel Robinson and an Illinois kinsman. In October 1864, as noted, Hurlbut issued stern pronouncements against the participation of his officers in illicit contraband trade, directing post commanders to prohibit all cotton trading outside the Union lines or suffer summary punishment.[36] Early in November 1864, Clark & Fulton, a thriving shipping house in New Orleans, secured a special presidential permit (actually an order issued by Secretary of the Treasury William P. Fessenden and endorsed by Lincoln) through Treasury Department agents in New Orleans to import a large quantity of cotton from a Confederate district in northern Louisiana. The traders presented their executive permit to Hurlbut on November 26, but he hesitated to endorse it, fearing that Confederate troops would seize the merchants' cotton in transit and possibly execute them as saboteurs or spies. But in mid-December the traders defiantly procured their 336 bales of cotton, justifying by presidential sanction their apparent violation of both Canby's General Orders No. 51 and Hurlbut's prohibition of trading contraband for cotton.

Suspicious of the authenticity of Clark & Fulton's presidential permit or preferring to have Canby accept the responsibility for the traders' success, Hurlbut commandeered and impounded the firm's cotton, pending Canby's action. Even when informed that Fessenden had authorized Clark & Fulton to procure cotton, Hurlbut refused to release the cotton because he believed that Fessenden had been misled by the traders' original representations. Canby then confiscated the cotton and had it stored in Treasury Department warehouses in New Orleans. However, independently, Hurlbut apparently obtained confirmation of the presidential permit. Meanwhile, in an obvious attempt to bribe Hurlbut, a representative of Clark & Fulton approached Provost Marshal Robinson and urged him to procure an order from Hurlbut for the release of their cotton. According to the report of an official investigation, Robinson accepted ten thousand dollars to obtain Hurlbut's signature. Shortly thereafter, a surprised Canby, who had belatedly learned of the validity of Clark & Fulton's permit, ordered Hurlbut to return the company's cotton. Hurlbut obeyed Canby's order, but not before profiting from the transaction. Fearing Hurlbut's retaliation should they apprise Canby of his duplicity, Clark & Fulton transported its cotton up the Mississippi and sold it in the North.

Meanwhile in November 1864 another large New Orleans cotton trading firm, Charles A. Weed & Company, apparently having learned of Hurlbut's unwillingness to honor a valid presidential permit, sent an accredited representative to pay Robinson ten thousand dollars for Hurlbut's permission to trade for Southern cotton. Robinson then wrung three thousand dollars from William Courtenay, the chief agent of the Star Line of riverboat steamers plying the Mississippi, to allow Courtenay to buy cotton within Confederate Louisiana without interference. Finally, the resourceful Robinson deposited his and Hurlbut's accumulated twenty-three thousand dollars in the First National Bank of New Orleans under the names of its president and cashier. Hurlbut claimed fourteen thousand dollars of this substantial sum, while Robinson retained $7,702 in gold bullion worth $2.25 per greenback dollar—or a realizable balance larger than Hurlbut's cash share.[37] Lincoln had thus unwittingly contributed to a highly ambiguous situation. Although he had continued to support Canby's, and Hurlbut's, policy on smuggling, he had exercised his authority as commander in chief to override it. However, the president had signally failed to apprise Canby and Hurlbut of his granting of special executive permits to certain cotton traders through Treasury Department agents in New Orleans, and he had consequently, although inadvertently, exposed those speculators to confiscation and extortion. Hurlbut had shrewdly—or cunningly—recognized the possibilities for profit.

But if Hurlbut believed that he could conceal these offences by denouncing the corruption of the legislature or by posing as a strict enforcer of Canby's prohibitive policy on smuggling, he deluded himself. Yielding to speculating interests from New Orleans lobbying in Washington (about which Hurlbut had self-servingly warned Lincoln the previous September), Lincoln on December 10, 1864, created a special commission to investigate military corruption in occupied Louisiana. By establishing this board, Lincoln pointedly contradicted Canby's contention that stringent enforcement of orders against smuggling would restrain military corruption. However, the president refrained from rescinding Canby's orders, although his special executive permits and his recommendation that Canby relax trade restrictions suggested his true purpose. Moreover, Lincoln doubtlessly created the commission as a means of terminating Hurlbut's military career. Although he could have summarily removed him from his Gulf command, Lincoln, probably to appease Hurlbut's few remaining but still influential supporters in Illinois, sought a legal foundation on which to court-martial him for misconduct and force him from the army. Lincoln undoubtedly recognized an opportunity to remove a strong opponent of presidential reconstruction in Louisiana and a central figure in the army's cotton ring at New Orleans.

Lincoln appointed Maj. Gen. William F. Smith as the investigating board's chairman. "Baldy" Smith, a forty-one-year-old Vermont native and an 1845 graduate of West Point, had compiled a mediocre record in the war. A War Democrat in 1861, he had served without distinction in the Army of the Potomac until the fall of 1863, when he had ably served Grant as an engineer during the

Chattanooga campaign. However, Smith had performed poorly as a corps commander in Butler's Army of the James in operations near Richmond and Petersburg; in July 1864 Grant had relieved him permanently from field command. On November 23 Lincoln appointed Smith as the senior commissioner of the special board of inquiry evaluating Hurlbut's Army and Department of the Gulf, and more generally the state of affairs in the whole Division of Western Mississippi. Formally establishing Smith as the chairman of the commission on December 10, Lincoln directed him to report his findings directly to Secretary of War Stanton. Smith, although egotistical, arrogant, and contentious, and actively seeking to return to field command under Grant, dutifully obeyed Lincoln's order of appointment.[38] Lincoln named James T. Brady of New York to be the second member of the commission. A noted lawyer and a onetime Douglas Democrat, Brady had gained a broad and enviable reputation for courageously seeking justice by having successfully defended an accused Confederate privateer in a New York state courtroom in a celebrated case in 1861.[39]

Oblivious to these preparations, Hurlbut continued in his willfully improper conduct. He proceeded to improve the financial fortunes of Lawrence L. Crandall, the husband of one of his wife's sisters. The Crandalls resided at the St. Charles Hotel, where Hurlbut had his headquarters. Hurlbut procured a War Department order making Crandall the superintendent of the property seized by Robinson, for a monthly salary of $125. Crandall's sinecure closely resembled James L. Loop's position on Hurlbut's staff in Memphis. In December 1864 Hurlbut repeatedly colluded in Crandall's illicit cotton speculations, issuing military permits for buyers of proscribed Confederate cotton, from whom Crandall received $5,250. Hurlbut also helped Crandall secure a commutation of sentence for James Holland of New Orleans, whom a provost court had sentenced to an extended term at hard labor in a U.S. military prison. For the consideration of $250, Holland's lawyer gained Crandall's intercession with Hurlbut, who thereupon reduced Holland's punishment to a nominal fine.[40] Hurlbut thereby unwittingly further compromised his position before the coming Smith-Brady investigation.

The formal announcement of the establishment of the Lincoln Commission in New Orleans early in January 1865 stunned Hurlbut. For Smith, who had preceded Brady to New Orleans, immediately informed Hurlbut of his mission to expose military corruption within the department. Shortly Smith began publishing appeals for information, even anonymously furnished, from "sufferers or . . . observers of corrupt and oppressive acts by persons acting as U.S. Government officials." Wholly disconcerted by Smith's resolution and zeal,

William F. Smith, principal member of the "Lincoln Commission." Prints and Photographs Division, Library of Congress.

Hurlbut refused his request for full cooperation, initially denying that the as-yet-incomplete commission constituted a legitimate tribunal—although he care-fully treated Smith with courtesy, in deference to Lincoln. Hurlbut attempted, in General Orders No. 35, to restrict the commission's investigative powers and repudiate its claim to presidential authority.[41] But Smith's discovery of both his and Robinson's First National Bank account aroused Hurlbut's apprehension. On February 12, Robinson hastened to protect himself by withdrawing Hurlbut's fourteen thousand dollars and handing him the money at the St. Charles Hotel. Hurlbut quickly locked his funds in a safety deposit box. Robinson, however, failed to remove his gold from the bank before Smith's detectives, under the famous Allan Pinkerton, discovered it; Robinson was arrested and imprisoned the following day.[42] It was in the following two months—unaccountably, since he was now under Smith's scrutiny—that Hurlbut tried, as previously described, to plunder the assets of the First National Bank during the banking scandal.

In the weeks following the seizure and imprisonment of Robinson, Hurlbut concocted an elaborate legal defense should, as was probable, Smith call him to testify. But Hurlbut's trust in Col. Harai Robinson's loyalty to him was mis-placed. He apparently expected Robinson to imitate the devotion of his prede-cessor, Williams. This error ultimately caused Hurlbut's downfall; Robinson presently broke the code of silence. Robinson secretly agreed to testify against Hurlbut in exchange for freedom and immunity—an understanding that led to his temporary release late in March 1865. Even before that, however, Robinson desperately attempted to entangle Hurlbut in his defense. On March 13, he had sent a letter to Hurlbut pleading for his help in countering Smith's accusations. Although anxious to dissociate himself from Robinson entirely, Hurlbut had to cooperate; Robinson threatened to release copies of the compromising letter, which had already begun "burning a hole in his [Hurlbut's] pocket." In any case, both men had by now been summoned to appear before the Smith-Brady commission on April 5. Hurlbut imprudently met with the now-released Robinson in his St. Charles Hotel quarters the day before their joint appear-ance. Hurlbut handed Robinson a set of fabricated documents designed to clear him; Hurlbut assured Robinson, "They will never bring you to trial, con-sequently you need not be afraid of anything." Hurlbut promised that he would perjure himself at the hearing to protect him and obtained Robinson's assur-ance that he would do the same in return. Moreover, Robinson persuaded Hurlbut to return eight thousand dollars of his secret funds to the War Depart-ment so as to forestall further investigation.[43]

On April 5, before the Lincoln Commission, Hurlbut listened in ill-con-cealed dismay as Robinson, who preceded him, gave Smith and Lt. Col. Nicholas Bowen, of the Office of the Judge Advocate General, a startlingly graphic account of his direct participation in Hurlbut's extortion ring, as well as of his and Hurlbut's plans to hide the evidence of their violation of Hurlbut's own orders against smuggling. During the grueling interrogation that followed, Hurlbut, shocked and confused by Robinson's unexpectedly hostile testimony, proceeded to perjure himself. Hurlbut denied that he had accepted payments from New Orleans merchant houses. Rather, he claimed that the money (now secured in a hotel safety deposit box, apart from the eight thousand dollars that he had relinquished) was part of a secret service fund for the surveillance and apprehension of cotton smugglers. As for its whereabouts, Hurlbut weakly explained, "I guess it has all been used up." He testified further that he had prepared a memorandum on November 19, 1864, instructing Robinson to expose and to entrap New Orleans commercial speculators by suggesting willingness to accept bribes—this was one of the spurious orders he had drawn up the day before.[44] This fabrication was designed to discredit and incriminate Robinson, by implying that he had actually taken the bribes, without Hurlbut's knowledge. Hurlbut disavowed personal responsibility for the illicit transactions of Crandall. Obviously disconcerted by what he himself understood to be the inconsistency, implausibility, patent falsehood of his testimony, Hurlbut returned to the St. Charles Hotel.

He agonized for a full week while the commission awaited the belated arrival of James T. Brady, who reached New Orleans on April 10. His having missed the testimony of Hurlbut and Robinson did not adversely affect Smith's and Bowen's work, for Lincoln had intended Brady primarily to review, analyze, and evaluate whatever evidence was uncovered, and assist in preparing the commission's preliminary report. On April 12, Smith and Brady announced their initial findings in a report to Canby. They pronounced Hurlbut guilty of serious misconduct and perjury, from motives of greed and deception. They concluded that he had unscrupulously reinforced and exploited the "lax morality" prevailing within his jurisdiction. The report cited Hurlbut's "official falsehood" in his having contrived in March (before his sworn testimony to the Lincoln Commission in April) an untruthful account of his and Robinson's deeds. Furthermore, Smith and Brady found both Hurlbut and Robinson guilty of extorting money from the firms of Clark & Fulton and Charles A. Weed & Company; they charged Hurlbut in particular as culpable for complicity with Crandall. The report urged Canby to place Hurlbut under house arrest pending court-martial in Washington, for proven extortionate and venal conduct, and other "evil practices" in which he had probably also "connived"; "The higher the rank of the officer who prostitutes his office the more prompt should be the method of dealing with him." Though probably concerned for himself, having failed to control his subordinate's behavior, Canby concurred with the commissioners' views. Canby arrested Hurlbut, confined him to the St. Charles Hotel, and urged the War Department to court-martial him.[45]

Hurlbut received another devastating blow when he learned of Lincoln's assassination. He requested permission to attend Lincoln's funeral in Springfield, but Smith persuaded Canby to detain Hurlbut in New Orleans while he reported to the War Department his findings.[46] Hurlbut, temporarily released from house arrest, reconciled himself to delivering a eulogy for the fallen president in Lafayette Square on April 22 in the presence of Banks, who had resumed command of the Department of the Gulf.[47] Standing proudly before "an immense throng of people" and raising his voice high above "martial music," Hurlbut "seemed greatly excited and spoke apparently with much feeling." Recalling how he had encountered Lincoln in the "ordinary walks of civil life" in Illinois, Hurlbut declared that he could not then have imagined that he would one day render tribute to him as a slain commander in chief. He regarded the assassin John Wilkes Booth's heinous crime as the "natural and necessary result" of treason and secession and vowed Northern vengeance on the Confederate authorities in Richmond should a War Department investigation prove they had conspired to murder Lincoln. Hurlbut expressed hope that the tragic death would usher in an era of enlightenment, racial justice, and harmony in the restored Union, in which both white and black citizens would "rejoice in the consummation of God's great purpose, the American nation."[48]

Hurlbut's sorrow notwithstanding, he undoubtedly recognized that Lincoln had effectively repudiated him. Furthermore, just as Hurlbut had always overestimated his own military ability, he had underestimated Lincoln's political astuteness. Hurlbut flattered himself that he had shrewdly exploited his close association with Lincoln to obtain brigade command and thereafter promotion, to avoid courts-martial, and implement presidential reconstruction in the West. The fact was that Lincoln had been shrewder, using Hurlbut to mobilize support of the war effort in northern Illinois and gratify the Illinois Clique that had originally supported him.

Meanwhile, Hurlbut had learned that Canby had come to doubt the wisdom of a court-martial on the basis of the Lincoln Commission's findings and that Canby would instead attempt to arrange a further and more thorough examination in Washington. Canby had recognized that he would himself bear a heavy burden of responsibility for his subordinate's conduct. Another board of inquiry, he believed, could conceivably arrive at wholly different conclusions. Canby still regarded Crandall as guilty and forced him to pay a bond of several thousand dollars to guarantee that he would not leave Louisiana. Hurlbut attempted to secure his release. Audaciously, in view of his own precarious position, he argued in a letter to Canby that if no military court had proved Crandall's guilt, Crandall should be released. Surprisingly, Canby obliged Hurlbut but forced Crandall to depart from New Orleans without his cotton proceeds or forfeited bond funds. Hurlbut himself never accounted for the disposition of his own remaining six thousand dollars.[49]

Hurlbut doubted Canby's ability or willingness to procure for him another War Department board of inquiry. In any case, Stanton and Grant had already shown signs of leniency toward Hurlbut, as they had when he faced charges of misconduct in Memphis. On May 11 Grant recommended that Stanton order the court-martial of Colonel Robinson but delay any official examination of Hurlbut pending the development of credible evidence. Stanton agreed with Grant, hesitating even to order a military trial for Robinson. Meanwhile, Hurlbut sought to discredit Smith and Brady (in terms reminiscent of the vituperation he had leveled at Trumbull and Pope in the fall of 1861 and at Hirsch and Beman in spring 1864), while carefully avoiding discussion of the evidence against himself. On May 14 he requested of President Andrew Johnson, through former Illinois governor Yates, now a U.S. senator, the "vindication of my personal honor against secret attacks." Hurlbut denounced Smith for "disgraceful and tyrannical" judicial conduct and accused him of suborning perjured witnesses to gratify his "gross self love" and "arbitrary temper." Hurlbut entreated the new president to grant him an early court-martial in Washington, at which he would expose Smith's "underhanded and cowardly practices."[50] Hurlbut complained to Yates on May 15 that Smith, like John Pope in Missouri, had deliberately attempted to destroy his reputation. Reflecting his almost paranoid distrust of the motives of certain members of the professional officer corps in their dealings with volunteer soldiers such as himself, Hurlbut angrily exclaimed, "A greater atrocity than has been committed by this d——d Copperhead West Pointer has not been known." Calling Smith "a bad combination of known fool & coward," Hurlbut sought Yates's intervention with Johnson to ruin Smith's reputation before a special court-martial could be convened in Washington.[51]

Hurlbut on May 21 also requested Illinois governor Richard J. Oglesby to intercede with Johnson. Smith, Hurlbut charged, had flagrantly violated the fundamental principles of military justice. He had "surrounded himself with bad men and worse women" in procuring "common whores" and forsworn witnesses to level false accusations. Attributing Smith's unscrupulous conduct chiefly to his "exaggerated self love," Hurlbut particularly feared that the unproven allegations of the Smith-Brady report would long "remain as a treasury of uncontradicted scandal for future malicious uses" against him in Illinois. He urged Oglesby to persuade Johnson to act on his (Hurlbut's) earlier request to establish a War Department board of inquiry before which he would rebut Smith's charges and "cashier him from the service."[52]

Hurlbut failed in his efforts to gain another court of inquiry. He had not really anticipated one. Hurlbut understood that Stanton had no serious intention of trying him for offenses against secessionists or Northern cotton speculators in occupied Southern cities; his denunciations of Smith amounted to posturing. Indeed, early in May 1865 Grant himself had cooperated with Stanton to ensure Hurlbut's freedom, although he had recommended that Stanton deny him another court of inquiry. In 1874 an anonymous political enemy of Hurlbut would explain what happened next to Illinois congressman William R. Morrison. Grant directed Maj. Gen. John A. Rawlins, his adjutant general and later the chief of staff of the U.S. Army, in June 1865 to request the secretary of war to "allow Hurlbut to go home & escape a trial; as the war was over & there was a disposition to let everybody off." Further, by this account, Grant and Stanton understood that Hurlbut "could do no further mischief as an officer, & there was a desire to save the army the disgrace of such an exposure," besides Rawlins's generous "wish to save Hurlbut & his family (whom he had formerly known)." On Grant's, Rawlins's, and Stanton's recommendations, Johnson on June 20, 1865, ordered Hurlbut honorably mustered out of the Union army. By September 23, 1865, when Smith and Brady submitted to Stanton the completed Lincoln Commission report, Hurlbut had long since returned to Belvidere.[53] Ultimately, Hurlbut's evasion of military justice in Louisiana resulted primarily from the War Department's recognition of his special status as a "political general" and of his prolonged and intimate association with Lincoln.

Hurlbut's departure from the Union army on honorable terms undoubtedly gratified David L. Phillips, editor of the *Illinois State Journal,* who visited New Orleans late in the winter of 1865. As Hurlbut's sincerest admirer and his most outspoken defender among Illinois Republican journalists since the beginning of the war, Phillips profusely praised Hurlbut's management of military affairs in the Crescent City. He attributed Hurlbut's success to a Southern background and inaccessibility to bribery and venality. "The keen perceptive faculties of the General, with his long legal and military training" as well as his intimate knowledge of "Southern habits, manners and modes of thought," Phillips asserted, had made ruling New Orleans "more easy than to a Northern man." Phillips was alluding to the earlier and highly controversial command of "Beast" Butler, a Massachusetts politician, who had thoroughly estranged the population of New Orleans. Phillips, however, pointedly neglected to mention that Butler's

Massachusetts-born successor, Nathaniel P. Banks, had largely succeeded in a more moderate and conciliatory policy. Further, ignorant of Hurlbut's involvement in profiteering, Phillips contended that Hurlbut's status as a temporary commander in Louisiana had protected him from temptation. Convinced that Hurlbut had steadfastly refused to be "feasted and flattered by designing financial schemers, brainless demagogues, and fashionable fools," Phillips attested to Hurlbut's honesty and probity.[54]

But the harsh truth was that in both Memphis and New Orleans Hurlbut had masterfully concealed a clear pattern of official misconduct under a facade of strict and efficient administration. Hurlbut's indictment and arrest on charges of corruption had stunned Phillips. Refusing to believe that Hurlbut had deceived him, Phillips lashed out at the Smith-Brady commission. In an editorial of June 7 he decried the "persecution" of Hurlbut by a "mousing military commission" that had sought to discredit this "gallant soldier and dashing General" by means of a "roving tribunal, *sitting in secret.*" Phillips further denounced the Lincoln Commission as the "offspring of vindictive malice" harbored by "men who are at heart traitors or disappointed speculators."[55] He had failed to understand that Lincoln's primary aim in creating the commission was to identify and remove from command officers whom he and the War Department suspected of engaging in cotton profiteering while defrauding legitimate traders.

Shortly before his release from military duty, Hurlbut addressed a political rally in New Orleans on the occasion of Governor Wells's return to Louisiana from Washington. Hurlbut told the conservative Unionists that Louisiana had resembled "a dead carcass on which a cloud of vultures had fattened," an unprotected and prostrate temple of wasted national wealth that a cabal of mercenary legislative "thieves" had ruthlessly plundered. Before a state like Louisiana could be restored to the Union, Hurlbut declared, "You must give evidence of sanity—that you are clothed and in your right mind, and sitting at the feet of Jesus." He urged Wells and his supporters to renounce both Republican radicalism and Democratic conservatism but to obey federal military authority and the terms of reconstruction as the surest means of rejoining the Union.

On June 24 Canby ordered Hurlbut to return to Belvidere, where he would receive official notification of his honorable discharge from the army.[56] In the end, Hurlbut could not deliver a farewell address to the Army of the Gulf—as he had not to the Sixteenth Corps in April 1864, after the Fort Pillow massacre—because of his further tarnished reputation.

Hurlbut reached Belvidere on July 4. There he delivered a speech for the Independence Day celebration. A gratified *Belvidere Standard* reported that "the General looks to be in first-rate health" and that the authorities had exonerated

Hurlbut of all charges laid against him in New Orleans. Actually, the *Standard* doubted "if there ever was [*sic*] any charges, more than existed in the fertile imagination of some lying newspaper correspondent." Heartened by the support of the *Standard* and his fellow townsmen, Hurlbut quickly resumed his law practice and political career. He also engaged in numerous social functions, including a journey to Springfield to confer with Richard Oglesby, and a welcome for Ulysses S. Grant to Belvidere and later to Galena.[57] But Hurlbut's connection with New Orleans had not yet concluded. In mid-November 1865, he returned to the Crescent City for reasons now unknown. Back in Belvidere early in December, Hurlbut informed the *Belvidere Standard* that he had perceived commercial and entrepreneurial activity there to be "extraordinarily lively, and politics rather more active and rabidly Secesh, because less restrained" than had been the case under his command. Amazingly, Hurlbut audaciously claimed that his—and Canby's—policies had worked to suppress secessionist elements among the Free State party and Lincoln's Ten Per Cent Plan government. Actually, of course, Hurlbut had systematically undermined the liberal Hahn and had effectively schemed to install the archconservative James Wells. The "rabidly Secesh" political maneuvering in postwar New Orleans that Hurlbut perceived and denounced had actually arisen as a result of his own repression of the racially enlightened and socially and fiscally responsible Hahn government.[58]

A calculating inconsistency of policy and a willful perversion of power marked the course of Hurlbut's final command in wartime New Orleans. Traditionally a moderately conservative Whig and Republican politician, he opposed Lincoln's free state government in Louisiana because he considered it excessively liberal; he consistently denounced its allegedly reckless fiscal and monetary policy and its too-generous provision for freedmen. If Hurlbut had conquered, or at least learned better to control, his excessive drinking, he had not demonstrated the ability to resist the temptation of cotton profiteering. Perhaps Lincoln, had he survived Booth's attack, would himself have granted Hurlbut an honorable discharge from the army, but he had repudiated Hurlbut for his betrayal of trust, obstruction of the war effort, and profiteering. As for Grant, in late June 1865 he still had a large measure of favor or forbearance for Hurlbut. Had Grant convened the special court-martial that Hurlbut had importunately requested, it probably would have convicted him. Oblivious to the narrowness of his escape, Hurlbut would thereafter depend as heavily on Grant's patronage as he had on Lincoln's before and during the war.

CHAPTER SIX

The Passing of a Diplomatic Partisan

The prairie community of Belvidere, Illinois, had acquired a more sophisticated look in the twenty years since Hurlbut had arrived there as a fugitive from his native Charleston, South Carolina. By 1865, although still an agricultural town set in the midst of vast expanses of rich corn-growing farmland, Belvidere had expanded from a population of only nine hundred in 1845 to over three thousand by 1865, including large numbers of recent Swedish immigrants. A newly constructed system of sidewalks and paved roads relieved the difficulties occasioned by seasonal mud and snow. There were fashionable new buildings and homes, six churches, two commodious assembly halls, the imposing First National Bank, and the admirable residence of Judge Allen C. Fuller, who had served as the adjutant general of Illinois during the war.[1]

General Hurlbut and his wife Sophronia and son George returned to their modest, two-story, redbrick home late in June 1865. He reestablished his legal practice, opening a new law office upon the upper floor of the Murch & Brothers General Store building, but he assigned what few cases he obtained (chiefly veterans' claims for federal pensions, land disputes, and probate conflicts) to Edward H. Talbott, his nephew-in-law and junior partner.[2] Meanwhile, perhaps envious of General Fuller's mansion (and perhaps also of Joseph Russell Jones's opulent Italian villa–style residence in Galena), Hurlbut early determined to build a home that befitted a man of his rank. Decidedly not a connoisseur of Victorian architectural styles, Hurlbut hired contractors who, with his cheerful approval, planned an elaborate mansion for a lot his wife had purchased in 1864. His new home on this property, adjacent to his older and humbler residence, would emphasize his improved financial fortunes. The *Belvidere Standard* reported in September 1867, "Gen. Hurlbut, we notice, has raised the frame of his new residence. It looks like a large building and we expect will be something quite handsome."[3] When it was finished in 1868, the three-story, wood-and-brick, Gothic Revival mansion exhibited (besides its imposing portico and balustrade that enclosed the entire porch and house) such classic Victorian architectural features as gables, bargeboards, and lofty chimneys. The large interior contained spacious dining and reading rooms, a kitchen, and a master bedroom—all lavishly furnished. Hurlbut's fireplace-equipped study included a law library of seventy-five books, while stables in the rear sheltered his riding horses and milk cows. Hurlbut had built the most opulent house in Belvidere, a residence that, observers agreed, surpassed in ostentation even Fuller's mansion.[4]

Hurlbut also purchased (for $625) four large pieces of land near his mansion. He assumed that proposed new railroad construction (particularly the extension of the Beloit & Caledonia Railroad to connect Belvidere and Madison, Wisconsin) would substantially increase the value of the property and more than compensate for his having overspent on his splendid new house. But Hurlbut's investment scheme failed. Desperate to recoup his losses, as late as August 1873 he urged local entrepreneurs to build more railroads, but unavailingly; he found himself forced to sell his property, piece by piece, to satisfy creditors.[5]

During the war Hurlbut had frequently complained of his poverty on a major general's pay. He managed to accumulate sufficient funds to construct a grand mansion and purchase property in Belvidere, but now he found it necessary to obtain an elective or appointive office for financial relief. Encouraged by Illinois senators Trumbull and Yates to seek the Republican state convention's nomination as congressman-at-large from the extensive First Congressional District, Hurlbut worked to consolidate electoral support among his rural constituency.

On July 4, 1866, exploiting Belvidere's Independence Day celebration, Hurlbut delivered an address that, rhetorically at least, continued the partisanship that he had begun in Illinois in 1845. He praised the martyred Lincoln as a true "child of the American soil" and the "plain citizen President," a man whose Confederate counterpart, Jefferson Davis, was the "son of Satan." Vigorously waving the "bloody shirt," Hurlbut also attacked President Andrew Johnson's "new fangled theory" of "restoration" of the conquered, but still seceded, Southern states. Defying powerful Republicans in Congress who wanted a harshly punitive process of political reconstruction, Johnson had also thwarted, Hurlbut charged, the will of the Northern people. Hurlbut won "three hearty cheers" of approval. Even earlier, however, in December 1865, Hurlbut had decried Johnson's reconstruction policies. In a letter to Congressman Thaddeus Stevens of Pennsylvania, the leading radical Republican in the House of Representatives, who had advanced the theory that Congress should treat the former seceded states as "conquered provinces," Hurlbut had asserted that the Northern people showed little interest in "Constitutional hair splitting as to the legal status of rebeldom & its communities." Rather, Hurlbut had urged Stevens to enforce the subordination of the rebellious states to the "National authority," block the admission to Congress of Southern members-elect (whom Hurlbut termed "all the old standard false leaders"), and "tie up the Executive by plain clear law" in order to preserve the fruits of victory.[6]

Unfortunately for Hurlbut, his electioneering could not overcome the challenge from John A. Logan, former general and a War Democrat turned radical Republican. The forty-year-old Logan, who had also fought in the Mexican War as a lieutenant of Illinois volunteers, had in the Civil War served under Grant in Tennessee and Mississippi (coming under Hurlbut's command at Shiloh and Hatchie Bridge) and under Sherman in Georgia and the Carolinas. He had ended his military career with the rank of major general of volunteers as commander of the Army of the Tennessee. Effectively exploiting his fame, the adoration of veterans, and support in the central and southern sections of Illinois, at the state Republican convention in Springfield in August 1866 Logan won unanimous nomination. In the November election Logan would soundly defeat his Democratic opponent.[7] Hurlbut had encountered the man who, as a radical, would be his arch political rival in the postwar period, as Elihu B. Washburne, an ideological conservative, had been in the antebellum years.

Hurlbut's unsuccessful campaign against Logan, however, coincided with his rapid accession as the national commander of the newly formed "Grand Army of the Republic" (GAR), a humanitarian and patriotic organization dedicated to the relief of needy Union veterans. Dr. Benjamin F. Stephenson, former regimental surgeon of the 14th Illinois Volunteers, had called for a convention to meet at Springfield on July 12, 1866, to promote efforts to ameliorate the plight of suffering veterans and preserve the institutions of republican government. Actually, the GAR had arisen from an astute political strategy crafted by Illinois governor Richard J. Oglesby and General Logan. Oglesby sought to exploit the GAR to promote Logan, who in turn hoped to use it to enter the Senate in the next election, unseating the more conservative Lyman Trumbull. (Trumbull's encouragement of Hurlbut to contend with Logan for a House seat probably resulted from the challenge he himself anticipated from Logan.) Hurlbut's own motives in the GAR were hardly altruistic; he saw in it a means of improving his prospects for the Republican nomination as congressman-at-large. Hurlbut eagerly attended the GAR convention in July. There he helped to frame its preliminary constitution and served on the Committee on Resolutions; in the latter capacity, Hurlbut proposed immediate and unconditional opposition to Johnson's lenient policy of reconstruction. The convention permanently established Springfield as the GAR's national headquarters and called upon Union veterans across the North to meet in national convention in Indianapolis in November 1866.[8]

At Indianapolis, Hurlbut served as presiding officer and chairman of the Select Committee on Permanent Organization. He promoted the incorporation of a radical Republican group, the "Soldiers and Sailors National Union League of Washington," into the GAR. Finally, he formulated policy concerning the payment and allocation of membership dues. Hurlbut specified that individual members would pay a dollar a year to their local posts; the several posts would pay 10 percent of their annual revenue to the regional departments; the regional departments would pay 10 percent of their yearly revenue directly to the national headquarters. As a reward for his efforts, Hurlbut was unanimously elected as the GAR's national commander.[9]

Hurlbut's selection suited both the founding Illinois members and the nationwide rank and file. Hurlbut hailed from Illinois and had commanded the "Fighting Fourth Division" of the Army of the Tennessee, which had contained Illinois regiments, whose veterans genuinely admired and esteemed their old commander. Moreover, Hurlbut was available; most other prominent Illinois Clique members held political or other office. Hurlbut's conspicuous address to the Illinois Freemasonry in Springfield before the war and prominent participation in a chapter of the "Royal Masons" in Belvidere shortly after the war increased his appeal among GAR Freemasons. Accepting the honor, and still acting as the presiding officer, "Comrade Hurlbut" formally closed the convention by pledging "to do what might be in his power to advance the order."[10]

Characteristically, Hurlbut quickly began to mismanage and even undermine the new organization. The GAR's permanent constitution of November 1866 called for annual conventions in January; Hurlbut refused to summon a national "encampment" in 1867. The eastern departments had soundly rejected his amendment to the preliminary constitution regulating dues. In particular, they strenuously objected to supporting Hurlbut's administration in Springfield while he continually failed to answer requests for instructions, rosters, rules, and for supplies. By the summer of 1867, the eastern wing of the GAR had raised a groundswell of protest against Hurlbut's apparent negligence. Dr. Stephenson, adjutant general of the GAR, declared that the convention of

November 1866 had rendered unnecessary a convention in January 1867 and that the eastern departments were isolating themselves. An extraordinary session of the "Boys in Blue," as the GAR members called themselves, met in Philadelphia in the fall of 1867; there James B. McKean, the GAR's senior vice commander, threatened to convene an independent national encampment.

Reluctantly, Hurlbut yielded and scheduled a convention in Philadelphia in January 1868. One hundred eight-six delegates represented twenty-one departments at the encampment; Hurlbut presided over three consecutive evening sessions and coordinated the floor proceedings and the production of committee reports. Reflecting the increasingly partisan spirit of the organization itself, Hurlbut addressed the convention and urged the Boys in Blue to support the presidential candidacy of Ulysses S. Grant. He denounced President Johnson's determined opposition to the radical Republican–supported Military Reconstruction Acts of 1867. The convention adopted a resolution that endorsed Grant but proceeded to elect Congressman Logan as national commander (in 1872, owing to his lack of active participation since 1868, the GAR would cancel Hurlbut's membership entirely).[11] Hurlbut had wasted an important opportunity; his sorry record as the GAR's national commander had resulted partly from his absorption in the construction of his mansion and his run for a seat in Congress. But it also reflected a lack of administrative ability or interest; Hurlbut had depended upon the inefficient Stephenson to manage GAR affairs. Hurlbut's short tenure as GAR national commander produced only dissension and factionalism.

A further distraction in the summer of 1866 was nomination by a Boone County Republican convention to the Illinois House of Representatives. Again waving the bloody shirt, Hurlbut easily overwhelmed his Democratic opponent at the polls. In contrast to a majority of his House colleagues, who "impress one unfavorably as to ability," Hurlbut struck the *Illinois State Journal* as a prepossessing figure, with a "compact, short, rotund body, smooth, round, pleasant face, [and] large head." As a legislator he had shown himself to be "fiery, brilliant, sound, eloquent in debate."[12] However, Hurlbut early dismayed his constituency when he supported a controversial bill to build a new state capitol in Springfield. The Illinois House, Republicans and Democrats alike, having rejected proposals to remove the capital to Peoria, Chicago, or Decatur, had finally agreed to appropriate three million dollars for a new statehouse by 1880. On April 21, 1868, Hurlbut attempted to defend his action in the *Belvidere Northwestern,* owned and edited by his young law partner, Edward Talbott. However, the *Belvidere Standard,* which had vigorously defended Hurlbut's controversial wartime record, criticized him. Declaring that he had "very much misrepresented the sentiments of the citizens" of Boone County upon the state

capitol bill, the *Standard* complained that they would have to pay heavier taxes
to raise "a vast architectural pile to adorn the little benighted hamlet known as
Springfield."[13] (The new capitol was to remain under construction long into the
1870s, crippled by deceitful contractors, faulty workmanship, and a shortage of
funds.) Hurlbut spent the rest of the winter of 1868 in Washington lobbying
influential congressmen for millions of dollars for navigation improvements to
the Illinois River and more locks and dams along the Illinois and Michigan
Canal. (He failed to obtain funding for the river project, but late in June 1868
Congress would allocate eighty-five thousand dollars for capital improvements
to the canal.)[14]

Meanwhile, the ever-ambitious Hurlbut had set his sights upon the governorship. His lobbying in Washington had ingratiated himself with Governor
Oglesby. Hurlbut reasoned that if Senator Yates, whose worsening alcoholism
had now nearly ruined his health, could not finish his term of office, the Illinois legislature would probably elect Oglesby as his successor, and that in turn
Oglesby would name him to the governorship. Nevertheless, as early as March
1867, Hurlbut had warned Yates to desist from heavy drinking and fulfill a
pledge of abstinence that Yates had made to Illinois voters. Hurlbut reminded
Yates that he himself had been constantly "'tempted in all things like as you' &
know how to feel for and with you," and assured him that "fame, home, family,
just influences all—should and will inspire you to whatever strength may be
needed" to renounce drinking and to strive against "'the world the flesh and the
devil.'"[15] Yates could not keep his pledge of abstinence and by early 1868 appeared to have reached the brink of death. "There is likely to be a vacancy in
the Senate," Hurlbut advised Oglesby in February 1868. "Yates cannot live three
months in Washington"; he would shortly "die like a dog . . . an early & wretched
death."[16] (Yates would in fact complete his senatorial term, drinking himself to
death only in September 1873.)

Hurlbut perceived in the rumored withdrawal of Gen. John M. Palmer from
the 1868 Illinois gubernatorial race another, and much better, opportunity. He
had by now concluded that Logan, not Oglesby, would probably succeed Yates
in the Senate. Accordingly, early in February 1868 Hurlbut informed Logan
that he proposed to pursue the gubernatorial nomination if Logan would support his candidacy. Not hearing from Logan, Hurlbut shifted his target to a seat
in Congress in a race against a radical Republican, Gen. John F. Farnsworth of
Kane County, west of Chicago. It was a prudent move: Palmer subsequently
declared his intention to run for governor after all, and Hurlbut quickly withdrew his name. Soundly defeated by Farnsworth in April 1868, Hurlbut then
sought the position of attorney general in a prospective Republican (presum-

ably Palmer) administration, but this prize also eluded him. The Republican nominating convention, held in Peoria in May, named him as one of the state's Republican presidential electors-at-large and as a member of the 1868 Republican National Platform's Subcommittee on Government Finance in Chicago, but Hurlbut failed to obtain a high position in Palmer's administration.

Thereafter, he no longer importuned Oglesby, Palmer, or other prominent figures for their patronage. Instead he turned to his old rival, Elihu B. Washburne, for help in gaining the position of U.S. attorney for the Northern District of Illinois—the post Lincoln had denied him in March 1861. Following Grant's election as president in November 1868, Hurlbut asked Washburne, as Hurlbut put it, "simply to ask of the men who have known me and who are near the fountainhead, to hold my pitcher when the stream begins to run." But neither Washburne nor Palmer could help Hurlbut, who returned to his declining law practice in Belvidere.[17]

Hurlbut, from 1865 to 1868, had reflected characteristic opportunism, both in seeking office and in attaching himself to increasingly influential new members of the Illinois Clique like Oglesby and Logan. An inept GAR administrator, a pork barrel legislator, and an unenterprising civil attorney, in the immediate postwar period Hurlbut had only his usual congeniality, adaptability, and loyalty to a circle of equally ambitious but more successful Illinois politicians.

The accession of Grant to the presidency in March 1869 revived Hurlbut's career. Generously rewarding Washburne, Jones, and Hurlbut for their political support and personal loyalty, Grant named Washburne to be ambassador to France, Jones as minister to Belgium, and Hurlbut minister to Colombia. The Washburne and Jones nominations produced acrimonious debates in the Senate prior to their confirmation, but the Hurlbut nomination gained approval without strong opposition.[18] By appointing Hurlbut to the Colombian post and giving him explicit instructions to negotiate a Panama Canal treaty, the president hoped to fulfill an ambition he had entertained for eighteen years. In the spring of 1851, Grant had trudged with troops of the 4th U.S. Infantry Regiment through the malarial jungles of Panama on a journey from New York to Fort Vancouver, Oregon Territory. That experience had convinced him of the need for a canal across the Isthmus of Panama. Shortly after the Civil War, he had attempted to obtain the permission of the Colombian government to conduct a land survey to determine the feasibility of a canal. When he appointed Hurlbut to the Colombian portfolio, Grant was still seeking authority to make that survey.[19] In the meantime, Grant instructed Hurlbut to negotiate another Isthmian treaty, since in February 1869 the senate of Colombia (of which Panama was then a province) had defeated the Cushing Convention of

January 14, 1869, which would have reaffirmed the U.S.-Colombian Treaty of 1846, which in turn had guaranteed the American right to march troops and transport goods across the Isthmus of Panama in exchange for the neutrality of any canal built by the United States, and for express assurances of Colombia's sovereignty over its increasingly rebellious province. However, the Colombian government had expressed its willingness to renew negotiations with the United States after the accession of Grant's administration.[20]

Having prepared himself and his family for an arduous journey to Bogota, the Colombian capital, Hurlbut proceeded to Washington early in August 1869 for consultations with Secretary of State Hamilton Fish. He also met with Caleb Cushing, who had been attorney general in the Johnson administration and the architect of the Cushing Convention, as well as Santos Acosta, the Colombian minister to the United States. Learning from Cushing that Hurlbut's predecessor, Peter J. Sullivan, had unsuccessfully attempted to obtain funds from the State Department with which to influence Colombian journalists, diplomats, and legislators, Hurlbut determined to procure such funds for his own use. Grant himself approved their disbursement, though he insisted that Hurlbut collect the money from a State Department official in New York, not in Washington. Having exchanged other memorandums with Fish in which he advocated the creation of an international consortium to control the construction and operation of the prospective Panama Canal—a plan that Fish quickly dismissed—Hurlbut and his family set sail for Colombia. Arriving there early in November 1869, Hurlbut presented his credentials to President Eustorgio Salgar and urged him to cooperate with him in negotiating an agreement that would guarantee exclusive American construction and maintenance of a canal. He diligently began cultivating the favor and support of influential journalists in Bogota, including the editors of the *Diario oficial, El liberal,* and *La revista de Colombia.* Hurlbut soon assured Fish that, furnished with American greenbacks, Bogota editors would begin advocating the construction of a "canal and the duties of this Republic to that work." After depleting his five-thousand-dollar fund, Hurlbut negotiated a protocol with the Salgar regime, which he and Salgar signed on January 26, 1870.[21]

The Hurlbut Convention, in preliminary terms, accorded to the United States all the privileges that the Cushing Convention had granted; in addition, Article XI provided for free passage of American troops and warships through the prospective canal during times of peace and war. Further, the armed forces of nations that had declared themselves at war with the United States or Colombia could not enter the canal. The Salgar government also conceded to the American navy the right to build and maintain docks and repair yards at each termi-

Hamilton Fish, secretary of state under President Grant. Prints and Photographs Division, Library of Congress.

nus of the canal. Finally, the Hurlbut Convention asserted the neutrality of the projected Panama Canal and again guaranteed Colombia's sovereignty over Panama.[22] Hurlbut had faithfully and effectively executed the instructions of President Grant and Secretary Fish, negotiating with the Salgar government a canal treaty that, in its substantive terms, favored the United States. Unfortunately, it also severely threatened the interests of European powers, particularly England and France. Consequently the Colombian Senate approved the Hurlbut Convention but, bowing to heavy pressure by European diplomats in Bogota (in particular the British chargé d' affaires, Robert Bunch) and in fearing augmented American economic, commercial, and military influence in Panama, early in July 1870 attached seventeen amendments to Article XI providing for English and French participation in the construction and operation of a Panamanian canal.[23]

The U.S. Senate Committee on Foreign Affairs objected to the amendments to Article XI, and the proposed treaty never reached the Senate floor for a vote.[24] The failure of the Hurlbut Convention sprang partly from Grant's and Fish's irresolution and ineptitude in working with the U.S. Senate toward an acceptable compromise. They also misunderstood Colombia's dependence upon large European loans and markets, and of the Salgar regime's dread of European retaliation if it extended overly favorable canal rights to the United States. Hurlbut should have urged an agreement that would threaten the vital interests of neither Colombia nor European powers, instead of promoting the extreme American position. Nonetheless, he blamed Grant alone.

Late in September 1871 Hurlbut criticized Grant, who he believed had betrayed him, in a letter to David L. Phillips, the former editor of the *Illinois State Journal* and a close friend of Horace White, who edited the *Chicago Tribune*. Besides blaming Grant for the failure of the canal treaty, Hurlbut attacked what a number of other Republicans, as well as Democrats, had already begun to denounce as "Grantism"—the president's enforcement of Reconstruction in the defeated South, his favoritism and flagrant misuse of even the much-abused spoils system, his diplomatic adventurism toward Great Britain in respect to the island of Santo Domingo, and his high tariff. In particular, Hurlbut believed Grant's policies had divided and weakened the Republican party across the North and simultaneously revived the Northern Democracy, especially over the racial question. "There comes the Everlasting African," Hurlbut complained to Phillips. In his opinion, Northerners had grown "exceedingly bored" with "the nigger" and "awfully tired of his special friends & prophets." Reminding Phillips of the Republican party's significant contributions to the black man's freedom, suffrage, and welfare, Hurlbut nonetheless asserted that the party had "done enough and it is time he [the black man] should walk alone. . . . The Country will not drynurse this nonpromising youngster any longer." Hurlbut suggested to Phillips that if the black man could not survive the challenges of his newly won freedom in the increasingly reactionary Southern states, he must perish, "as all weak & worthless races inevitably do." Finally, Hurlbut condemned Grant's military rule in the South, declaring, "The time for the dominion of force is over—the dominion of law, equal justice, and as far as possible oblivion for the past is on us."[25] Thus Hurlbut had secretly repudiated Grant and had begun his flirtation with the "Liberal Republican" revolt of 1872.

Hurlbut was involved in two grave maritime incidents that occurred within

Colombian waters—episodes in which he would express his chauvinistic and decidedly jingoistic attitudes toward the governments of Colombia and of Spain. Hurlbut would eventually succeed in procuring compensation from Colombia for losses sustained by owners of an American ship, the *Montijo,* at the hands of Panamanian rebels. But he would fail, ultimately, to ensure American naval protection of the Cuban-owned *Virginius* from the Spanish authorities who, in 1873, would cruelly execute its crew of fifty-three Cuban sailors, even though their ship had flown (if illegally) American colors.

In the *Montijo* affair of June 1871, the Colombian foreign secretary, Felix Zapata, vehemently denied his country's alleged responsibility for the seizure of the ship by Panamanian secessionists. Hurlbut, who tried but altogether failed to negotiate a prompt settlement of the dispute with Zapata, denounced Colombia as "an organized anarchy, most skillfully directed to the perpetuation of revolution and the consecration of secession." In the *Virginius* affair, Hurlbut urged Fish to threaten Spain with war; he himself ordered the commanding officer of an American warship, the *Kansas,* to protect the *Virginius* against Spanish search or seizure.[26]

Despite such bellicosity, Hurlbut performed well as his country's ranking diplomatic officer in Colombia before departing in April 1872 on leave and returning to Belvidere (he resigned his commission in the diplomatic corps shortly thereafter). He aggressively negotiated a canal treaty with the Salgar government in Bogota—though he utilized the questionable method of influencing, perhaps buying outright, the favorable opinion of journalists and legislators to achieve his goal. Moreover, he clearly demonstrated a realistic and perceptive understanding of the close interrelationships between international power politics, competing hemispheric and regional economic and commercial interests, and the spread of insurrection and civil war in Panama. Thus, Hurlbut had shown promise as a diplomat, if he could restrain his jingoistic impulses and change his view of diplomacy as essentially a larger arena for partisan rivalry and conflict. Unfortunately, he would adopt this same attitude in Peru in 1881 and almost embroil the United States in war.

After arriving in Belvidere in May 1872, Hurlbut began to lay the foundation for another bid for a seat in Congress, this time from the recently created Fourth Congressional District, which embraced Boone, Lake, Kane, McHenry, De Kalb, and Winnebago counties. Early in June he delivered two well-received lectures on Colombia to townsmen in the First Baptist Church, of which he and his wife and son remained members. "As a whole his portrait of the people was not flattering," the *Belvidere Standard* reported, "though they have some good traits." On June 11 Hurlbut showed off colorful Colombian coffee beans and "curious and valuable woods" that he had brought from Bogota. He also attended the Old Settlers Annual Picnic in Belvidere on June 12 and reminisced about his early days in Boone County.[27]

Apart from such preliminary electioneering, Hurlbut faced a serious ideological dilemma. In May 1872, the national Liberal Republican convention at Cincinnati had chosen Horace Greeley, the eccentric and controversial editor of the *New York Tribune,* to lead the Liberal charge (which Democrats supported) against Grant in the November 1872 election. Widespread discontent in the Republican party over "Grantism" disaffected Republicans including Charles Sumner, Carl Shurz, and Lyman Trumbull to create a reform movement that observers called the "Liberal Republican" party. Their advocacy of civil service and federal tariff reform, universal pardon for prominent Confederates, and a prompt withdrawal of federal troops from occupied southern states also commanded substantial Democratic support.[28] But Hurlbut found it necessary or expedient to suppress his political dissent and proclaim support of Grant. By condemning Greeley's defection, applauding Grant's loyalty to the Republican party, and winning—at the last moment—the support of De Kalb County's whole delegation, Hurlbut defeated William Lathrop (a strong Washburne supporter in the 1850s) at the Republican nominating convention, held in June 1872 at Elgin, in Kane County.[29]

Flushed with victory over Lathrop, Hurlbut attended a Grant rally in Madison, Wisconsin, on Independence Day, 1872. There he delivered an anti-Greeley speech before several thousand Army of the Tennessee veterans who had gathered to support Grant for reelection. But, apparently unknown to Hurlbut, the rally's organizers desired to appease and possibly win back numerous Greeley men in their midst by carefully refraining from denouncing either the Liberal Republican party leaders or their reform movement. Perhaps they did not intend for Hurlbut to ascend the speaker's platform, from which he called the Liberal Republicans a cabal of "burglars" who sought to rob the country of the benefits of Northern victory. He also castigated Greeley as a "slippery, egotistical" editor whose "growing imbecility and most egregious vanity" threatened to disrupt the party of Lincoln and Grant. Disparaging Liberal Republicans as either "great fools or great knaves," Hurlbut quoted Milton in warning that Greeley could yet "crawl like a toad, or whisper evil counsel in our dreaming ears. Let but the spear of Ithuriel touch him" (a reference to the archangel Ithuriel in *Paradise Lost,* Book IV, whose spear exposed all deceit), and he would spring up revealed in all his "dark malignity." Loudly heckled by Greeley supporters, Hurlbut left the speaker's platform and boarded a train for Belvidere.[30]

Hurlbut sustained a barrage of criticism from Democratic and Liberal Republican editors for his speech. The *Madison Democrat* called his ostensibly patriotic oration "a political harangue, pregnable in its argument, abusive in its censure, low in its rhetoric," prepared during one of his "hilarious conditions, induced by a superabundance of tangle-leg." The Republican *Madison Journal* agreed that Hurlbut had politicized the Independence Day proceedings, but it avoided reviving memories of Hurlbut's wartime intemperance. However, the *Chicago Tribune,* edited by the Liberal Republican Horace White, exercised no such restraint. Angered by Hurlbut's speech but even more incensed over his apostasy (he had obtained from Phillips Hurlbut's September 1871 letter expressing his opposition to "Grantism"), White declared that Hurlbut's oration had not "even the questionable excuse that it was delivered after dinner." Describing Hurlbut as "a man of grossly intemperate habits, unless he has improved at the Bogota reformatory," White expressed doubt as to whether Hurlbut had fallen "more under the influence of nervous excitement and paroxysmal insanity at Bogota or at Elgin." For the rest of the campaign White would challenge Hurlbut to publish the letter to Phillips, threatening to publish it himself if Hurlbut refused to withdraw from his congressional race. White doubted that Hurlbut would have the boldness to publish his letter to Phillips; that would show Judge Allen C. Fuller and "the smaller creatures" of the Republican party in Hurlbut's congressional district "how vigorously the General can fight when he undertakes to slay vermin of more exalted rank," such as Grant. In the end, both Greeley's candidacy and White's strategy failed; in the November elections Grant overwhelmed Greeley, and Hurlbut crushed his Democratic opponent.[31]

Winning a seat in the House of Representatives was an ambition he had cherished since 1852. Hurlbut hastened to Washington late in November 1873 to take his seat in the Forty-third Congress. He stayed in a boarding house at 810 Twelfth Street, where he lodged and dined with Congressmen Charles B. Farwell and William R. Ray of Illinois, Robert S. Hale of New York, and James Monroe of Ohio. In the House chamber, he and his colleagues supported the election of James G. Blaine of Maine as speaker.[32] Hurlbut quickly gained recognition when he sponsored a compromise bill to deal with a controversial question of congressional pay. The previous Congress had in early 1873 passed what many editors across the country had denounced as a Republican "Salary Grab" bill ($7,500 a year for each representative). With droll humor, Hurlbut persuaded the House to take but a thousand-dollar increase in pay, a raise from five to six thousand. Having displayed his ability as a legislator and coalition builder, Hurlbut addressed other issues. He advocated federal legislation to strengthen the regulation of the increasingly monopolistic railroads; he urged a more vigorous prosecution of the war in the West against Plains Indians who impeded the movement of American settlers beyond the Mississippi River; and he called for an investigation of scandalous War Department contract frauds. Finally, in March 1874, Speaker Blaine selected Hurlbut to head the honorary committee to attend the funeral of Charles Sumner in the Senate chamber and escort the body to Boston for burial.[33] This appointment was ironic; Sumner had voted against Hurlbut's confirmation as a major general, and Hurlbut during the war had adopted policies, and expressed views, regarding blacks that Sumner would have found anathema.

Convinced that he had served his constituency with distinction in Congress, Hurlbut confidently returned to Belvidere in July 1874 to campaign for a second term. (Despite Horace White's opposition, Hurlbut would defeat both Charles W. Marsh of De Kalb County—his rival for the Republican nomination—and also Farnsworth of Kane County, who had now turned Democrat.)[34] Hurlbut returned to Washington late in November 1874 to attend the second session of the Forty-third Congress. Appointed by Blaine to a House committee investigating bloody race riots at Vicksburg in December 1874, Hurlbut and four colleagues immediately proceeded to Mississippi. For two weeks they compiled sworn testimony from 115 persons who had either witnessed or participated in the repeated clashes between black and white militia companies in Warren County.

In September, Mississippi Democrats had regained control from the "carpetbaggers" of the municipal government of Vicksburg. In December white Democrats had attempted to overthrow as well the black-dominated government of Warren County. According to the committee's majority report, white partisans of Warren County instigated disturbances. Hurlbut would join in accusing "White Line" armed bands of Mississippi Democrats (most of whom had served as Confederate soldiers) of attempting to deprive black citizens of their constitutionally guaranteed civil and political rights. Hurlbut had never before shown an interest in the plight of blacks in the deep South states, but he seized upon the Vicksburg riots as an opportunity to reaffirm his opposition to the Democratic party and his support of Grant's policy of military Reconstruction. In the months following, Hurlbut engaged in heated debates with Democrats on the House floor, where he supported Republican-sponsored "Force Bills" that authorized military suppression of the widespread intimidation of and violence against black voters in the South.[35]

In 1876 Hurlbut turned his main efforts to civil service reform and his prospects for reelection. Hurlbut's participation in a civil service controversy that involved his former patron, Joseph Russell Jones, drew attention to the disinte-

Stephen A. Hurlbut, diplomat and Republican congressman. From Stephen
A. Hurlbut, L.H.D., *Between Peace and War* (1953).

gration of the Illinois Clique of Republican politicians since the deaths of Lincoln and Yates and the Liberal defection of Trumbull. In 1871, Congress had
created a civil service commission that had sought to abolish the "spoils system"
of filling political offices, but Grant had effectively resisted its recommendations
for reform. Although Hurlbut himself had never supported civil service reform
(having benefited from the spoils system since 1861), as a member of the House
Civil Service Committee he found it necessary to do so. In 1869, Jones had been
on diplomatic service in Belgium; before that he had been a broker for Benjamin J. Sweet, once commandant of the Camp Douglas prison in Chicago,

and for George W. Campbell of Chicago. Jones had arranged to have Grant make Sweet the head of the U.S. Pension Agency in Chicago if Sweet would employ Campbell as his clerk, at an annual salary of six thousand dollars. Sweet hired Campbell and therefore received the federal post. But Campbell had continued to draw full pay from Sweet even after quitting in 1870.[36] Returning to America in 1875, Jones had declined the position of secretary of the interior but had accepted the lesser post of port collector in Chicago. At this point an obscure and disappointed Pension Agency office seeker, William Tourtelotte of Chicago, learned of Jones's secret agreement with Sweet and Campbell and filed charges against him with the House Civil Service Committee.[37]

Hurlbut, who had forfeited Jones's patronage in 1861 by his intemperance in Civil War Missouri, informed Jones of the charges, attempting either to force him to resign or at least protect Grant from further embarrassment and scandal. Jones, however, summoned before the House Civil Service Committee in June 1876, strongly denied wrongdoing. Fearing that the committee had already determined to ruin him, Jones sought to destroy Hurlbut's credibility by releasing his own statement on the Chicago Pension Agency affair and reviving stories of Hurlbut's intemperance and profiteering during the Civil War. His efforts, however, failed. Former Illinois governor Richard Oglesby, who had succeeded Richard Yates in the Senate in 1873, demanded Jones's resignation as the collector; Grant also urged Jones to resign. Perceiving a conspiracy among Hurlbut, Oglesby, Logan, and other Illinois Republicans in Washington to hound him from office, Jones angrily complained to Grant: *"I can't afford to be thus publicly disgraced by you!"* Jones would defy Grant until 1877, when he attempted to defeat Logan's reelection by bribing Illinois legislators; Grant threatened forcible removal from office if he should succeed. Jones would remain in office long after the end of Grant's presidency in March 1877, virtually banished from the Illinois Clique.[38] However, the close ring of Illinois Republicans would lose much of its vitality by the conclusion of Grant's presidency.

Hurlbut now returned his attention to his uncertain reelection prospects. Republican party leaders having rejected a possible third term for Grant, Hurlbut obliged Blaine, himself a presidential hopeful, by inducing Robert G. Ingersoll, former Illinois attorney general, to place Blaine's name into nomination at the Republican national convention in Cincinnati. Then, to avert a threatened movement of the Illinois delegation to Elihu B. Washburne, the state's favorite son, Hurlbut hurried to Springfield, where, according to the Democratic *Chicago Times,* he "'fixed' the state delegation" and "knocked the wind out of Joe Medill, Russell Jones" and all the rest of the "Washburne crowd."[39] Having secured the Illinois delegation for Blaine, Hurlbut proceeded to Cincinnati, where he heard Ingersoll introduce Blaine. "Like an armed warrior, like a plumed knight," Ingersoll proclaimed, Blaine had confronted his opponents in Congress and had hurled "his shining lance full and fair, against the brazen foreheads of the defamers of his country, and the maligners of his honor." Despite Ingersoll's eloquence and Blaine's convention strategy, Rutherford B. Hayes of Ohio won the nomination.[40]

Reconciled to the defeat of Blaine, Hurlbut counseled Hayes's campaign managers on strategy (particularly for carrying Indiana), denounced the opposition, and ridiculed Governor Samuel J. Tilden of New York, the Democratic candidate.[41] Unfortunately for Hurlbut, these preoccupations gave Republican rivals in his home district time to campaign against his renomination for Congress. His Republican opponent, William Lathrop, defeated Hurlbut at the convention in Elgin by a narrow plurality. Stunned, Hurlbut nevertheless determined to defeat both Lathrop and their common Democratic opponent in the fall election by offering himself as an independent candidate. William H. Smith of Chicago warned Hayes late in October 1876 that division in the Republican ranks in the Fourth Congressional District—as well as in the Ninth Congressional District, where the Republican party's candidate was Richard H. Whiting—would reduce his congressional support should he win the presidency. Smith, the founder of the Western Associated Press and Hayes's principal adviser in Illinois, informed Hayes, "There are two Rep. Congressional districts, too, in danger of being thrown away on account of the selfishness of two men—Hurlbut in [the] Fourth, and Whiting in the Peoria district. . . . Everything possible has been done to heal the breach, but in vain."[42]

But Smith's forebodings proved incorrect. In the November 1876 election, a heavy Republican voter turnout in the Fourth Congressional District elected Lathrop over both Hurlbut and General Farnsworth, even in Hurlbut's Boone County. Acknowledging his defeat, Hurlbut nonetheless urged the Republican presidential electors in Illinois (who included Judge Allen C. Fuller) to adopt an open rather than a secret balloting system, which the Democrats were demanding. The presidential election was bitterly contested; Tilden had gained 184 electoral votes to 165 for Hayes, but twenty votes remained undecided in Louisiana, Florida, South Carolina, and Oregon. Hayes needed all twenty to defeat Tilden; Hurlbut believed that secret balloting in the electoral college would allow a subterfuge to elect Tilden even if Hayes gained all the contested votes. "We are on the edge of revolution already," Hurlbut warned Fuller; "Things are miserably bad, but do not leave a single loop-hole unguarded."[43]

Hurlbut returned to Washington as a lame-duck representative to the second session of the Forty-fourth Congress. Challenging Democratic claims to victory in the contested Southern states, Hurlbut (and other House members) traveled to New Orleans as a "Visiting Statesman"; he returned to Washington angrily denouncing what he deemed to be fraudulent election returns from Louisiana. Amid the growing constitutional crisis, Hurlbut unsuccessfully opposed the passage late in January 1877 of a bill that created a bipartisan electoral commission; Hurlbut feared that Judge David Davis, a staunchly independent Republican from Illinois (and the commission's last selected member), would break the electoral stalemate by supporting Tilden. However, another Republican replaced Davis, and the electoral board decided every disputed vote in favor of Hayes. Early in March 1877, not Tilden but Hayes succeeded Grant to the presidency.[44]

On balance, Hurlbut's service in the House of Representatives reflected his inclination to exploit postwar political instability for personal advantage. By posing as a patriotic opponent of the Liberal Republican candidacy of Horace Greeley and as a true "stalwart" Republican adversary of the resurgent Negrophobic Southern Democracy, Hurlbut rode upon the tides of Northern indignation to gain congressional victories in 1872 and 1874. Moreover, Hurlbut vainly endeavored to seize Washburne's still-dominant position in the Illinois Clique; in the end, it was Logan and Oglesby—not Hurlbut—who grew into increased prominence in Washington and won Grant's trust. Finally, the astute political maneuverings of his opponents, and the effective breakup of the Illinois Clique not only contributed to his defeat for reelection but left him in an isolated political and ideological position. His move to Blaine in 1876 clearly revealed a desperate search for steadier political bearings under an eastern, not an Illinois or western, standard-bearer.

Recognizing the rise of a circle of Ohio Republicans headed by President Hayes himself, Hurlbut hastened to seek the patronage of Hayes, notwithstanding his own work on the House Civil Service Committee against such practices. Late in March 1877 Hurlbut sought the intercession of Ohio congressman James A. Garfield to procure the position of commissioner for the District of Columbia.[45] Garfield could not help Hurlbut, who had antagonized Hayes over civil service reform and Reconstruction. Hayes insisted upon abolishing the spoils system, which Grant had not, and wished to withdraw troops from South Carolina and Louisiana. Hurlbut then sought the post of ambassador to Brazil, obtaining recommendations from Generals Philip H. Sheridan and William T. Sherman as well as prominent Illinois Republicans, chiefly Senator Oglesby. But he failed to secure the support of John A. Logan, now the leading Illinois Republican in the Senate.[46] Hayes did consider Hurlbut but instead appointed Henry W. Hilliard of Georgia, in order to conciliate Confederate expatriates in Brazil.[47] Hurlbut returned to Washington late in 1877 to

practice law in the Supreme Court, the Court of Claims, and District of Columbia courts.[48] However, he had already determined to run again for Congress
from his home district. Therefore, Hurlbut returned to Belvidere early in February 1878 and began planning a shrewd campaign strategy.

As the most important part of that strategy, Hurlbut joined the Belvidere
chapter of the American Red Ribbon Club (ARRC). Founded in 1875 in New
York by two reformed drinkers, Dr. Henry A. Reynolds and Francis Murphy,
the ARRC was a temperance organization; its members forswore alcohol and
tied red ribbons around their arms as a token of abstinence. Though during the
Civil War heavy drinking threatened to destroy his career, he associated himself
with the ARRC to revive his rapidly ebbing political fortunes. Horace White
and Democratic editors had damagingly resurrected stories of his wartime intemperance, despite his apparent sobriety since 1864; moreover, the National
Prohibition party, established in 1869, had drawn numerous Republicans into
its ranks, seriously weakening the Republican party, although mostly in close
state and local races.[49] For much of the war Hurlbut had not responded to the
moral suasion of his wife, Joseph Russell Jones, Orville H. Browning, or other
figures to desist from drinking, nor had he abstained upon a purely voluntary
basis. Yet as an ARRC member Hurlbut would recommend these approaches
for the reformation of heavy drinkers.

In a "stirring speech" before 2,700 of the ARRC's "boys" on February 21 at
Belvidere, Hurlbut made his initial effort to forestall a Prohibition party victory
in his congressional district. In August, after another five months in Washington, Hurlbut returned to Belvidere to resume his campaigning. Not content
merely to profess his own reformation, Hurlbut boldly endeavored to win ab-
stinent Republicans' votes and even those of Prohibition supporters at a temperance camp meeting at Cherry Valley, in Winnebago County. Emphasizing
the supposed power of "moral suasion" and "voluntarism" in curbing the use of
alcohol, Hurlbut recommended against federal or state legislation that would
prohibit the manufacture or sale of alcoholic beverages. Thus "General Hurlbut's
temperance speech at Cherry Valley," the *Belvidere Standard* reported, "did not
suit the prohibitionists present"; they had expected him to advocate the creation of legislation to slay "Demon Rum." Hurlbut's moderate stand on the
liquor question not only alienated Prohibition party members but antagonized
the "dry" wing of the local Republican party and led to his defeat. (Commend-
ably, he would afterward help John C. Sherwin, the successful nominee, defeat
Democratic, Prohibition, and Greenback party candidates in the 1878 fall election.) Hurlbut thereupon returned to Washington, where for most of 1879 he
practiced law. Late in October he traveled to Janesville, Wisconsin, where he,

Logan, and other Republican politicians welcomed Grant, who was returning to the United States after a triumphant world tour.[50]

Hurlbut's praise of Grant in Janesville and, a month later, at a gala banquet in Chicago, belied his imminent involvement in a campaign to deny Grant the support of the Illinois Republican party for a possible third term in the White House. Having become one of Senator Blaine's campaign managers in Illinois, early in March 1880 Hurlbut proceeded to Chicago to confer with co-managers Charles Farwell, an Illinois congressman, and Joseph Medill, former editor of the *Chicago Tribune.* Thereafter, the sixty-four-year-old Hurlbut (whose energy and enthusiasm for politicking had scarcely diminished since the 1850s) flung himself into the campaign. Logan, then directing Grant's Illinois campaign from Washington, complained to Elihu B. Washburne (who himself aspired to the Republican presidential nomination) about Hurlbut's allegedly deceitful maneuverings. On April 4, Logan reported to Washburne that the Knox and Champaign County Republican conventions originally "were seemingly [for] Grant" but that in a "very strange" manner both had appointed Blaine delegates to the Republican state convention in May. "Hurlburt [*sic*] and other of Bs. [Blaine's] Paid emissaries are traveling all over the state setting up conventions" in nearly every county, Logan charged, "sending delegates professedly Grant until appointed. . . . The dirtiest race that can be conceived is now being made on Grant."[51] In short, according to Logan, Hurlbut had stacked county conventions with Blaine men wearing Grant hats. Longtime Grant Republican Jesse Spalding advised Logan on April 6 that the "Blaine boom" in Illinois had arisen because of "Gen'l Hurlbert [*sic*] and others of the same class" of politicians, while "it is currently reported here that money is being spent in the effort to get up this boom" in Chicago and Cook County.[52] Grant's managers determined to deny, by whatever means they could, convention seats to Blaine delegations from Chicago, Cook County, and Hurlbut's legislative district.

Appointed as a Boone County delegate to the Republican state convention at the Illinois capital, Hurlbut and Farwell immediately formed an "anti-Grant gang" of Blaine Republicans, including the former congressman "Long John" Wentworth. Developments on the convention floor (in the new capitol building) threatened to defeat their efforts. Grant Republicans, led by Logan and by Emory A. Storrs (a prominent Chicago lawyer), benefited from the partisan chairmanship of Green B. Raum, the federal commissioner of internal revenue and a former Union general and Republican congressman who had strongly opposed Andrew Johnson's lenient Reconstruction policy. Although Hurlbut and Farwell vigorously sought to have the several Blaine delegations recognized as properly elected and representative, Raum, closely cooperating with Logan,

John A. Logan, Republican U.S. senator from Illinois. Prints and Photographs Division, Library of Congress.

recognized only the Grant delegations—particularly the larger ones, from Chicago and Cook County. Consequently, the convention was preponderantly pro-Grant. Raum then proposed (contrary to the traditional method) a "unit rule," whereby a special committee, which he would appoint, would select all the members of the Illinois delegation to the national Republican convention in Chicago; that delegation would vote as a single bloc for either Grant or Blaine.

Given its dominant pro-Grant composition, on May 20 the delegates predictably voted to adopt Raum's unit-rule and single-bloc proposals. The Democratic *Illinois State Register* of Springfield, sarcastically asked, "Does Gen. Hurlburt [*sic*], with his bright brain, keen eye and quick ear, really suppose that the convention, with the Grant flag waving triumphantly above it," would consent to "any division of the delegation to be sent to Chicago? Never!"[53]

Desperate to avoid a unanimous Grant delegation to the national convention, Hurlbut devised a bold plan to force Logan and Raum either to abolish the unit rule or risk a bolt of the Blaine men. If the Springfield convention was disrupted, Hurlbut believed, the Chicago convention might not seat the Grant delegation. Specifically, Hurlbut planned to present Chairman Raum on the last day of the convention with a resolution calling for the immediate nomination of a candidate for governor of Illinois. Knowing that the Grant delegates at the convention had already divided sharply over the prospective candidacy of Shelby M. Cullom, a Grant man, Hurlbut planned to support the anti-Cullom faction, in the expectation that Cullom's supporters would themselves bolt, leaving a solidly pro-Blaine convention to send a delegation to Chicago. But Hurlbut underestimated Raum's determination. On May 21, when Raum called the last day's session to order, "General Hurlbut was instantly on his feet and demanded recognition." Raum coolly ignored Hurlbut, who stormed down the aisle waving his draft resolution and shouting, "Will the Commissioner of Internal Revenue give me the floor?" Bedlam erupted; Raum's "vigorous rapping" of the gavel only slowly restored order. Hurlbut shrank back to his seat in defeat.[54]

The pro-Grant *Illinois State Journal,* evaluating the performance of Blaine's campaign managers at Springfield, declared, "The man who felt worst was Gen. Hurlbut of Boone. He had simply taken too large a contract, and wasn't able to deliver." The more censorious Democratic *Illinois State Register* gleefully asserted that Logan ("the swarthy-faced senator" and "imperious boss" of the Grant Republicans in Illinois) had come to Springfield with "relentless vim" to "grind Charley Farwell and Gen. Hurlbut in the dust, and he departed over the lifeless forms of his embittered foes."[55] Yet Hurlbut was not Blaine's problem; Blaine had underestimated the strength of the third-term Grant movement in the Prairie State, and he should not have pitted the like of Hurlbut and Farwell against such skillful politicians as Logan and Raum.

But even Logan and Raum could not prevent the Credentials Committee at the national convention that June from admitting Blaine delegates from Springfield and overruling Raum's unfair unit rule. Moreover, neither Grant nor Blaine gained the nomination at Chicago. Instead, the prize fell to Senator Garfield, still another dark horse candidate from Ohio, who afterward defeated his popular Democratic opponent and won the White House. Hurlbut supported Garfield's candidacy, offering counsel on campaign strategy and making speeches for him in Illinois and Indiana.[56] Following the election, Hurlbut continued to advise Garfield on matters ranging from the selection of cabinet officers to American participation in the construction of a Panama canal. However, Garfield declined Hurlbut's numerous applications for the position of minister to Mexico, whereupon Hurlbut again returned to Belvidere.[57]

From 1877 to 1881, as we have noted, Hurlbut had scrambled to secure more stable political moorings, particularly in view of the steady decline of the Illinois Clique, of which he had remained a member until its final disintegration upon the defeat of Grant in 1880. In this respect, Hurlbut himself had helped to effect its dissolution. However, associating him with the "Grantism" that he himself had since 1871 repudiated, the "Ohio Clique" did not admit Hurlbut. Thus, with the patronage of neither Illinois nor Ohio politicians, Hurlbut grew increasingly isolated. But he had also followed an erratic course since his departure from Congress in 1877, ranging himself with the anti-Grant Republicans and consequently opposing a decidedly superior John A. Logan. Hurlbut had courted the support of Prohibition party members in 1878 but had adopted a position that estranged him from both the Prohibitionists and the "drys" of his own party. His lack of clear conviction or direction after 1877 accounted for his deepening obscurity.

However, Hurlbut's political fortune was now revived by the expansion of the War of the Pacific in South America, somewhat as the outbreak of the Civil War had done. In April 1879, Chile had declared war on Bolivia and Peru; the Santiago government's military and naval forces had vanquished its enemies late in 1880. Chilean troops had marched into the mineral-rich Peruvian province of Tarapaca and seized also the fertile regions of Tacna and Arica. After an unsuccessful American mediation effort in October 1880, Chile had demanded huge territorial concessions from Peru as a precondition of a comprehensive peace settlement. Bolivia had previously capitulated to Chile and had already granted valuable economic and commercial rights in its own territory. Finally, in January 1881, Chilean troops captured Lima, the Peruvian capital; there the Chilean naval commander called on the Peruvian government for a prompt accommodation of all outstanding disputes.[58] The steadily deteriorating situation in Peru in the spring of 1881 alarmed and disappointed the newly appointed American secretary of state, James G. Blaine. Blaine had envisaged a "Pan-American Alliance," a reciprocal economic and commercial relationship between the United States and the more prosperous countries of Latin America. Such a trade partnership would necessitate the expulsion of British economic influence from Chile. Convinced that the British had instigated the War of the Pacific, in an attempt to assert neocolonial rule over Chile in defiance of the Monroe Doctrine, Blaine hastily endeavored (as noted above) to negotiate a peace treaty between Chile and Peru in order to prevent the expansion of British interests into the newly

James G. Blaine, Republican U.S. senator from Maine. Prints and Photographs Division, Library of Congress.

occupied Peruvian territories. He also sought to replace the growing British
influence with an expanded American economic and commercial presence.[59]

Blaine now recommended the appointment of two former Union army generals who had diplomatic experience in South America. He asked Garfield to
nominate them and urged Republican senators on the Foreign Affairs Committee, particularly John A. Logan, quickly to confirm them. To serve as his ambassador to Peru, Blaine recommended Hurlbut. Blaine's prospective minister to
Chile, Gen. Hugh Judson Kilpatrick, had previously served in Santiago, from
1865 to 1868. A forty-five-year-old native of New Jersey, Kilpatrick had graduated from West Point in 1861 and during the Civil War had rapidly risen to

command cavalry brigades and divisions. But he had also earned the dubious sobriquet "Kill-cavalry" for his reckless aggressiveness. Hurlbut and Kilpatrick brought to the foreign service a revived spirit of militant partisanship. But Blaine anticipated close and effective cooperation between the two men in executing his instructions to mediate the conflict between Peru and Chile.[60]

Confirmed by the Senate on May 19, 1881, Hurlbut hurried to Washington from Belvidere to discuss his assignment with Blaine. Blaine ordered him to support the provisional Peruvian government under Francisco Garcia Calderon (whose regime Hurlbut's immediate predecessor, Judge Isaac P. Christiancy, had tentatively recognized) and not to recognize the deposed Peruvian president, Nicholas de Pierola. Fifteen thousand Chilean troops occupied Lima; Hurlbut was to urge the Peruvian government to negotiate quickly a peace treaty. If Peru could not pay the demanded reparations, Hurlbut should persuade Calderon to consider ceding the provinces of Tarapaca, Tacna, and Arica. Blaine further instructed Hurlbut to defend (otherwise) the territorial integrity of Peru and to oppose British economic and commercial influence in that country. On June 15, Blaine sent Hurlbut (who had returned to Belvidere) written instructions that essentially repeated those conveyed in Washington in May. Overall, then, Blaine had given Hurlbut to understand that the American government stood willing to support Chile's demands for substantial reparations, either financial or territorial. Blaine had likewise clearly instructed Kilpatrick to support Chilean claims against Peru, although he was to discourage the further British influence in Chile.[61] In short, Blaine's policy included contradictory elements: to support the demands of Chile against Peru, to defend the territorial integrity of Peru against Chilean aggression, to check the spread of British neocolonial influence, and to establish the Pan-American Alliance upon resolving the diplomatic crisis and ending British influence.

Thrown headlong into this imbroglio, Hurlbut, Sophronia, and George proceeded to New York to begin their voyage to Peru. On July 2, 1881, only hours before they left New York aboard the steamer *Alaska*, Hurlbut learned that President Garfield had been shot. Unknown to either Blaine or Hurlbut, Garfield's death on September 19 and the accession of Chester A. Arthur would complicate Blaine's plan for ending the War of the Pacific. Meanwhile, the Hurlbuts arrived in the port of Callao, west of Lima, late in July and proceeded by rail to the ancient Incan village of Magdalena, outside Lima, where Hurlbut was presented to President Calderon. Speaking in Spanish (but apparently in seriously misconstruing or disregarding the substance of Blaine's instructions), Hurlbut declared to Calderon that "the abuse of victory more frequently becomes a curse to the conqueror" than to the conquered. He thereby immediately contradicted the fundamental proposition underlying Blaine's policy—that Chile had won the war and that accordingly Peru must either pay reparations or surrender provinces. He and his family then accompanied Calderon to the capital, where Hurlbut found himself "carried with great ceremony to the handsomest palace in Lima," adjoining the residence of Calderon, "whose position and power had been given to him through the kindness of Chile."

Meanwhile, Kilpatrick had already begun to suspect the looseness of Hurlbut's adherence to Blaine's instructions. Kilpatrick's own increasingly partisan support of Chilean demands arose in part from his recently consummated marriage to a young niece of a rabidly anti-Calderon Chilean cleric, and in part from an incurable kidney disease; he was resolved to vindicate the Chilean cause before his rapidly approaching death. Further, Kilpatrick, like Hurlbut, had begun to deviate from Blaine's instructions. Kilpatrick had begun to express willingness to promote British commercial influence in Chile, particularly if the United Kingdom would help Chile achieve her war aims.[62]

Hurlbut reminded Kilpatrick of his duty to oppose any gratuitous Chilean seizure of land from Peru. Hurlbut also reminded him that Washington had, since the proclamation of the Monroe Doctrine in 1823, consistently refused to recognize "the European notion of addition to territory by conquest." Grossly misinterpreting Blaine's instructions, Hurlbut expressed his opinion that the United States would repudiate Chilean demands for cessions of land as the precondition of negotiated peace, and he suggested that Kilpatrick warn the Chilean government of the American government's resolve to defend Peruvian territorial integrity and to curb British and other European influence. Hurlbut then dispatched a letter to Blaine in which he described the unsettled conditions in Peru under Chilean occupation and assured Blaine of his support of the Calderon regime. The fugitive President Pierola had reorganized his government and established a guerrilla insurgency in the mountainous country of northern Peru; Hurlbut called the exiled regime "a violent usurpation, autocratic and despotic." Reflecting his conservative and elitist bias (the Peruvian people generally supported the resistance movement), he asserted that around the Calderon government "all the better class of men, the holders of property, the men of education, the friends of constitutional order and of peace, are disposed to assemble." Hurlbut further advised Blaine that the Chilean government intended to negotiate informally with the Calderon regime, pending formal recognition. Finally, however, Hurlbut urged Blaine to threaten Chile with military intervention to deter its "greed of conquest" and to ensure the speedy expulsion of British interests.[63]

On August 24, 1881, Hurlbut confronted Rear Adm. D. Patricio Lynch, the Chilean commander in Lima. At both a private conference and in a formal memorandum that followed, Hurlbut warned Lynch that the United States would oppose a Chilean appropriation of land from Peru, despite the commencement of peace negotiations. Moreover, exceeding his instructions, Hurlbut suggested the strong possibility of American military intervention should Chile spurn Peru's conciliatory overtures—those short of the cession of lands—and seize the province of Tarapaca. Hurlbut then apprised Blaine and Kilpatrick of the contents of his so-called Lynch Memorandum, boasting to Blaine that the "English and French ministers seem somewhat aggrieved, or pretend to be" at his taking of independent action without their concurrence. Hurlbut had declared to the British minister in Lima that "the position of the United States is its own, and only to be determined by itself." Hurlbut then opened communication with Pierola, a man he regarded as a bandit and petty dictator. Overlooking Pierola's broad popular support and his fierce rivalry with Calderon, Hurlbut suggested the possibility of a truce between them and of a war against the "common enemy," Chile. Pierola replied by accusing Calderon of collaborating with the despised enemy and of plotting to cede valuable lands. Hurlbut, in turn, denied the charges. He informed Blaine that Pierola's insurgency had begun to weaken and would probably collapse before the conclusion of the negotiations then in progress in Lima. His prediction proved accurate; denied American diplomatic recognition, Pierola late in November 1881 relinquished his claim to the presidency. Admiral Lynch, meanwhile, finding his own position growing stronger, late in September 1881 suspended the negotiations, dispersed the Peruvian congress, attempted to plunder the Peruvian treasury, and established rigorous martial law in Lima. Hurlbut allowed the Peruvian archives to be hastily removed to the U.S. legation and apprised Blaine of Lynch's actions.[64]

This unexpected turn of events discredited Hurlbut and frustrated his diplomatic efforts. Marcial Martinez, the Chilean minister to Washington, attempted to curb Hurlbut's clearly partisan interference with the peace negotiations in Lima. He urged the secretary of state to publicly make "some act or declaration which will tend to destroy the bad impression" created by Hurlbut's conduct.[65] Influential editorialists in South America and in the United States also expressed displeasure with Hurlbut. For example, the *Cochabamba el Heraldo,* in Bolivia, criticized the Lynch Memorandum and accused Hurlbut of having opposed Lynch's dissolution of the Calderon government "with all the slowness of the yankee." The *New York Tribune,* which had earlier supported Hurlbut's interventionist policy, began to declare grave doubts. The *New York Times,* evaluating "Gen. Hurlbut's Mentorship" in Peru, decried his interference with the peace negotiations; "Gen. Hurlbut may have a timely admonition from Washington against too great epistolary zeal at this juncture." According to the *Times,*

Hurlbut had now "twice gone a little beyond the custom of our diplomacy." Finally, *The Nation* observed sarcastically, "We believe this is the first time any such limitation on the rights of a conqueror has been produced by any diplomatist" in the history of European or American foreign policy.[66] Hurlbut had become the butt of ridicule.

He blamed neither Blaine nor himself, however, but Kilpatrick. From the time of his arrival in Lima, Hurlbut had sent numerous official notes to Kilpatrick in Santiago but had not received a reply until late September. The increasing gravity of Kilpatrick's illness had largely accounted for his silence; Hurlbut thus informed Blaine, "I fear his situation is dangerous, and he evidently thinks so." Hurlbut also objected to Kilpatrick's continued support of Chilean annexation of Peruvian land and his strong opposition to Hurlbut's Lynch Memorandum. Insinuating that Kilpatrick had contravened Blaine's instructions in order to advocate the territorial dismemberment of Peru if that was the only means of achieving peace with Chile, Hurlbut advised Blaine that "there would seem to be a radical difference between General Kilpatrick and myself, which demands the attention of the Department."[67]

Meanwhile, editors in the United States continued their criticism of Hurlbut's policy. Accusing both Hurlbut and Kilpatrick of partisanship, the *New York Times* asserted that Hurlbut had "invented" the provisional Calderon government and had attempted to dictate peace terms to Chile. The *Times* declared that Blaine should recall Hurlbut, who, it claimed, had begun the "present extraordinary quarrel" and was "not designed by nature for the diplomatic service." By causing "hopeless confusion" in Lima through his "insane attempts" to impose peace terms on Chile, Hurlbut had threatened to embroil the United States in a potentially renewed and wider War of the Pacific. The formerly charitable *New York Tribune* now abandoned Hurlbut, declaring bluntly, "Men may be popular politicians and energetic stump speakers without having the capacity to succeed in the career of diplomacy."[68]

Blaine himself by this time faced the prospect of imminent replacement in office by Frederick T. Frelinghuysen. President Arthur had decided to replace Blaine, in an effort to break the diplomatic deadlock in Peru. Meanwhile, the House Committee on Foreign Affairs had called for a congressional investigation of his Latin American policy and had begun summoning witnesses. An alarmed Blaine immediately announced a special diplomatic mission to mediate the conflict between Chile and Peru. In November 1881, while the committee examined his policy, Blaine sought to shift the blame for his failed policy to Hurlbut and Kilpatrick. For instance, when Ambassador Martinez personally complained to Blaine in mid-November about some particularly truculent anti-

Chilean pronouncement by Hurlbut, Blaine bellowed, "He must have been drunk at the time." Later in November, Blaine repudiated the Lynch Memorandum (which he had not done before the formation of the House's investigating committee); he criticized Hurlbut for involvement in dubious American investment schemes and foreign land claims in Peru; and he censured him for assuming trusteeship over Peru's Chimbote Railroad and a naval coaling station on the Pacific coast. (As to the latter, Hurlbut had previously considered, albeit briefly, supporting the ambitious enterprises of a Chicago investor, Jacob R. Shipherd, relating to the recovery of valuable guano from coastal Peru. His trusteeship had attempted to deprive Chile of these important strategic assets.)

Nonetheless, Hurlbut continued to encourage the Calderon government to believe that the United States would oppose annexation of Peruvian lands—a position he made clear in a proclamation he circulated among "The Notables of Lima." On December 2, 1881, Kilpatrick died in Santiago. His expected death had left Hurlbut as the only American envoy to mediate the disputes between Chile and Peru. Fortunately for Blaine, however, his newly formed "Trescot Mission" arrived in Lima early in January 1882. This mission comprised William Henry Trescot, a distinguished South Carolina lawyer and diplomat whom Hurlbut had known in Charleston, and the young Walker Blaine, Blaine's eldest son and the third assistant secretary of state. Receiving a tumultuous welcome in occupied Lima, Trescot and Blaine proceeded to Santiago, where they enjoyed a decidedly less enthusiastic reception and were struck by the Chilean people's hatred of Hurlbut and by their love for the late Kilpatrick. Trescot and Blaine invited Peruvian and Chilean delegations to a peace conference in Washington that, Secretary Blaine hoped, could yet implement his South American policy.[69] The Trescot Mission quickly failed, because the House investigating committee had just released compromising State Department documents documenting Hurlbut's diplomatic adventurism and also connections with speculative schemes of American capitalists in Peru, particularly with Shipherd.[70]

Now thoroughly isolated, Hurlbut tried to protect himself from further investigation by the House Committee on Foreign Affairs. He had already requested John A. Logan to obtain permission for him to return to the United States on leave to avoid being "peremptorily recalled." Logan obliged.

But Hurlbut did not live to take his case to Washington. On the morning of March 27, 1882, Hurlbut (who had first complained of severe chest pains in 1879) collapsed and died of a massive heart attack. A hysterical Sophronia would later accuse Chilean partisans of having poisoned her husband, but an autopsy performed aboard an American warship at Callao confirmed Hurlbut's death from natural causes.[71] In New York, Hurlbut's former State Department chief,

Hamilton Fish, exclaimed to Blaine's former under secretary of state, John C. B. Davis, "Hurlbut dead! Just as Trescot arrives!! Is Blaine jubilant today? Hurlbut cannot testify."[72] However, the Peruvians lamented Hurlbut's death. Trescot and Walker Blaine, having returned to Lima on March 28, observed throngs of mourners in the streets and in the churches of the capital. Walker Blaine described to his mother the "very grand and impressive" ceremonies held in Lima in Hurlbut's memory: "It's very strange, and makes me feel almost superstitious to think of both Hurlbut and Kilpatrick" dying at their posts.[73] Hurlbut's embalmed body lay in state at Lima for a week before Sophronia and George had it shipped to Belvidere, where it was buried on April 30, 1882.

The Hurlbut connection to Belvidere ended many years later. Senator Logan supported a bill to provide Sophronia with a pension to supplement the estate her husband had left her, while George sold his father's mansion in 1899 and moved to New York City, where he gained distinction as a civil engineer.[74]

Hurlbut's record of service as minister to Peru demonstrated that he had not learned the rudiments of diplomacy. As in Colombia, he showed himself in Peru to be an effective negotiator, an aggressive proponent of what he perceived to be his country's strategic interests; he was also a charismatic and heroic figure among the Peruvians, whose behalf he had so zealously served. However, Hurlbut had committed egregious errors of judgment. He had stretched considerably, or seriously misunderstood, Blaine's written—and apparently also oral—instructions regarding territorial concessions to Chile. Moreover, Hurlbut, without the slightest authority, had threatened the Chilean commander in Lima with American military intervention—a rash move that apparently led Lynch to terminate the peace negotiations then progressing. Hurlbut's partisanship delayed but did not prevent the seizure by Chile of the spoils of war. By the Treaty of Ancon of 1883, Chile acquired Tarapaca outright, as well as Tacna and Arica through 1893. In the end, however, the House Committee on Foreign Affairs refused to censure Hurlbut for diplomatic adventurism. Rather, the committee judged that Hurlbut, however imprudently and ineptly, had largely pursued Blaine's contradictory foreign policy, which it censured.[75]

But Hurlbut's overall record of political and diplomatic service following the Civil War surpassed that of rival Kilpatrick. His career as a general brought him prominence as a Republican politician that he had been unable to attain before the war. His wartime reputation for drinking and corruption hounded him. Still, he contributed significantly to the organization of the Grand Army of the Republic in 1868; he served his constituency with credit, if not brilliance, in the House of Representatives in the 1870s; and he laid in 1870 the groundwork for a future American treaty with Colombia to build a canal across the Isthmus of Panama. If Hurlbut's overzealous support of the Peruvian cause during the War of the Pacific hindered the conclusion of a just peace treaty, his adventuristic diplomacy nonetheless helped expose (if unwittingly) the fundamentally flawed policy of Secretary of State Blaine in that faraway conflict.

Evaluation of Generalship

Stephen Augustus Hurlbut was a Southerner with a Yankee heritage. His ante-bellum career as a militarily minded lawyer and Whig and Republican politician in South Carolina and in Illinois scarcely prepared him for high military rank and command; not surprisingly, he compiled a mixed record of success and failure as a Union army general during the Civil War. As a field commander in Missouri in 1861, campaigning against the Missouri State Guard under Col. Martin E. Green, he showed a decided incapacity for formulating and executing strategic plans, operations, and maneuvers. However, Brig. Gen. John Pope's calculated policy of depriving Hurlbut of infantry, cavalry, and artillery contributed to his inability to plan or mount a coordinated offensive campaign against Green. Hurlbut understood the logistical importance of protecting railroads and strategic points near them, but he failed to grasp the nature and extent of the guerrilla warfare then occurring across the largely pro-Confederate border state. He attempted to employ conventional methods against marauding raiders along the Hannibal & St. Joseph Railroad and treated the state militia forces as purely a plundering guerrilla band—a fundamental miscalculation that precipitated the fall of Shelbina and his own summary removal from command in 1861. Subsequently, however, at the Battle of Shiloh in April 1862, Hurlbut showed a marked tactical ability; his gallant and dogged defense of the Union left flank contributed significantly to the Union victory. Undoubtedly, Hurlbut's finest hour in the Union army occurred near Pittsburg Landing, where in stark contrast to his earlier reprehensible behavior he exhibited an exemplary valor, tactical prowess, and his peculiarly charismatic style of combat leadership. He demonstrated resolute determination to remove the disgrace of his Shelbina blunder, even if that should mean his death on the Shiloh battlefield. He showed a further developed tactical skill at the Battle of Hatchie Bridge later in 1862, though his disappointing failure under Rosecrans to pursue the defeated Confederate army promptly once again indicated his unsuitability for responsible field command. However, during the successive Corinth and Meridian campaigns of 1862 and 1864, where deliberate pursuit and engagement of regular troops was the objective, Hurlbut exhibited sense and ability, in contrast to his previous ineffectual preoccupation with elusive guerrillas and irregular forces. Throughout the war Hurlbut demonstrated commendable subordination and constant loyalty to superior officers, particularly to several West Point–educated commanders. Although he sought to discredit Pope after his own arrest in Missouri in 1861, endeavored to arrange the reassignment of Hamilton from Memphis in 1863, and attempted to ruin the reputation and career of "Baldy" Smith in New Orleans in 1865, Hurlbut rendered dutiful obedience to Halleck, Grant, Sherman, and Canby.

As the commander of the Sixteenth Corps of the Army of the Tennessee at Memphis from 1862 to 1864 and as the commander of the Army and the Department of the Gulf in New Orleans from 1864 to 1865, Hurlbut miserably failed to fulfill the expectations of Grant, Sherman, and Canby. As the Sixteenth Corps commander in Memphis, with administrative oversight of Memphis briefly in 1862 and again in 1864, he failed to eliminate or ameliorate the inhumane conditions within army hospitals and military prisons. He also created arbitrary policies regarding liquor, prostitution, and contraband blacks, even though he dutifully sought and obtained Grant's and Sherman's authorization for them. At New Orleans, Hurlbut also neglected to develop systematic regulations to implement Canby's orders regarding smuggling, freedmen, and cotton speculators. Furthermore, as an operational commander charged to protect strategically important posts on the Mississippi, Hurlbut failed to deal effectively with Confederate cavalry incursions and infantry infiltrations into West Tennessee. He failed, moreover, to employ aggressively the Army of the Gulf to disperse those Confederate forces; instead they protected the Southern, and often the Northern, cotton smugglers whose speculative enterprises contributed substantially to unauthorized trading at New Orleans.

As a leader of men also, Hurlbut's qualities were mixed. Unquestionably he exhibited conspicuous bravery under fire, particularly at Shiloh. He gained popularity and admiration among his troops in Missouri and Tennessee for his courage, eloquence, and patriotism, and he inspired s strong loyalty in most of his staff officers and subordinate commanders—although Robinson finally betrayed him in 1865. Hurlbut seriously failed, however, as a disciplinarian. Despite his express orders, his troops often committed offenses and depredations against civilians or their property; Hurlbut responded only by condemning the disloyalty of the secessionist inhabitants of his district. Further, he was excessively harsh toward Southern sympathizers, as demonstrated by the controversial McAfee, Frankland, Meyer, Kenosskey, and Hallum affairs in Missouri and Memphis. There followed his intimidation of the Belgian journalist Houzeau and his defrauding of the Committee of Safety and the hapless deacons of Christ Church in New Orleans. Throughout the Civil War Hurlbut manifested hostility toward blacks, Jews, and foreigners—racial and ethnic prejudices he had harbored before the conflict. Worse still, Hurlbut's chronic heavy drinking from 1861 to 1864, apparently brought under a measure of control by the vigilance and intervention of his wife and son in New Orleans in only 1864 and in 1865, exacerbated his vindictiveness while it impaired his ability to function effectively. His persistent intemperance, involvement in cotton and extortion rings, and exploitation of his rank for political advancement further reduced his military usefulness and effectiveness.

Hurlbut's military fortunes rose steadily with those of Grant and Sherman in the West, but they fell sharply when he lost Lincoln's support in the fall of 1864. Grant since 1861, and Sherman after 1862, sincerely appreciated Hurlbut's loyalty and service, and they had repeatedly interceded with Lincoln and Stanton on his behalf. It is ironic that Hurlbut's personal and professional relationships with Grant proved the most vexed of his overall career. Hurlbut easily gained and effectively exploited Petigru's patronage in his native Charleston before the war; reconciled himself to the insurmountable obstacle represented by Washburne in northern Illinois throughout the 1850s; and acknowledged his arch rival Logan as the preeminent Illinois Republican politician following the war. Hurlbut also established a mutually advantageous relationship with Lincoln both before and during the conflict and more or less managed his relationships, harmonious or antagonistic, with a mixed procession of West Point–trained officers and "political generals" alike—Frémont, Pope, Halleck, Sherman, McClernand, Oglesby, Ord, Rosecrans, Hamilton, Canby, Smith, and others.

But Hurlbut could never understand Ulysses S. Grant. He held a simultaneous admiration and disdain for Grant the soldier and Grant the politician. As for Grant himself, he eventually found Hurlbut a highly troublesome subordinate in the Western theater, only slightly less so than the War Democrat John A. McClernand. Jealous and envious of Grant throughout the war, Hurlbut nevertheless acknowledged and acclaimed Grant's genius after the fall of Vicksburg in 1863—although he continued to regard Grant as "an accident with few brains," as he had complained to his wife after Shiloh.

But it was the president himself who appointed Hurlbut a brigadier general in 1861, promoted him to major general in 1862, gave him the Sixteenth Corps command at Memphis in 1863, and assigned him to serve under Canby at New Orleans in 1864. Lincoln found it variously necessary or expedient to trust and use Hurlbut, a fellow Illinoisan in the West; without Lincoln's patronage and approval, Hurlbut would have had to content himself with at most a colonel's commission from Governor Yates and obscure service in command of a regiment. The president long tolerated Hurlbut's deficiencies as a commander and bore with Hurlbut's active or complicit corruption. Lincoln, however—who had sagaciously used Hurlbut and other "political generals" to counterbalance West Point officers, who might resist presidential reconstruction in the West—repudiated him when in November 1864 Hurlbut betrayed his trust in New Orleans. Ultimately, even the combination of Hurlbut's abilities as a lawyer, politician, and volunteer soldier could not compensate for his intemperance, cupidity, and abuse of power.

NOTES

PREFACE

1. Grant the president is portrayed in these stark terms in William B. Hesseltine, *Ulysses S. Grant: Politician,* but see Jean E. Smith, *Grant,* for a more favorable assessment of Grant's capacity for leadership.

2. For equally trenchant analyses of Banks and Butler as "political generals," see James G. Hollandsworth Jr., *Pretense of Glory: The Life of General Nathaniel P. Banks;* Fred H. Harrington, *Fighting Politician: Major General N. P. Banks;* Dick Nolan, *Benjamin Franklin Butler: The Damnedest Yankee;* Hans L. Trefousse, *Ben Butler: The South Called Him Beast!;* and Howard P. Nash Jr., *Stormy Petrel: The Life and Times of General Benjamin F. Butler, 1818–1893.*

3. Two authoritative Civil War studies of McClernand are: Richard L. Kiper, *Major General John Alexander McClernand: Politician in Uniform,* and Victor Hicken, "From Vandalia to Vicksburg: The Political and Military Career of John A. McClernand." For Prentiss, see James L. McDonough, *Shiloh: In Hell before Night,* and Wiley Sword, *Shiloh: Bloody April.* For Logan, see James P. Jones, *"Black Jack": John A. Logan and Southern Illinois in the Civil War Era,* and *John A. Logan: Stalwart Republican from Illinois.* For Oglesby, see Mark A. Plummer, *Lincoln's Rail-Splitter: Governor Richard J. Oglesby.* A definitive treatment of William H. L. Wallace's career is lacking, but see Isabel Wallace, *Life & Letters of General W. H. L. Wallace.* For a scholarly—although largely anecdotal—article on Hurlbut, see Juliet G. Sager, "Stephen A. Hurlbut, 1815–1882."

4. From a letter of Oct. 4, 1863, to the *Springfield Republican* and reprinted in the *Cincinnati Daily Times,* Nov. 23, 1863, and *Memphis Daily Appeal,* Nov. 22, 1863. See also Stephen W. Sears, ed., *Mr. Dunn Browne's Experiences in the Army: The Civil War Letters of Samuel W. Fiske,* 95–97, 176–78, 226–29. Some Union generals, however, endeavored to control the consumption of hard liquor by both officers and enlisted men. Benjamin F. Butler, for one, forbade the sale of "King Alcohol" to his forces at Fortress Monroe, Va., in the summer of 1861; *New York Daily Tribune,* Aug. 5, 1861, and *Quincy (Illinois) Daily Whig and Republican,* Aug. 12, 1861. Other Union commanders incurred severe criticism for excessive drinking. For example, late in May 1863 a *New York Times* editor, comparing the campaign records of several eastern officers with the more successful generalship of Grant in the West, particularly censured Brig. Gen. Henry W. Benham's "proneness to strong drink" and the alleged "drunkenness" in a battle of Col. Dixon S. Miles, both of whom (Benham later) served in the Army of the Potomac; *New York Times,* May 26, 1863. See also *Quincy Daily Whig and Republican,*

July 29, 31, 1861; *Quincy Herald,* Dec. 16, 1861; and *Des Moines Daily State Register,* Dec. 3, 1862.

5. John D. Billings, *Hardtack and Coffee, Or the Unwritten Story of Army Life,* 139, 140. Billings further asserted, "The officers who did not drink more or less were too scarce in the service." But numerous others had succumbed to a strong "appetite in a crisis," and he still had to question, if also admire, the sense of patriotic duty whereby Union soldiers had nonetheless obeyed a commander "whose head at a critical moment might be crazed with commissary whiskey? Hundreds if not thousands of lives were sacrificed by such leadership." But, Billings concluded: "I may state here that drunkenness was equally as common with the Rebels as with the Federals"; ibid., 141, 145, 219. For a Southern journal's criticism of rampant intemperance among the Confederate forces in Virginia, see *Norfolk Day Book,* Feb. 21, 1862, as qtd. in *Rockford [Illinois] Republican,* Mar. 20, 1862.

INTRODUCTION: YANKEE HERITAGE

1. Henry H. Hurlbut, *The Hurlbut Genealogy, Or Record of the Descendants of Thomas Hurlbut, of Saybrook and Wethersfield, Conn., Who Came to America as Early as the Year 1637,* 15–17, 18; *Proceedings of the Massachusetts Historical Society,* 2d ser., 12: *1897–1899,* 204–206; John Mason, "A Brief History of the Pequot War; Especially of the memorable Taking of Their Fort at Mistick in Connecticut in 1637. Written by Captain John Mason, a principal Actor therein, as then chief Captain and Commander of Connecticut Forces," 8: 131–32; Timothy Dwight, *Travels in New England and New York,* 3: 9, 381; J. Hammond Trumbull and Charles J. Hoadly, eds., *The Public Records of the Colony of Connecticut, Prior to the Union with New Haven Colony, May, 1665,* 1: 81, 82, 102, 129, 136; 2: 161, 329, 520. James Savage, *A Genealogical Dictionary of the First Settlers of New England, Showing Three Generations of Those Who Came before May, 1692, on the Basis of the Farmer's Register,* 2: 506; Ida P. Jenkins, Ruby H. Ellis, et al., comps., *Lineage Book: National Society of the Daughters of the American Colonists,* 5: 47; 11: 279; 13: 143; 26: 234; 31: 97. *Encyclopedia of Connecticut Biography: Genealogical-Memorial, Representative Citizens,* 174–76; R. R. Hinman, *Catalogue of the Names of the First Puritan Settlers of the Colony of Connecticut, with the Time of Their Arrival in the Colony,* 39, 149, 164, 192, 220.

2. Hurlbut, *Hurlbut Genealogy,* 90; Julian P. Boyd and Robert J. Taylor, eds., *The Susquehanna Company Papers,* 3: *1768–1769,* 172; 8: *1784–1786,* 215, 218, 227, 234, 326, 381; 9: *1787–1788,* 17–20, 32, 40, 53, 58–59, 69, 96–97, 107–108, 112–13, 115–16, 269, 312, 457, 494, 513; and Forrest Morgan, ed. *Connecticut as a Colony and as a State, Or One of the Original Thirteen,* 1: 461–65.

3. Hurlbut, *Hurlbut Genealogy,* 175–76; Stephen A. Hurlbut, "Late Martin L. Hurlbut: With a Memoir of the Author," 44. See also Hurlbut to Appleton, Feb. 15, June 24, 1808, Jan. 28, 1812, Jesse Appleton Papers, 1772–1819, Bowdoin College Library, Brunswick, Maine.

4. David Ramsay, *Ramsay's History of South Carolina, from Its First Settlement in 1670 to the Year 1808,* 2: 246, 360–61.

5. Jedidiah Morse, *The American Universal Geography: Or a View of the Present State of All the Empires, Kingdoms, States and Republiks in the Known World, and of the United States in Particular,* pt. 1: 706, 715. Morse described Beaufort as "a pleasant little town, of about 50 or 60 houses, and 200 inhabitants, who are distinguished for their hospitality and politeness"; ibid., 706. See also Hurlbut to Morse, Mar. 11, 1812, Manuscript Division, South Caroliniana Library, Univ. of South Carolina, Columbia, S.C.; and Hurlbut to Appleton, May 9, 1812, Appleton Papers.

6. William J. Grayson, *James Louis Petigru: A Biographical Sketch,* 66–67; James P. Carson, *Life, Letters and Speeches of James Louis Petigru, the Union Man of South Carolina,* 37–38.

7. Hurlbut to Morse, Mar. 11, 1812, South Caroliniana Library. See also Hurlbut to Appleton, May 9, 1812, Appleton Papers; Grayson, *Petigru,* 66–67; and Carson, *Petigru,* 37–38.

8. William H. Pease and Jane H. Pease, *James Louis Petigru: Southern Conservative, Southern Dissenter,* 19, 37–38, 165; and Michael O'Brien and David Moltke-Hansen, eds., *Intellectual Life in Antebellum Charleston,* 158.

9. Hurlbut to Appleton, Sept. 22, 1813, Appleton Papers. For a penetrating study of the historical, social, and psychological origins of European and American antipathy toward blacks in the colonial and early national periods of American history, see Winthrop D. Jordan, *White over Black: American Attitudes toward the Negro, 1550–1812.*

10. Thomas C. Johnson, *The Life and Letters of Benjamin Morgan Palmer,* 15–17. See also Carson, *Petigru,* 37.

11. Martin Luther Hurlbut afterward explained to the Reverend Dr. Appleton that "Mrs. H. was no better than myself—for she too was a Yankee—& from the most yankeefied of all Yankee places, *Connecticut.*" See Hurlbut to Appleton, Feb. 1, 1819, Appleton Papers. For other references to the Palmers of South Carolina, see Alexander S. Salley, ed. *The South Carolina Historical and Genealogical Magazine* 9 (July 1908): 132–33; 29 (July 1928): 310; 31 (Jan. 1930): 69. Robert M. Myers, ed., *The Children of Pride: A True Story of Georgia and the Civil War,* 39, 123, 138, 218, 309–10, 389, 411, 414, 607, 679, 687–88, 738–39, 810, 813, 820, 1005, 1034, 1128, 1277, 1349, 1365, 1379, 1381–82, 1384, 1397, 1399, 1400, 1416, 1639; Clement Eaton, *The Freedom-of-Thought Struggle in the Old South,* 59, 291, 319, 347–48; and Dumas Malone and Allen Johnson, eds., *Dictionary of American Biography* [hereafter *DAB*], 14: 175–76.

12. Hurlbut, *Hurlbut Genealogy,* 175–76; Hurlbut, "Memoir," 45. As the catastrophe at Beaufort that followed showed, Martin Hurlbut had acted prudently. William J. Grayson, who taught at Beaufort College after 1815, later described the devastating disease of 1817: "We began the year with favourable auspices," because he and his colleagues had prepared the college to be "a great resort with the country about for all ingenuous youth ambitious of learning and its honours." But the 1817 malarial pestilence killed 126 of the town's six hundred "white inhabitants," while "among the survivors more than half were sick. The whole village was a hospital. The College suffered with the town. The boys were dispersed. The College building was abandoned. A small schoolhouse was erected in the town in what was judged to be a more healthy quarter and trustees and teachers gave up their hopes and expectations of future greatness. The site of the large

college building proved permanently sickly"; therefore, "the building was pulled down"; Samuel G. Stoney, ed., "The Autobiography of William John Grayson," 126–27, 166–67. See also Hurlbut to Appleton, Mar. 18, 1819, Appleton Papers.

13. *Charleston Courier,* Dec. 13, 15, 22, 29, 1814; Jan. 2, 1815. See also Lawrence S. Rowland, Alexander Moore, and George C. Rogers Jr., *The History of Beaufort County, South Carolina,* 1: *1514–1861,* 259, 284–86, 291, 318, 336, 338–39, 343, 382, 396–98, 400–406, 422, 424–25.

CHAPTER 1: THE MAKING OF A CAROLINA YANKEE

1. For a picturesque description of antebellum Charleston, see William B. Hesseltine, *The South in American History,* 285–87; and Robert Molloy, *Charleston: A Gracious Heritage,* 79–94.

2. Richard C. Wade, *Slavery in the Cities: The South 1820–1860,* 3, 11, 17, 25, 70, 76, 78, 277, 326; and *Charleston Courier,* Jan. 9, 10, 11, 12, 1837.

3. *Charleston Courier,* June 19, 29, 1816; Mar. 27, Apr. 28, Dec. 17, 1817. "Typed Newspaper articles on the College of Charleston and on Education in South Carolina generally, 1798–1841," 43, 54, Archives Division, College of Charleston Library, Charleston, South Carolina; James H. Easterby, *A History of the College of Charleston, Founded 1770,* 64, 347; "Minutes of the Journals of the Board of Trustees, 1791–1870," box 1 (1918), 12, Archives Division, College of Charleston Library; Jasper Adams, *A Historical Sketch of the College of Charleston, South Carolina,* 8; John H. Moore, ed., "The Abiel Abbot Journals: A Yankee Preacher in Charleston Society, 1818–1827," 56, 64, 68; Elizabeth H. Jewey, ed., "Marriage and Death Notices from *The City Gazette* of Charleston, S.C.," 152; and Hurlbut to Appleton, Feb. 1, Mar. 18, 1819, Appleton Papers.

4. Eaton, *Freedom-of-Thought,* 316–20; David Robinson, *The Unitarians and the Universalists,* 9–46; Conrad Wright, *The Beginnings of Unitarianism in America,* 200–22; Earl W. Cory, "The Unitarians and the Universalists of the Southeastern United States during the Nineteenth Century," 2–4, 29–30; George N. Edwards, *A History of the Independent or Congregational Church of Charleston, South Carolina, Commonly Known as Circular Church,* 59–64; Arthur A. Brooks, *The History of Unitarianism in the Southern Churches, Charleston, New Orleans, Louisville, Richmond,* 3–10; *Rent Lists of Pews and Accounts, the Independent or Congregational Church, S.C., 1806–1820,* 188, 206; *Record Book of Independent or Congregational Church, 1796–1824, Charleston County,* 222, 232, 237–38, 241; Hurlbut to Appleton, Feb. 1, 1819, Appleton Papers. A faithful pictorial likeness of Martin Luther Hurlbut is shown in the *Catalogue of an Exhibition of Portraits by John Neagle,* 29.

5. For instance, see Martin Luther Hurlbut, "Reply to the Charleston *Southern Intelligencer,*" 1–2. This particular edition of the *Unitarian Defendant* is on microfilm at the Kent State Univ. Library, Kent, Ohio. See also Cory, "Unitarians," 83–84, 95–96, 103–106, 113; and Hurlbut, "Memoir," 42–43.

6. William Way, *History of the New England Society of Charlestown, South Carolina for One Hundred Years, 1819–1919,* 1–2, 4, 27, 31–32, 38, 44, 48, 56–57, 60, 76, 83–84, 96, 98–99, 112–13, 114–56, 268–69. See also Eaton, *Freedom-of-Thought,* 260–61.

7. Hurlbut to Appleton, Feb. 1, 1819, Appleton Papers. See also Way, *New England Society*, 188–238; Barbara L. Bellows, *Benevolence among Slaveholders: Assisting the Poor in Charleston, 1670–1860*, 40; and Cory, "Unitarians," 112.

8. Hurlbut to Appleton, Feb. 1, 1819, Appleton Papers; Colyer Meriwether, *History of Higher Education in South Carolina with a Sketch of the Free School System*, 58. Meriwether describes William Henry Hurlbut as having been "a very quick, bright boy," while his younger brother, Stephen Augustus, in overall comparison, "was somewhat slower in apprehension."

9. "Mortgage Book RRR, Oct. 13, 1818–Aug. 28, 1828," vol. 28: 162; and "Mortgage Book TTT, Sept. 4, 1822–June 16, 1826," vol. 30: 207, in South Carolina Department of Archives and History, Columbia, South Carolina [hereafter SCAH]. See also Hurlbut, *Hurlbut Genealogy*, 176.

10. Caroline Gilman, *Record of Inscriptions in the Cemetery and Building of the Unitarian, Formerly Denominated the Independent Church, Archdale Street, Charleston, S.C., from 1777 to 1860*, 97; Hurlbut, "Memoir," 42. For a list of birth and death notices, see Hurlbut/Hurlbert Family Folder, South Carolina Historical Society, Charleston, South Carolina.

11. John Lofton, *Insurrection in South Carolina: The Turbulent World of Denmark Vesey*, 75–239; Herbert Aptheker, *American Negro Slave Revolts*, 264–76; Wade, *Slavery*, 102, 129, 168, 191, 193, 194, 217, 228–41, 263, 272.

12. "Minutes, 1818–1830," 2: 5–6, 8–12, 14–15, 17–22, 32, 303; Easterby, *College of Charleston*, 67–68, 347–48; *Charleston Courier*, Jan. 20, 1823; Hurlbut/Hurlbert Folder, South Carolina Historical Society; Hurlbut, "Memoir," 42; "Mortgage Book, TTT," 30: 207, SCAH; "Miscellaneous Bills of Sale, 5A, 1823–1825," 121: 461, SCAH.

13. Elizabeth M. Geffen, "Philadelphia Unitarianism (1796–1861)," 200.

14. Martin Luther Hurlbut joined the South Carolina Society in June 1828; his son, Stephen, joined in 1842. *The Rules of the South Carolina Society Established at Charlestown in the Said Province, September, 1737, Originally Incorporated, May 1, 1751*, 49–50, 122. See also "Typed Articles," 54.

15. William W. Freehling, *Prelude to Civil War: The Nullification Controversy in South Carolina, 1816–1836*, 41–42, 89–133; William W. Freehling, *The Road to Disunion*, 1: *Secessionists at Bay, 1776–1854*, 213–307; Gerald M. Capers, *John C. Calhoun: Opportunist, A Reappraisal*, 99–165; Way, *New England Society*, 83. William Henry Hurlbut II, who afterward changed the spelling of his surname to "Hurlbert," later proudly recalled that his father had adopted, with "other strong men" in Charleston, a defiant posture, opposing Calhoun and nullification. *New York World*, Apr. 3, 1882.

16. Hurlbut/Hurlbert Folder, South Carolina Historical Society; Hurlbut, *Hurlbut Genealogy*, 176; U.S. Department of the Interior, Bureau of the Census, microfilm copy of the "Fifth Census of the United States, South Carolina, 1830," Population Schedules, Ward I, vol. 2: 6, SCAH. See also James W. Hagy, *Directories for the City of Charleston, South Carolina for the Years 1830–31, 1835–36, 1836, 1837–38, and 1840–41*, 14.

17. Hurlbut, "Memoir," 42–43; Hurlbut, *Hurlbut Genealogy*, 176; Geffen, "Philadelphia Unitarianism," 200–201; Charles G. Leland, *Memoirs, by Charles Godfrey Leland (Hans Breitman)*, 73, 80–81. See also Hurlbut to Webster, Mar. 17, 1851, Daniel Webster Papers, Manuscript Division, Library of Congress, Washington, D.C.

18. *Charleston Courier,* Jan. 9, 10, 11, 12, 1837, Dec. 24, 1840, Jan. 4, 1841; and *Charleston Mercury,* Jan. 9, 1841.

19. Malone and Johnson, *DAB,* 9: 425; *Charleston Courier,* Jan. 9, 1837. Hurlbut eventually rose to serve as the secretary of the Charleston bar; *Charleston Mercury,* June 27, 1843. Before he left Charleston in 1845, Hurlbut acted as one of two U.S. district commissioners for South Carolina taking acknowledgments of bail and affidavits in federal civil cases, and he served as the South Carolina commissioner for taking acknowledgments of deeds for the state of New York; *Charleston Mercury,* Jan. 15, 16, 1845; and *Charleston Courier,* July 7, 30, Dec. 31, 1845.

20. Carson, *Petigru,* 1–220; Grayson, *Petigru,* 1–90; *Charleston Courier,* Sept. 1, 1838; Hagy, *Directories,* 111. See also James Louis Petigru to Susan Petigru (Mrs. Susan King), July 24, 1861, James Louis Petigru Letters, 1812–1863, Manuscript Division, Library of Congress, Washington, D.C.

21. Petigru to Susan Petigru, Apr. 12, 1842, Petigru Letters; Carson, *Petigru,* 214–15; autograph letter of Stephen A. Hurlbut, May 17, 1842, "Miscellaneous Records, 5Z, 1842–1843," 145: 214, SCAH.

22. *Charleston Mercury,* Oct. 14, 1842; July 22, Aug. 2, 4, 9, 24, 25, 28, 29, Sept. 4, 6, 7, 11, 1843; *Charleston Courier,* July 12, 20, 22, Aug. 2, 4, 9, 16, 24, 25, 28, Sept. 2, 4, 6, 11, 27, 1843. For another case Hurlbut handled, see "Records of the Court of Equity, Charleston District, Court Minute Book, Feb. 5, 1844–Dec. 16, 1845," Gan–H Register, vol. 28: 96, SCAH.

23. *Charleston Courier,* Feb. 24, Mar. 2, 1840. On July 4, 1843, Hurlbut's comrades in arms elected him to be the "orator" for the "Washington Society" for the following year; *Charleston Mercury,* July 6, 1843.

24. *Charleston Courier,* Jan. 21, Feb. 11, 1841; *Charleston Mercury,* Jan. 28, 1841, Feb. 24, 27, Mar. 5, Apr. 4, 1845. For an analysis and evaluation of the strength, efficiency, and morale of northern and southern militia organizations before the Civil War, including the Washington Light Infantry, see R. Don Higginbotham, "The Martial Spirit in the Antebellum South: Some Further Speculations in a National Context," 3–26, particularly 16–18.

25. William T. Sherman, *Memoirs of Gen. W. T. Sherman, Written by Himself,* 1: 247. See also Lloyd Lewis, *Sherman: Fighting Prophet,* 66–75; and Lee Kennett, *Sherman: A Soldier's Life,* 25–33.

26. Way, *New England Society,* 154.

27. *Charleston Mercury,* Apr. 13, 1840; Dec. 25, 1843; Dec. 23, 1844; June 4, 27, 1845. *Charleston Courier,* Dec. 23, 1843; Dec. 24, 1844; Dec. 23, 1845.

28. *Charleston Daily Courier,* Mar. 26, 1863. See also *Memphis Daily Appeal,* Apr. 2, 7, 1863.

29. *Charleston Mercury,* Feb. 11, 12, Dec. 30, 1840.

30. The duties of a "noble grand" are minutely explained in Theodore A. Ross, *Odd Fellowship: Its History and Manual,* 383, and Aaron B. Grosh, *The Odd Fellow's Manual: Illustrating the History, Principles, and Government of the Order, and the Instructions and Duties of Every Degree, Station, and Office,* 246–47. See also *Charleston Courier,* Oct. 5, 1843.

31. *Most Worthy Grand Lodge of Charleston, South Carolina, First Public Procession of the Independent Order of Odd Fellows, of the State of South-Carolina, Saturday, January 1st, 1842*, 3–5; Stephen A. Hurlbut, *Oration Delivered at the Anniversary Celebration of the Independent Order of Odd Fellows, of the State of South-Carolina, January 1, 1842*, 2–19.

32. *Charleston Courier*, Jan. 4, 1842; Sept. 11, 22, Oct. 5, 1843. Hurlbut's aspiration for oratorical renown coincided with his production of poetry, which, along with compositions of other Charleston lawyers and professionals, appeared in literary journals edited by contemporaries; O'Brien and Moltke-Hansen, *Intellectual Life*, 34. In July 1841, "S. A. Hurlbut" was identified as one of numerous "able writers" then producing literary works in Charleston; Mary C. Simms Oliphant, ed., *The Letters of William Gilmore Simms*, 1: *1830–1844*, 268.

33. *Charleston Courier*, Jan. 13, Mar. 1, Sept. 11, Oct. 5, 1843; *Charleston Mercury*, Jan. 2, 13, 14, 15, 16, 18, 19, 24, 25, 26, 27, 28, Sept. 11, 22, 1843.

34. *Charleston Courier*, Sept. 22, 1843, Jan. 3, 1844; Ross, *Odd Fellowship*, 383; Grosh, *Odd Fellow's Manual*, 304, 306–307, 309.

35. *The Rules of the South Carolina Society*, 40, 122, 144; Bellows, *Benevolence among Slaveholders*, 16–17, 44.

36. *Charleston Courier*, May 31, June 14, 1844; *Charleston Mercury*, May 16, 31, June 17, July 30, 1844, and for arguments for and against the ARA, see the *Mercury*, May 18, June 19, 21, July 10, 11, 12, 13, 15, 19, 24, 1844; Michael E. Bell, "Regional Identity in the Antebellum South: How German Immigrants Became 'Good' Charlestonians," 9, 15–17. See also Ray A. Billington, *The Protestant Crusade, 1800–1860: A Study of the Origins of American Nativism*, 1–430, particularly 10, 18, 21, 23, 36, 38, 65, 90, 139, 200–201, 311, 333, 422; William D. Overdyke, *The Know-Nothing Party in the South*, 1–295, especially 4, 12, 14, 33, 70, 95–96; David W. Howe, *The Political Culture of the American Whigs*, 1–122, 201–37, 248–49, 262; Michael F. Holt, *The Rise and Fall of the American Whig Party: Jacksonian Politics and the Onset of the Civil War*, 190–91. Freehling, *Civil War*, 134–297, 301–60; and William J. Cooper, *The South and the Politics of Slavery, 1828–1856*, 237–38.

37. Cooper, *Politics of Slavery*, 98–148; Hesseltine, *The South*, 239–52; Holt, *Whig Party*, 89, 104–13, 190.

38. *Charleston Mercury*, Sept. 19, Oct. 8, 9, 10, 1840; *Charleston Courier*, Sept. 19, 1840.

39. *Charleston Courier*, Dec. 24, 25, 1840, Jan. 4, 1841; *Charleston Mercury*, Jan. 7, 9, 15, 1841.

40. *Charleston Courier*, July 3, 1841, Sept. 6, 8, 1841; *Charleston Mercury*, Jan. 15, 1841.

41. Cooper, *Politics of Slavery*, 149–81; Glyndon G. Van Deusen, *The Life of Henry Clay*, 60, 164, 165, 215, 237, 269; Maurice G. Baxter, *Henry Clay and the American System*, 16–33, 108–20; Howe, *American Whigs*, 2, 18, 49, 136–39, 145–46, 149, 167, 172, 213, 217–18, 272, 292; Hesseltine, *The South*, 237–38; Arthur C. Cole, *The Whig Party in the South*, 64–103; Holt, *Whig Party*, 2, 13, 15, 19, 46, 94, 447.

42. *Charleston Mercury*, Dec. 11, 1843, Feb. 1, 7, 12, Mar. 1, 26, Apr. 2, 3, 4, 8, Oct. 29, 1844; *Charleston Courier*, Dec. 4, 12, 28, 1843, Feb. 5, 7, Mar. 1, 12, Apr. 1, 3, 4, 5, 22, 24, 1844; Cooper, *Politics of Slavery*, 165–66, 182–224; Van Deusen, *Henry Clay*, 358–63; Howe, *American Whigs*, 143–44, but see also 123–42, 145–49; Hesseltine, *The South*, 253–55; Cole, *Whig Party*, 114; Holt, *Whig Party*, 166, 176–83, 189–90, 199.

43. *Baltimore Sun,* Apr. 30, May 2, 3, 1844; *Charleston Courier,* May 7, 30, 1844; *Charleston Mercury,* Apr. 25, May 28, 30, 1844. See also Charles Sellers, "The Election of 1844," 1: *1789–1844,* 761; Howe, *American Whigs,* 215–17, 220–21; O'Brien and Moltke-Hansen, *Intellectual Life,* 18, 28, 40, 127, 152–85, 237, 308; and Hurlbut to Caleb B. Smith, Feb. 1, 1849, Caleb B. Smith Papers, 1808–1862, Manuscript Division, Library of Congress, Washington, D.C.

44. *Charleston Courier,* Aug. 19, 1844; Cooper, *Politics of Slavery,* 206–24; Freehling, *Road to Disunion,* 1: 355–439.

45. Philip M. Hamer, "Great Britain, the United States, and the Negro Seamen Acts, 1822–1848," 3–28.

46. Hurlbut recounted this incident to Sen. George F. Hoar, Samuel Hoar's son, on some occasion after 1874 when Hurlbut served as a Republican member of Congress; George F. Hoar, *Autobiography of Seventy Years,* 1: 25–26. *Charleston Mercury,* Dec. 3, 9, 11, 17, 1844, Jan. 13, 17, 1845. See also Hamer, "Negro Seamen Acts," 22–23; Carson, *Petigru,* 240; and O'Brien and Moltke-Hansen, *Intellectual Life,* 419.

47. *Philadelphia Inquirer & National Gazette,* Jan. 20, 1843; Hurlbut, "Memoir," 32–44.

48. Charles Godfrey Leland, the Philadelphia philologist and a boyhood playmate of William Henry Hurlbut in 1838, witnessed this nearly fatal shooting incident. Leland, as a pupil, had found Martin Luther Hurlbut's institution "simply intolerable" because of Hurlbut's oppressive discipline and pedantic didacticism. He described William Henry Hurlbut as prone to fits of blind rage. The younger Hurlbut had, Leland surmised, "a screw loose"; Leland, *Memoirs,* 73, 80–81, 233–34. See also a letter of July 26, 1861, from William Henry Hurlbert to the Confederate States Congress, concerning Philadelphia and Charleston antecedents, in *The War of the Rebellion: A Compilation of the Official Records of the Union and Confederate Armies,* ser. 2, vol. 2: 1492–95.

49. *Charleston Mercury,* Jan. 22, 1844; *Charleston Daily Courier,* Mar. 26, 1863. For other accounts, see *Memphis Daily Appeal,* Apr. 2, 7, 1863; and *Belvidere Standard,* July 30, 1872.

50. Theodore Rosengarten, *Tombee: Portrait of a Cotton Planter, with the Journal of Thomas B. Chaplin (1822–1890),* 120, 332, 359, 364.

51. *Charleston Courier,* Mar. 12, 1844, Dec. 12, 1843; *Charleston Mercury,* Apr. 2, 3, 4, 8, 1844.

52. *Charleston Daily Courier,* Mar. 26, 1863; *Memphis Daily Appeal,* Apr. 2, 7, 1863; *Richmond Sentinel,* Mar. 24, 1863. For a northern correspondent's account of the circumstances surrounding Hurlbut's departure from Charleston, however, see *New York Daily Tribune,* Mar. 30, 1861. See also an obituary of Stephen A. Hurlbut by William Henry Hurlbert, in *New York World,* Apr. 3, 1882. The foregoing southern editorial references to Hurlbut's fraudulent misconduct in Charleston cannot be dismissed as Confederate propaganda. Besides accurately establishing the personal relationships involved in the Dickson affair, the *Courier's* account accords with the pattern of misconduct in which Hurlbut subsequently engaged in Memphis and New Orleans during the Civil War. Moreover, James Petigru Carson, the grandson of James Louis Petigru, corroborated the *Courier's* charges, albeit euphemistically, alluding to the swindling of Dickson as "some unedifying frolic" that compelled Hurlbut's departure from Charleston in 1845; Carson, *Petigru,*

374–75. As for his drinking in Charleston, twenty-seven years later, in 1872, Hurlbut admitted that in his "earlier years" he had overindulged "when he may have been a little wild"; *Belvidere Standard,* July 30, 1872.

53. *Belvidere Standard,* June 18, 1872; Sager, "Hurlbut," 53–54. The Illinois legislature in 1854 renamed the Fever River the Galena River.

CHAPTER 2: LAWYER, WHIG, AND REPUBLICAN

1. Sager, "Hurlbut," 53–56; Richard V. Carpenter, ed., *Historical Encyclopedia of Illinois and History of Boone County,* 2: 661–942; Virginia B. Moorhead, ed., *Boone County Then and Now, 1835–1976: A History in Words and Pictures by Her Sons and Daughters to Celebrate the Bicentennial of the Signing of the Declaration of Independence,* 1–165. Ten years later, in 1855, the population of Belvidere and surrounding countryside had grown to include 3,406 whites and six blacks. For the 1855 census, see *Belvidere Standard,* Sept. 4, 1855.

2. William V. Pooley, "The Settlement of Illinois from 1830 to 1850," 352–74, 421–39, 491; *Belvidere Illustrated: Historical Descriptive and Biographical,* 7–9.

3. A daguerreotype image of Hurlbut in the 1840s is shown in Francis T. Miller, ed., *The Photographic History of the Civil War, in Ten Volumes,* 10: 191.

4. *Belvidere Republican,* Aug. 3, 1848; Sager, "Hurlbut," 56. Hurlbut removed his office to larger quarters on the upper floor of C. M. Castle's General Store, next to the Belvidere Bank, in mid-October 1853; *Belvidere Standard,* Oct. 18, 1853.

5. Sager, "Hurlbut," 56; Carpenter, *Boone County,* 2: 666–80, 713; *Belvidere Illustrated,* 70–77; *Portrait and Biographical Record of Winnebago and Boone Counties, Illinois,* 516–17. See also Hurlbut to Calvin DeWolfe, Mar. 29, 1848, Zebina Eastman Collection, 1842–1883, Chicago Historical Society, Chicago, Illinois; and *Chicago Democrat,* Aug. 24, 1849.

6. "Circuit Court Record, Boone County, 1843–1848," book C1, 139, 176, 219, 236, 241, 262, 285, 292, 309, 321, 337, 343, 346, 377, Boone County Courthouse, Belvidere, Illinois [hereafter BCCH]. See also *Belvidere Standard,* Oct. 21, Nov. 4, 1851.

7. Stephen A. Hurlbut, L.H.D., *Between Peace and War: A Report to Lincoln from Charleston, 1861. In the Midst of War: A Letter from Shiloh, 1862. Edited from the Manuscripts of Maj.-Gen. Stephen A. Hurlbut,* 4; Sager, "Hurlbut," 56; *Belvidere Standard,* Feb. 14, 1865.

8. Robert L. Steenrod, comp., *Boone County, Illinois: Marriage Records, 1838–1860,* 9; Carpenter, *Boone County,* 2: 682; "Mortgage Record D, 1844–1857," 323, BCCH; *Belvidere Illustrated,* 13, 19, 24, 27.

9. Theodore C. Pease, ed., *Illinois Election Returns, 1818–1848,* 438; *Sangamo (Springfield) Journal,* May 6, 13, 1847.

10. *Sangamo Journal,* June 15, 17, 1847.

11. Arthur C. Cole, ed., *The Constitutional Debates of 1847,* 65, 85–86, 170, 214, 365, 369, 539.

12. *"Foreigners"* comment in *Weekly Chicago Democrat,* July 6, 1847.

13. Ameda R. King, "The Last Years of the Whig Party in Illinois: 1847 to 1856," 32: 110–20, 123, 136, 146; Mark E. Neely, ed., "Lincoln's Springfield Friends: Friends of the

Negro," 1–3; Leon F. Litwack, *North of Slavery: The Negro in the Free States, 1790–1860*, 61–71; N. Dwight Harris, *The History of Negro Servitude in Illinois and of the Slavery Agitation in That State, 1719–1864*, 16–26, 50–67, 160–61, 233, 235–38; Emil J. Verlie, ed., *Illinois Constitutions*, 5, 51; Charles A. Church, *History of Rockford and Winnebago County Illinois from the First Settlement in 1834 to the Civil War*, 264–65.

14. David M. Potter, *The Impending Crisis, 1848–1861*, 18–27, 57–59, 81.

15. David H. Donald, *Lincoln*, 19–161; Roy P. Basler, ed., *The Collected Works of Abraham Lincoln*, 1: *1824–1848*, 498.

16. *Illinois State Journal*, July 20, 1848; *Belvidere Republican*, Aug. 3, 1848; *Galena Weekly Northwestern Gazette*, Sept. 6, 1848. See also Holt, *Whig Party*, 273.

17. *Chicago Journal*, Oct. 6, 7, 1848.

18. Colfax to Smith, Nov. 17, 1848, Jan. 11, 27, 1849, Hurlbut to Smith, Feb. 1, Mar. 24, 1849, Smith Papers. See also Richard J. Thomas, "Caleb Blood Smith: Whig Orator and Politician: Lincoln's Secretary of Interior," 3–86, 105–20; Donald W. Riddle, *Congressman Abraham Lincoln*, 192, 194–95. The English-born Edward D. Baker of Springfield had represented Sangamo County in the Illinois House and Senate before serving in the Mexican War and winning reelection to Congress after the war. "Long John" Wentworth had edited the *Chicago Daily Democrat* after 1840 and had then served in Congress; John T. Hubbell and James W. Geary, eds., *Biographical Dictionary of the Union: Northern Leaders of the Civil War*, 21–22, 579–80.

19. "Circuit Court Record, Boone County," book 2, 1849–1851, and book 3, 1851–1854, BCCH. See also *Belvidere Standard*, July 20, 27, Sept. 7, 1852. In 1850 Hurlbut helped to prepare federal census returns for Boone and McHenry counties. Moreover, he described the region's topographical and geological features as well as the prevalent climatic conditions in northern Illinois; Wesley Johnston, "Mortality Schedule Remarks," 47; and *Illinois State Journal*, July 23, 1850.

20. *Belvidere Standard*, Apr. 26, May 3, 10, 1853, Apr. 11, 1854. Hurlbut later handled five lesser criminal cases. He prevailed (with or against Fuller and other counsel) in two unrelated larceny and bastardy cases but lost three cases of slander and assault and battery; *Belvidere Standard*, Apr. 24, May 1, 1855.

21. *Belvidere Standard*, Oct. 19, 1852, Apr. 26, May 3, 1853, Oct. 17, 1854. The most important civil case Hurlbut handled in the mid-1850s occurred in February 1854, when Fuller defeated his efforts to recover seventy dollars in damages for a farmer whose bull and two-year-old steer had been struck and killed by a Galena & Chicago Union locomotive. But in lesser cases, Hurlbut and Fuller jointly won a breach-of-promise-of-marriage suit, although Hurlbut himself lost a divorce case; see *Belvidere Standard*, Feb. 14, 1854, Apr. 24, May 1, 1855.

22. "Mortgage Record D, 1844–1857," 323, 414, 445–46, BCCH.

23. *Belvidere Standard*, Nov. 25, Dec. 2, 8, 1851, May 7, 1854 (as to a proposed "State Industrial University"); June 19, July 17, Oct. 30, Dec. 11, 1855, June 10, 1856, June 22, 30, 1857. The "beautiful company" remark in *Freeport Bulletin*, July 8, 1858.

24. *Illinois State Journal*, July 9, 1852; *Belvidere Standard*, Aug. 3, Sept. 21, 1852.

25. Russell K. Nelson, "The Early Life and Congressional Career of Elihu B. Washburne," 86. See also William E. Gienapp, *The Origins of the Republican Party, 1852–1856*, 24; and Holt, *Whig Party*, 744.

26. *Belvidere Standard,* Oct. 12, Nov. 9, 1852.

27. Hurlbut to Washburne, Nov. 8, 1852, Elihu B. Washburne Papers, 1829–1892, Manuscript Division, Library of Congress, Washington, D.C.

28. Potter, *Impending Crisis,* 145–77; Freehling, *Road to Disunion,* 1: 536–65; Robert W. Johannsen, *Stephen A. Douglas,* 206–544; Gerald M. Capers, *Stephen A. Douglas: Defender of the Union,* 87–112; Stephen B. Oates, *With Malice toward None: The Life of Abraham Lincoln,* 111–22.

29. Charles A. Church, *History of the Republican Party in Illinois, 1854–1912, with a Review of the Aggressions of the Slave-Power,* 20–22; Church, *History of Rockford,* 329–30; Nelson, "Life of Washburne," 109; *Belvidere Standard,* Sept. 5, 1854. See also Gienapp, *Republican Party,* 124.

30. "Frightful limitations" and preceding remarks quoted in Church, *History of Rockford,* 330. Also, on September 6, 1854, Hurlbut approached Hiram H. Waldo, another convention delegate and a strong Washburne supporter, and "complimented him on his splendid fight, and said that, considering the material at hand, he had done well" in securing Washburne's nomination. Church, *History of Rockford,* 330. "Loco Hunker candidate" remark of Benjamin S. Hurton to Washburne, Sept. 17, 1854, Washburne Papers.

31. "Circuit Court Record, Boone County," book 4, 1855–1860, BCCH. See also *Belvidere Standard,* Apr. 24, May 1, Aug. 14, 1855, Jan. 22, Feb. 12, June 10, July 8, 1856; Carpenter, *Boone County,* 2: 720.

32. Potter, *Impending Crisis,* 199–213.

33. Hurlbut to Trumbull, May 2, 1856, Lyman Trumbull Papers, 1855–1872, Manuscript Division, Library of Congress, Washington, D.C. See also Mark M. Krug, *Lyman Trumbull: Conservative Radical,* 94–132.

34. Church, *Republican Party,* 30–33; Gienapp, *Republican Party,* 28–43 and passim.

35. *Belvidere Standard,* June 24, 1856; Smith to Washburne, Aug. 14, 1856, Washburne Papers. See also Anson S. Miller to Washburne, Aug. 27, 1856, and Elijah W. Blaisdell to Washburne, Aug. 28, 1856, Washburne Papers.

36. *Belvidere Standard,* Aug. 19, 25, Sept. 2, 16, Oct. 21, Nov. 4, 1856; *Rockford Republican,* Aug. 27, 1856; Allan Nevins, *Frémont, Pathmarker of the West,* 2: *Frémont in the Civil War,* 439–58.

37. Potter, *Impending Crisis,* 267–327.

38. Hurlbut to Trumbull, Dec. 14, 22, 1857, Trumbull Papers. See also Horace White, *The Life of Lyman Trumbull,* 74. Hurlbut's view proved partially correct. The 1860 national Democratic convention in Charleston broke up over this question, with Southern Democrats rejecting Douglas's formulation of popular sovereignty and demanding federal protection of slavery in the territories and rigid observance of the principles laid down in the clearly pro-Southern Dred Scott decision.

39. Hurlbut to Douglas, Dec. 25, 1857, Stephen A. Douglas MSS, 1833–1861, Univ. of Chicago Library, Chicago, Illinois. See also John S. Wright, "The Background and Formation of the Republican Party in Illinois, 1846–1860," 218–19; and Oates, *Lincoln,* 137–41.

40. Hurlbut to Trumbull, May 16, 1858, Trumbull Papers. See also Potter, *Impending Crisis,* 323–25. Here again, Hurlbut proved only partially accurate in his predictions. Kansans rejected the Lecompton Constitution in 1858, but Douglas refrained from en-

dorsing the Topeka Constitution. Rather, ultimately he favored a compromise measure that never received Senate approval; see Johannsen, *Douglas,* 545–613; Capers, *Douglas,* 132–75; Donald, *Lincoln,* 162–215; and David E. Meerse, "Buchanan, the Patronage, and the Lecompton Constitution: A Case Study," 291–312.

41. Compared with his regular attendance late in the 1840s and early in the 1850s, Hurlbut compiled an uneven and sporadic record of courtroom appearances later in the 1850s. "Circuit Court Record, Boone County," book 4, 1855–1860, BCCH.

42. Hurlbut to Lincoln, May 29, 1858, Robert Todd Lincoln Collection of the Papers of Abraham Lincoln, Manuscript Division, Library of Congress, Washington, D.C. (microfilm copy, Kent State Univ. Library, Kent, Ohio).

43. Basler, *Collected Works,* 2: *1848–1858,* 456. See also *Illinois State Journal,* June 17, 1858.

44. Fuller to Washburne, July 13, 1858, Washburne Papers. See also Blaisdell to Washburne, May 27, 1858, ibid; *Belvidere Standard,* June 1, July 20, 1858. The Democratic *Freeport Bulletin,* considering the professedly antislavery Republican candidates running for office from the First Congressional District, cynically asserted that these aspirants "are willing to sacrifice their own interests and convenience for the *dear people,* and are ready to take the nomination for Congress. They will mount the woolly horse"— that is, the cause of the "colored man"; *Freeport Bulletin,* July 8, 1858.

45. Flynn to Washburne, July 19, 1858, Washburne Papers. See also Lawrence S. Church to Washburne, Aug. 9, 1858, ibid. Nevertheless, as early as November 1852, the formerly Democratic *Belvidere Standard* had wondered if "'the *root of all evil*' entered largely into the canvass, (as has been pretty generally understood)" in accounting for Washburne's nomination as the Whig candidate representing the First Congressional District in northern Illinois; *Belvidere Standard,* Nov. 9, 1852.

46. "Monopoly" and succeeding remarks in *Belvidere Standard,* Aug. 17, 1858. See also Aug. 12, 19, Nov. 2, 11, 1858. Besides serving as the principal Boone County delegate to the Whig congressional nominating convention at Rockford, Hurlbut also acted as a county delegate to the Republican senatorial convention from the Third Senatorial District to nominate a Whig party candidate; *Rockford Republican,* Sept. 30, 1858. See also *Freeport Bulletin,* Aug. 19, 1858, and Potter, *Impending Crisis,* 328–38, 354–55.

47. Church to Washburne, Nov. 11, 1858, Washburne Papers; John Clayton, comp., *The Illinois Fact Book and Historical Almanac, 1673–1968,* 223; Sager, "Hurlbut," 57–60; *Illinois State Journal,* Nov. 13, 1858. Regarding Hurlbut's candidacy for a seat in the Illinois House, an editor declared, "Our nominee for Representative is a man who has the ability and inclination to do service in the cause of Republican principles"; *Belvidere Standard,* Oct. 19, 1858 and Nov. 9, 1858.

48. *Belvidere Standard,* Aug. 24, 31, 1858; *Rockford Republican,* Aug. 19, 1858; "perpetual" remark in *Freeport Bulletin,* Sept. 2, and 23, 1858; Johannsen, *Douglas,* 614–874; Capers, *Douglas,* 177–88; Donald, *Lincoln,* 215–29; Oates, *Lincoln,* 149–60. See also Harold Holzer, ed., *The Lincoln-Douglas Debates: The First Complete, Unexpurgated Text,* 3, 18, 24, 86–135, 226, 329.

49. Hurlbut to Hatch, Dec. 1, 1858, Ozias M. Hatch Papers, 1818–1875, Illinois State Historical Library, Springfield, Ill.; *Journal of the House of Representatives of the Twenty-first General Assembly of the State of Illinois, at Their Regular Session, Begun and Held at Springfield, January 3, 1859,* 19, 32.

50. John Moses, *Illinois: Historical and Statistical, Comprising the Essential Facts of Its Planting and Growth as a Province, County, Territory, and State,* 2: 621–23; *Journal of the House,* 880–89; *Belvidere Standard,* Feb. 1, 19, Mar. 1, Apr. 19, 1859; "lion's den" remark in *Belvidere Standard,* Nov. 13, 1860.

51. Hurlbut to Hatch, Mar. 8, 1859, Hatch Papers. See also *Portrait and Biographical Album of McLean County, Ill.,* 147–48; David W. Lusk, *Politics and Politicians: A Succinct History of the Politics of Illinois from 1856 to 1884, With Anecdotes and Incidents, and Appendix from 1809 to 1856,* 95, 96, 218–20; and *St. Louis Missouri Democrat,* Feb. 26, 1861.

52. *The Past and Present of Boone County, Illinois,* 303; *Belvidere Standard,* Dec. 28, 1858; *Illinois State Journal,* Oct. 6, 1859. Hurlbut might have derived satisfaction from learning that Democratic senator Stephen A. Douglas, long renowned for his eloquence, had served as Illinois's Masonic grand orator in 1840; Henry Horner, "Grand Orators of Illinois: Eloquent Address Delivered at the 1924 Grand Lodge Meeting," 16–18.

53. Charles W. Marsh (?) to Washburne, Nov. 4, 1859, Washburne Papers; Hurlbut to Hatch, Nov. 14, 1859, Hatch Papers; *Journal of the House,* 954–1136.

54. Holm to Washburne, Jan. 5, 1860, and Frederick Brown to Washburne, July 22, 1860, Washburne Papers.

55. *Rockford Republican,* Aug. 2, 1860. See also *Belvidere Standard,* July 17, 31, 1860, and *Freeport Bulletin,* Nov. 1, 1860.

56. Hurlbut to Trumbull, Apr. 18, 1860, Trumbull Papers; Jesse P. Weber, ed., "Dedication of a Tablet Marking the Site at Decatur, Illinois, of the Old Wigwam in Which the Illinois State Republican Convention of 1860 Was Held," 151. See also Jane M. Johns, *Personal Recollections of Early Decatur: Abraham Lincoln, Richard J. Oglesby, and the Civil War, 1849–1865,* 79–80; Church, *Republican Party,* 79–80; and *Illinois State Journal,* May 12, 1860.

57. Oates, *Lincoln,* 175–79.

58. "Circuit Court Record, Boone County," book 4, 1855–1860, and book 6, 1860–1866, BCCH; *Belvidere Standard,* May 29, 1860. The lapses in his law practice notwithstanding, on March 14, 1861, Hurlbut's colleagues appointed him chairman of the Boone County bar; *Belvidere Standard,* Mar. 19, 1861.

59. "Old Abe," in *Illinois State Journal,* Aug. 9, 13, 17, 1860; "fagged out" in *Belvidere Standard,* Aug. 21, 1860. A Republican supporter of Lincoln during the 1860 presidential campaign later recalled that "Abraham Lincoln once said that Stephen A. Hurlbut was the ablest orator on the stump that Illinois had ever produced"; Church, *History of Rockford,* 331.

60. Basler, *Collected Works,* 4: 1860–1861, 124, 134. See also *Illinois State Journal,* Oct. 5, 27, 1860, and *Belvidere Standard,* Sept. 4, 1860. For a reminiscence of Hurlbut's (concerning his canvassing of the Springfield area for Lincoln), see *New York Times,* Aug. 30, 1872.

61. *Belvidere Standard,* Sept. 25, Oct. 2, 30, Nov. 6, 1860.

62. *Belvidere Standard,* Nov. 13, 1860; Hurlbut to Washburne, Dec. 18, 1860, Washburne Papers.

63. Hurlbut to Davis, Dec. 18, 1860, David Davis Papers, 1815–1921, Chicago Historical Society, Chicago, Illinois. See also Benjamin P. Thomas, *Abraham Lincoln: A Biography,* 157, 165, 179, 193–94, 200–201, 208, 212, 235.

64. *Illinois State Journal,* Feb. 1, 1861.

65. Cullom later recalled, "I might say that General Hurlbut and Lawrence Church were two very strong men, both from the northern part of the State, and both became prominent in the public service. I might also say that but for those two men, who put me forward as a candidate for the Speaker-ship, I probably would not have become a candidate"; Shelby M. Cullom, *Fifty Years of Public Service: Personal Recollections of Shelby M. Cullom, Senior United States Senator From Illinois,* 77. See also James W. Neilson, *Shelby M. Cullom: Prairie State Republican,* 7.

66. *Journal of the House of Representatives of the Twenty-second General Assembly of the State of Illinois, at Their Regular Session, Begun and Held at Springfield, January 7, 1861,* 477–79, 488. Hurlbut also served on the Illinois House committees of apportionment and of the militia and voted for the Reapportionment Bill of January 31, 1861, which created twenty-five senatorial and sixty-five representative districts with substantially increased proportionate Republican representation from the House districts in comparison to what the Democratic measure of 1859 had proposed to assign to them; ibid., 79; Church, *Republican Party,* 82. See also Hurlbut to Hatch, Nov. 27, 1860, Hatch Papers, and Hurlbut to Trumbull, Jan. 22, 1861, Trumbull Papers.

67. Hurlbut to Trumbull, Feb. 27, Mar. 13, 1861, Trumbull Papers; Hurlbut to Nicolay, Mar. 4, 1861, Lincoln Papers.

68. Letter from Washington, Mar. 23, 1861, from "Belvidere," printed in *Belvidere Standard,* Apr. 2, 1861; Fuller to Trumbull, Mar. 4, 1861; and C. Vincent Roscoe to Trumbull, Mar. 19, 1861, Trumbull Papers.

69. John G. Nicolay and John Hay, *Abraham Lincoln: A History,* 3: 390–92; Malone, *DAB,* 5: 562–63; Sager, "Hurlbut," 60–61.

70. Scott to Anderson, Mar. 22, 1861, Winfield Scott Folder, Chicago Historical Society, Chicago, Illinois. Scott recommended that Lincoln evacuate Fort Sumter to conciliate the South, but officers in the War Department ultimately overruled his counsel. For recent studies of Scott's antebellum career and a discussion of his role in the momentous Fort Sumter affair, see Timothy D. Johnson, *Winfield Scott: The Quest for Military Glory,* 7–225, and John S. D. Eisenhower, *Agent of Destiny: The Life and Times of General Winfield Scott,* 1–349, 356–68.

71. Ward H. Lamon, *Recollections of Abraham Lincoln, 1847–1865,* 68–79; Philip Van Doren Stern, *Prologue to Sumter: The Beginnings of the Civil War from the John Brown Raid to the Surrender of Fort Sumter,* 460–66; Hurlbut to Lincoln, Mar. 27, 1861, Lincoln Papers; and Hurlbut, *Between Peace and War,* 5–6. Hurlbut proudly recounted to his son his confrontation in Charleston with Confederate soldiers. George Hurlbut, by then seventy years old, described in 1918 his father's Fort Sumter adventures of 1861 to George V. Lauman, the son of Brig. Gen. Jacob G. Lauman of Iowa and a man who had fought gallantly under Hurlbut at Shiloh; see Hurlbut to Lauman, Oct. 25, 1918, Winfield Scott Folder.

72. "Ambassador" remark quoted in Carson, *Petigru,* 374–75. See also Pease, *Petigru,* 156–58; Hurlbut to Lincoln, Mar. 27, 1861, Lincoln Papers; Hurlbut, *Between Peace & War,* 6; and *Charleston Daily Courier,* Mar. 23, 25, 26, 29, Apr. 1, 3, 1861. Lamon (and probably Hurlbut besides) sought to enlist Petigru's help in reaching Major Anderson in

Fort Sumter. On the morning after he had met Lamon, Petigru informed his first cousin, J. Johnston Pettigrew, "There is no doubt that Anderson will be off in a few days and I don't see why the order was not given weeks ago. Lamen [?], a friend of Lincoln called on me last evening; said he wanted to see Anderson and I advised him to go boldly to [South Carolina governor Francis W.] Pickens and say so. He has here closeted with Pickens, but I don't know whether he has seen the inside of the Fort or been allowed to do so"; Petigru to Pettigrew, Mar. 25, 1861, J. Johnston Pettigrew Papers, Department of Cultural Resources, Division of Archives and History, Raleigh, North Carolina.

73. Hurlbut to Lincoln, Mar. 27, 1861, Lincoln Papers; Hurlbut, *Between Peace & War,* 6–7; "laughed at me" remark, included among Hurlbut's reminiscences of his encounters with secessionists whom he "had known in my boyhood," qtd. in *New York Times,* Sept. 11, 1872. See also *New York Daily Tribune,* Mar. 30, 1861.

74. *The War of the Rebellion: A Compilation of the Official Records of the Union and Confederate Armies,* ser. 1, vol. 1: 218, 221, 222, 230, 237, 281–82, 294 [hereafter *OR;* all references are to series 1, unless otherwise noted].

75. *New York Daily Tribune,* Mar. 26, 27, 28, 29, 30, Apr. 2, 4, 1861; *New York Times,* Mar. 26, 28, 29, Apr. 2, 6, 1861; *New York Herald,* Mar. 25, 28, 1861; *Charleston Daily Courier,* Mar. 26, 28, 29, Apr. 3, 1861; "danger ahead" remark qtd. in Lamon, *Lincoln,* 78–79; Stern, *Prologue to Sumter,* 466. Lamon later recalled, "I learned afterward that about all of Hurlbut's time in Charleston had been employed in eluding the search of the vigilants, who, it was feared, would have given him a rough welcome to Charleston if they had known in time of his presence there." Upon Lamon's return to Washington, "the President learned for the first time that Hurlbut had been in South Carolina. He laughed heartily over my unvarnished recital of Hurlbut's experience in the hotbed of secession." Lamon, *Lincoln,* 79. Lincoln, of course, contrary to Lamon's anecdote, had in fact dispatched Hurlbut to Charleston; see Nicolay and Hay, *Abraham Lincoln,* 3: 390–92.

76. *New York Daily Tribune,* Mar. 26, 30, 1861. *Freeport (Illinois) Bulletin,* describing Hurlbut as "an Illinoisan in Limbo," reprinted in a *New York Herald's* account of March 26, 1861, asserting that municipal authorities had arrested one "S. Hurlbut" shortly following his arrival in Charleston "for a debt contracted in South Carolina before removing from that State some years ago"; *Freeport Bulletin,* Apr. 11, 1861.

77. Hurlbut to Lincoln, Mar. 27, 1861, Lincoln Papers; Hurlbut, *Between Peace & War,* 7–13; *Charleston Daily Courier,* Apr. 1, June 21, 26, 1861; *Charleston Mercury,* Mar. 26, 1861. "S A Hurlbut and lady" stayed at Willards' Hotel in Washington both before and after their trip to Charleston. *Washington Evening Star,* Mar. 21, 28, 1861. See also Maury Klein, *Days of Defiance: Sumter, Secession, and the Coming of the Civil War,* 341–43, and Allan Nevins, *The War for the Union,* 1: *The Improvised War, 1861–1862,* 48, 53–54.

78. Richard N. Current, *Lincoln and the First Shot,* 15–125. See also Donald, *Lincoln,* 230–94; Klein, *Days of Defiance,* 403–20; Oates, *Lincoln,* 219–27; Albert Castel, "Fort Sumter: 1861," 4–50; *Charleston Daily Courier,* Apr. 13, 15, 1861; *Charleston Mercury,* Apr. 13, 1861; and Hubbell and Geary, *Northern Leaders,* 8–9, 460. The fall of Fort Sumter aroused Hurlbut's fear of an imminent Confederate capture of Washington—"Mr. H. believes that nothing will prevent an attack upon the Capitol by the Seceders" barring the prompt demonstration of superior military might from mobilized Northern forces; *Belvidere Standard,* Apr. 16, 1861.

CHAPTER 3: SUPPRESSOR OF REBELLION:
GENERAL HURLBUT INVADES THE CONFEDERACY

1. *Belvidere Standard,* Apr. 16, 23, May 14, 1861; *Chicago Evening Journal,* Apr. 27, 1861. See also Hurlbut to Lincoln, Apr. 23, 1861, Lincoln Papers.

2. *Illinois State Register,* July 16, 1861; *Belvidere Standard,* May 21, 28, June 4, 1861, see also Jan. 8, 29, 1861. See also *Illinois State Journal,* May 17, 23, 1861; *Chicago Tribune,* May 24, 1861; *Chicago Evening Journal,* June 18, 1861; Lucius W. Barber, *Army Memoirs of Lucius W. Barber, Company "D," 15th Illinois Volunteer Infantry, May 24, 1861, to Sept. 30, 1865,* 11, 13, 77; Edwin E. Sparks, ed., *Collections of the Illinois State Historical Library,* 3: *Lincoln Series,* 1: *The Lincoln-Douglas Debates of 1858,* 147, 189, 196; Holzer, *Debates,* 91, 117–18, 121–22; *Portrait And Biographical Album of Stephenson County, Ill., Containing Full Page Portraits and Biographical Sketches of Prominent and Representative Citizens of the County,* 733–34; and *Who Was Who In America: Historical Volume (1607–1896),* 541.

3. Yates to Hurlbut, May 29, 1861, qtd. in Hurlbut, *Between Peace & War,* 15. Yates, however, in his letter from Washington, added: "Now, Hurlbut, I do not write this to excite hopes, for he may not offer it to you, but this is what he said"; ibid. For a contemporary sketch of Yates and his antecedents, see *Rockford Republican,* May 31, 1860.

4. Washburne to Lincoln, June 11, 1861, Lincoln Papers.

5. George R. Jones, *Joseph Russell Jones,* 1–28. See also Jack J. Nortrup, "Richard Yates: Civil War Governor of Illinois," 1–211; Richard Yates II and Catherine Y. Pickering, *Richard Yates: Civil War Governor,* 149–59, 199–210; Lloyd Lewis, *Captain Sam Grant,* 406, 417, 419; and Robert M. Hutchins, ed., *Letters from Lloyd Lewis, Showing Steps in the Research for His Biography of U. S. Grant,* 13.

6. Jones, *Jones,* 1–22, 38–39; Jones to Washburne, June 13, 1861, Washburne Papers. Eleven years after the war, Jones continued to claim that he had procured the Hurlbut appointment. But in truth, Washburne, not Jones, finally persuaded Lincoln to make Hurlbut a brigadier general. For Jones's account, see *Chicago Pension-Agency, Sworn Statement of Joseph Russell Jones, Chicago, Illinois, July 3, 1876,* 6–7.

7. Christopher Dell, *Lincoln and the War Democrats: The Grand Erosion of Conservative Tradition*—as for Butler, 44–316 and passim; as for McClernand, 38–304 and passim; and as for the Union party, 18, 21–22, 105, 309; Victor Hicken, *Illinois in the Civil War,* 12; Ezra J. Warner, *Generals in Blue: Lives of the Union Commanders,* 245. To clarify terminology—"Union party" refers to an actual historical entity, while "Illinois Clique" is my own expression to describe the closely integrated political circle of Lincoln, Yates, Washburne, Jones, and Hurlbut.

8. *Belvidere Standard,* June 18, 1861; *Chicago Evening Journal,* June 18, 1861; *Rockford Republican,* June 20, 1861; *Chicago Post,* June 16 (?), 1861, qtd. in *Chicago Times,* June 18, 27, 1861; "English nobleman" remark in T. D. M'Gillicudy, "General Grant's First Service in the War," 62; James H. Wilson, *The Life of John A. Rawlins: Lawyer, Assistant Adjutant-General, Chief of Staff, Major General of Volunteers, and Secretary of War,* 51; John Y. Simon, ed., *The Papers of Ulysses S. Grant,* 2: *April–September 1861,* 30n, 41n, 43n–44n; *National Tribune,* Jan. 14, 1886. For other editorial comments on the Hurlbut appointment, see *St. Louis Missouri Republican,* July 3, 1861; *New York Times,* June 23, 1861; *Quincy Daily Whig and Republican,* June 18, 1861; *Illinois State Journal,* May 21, 23, June 17, 1861; *St. Louis Missouri Democrat,* July 9, 1861; and *Cincinnati Daily Commercial,* Aug. 10, 1861.

9. *Illinois State Register,* June 17, 20, 1861; *Freeport Bulletin,* July 4, 1861; the "one-horse lawyer" and succeeding remarks of the *Free Trader* are quoted in the *Quincy Herald,* July 1, 8, 1861. See also *Cincinnati Daily Enquirer,* June 20, 1861.

10. *OR,* 3: 390, 396–97. See also Simon, *Papers of Grant,* 2: 71; and Hubbell and Geary, *Northern Leaders,* 323. The Democratic *Illinois State Register* of Springfield, commenting upon Hurlbut's assignment to Quincy (a point of rendezvous where no Union troops had yet assembled), sarcastically remarked that he would consequently qualify as "the right man in the right place." *Illinois State Register,* July 10, 1861. See also *Rockford Republican,* July 11, 1861. For a favorable description of Hurlbut and the Boone Rifles at Camp Scott, see *Freeport Bulletin,* May 23, 1861.

11. Jones to Washburne, July 12, 1861, Washburne Papers.

12. Ibid. For "rousing" remark, see *Belvidere Standard,* Feb. 2, 1858, but see also Feb. 3, 8, 1853, and May 29, 1855.

13. Fitch to Trumbull, June 26, 29, 1861, Trumbull Papers; Fitch to Washburne, July 13, 1861, Washburne Papers. In 1858, Fitch had served as the U.S. district attorney at Chicago for the District of Northern Illinois. Later, in 1862, eight months after Hurlbut received Senate confirmation as a brigadier general, Fitch served in Tennessee. But presently, tiring of field duty, he obtained a position on Maj. Gen. William T. Sherman's staff as chief quartermaster at Memphis. See *OR,* 17, pt. 2: 156, 159, 170, 237, 243, 277, 289, 345, 406, 426, 480; and *Freeport Bulletin,* Oct. 14, 1858.

14. Medill to Trumbull, July 13, 1861, Trumbull Papers; Nevins, *War for the Union,* 1: 230; Browning to Lincoln, Sept. 11, 30, 1861, Lincoln Papers. See also Maurice Baxter, *Orville H. Browning: Lincoln's Friend and Critic,* 130; Basler, *Collected Works,* 4: *1860–1861,* 531.

15. Long to Trumbull, July 13, 1861, Trumbull Papers.

16. Browning to Hurlbut, July 18, 1861, Orville H. Browning Folder, Chicago Historical Society, Chicago, Ill. See also Harlan H. Horner, "Lincoln Rebukes a Senator," 103–106, 111; and Hubbell and Geary, *Northern Leaders,* 63–64.

17. Leslie Anders, *The Twenty-first Missouri: From Home Guard to Union Regiment,* 6–21; Basler, *Collected Works,* 4: 407; *OR,* 3: 390. See also Mark M. Boatner III, *The Civil War Dictionary,* 314–15; Andrew F. Rolle, *John Charles Frémont: Character as Destiny,* 191; and Hubbell and Geary, *Northern Leaders,* 187.

18. *OR,* II, 1: 185, 186–87; *Chicago Tribune,* July 23, 1861; Nevins, *War for the Union,* 1: 319.

19. George T. Palmer, *A Conscientious Turncoat: The Story of John M. Palmer, 1817–1900,* 1–66; Boatner, *Dictionary,* 617, 774, 853; Moses, *Illinois: Historical and Statistical,* 1: 481–84; Harry M. Beardsley, *Joseph Smith and His Mormon Empire,* 337–68; John H. Evans, *Joseph Smith: An American Prophet,* 191–207; Daniel H. Ludlow, ed., *Encyclopedia of Mormonism: The History, Scripture, Doctrine, and Procedure of the Church of Jesus Christ of Latter-Day Saints,* 1: 255–56, 2: 860–62, 3: 1329–39, 1347; Dallin H. Oaks and Marvin S. Hill, *Carthage Conspiracy: The Trial of the Accused Assassins of Joseph Smith,* 18, 20, 121, 143, 160, 218; Hubbell and Geary, *Northern Leaders,* 207–209, 391–92.

20. Patricia L. Faust, ed., *Historical Times Illustrated Encyclopedia of the Civil War,* 766; Theodore J. Karamanski, *Rally 'Round the Flag: Chicago and the Civil War,* 111–13; and Mary A. Livermore, *My Story of the War: A Woman's Narrative of Four Years Personal Experience,* 114–16. Toward the end of the war, the Democratic *Chicago Times,* review-

ing *Military Rambles* (Turchin's war reminiscences), declared that he had distinguished himself chiefly by the "efficient manner in which his command disposed of the jewelry and under clothing of she rebels, and for the signal manner in which he took the nonsense out of a bevy of misses at the Athens female seminary." Reprinted in *Illinois State Register,* Feb. 24, 1865. See also *St. Louis Missouri Republican,* Aug. 21, 1862.

21. Turchin to Hurlbut, July 17, 1861, Stephen A. Hurlbut Folder, Stephenson County Historical Society Museum, Freeport, Illinois; "Russo-Yankee dog" remark in *Richmond Daily Dispatch,* Apr. 23, 1863. See also *Illinois State Register,* Aug. 5, 1861, and *Quincy Daily Whig and Republican,* Aug. 6, 8, Sept. 16, 1861.

22. *OR,* 3: 135, 390, 396–97, 401–402, 406, 415, 434, 447, 459; II, 1: 185, 186–87, 188, 194, 202–203, 206–207, 208–209. See also Simon, *Papers of Grant,* 2: 68–69, 73, 124; Rolle, *Fremont,* 191; Benjamin F. Gue, *History of Iowa, from the Earliest Times to the Beginning of the Twentieth Century, Four Volumes,* 2: *The Civil War,* 136, 141, 143; and *Cincinnati Times,* July 31, 1861.

23. *OR,* 3: 402–405, 423–24, 458–59; *Illinois State Journal,* Apr. 24, May 4, 29, 31, June 20, 22, 1861; *New York World,* July 5, 1861; *St. Louis Missouri Democrat,* July 30, 1861; Peter Cozzens, *General John Pope: A Life for the Nation,* 3–35; Peter Cozzens and Robert I. Girardi, eds., *The Military Memoirs of General John Pope,* 3–39, 245–54; Wallace J. Schutz and Walter N. Trenerry, *Abandoned by Lincoln: A Military Biography of General John Pope,* 3–61; Hubbell and Geary, *Northern Leaders,* 410–11; Boatner, *Dictionary,* 658–60; Richard S. Brownlee, *Gray Ghosts of the Confederacy: Guerrilla Warfare in the West, 1861–1865,* 3–52; and Michael Fellman, *Inside War: The Guerrilla Conflict in Missouri During the American Civil War,* 81–192.

24. *Illinois State Journal,* July 16, 1861; *Quincy Daily Whig and Republican,* July 15, 1861; *St. Louis Missouri Democrat,* July 16, 23, 1861; Frank Moore, ed., *The Rebellion Record: A Diary of American Events,* 2: 304–305, 442–43; *New York Times,* July 16, 1861.

25. *OR,* 3: 402–405, 423–24, 458–59; II, 1: 184–217. Cozzens, *Pope,* 36–42; Cozzens and Girardi, *Memoirs,* 21–28; Schutz and Trenerry, *Pope,* 62–68; Brownlee, *Gray Ghosts,* 33–36; Moore, *Rebellion Record,* 2: 64, 72, 522, 537; *Illinois State Journal,* Aug. 20, 1861; *Quincy Herald,* Aug. 26, Sept. 2, 1861; *St. Louis Missouri Republican,* Sept. 3, 1861; *St. Louis Missouri Democrat,* Aug. 6, 27, 1861; *Cincinnati Daily Commercial,* Aug. 20, 1861.

26. *OR,* II, 1: 194; Simon, *Grant,* 2: 74–75, 81–82, 85–86, 124; Brooks D. Simpson, *Ulysses S. Grant: Triumph over Adversity, 1822–1865,* 78–90; Hurlbut to William P. Dole, Oct. 15, 1861, Lincoln Papers. See also *Illinois State Journal,* July 31, 1861, and *St. Louis Missouri Republican,* Sept. 3, 1861. For a favorable assessment of Frémont's leadership, see Robert L. Turkoly-Joczik, "Frémont and the Western Department," 363–85.

27. *New York Times,* Sept. 19, 1861.

28. *OR,* 3: 135, 390, 396–97, 415, 434, 447, 457–59; II, 1: 185–87, 202–203, 206–209, 218–19; *Quincy Herald,* Aug. 5, 12, 19, Sept. 23, 1861; Brownlee, *Gray Ghosts,* 34–36.

29. Browning to Hurlbut, Aug. 5, 1861, Browning Folder; *Journal of the Executive Proceedings of the Senate of the United States of America, from December 6, 1858, to August 6, 1861, Inclusive,* 11: 489, 493, 533, 554; *Washington Evening Star,* Aug. 6, 1861.

30. *Keokuk Gate City,* Aug. 5(?), 1861, qtd. in the Republican *St. Louis Missouri Democrat,* Aug. 6, 1861; *Illinois State Journal,* Aug. 9, 1861; *Quincy Herald,* Sept. 2, 9, 1861.

31. *OR*, 3: 133, 156–70; II, 1: 223, 233. "Gnashed their teeth" remark in Seymour D. Thompson, *Recollections with the Third Iowa Regiment*, 93, also 73–111.

32. Ibid. See also Pope to John C. Kelton, Aug. 9, 1861, Pope to Frémont, Sept. 8, 1861, including "Charges and Specifications against Brig. Genl S. A. Hurlbut U.S.A., with lists of witnesses" [hereafter "Charges and Specifications"] in U.S. War Department, "Generals' Papers and Books," John Pope File, Record Group [hereafter RG] 94, National Archives [hereafter NA], Washington, D.C.

33. *OR*, 3: 133, 156–70; II, 1: 223, 233. Thompson, *Third Iowa*, 73–111.

34. *OR*, 3: 133, 156–70; II, 1: 223, 233.

35. *OR*, 3: 133, 156–70; II, 1: 223, 233. *St. Louis Missouri Democrat*, Aug. 12, 21, 27, Sept. 3, 6, 7, 10, 1861; Franklin D. Nickell, "Grant's Lieutenants in the West, 1861–1863," 326–27; Anders, *Twenty-first Missouri*, 34–36; Leslie Anders, "'Farthest North': The Historian and the Battle of Athens," 147–68. Capt. Addison A. Stuart, a member of the 17th Iowa Infantry, before the end of the war candidly concluded that Green's unopposed sweeping movement around Hurlbut's combined command near Kirksville "was the result of a blunder, for which one, who subsequently became distinguished, was responsible. It was positively asserted at the time, that, had General Hurlbut used more powder and fewer proclamations, the result would have been different." Addison A. Stuart, *Iowa Colonels and Regiments: Being a History of Iowa Regiments in the War of the Rebellion; And Containing a Description of the Battles in Which They Have Fought*, 85–86, and for related comments 83–84, 87.

36. *St. Louis Missouri Democrat*, Sept. 7, 10, 1861.

37. *St. Louis Missouri Republican*, Sept. 7, 20, 1861. See also *Quincy Daily Whig and Republican*, Sept. 18, 1861.

38. "Charges and Specifications," in "Generals' Papers and Books," John Pope File, RG 94, NA; Hurlbut to Dole, Oct. 15, 1861, Lincoln Papers. See also letters from Hurlbut to Frémont on the Shelbina affair in "Generals' Papers and Books," Stephen A. Hurlbut, file no. 159, RG 94, NA; and official reports on the affair in *OR*, 3: 473–75, 479, 496.

39. *OR*, 3: 473–75, 479, 496; *Hannibal Messenger*, Sept. 10, 1861, qtd. in *Quincy Daily Whig and Republican*, Sept. 11, 1861 (see also Sept. 12, 1861); *New York Times*, Sept. 19, Nov. 25, 1861; "mutinous conduct" remark in *St. Louis Missouri Republican*, Sept. 20, 1861 (see also Sept. 12, 1861); *St. Louis Missouri Democrat*, Sept. 19, 1861; *Cincinnati Daily Commercial*, Oct. 14, 1861. Captain Stuart afterward recalled of Williams, "It was said that the Colonel was drunk at Paris; but the general, with his *own weaknesses*, would hardly have put him under arrest for that." Of Williams's redoubtable reputation as a martinet, Stuart concluded that "he was tyrannical, and, by a majority of both the officers and men, sincerely hated." Stuart, *Iowa Colonels and Regiments*, 95–96, and 86–87, 92. A 3d Iowa veteran asserted that Williams (and also Lieutenant Colonel Blair of the 2d Kansas), while "too much under the influence of liquor to be in a condition to command men," had "behaved most ridiculously" at Paris and had negligently committed the "crime" of getting "drunk in the presence of a superior enemy." Thompson, *Third Iowa*, 105–106, and 67–71, 112–19. See also Cozzens and Girardi, *Memoirs*, 28–39.

40. *Quincy Daily Whig and Republican*, Sept. 18, 1861; Pope to Frémont, Sept. 8, 1861, with "Charges and Specifications," in "Generals' Papers and Books," John Pope File, RG 94, NA; Jones, *Sworn Statement*, 6–7. Jones withheld his letter from the president, because

he feared he could only stand to lose further influence with Lincoln, since he had sponsored Hurlbut's candidacy for a military appointment in June 1861. See also Donald, *Lincoln*, 314–17, 363, 425, 479.

41. *Belvidere Standard*, Sept. 10, 17, 1861; *Chicago Tribune*, Sept. 10, 1861; *Rockford Republican*, Sept. 19, 1861.

42. *Chicago Evening Journal*, Sept. 9, 1861; *Illinois State Journal*, Sept. 11, 1861, also Sept. 14, 1861; *Quincy Daily Whig and Republican*, Sept. 12, 1861; *St. Louis Missouri Democrat*, Sept. 7, 10, 1861; *Hannibal Messenger*, Sept. 10, 1861, qtd. in *Quincy Whig and Republican*, Sept. 11, 1861.

43. *Illinois State Register*, Sept. 2, 9, 10, 21, and July 19, 1861; *Quincy Herald*, Sept. 16, 1861 (see also Oct. 21, 1861). The *Herald* further declared: "Two or three more such Generals as Hurlbut in N.E. Missouri, would put an end to Unionism within the range of their jurisdiction in a very short time"; ibid.

44. "Dead drunk" and "drunken loafer" remarks quoted in the Democratic *Dubuque Herald*, Sept. 10, 15, 1861 (on September 20, 1861, the *Herald* asserted in reference to Hurlbut's furlough and return to Belvidere, "He ought not only to stay at home but should have been kept at home"), and *Davenport Democrat and News*, Sept. 12, 20, 1861; "political hacks" and the succeeding remark in *Davenport Democrat and News*, Sept. 20, 1861; *Galena Weekly Northwestern Gazette* (concerning the charges leveled at Hurlbut: "The lives of our soldiers must not be hazarded by drunken officers"), Sept. 17, and Sept. 24, 1861. See also *St. Louis Missouri Democrat*, Sept. 20, 1861; and *Cincinnati Daily Times*, Sept. 10, 24, 1861.

45. *New York Times*, Sept. 19, 1861; *New York Tribune*, Sept. 12, 1861.

46. Browning to Lincoln, Sept. 11, 30, 1861, Lincoln Papers; Lincoln to Browning, Sept. 22, 1861, in Roy P. Basler, ed., *Abraham Lincoln: His Speeches and Writings*, 615; Basler, *Collected Works*, 4: 531, 533. See also Theodore C. Pease and James G. Randall, eds., *The Diary of Orville Hickman Browning*, 1: *1850–1864*, 507; and Baxter, *Browning*, 130.

47. Palmer to Trumbull, Sept. 22, 1861, Trumbull Papers. See also Palmer, *John M. Palmer*, 66–75.

48. Simon, *Papers of Grant*, 3: *October 1, 1861–January 7, 1862*, 207; Hubbell and Geary, *Northern Leaders*, 567.

49. *Belvidere Standard*, Sept. 10, 17, 1861; *Quincy Daily Whig and Republican*, Sept. 12, 18, 1861; *Quincy Herald*, Sept. 24, 1861.

50. Hurlbut to Frémont, Oct. 3, 1861, "Generals' Papers and Books," Stephen A. Hurlbut, file no. 159, RG 94, NA.

51. Hurlbut to Dole, Oct. 15, 1861, Blair to Lincoln, Oct. 2, 1861, Lincoln Papers. See also William E. Parrish, *Frank Blair: Lincoln's Conservative*, 79–145; Allan Nevins, *Frémont*, 2: 473–549, particularly 503–28; Oates, *Lincoln*, 259–63; Boatner, *Dictionary*, 67; and Hubbell and Geary, *Northern Leaders*, 43.

52. Hurlbut to Dole, Oct. 15, 1861, Lincoln Papers.

53. Hurlbut to Yates, Nov. 15, 1861, Richard Yates Papers, 1815–1873, Illinois State Historical Library, Springfield, Illinois; Hurlbut to Trumbull, Dec. 18, 1861, Trumbull Papers.

54. *Quincy Herald*, Jan. 13, 1862; *Belvidere Standard*, Dec. 31, 1861; Halleck to Hurlbut, Jan. 1, 1862, "Generals' Papers and Books," Stephen A. Hurlbut File, RG 94, NA. See also *Belvidere Standard*, Jan. 14, 1862; *St. Louis Missouri Republican*, Dec. 1, 1861; *New*

York Times, Sept. 29, Dec. 1, 7, 1861; *Memphis Daily Appeal,* Sept. 1, 1861; *Cincinnati Daily Enquirer,* Oct. 8, 1861; and Stephen E. Ambrose, *Halleck: Lincoln's Chief of Staff,* 11–24, 36–40.

55. Lucien B. Crooker, et. al., *The Story of the Fifty-fifth Regiment Illinois Volunteer Infantry in the Civil War, 1861–1865.* Pt. 1: *From Chicago to Arkansas Post, October, 1861, to January 1863,* 94. A 15th Illinois Volunteer Infantry veteran recalled that late in February 1862, "Hurlbut's reputation was resting under a dark cloud" while "that black stain which sullied his reputation in Missouri had to be wiped out and he set to work in good earnest to do it. He proved to be a brave and efficient officer." Barber, *Memoirs,* 45. See also *Indianapolis Daily Journal,* Jan. 21, 1862.

56. Sherman, *Memoirs,* 1: 246–47; *New York World,* Dec. 21, 1861; *Belvidere Standard,* Mar. 4, 1862; Lewis, *Fighting Prophet,* 66–75, 188–207; Kennett, *Sherman,* 151–55; Michael Fellman, *Citizen Sherman: A Life of William Tecumseh Sherman,* 3–83; Hubbell and Geary, *Northern Leaders,* 475–76.

57. Fritz Haskell, ed. and comp., "Diary of Colonel William Camm, 1861 to 1865," 830. See also James Dugan, *History of Hurlbut's Fighting Fourth Division: And Especially the Marches, Toils, Privations, Adventures, and Battles of the Fourteenth Illinois Infantry,* 94; Simon, *Papers of Grant,* 4: *January 8–March 31, 1862,* 236, 238, 241, 252–54, 265, 276–77.

58. Lewis, *Grant,* 3–492; Bruce Catton, *Grant Moves South,* 3–43; Smith, *Grant,* 21–166; Simpson, *Grant,* 1–122; William S. McFeely, *Grant: A Biography,* 50, 55, 74, 77, 77, 88, 96–97, 109, 120, 132–35, 140, 147–48, 153, 283, 341, 351, 472–73; Geoffrey Perret, *Ulysses S. Grant: Soldier & President,* 3–182; John Y. Simon, "From Galena to Appomattox: Grant and Washburne," 165–75, 188; Hubbell and Geary, *Northern Leaders,* 207–208.

59. *OR,* 7: 650; Catton, *Grant,* 44–197; Nathaniel C. Hughes Jr., *The Battle of Belmont: Grant Strikes South,* 1–208; Benjamin F. Cooling, *Forts Henry and Donelson: The Key to the Confederate Heartland,* 1–279; Simon, *Papers of Grant,* 4: 236–37, 241, 253–54, 265, and 9 *(July 7–December 31, 1863):* 185.

60. Haskell, "Diary of Camm," 839; Dugan, *Fighting Fourth Division,* 97–99; Thompson, *Third Iowa,* 192–205. Hurlbut himself believed that Halleck and Grant had not designated Corinth but rather Montgomery, Alabama, as the Army of the Tennessee's ultimate objective; Benjamin F. Cooling, *Fort Donelson's Legacy: War and Society in Kentucky and Tennessee, 1862–1863,* 16.

61. Isaac C. Pugh to his wife, Mar. 22, 1862, Isaac C. Pugh Letters, 41st Illinois File, Shiloh National Military Park, Shiloh, Tennessee. Besides censuring Hurlbut, the Fourth Division's commander, Pugh also criticized his own brigade commander, Col. Nelson G. Williams. Reviving earlier charges of cowardice at the Battle of Shelbina in September 1861, Pugh described Williams and, by association, Hurlbut as "drunken cowardly dogs" who had undeservedly gained high command. See also Larry J. Daniel, *Shiloh: The Battle That Changed the Civil War,* 109; and Barber, *Memoirs,* 47.

62. "Shirt sleeves" remark in Haskell, "Diary of Camm," 841–42; "long-roll" and succeeding remarks in Thompson, *Third Iowa,* 206–207; *Des Moines Daily State Register,* June 8, 1862. See also *New York Times,* Apr. 13, 1862, Aug. 30, 1872. *National Tribune.* Dec. 24, 1885, Feb. 4, 1886. McDonough, *Shiloh,* 18–21; Sword, *Bloody April,* 13–14; and W. Wiley Sword, "The Battle of Shiloh," 4–50. Earlier, following the forward deployment of Union

forces south and west of Pittsburg Landing, Grant had repeatedly refused Hurlbut's requests that the "old troops" of the Fourth Division should replace Brig. Gen. Benjamin M. Prentiss's less seasoned Sixth Division on the vulnerable advanced position. See Hurlbut to Sophronia R. Hurlbut, Apr. 10, 1862, qtd. in Hurlbut, *In the Midst of War,* 17.

63. Hubbell and Geary, *Northern Leaders,* 300, 324, 390, 415–16, 555–56; Boatner, *Dictionary,* 525, 667, 887.

64. Hurlbut, *In the Midst of War,* 17–18; Crooker, *Fifty-fifth Regiment,* 66–134; Dugan, *Fighting Fourth Division,* 99–106; Leander Stillwell, "In the Ranks at Shiloh," 469, 471; "men in blue" and "Sheneral Hurlbut" remarks in Leander Stillwell, *The Story of a Common Soldier of Army Life in the Civil War, 1861–1865,* 46, and see also 37–68; McDonough, *Shiloh,* 91–93; Sword, *Bloody April,* 230, 234, 238–39, 256, 259, 264, 268, 277–78. For Hurlbut's reminiscences of Shiloh, see Hurlbut to William P. Johnston, Nov. 22, 1877, William Preston Johnston Papers (in Mrs. Mason Barret Collection), Howard-Tilton Memorial Library, Tulane Univ., New Orleans, La. See also Don Carlos Buell, "Shiloh Reviewed," 1: 523.

65. *OR,* 3: 203–11; 10, pt. 1: 103, 110, 119, 122, 131, 135, 151, 153–54, 162, 168, 181, 203–204, 207, 211–12, 239–40; "Dutchmen" remark in Thompson, *Third Iowa,* 218, and see also 207–20; "We generals" remark in a letter from Smith D. Atkins to Sophronia R. Hurlbut, Apr. 13, 1862, as qtd. in *Belvidere Standard,* Apr. 22, 1862; *Cincinnati Gazette* "Turks" remark quoted in Moore, *Rebellion Record,* 4: 392, and see also 400–403.

66. *OR,* 3: 203–11; 10, pt. 1: 103, 110, 119, 122, 131, 135, 151, 153–54, 162, 168, 181, 203–204, 207, 211–12, 239–40. Thompson, *Third Iowa,* 207–20; Gue, *Iowa,* 2: 143; "rash movement!" remark in *New York World,* Apr. 26, 1862, and see also Apr. 12, 19, May 3, 31, 1862, and *Des Moines Daily State Register,* May 2, 1862; *Belvidere Standard,* Apr. 22, 1862; *New York Tribune,* Apr. 16, 18, 1862; *New York Times,* June 16, 1861, Apr. 10, 11, 13, 14, 1862. Sword, *Bloody April,* 230, 234, 238–39, 256, 259, 264, 268, 277–78. For a surviving 44th Indiana soldier's description of his regiment's earlier participation in the Battle of Shiloh, see Julie A. Doyle, John D. Smith, and Richard M. McMurry, eds., *This Wilderness of War: The Civil War Letters of George W. Squier, Hoosier Volunteer,* 8–16. Of Jacob Lauman's characteristic impetuosity, the historian Captain Stuart of Iowa observed that, "As a military leader, he is brave to a fault, but he lacks judgment. He would accomplish much more by intrepidity, than by strategy; and, if his intrepidity failed him, he might lose everything." Stuart, *Iowa Colonels and Regiments,* 170, and 93–95, 163–70. As for Veatch's participation in the battle, see a reporter's account in *Indianapolis Daily Journal,* Apr. 29, 1862, and Veatch's autograph histories of both the 25th Indiana and of Shiloh, with a related memorandum and letter, in boxes 1, 5, and 6, of the James C. Veatch Papers, 1843–1895, William Henry Smith Library, Indiana Historical Society, Indianapolis, Ind.

67. John P. Broome, "How Gen. A. S. Johnston Died," 629. See also William P. Johnston, "Albert Sidney Johnston at Shiloh," 1: 564–65; and *Memphis Daily Appeal,* Apr. 10, 1862.

68. *OR,* 10, pt. 1: 203–208; Hurlbut to Sophronia R. Hurlbut, Apr. 10, 1862, qtd. in Hurlbut, *In the Midst of War,* 18–19; Moore, *Rebellion Record,* 4: 400–403; "mowed down" remark in *New York Tribune,* Apr. 16, 1862. See also *Memphis Daily Appeal,* Apr. 11, 15, 17, 1862; Thompson, *Third Iowa,* 221–32; and Stillwell, *Common Soldier,* 48.

69. "Watery eyes" and "mourned" remarks in Barber, *Memoirs,* 57, also 54–55; "against the enemy" and "shot and shell" and succeeding remarks in Thompson, *Third Iowa,* 235–36, also 233–56; *OR,* 10, pt. 1: 203–207, 208–11, 218, 221, 227, 229, 239–40, 245, 247–48, 250, 257–58, 278–79, 286, 304; Hurlbut to Sophronia R. Hurlbut, Apr. 10, 1862, qtd. in Hurlbut, *In the Midst of War,* 20–21; *Belvidere Standard,* Apr. 15, 22, 1862; *Des Moines Daily State Register,* Apr. 12, 17, 19, June 8, 1862; Mildred Throne, ed., *The Civil War Diary of Cyrus F. Boyd, Fifteenth Iowa Infantry 1861–1863,* 27–39; Daniel, *Shiloh,* 15–317, particularly 82, 86, 100, 102, 106, 109, 111, 135, 191–93, 195, 197, 206, 211, 218, 221–22, 224–25, 245, 281; McDonough, *Shiloh,* 185–213; Sword, *Bloody April,* 284–434; Kiper, *Politician,* 170–203, 543; Charles C. Anderson, *Fighting by Southern Federals,* 12, 71–74, 321–22; Boatner, *Dictionary,* 899. Col. Thomas J. Turner missed the battle because he had returned home to treat his case of "erysipelas." See *Freeport Bulletin,* Mar. 6, 13, 20, Apr. 3, May 22, 1862.

70. *OR,* 10, pt. 1: 110. See also *National Tribune,* Dec. 24, 1885, and Nickell, "Grant's Lieutenants," 331–35.

71. "Frightened sheep" and succeeding remarks in J. O. Harris, "Recollections of an Army Surgeon," 140–41; "few brains" remark of Hurlbut to Sophronia R. Hurlbut, Apr. 10, 1862, qtd. in Hurlbut, *In the Midst of War,* 21. Hurlbut's contempt for poltroons had arisen late on April 6 when "10,000 cowards were skulking under the Landing who might have aided us largely had they dared"; ibid., 19. See also Hurlbut to Yates, Apr. 10, 1862, Yates Papers; Catton, *Grant,* 198–264; Moore, *Rebellion Record,* 4: 392, 400–403; and Gue, *Iowa,* 2: 143.

72. *Illinois State Journal,* Apr. 10, 14, 17, 23, 1862; *Belvidere Standard,* Apr. 15, 1862; *Illinois State Register,* Apr. 15, 1862. The Republican *Des Moines Daily State Register,* concurring with the opinion of war correspondent "Winfield" of the *Charles City (Iowa) Intelligencer,* asserted: "Gen Hurlbut was the man who saved the army. He is the bravest, coolest man I ever saw." *Daily State Register,* May 8, 1862. For an equally favorable Republican estimate of Hurlbut's perceived tactical skill at Shiloh, see *Indianapolis Daily Journal,* Apr. 16, 1862.

73. Simon, *Papers of Grant,* 5: *April 1–August 31, 1862,* 55, 71; *OR,* III, 3: 135, 139; Dugan, *Fighting Fourth Division,* 127–29; Haskell, "Diary of Camm," 870, 878–79, 881–82, 894. See also Hurlbut to Yates, Aug. 18, 1862, Yates Papers; Henry Villard, *Memoirs of Henry Villard: Journalist and Financier, 1835–1900,* 1: *1835–1862,* 272; James G. Smart, ed., *A Radical View: The "Agate" Dispatches of Whitelaw Reid, 1861–1865,* 1: 144; *Belvidere Standard,* May 13, 1862; and *New York Times,* May 23, 1862. After Shiloh, Hurlbut had numerous soldiers arrested for cowardice in the late battle. However, his reputation for intemperance provided an Indiana soldier with a means to remedy "my troubles with the General." In a letter to Colonel Veatch—also from Indiana and a brigade commander in Hurlbut's Fourth Division—he complained that "I learned just before leaving Pittsburgh that the Genl was in the habit of taking a little too much of the *ardent;* if so he must have taken an over dose about the time he ordered so many of us under an arrest"; William H. Morgan to Veatch, Apr. 25, 1862, Veatch Papers. Clearly, then, Hurlbut's association with heavy drinking continued to furnish his detractors with justification for attacks upon his fitness for command.

74. *OR,* 17, pt. 2: 11–12, 23, 27, 32, 34, 37–40, 49–51, 58, 60, 72–73, 99, 114, 118–19, 122, 168, 204, 210–11, 215–16, 220, 226; Hurlbut to Sherman, June 16, 24, 1862, Hurlbut

Folder; Simon, *Papers of Grant*, 5: 150, 408; Ulysses S. Grant, *Personal Memoirs of U. S. Grant*, 1: 386–87; Barber, *Memoirs*, 74–75, 77, 80. See also *Belvidere Standard*, Sept. 16, 1862, *St. Louis Missouri Republican*, June 16, 1863, *Cincinnati Daily Commercial*, July 30, Oct. 2, 1862, and *Memphis Bulletin*, Aug. 27, 1862.

75. *Journal of the Executive Proceedings of the Senate of the United States of America, from December 1, 1862, to July 4, 1864, Inclusive*, 13: 59, 128–29, 188, 229, 260, 273. Hurlbut's confirmation as major general followed in March 1863 by a Senate vote of twenty-two to thirteen. His Western supporters included Trumbull and John Sherman (William T. Sherman's younger brother). Two eastern radical Republicans, Henry Wilson and Charles Sumner, both from Massachusetts, attempted to block Hurlbut's promotion, perhaps because of his southern background and his somewhat conservative views on reconstruction; ibid., 309; *OR*, 17, pt. 2: 307. Regarding Hurlbut's threatened refusal of a promotion to major general, see a letter of September 24, 1862, in the *Chicago Post*, from an officer in Hurlbut's division, reprinted in the *Quincy Daily Whig and Republican*, Oct. 18, 1862.

76. "Rode across the bridge" remark in Thompson, *Third Iowa*, 311, and see 303–28. *OR*, 17, pt. 1: 225, 301–35, 368, 380–81, 396; pt. 2: 204–205, 210–11, 216, 228–29, 234, 238–39, 250–52, 268, 274, 277; Dugan, *Fighting Fourth Division*, 173–201; Throne, *Civil War Diary*, 77; Barber, *Memoirs*, 81–85; *Belvidere Standard*, Oct. 21, Nov. 4, 1862; *New York Times*, Oct. 7, 8, 11, 12, 23, 1862; *Illinois State Journal*, Oct. 16, 1862; *St. Louis Missouri Republican*, Oct. 15, 1862; *Des Moines Daily State Register*, Oct. 14, 19, 1862; *Cincinnati Daily Commercial*, Oct. 17, 1862. "Murderous fire" and "colors" remarks in *National Tribune*, Jan. 14, 1886; "devil" remark in a letter of Oct. 9, 1862, from R. B. Leonard, 53d Indiana, to his father, as qtd. in *Memphis Bulletin*, Oct. 20, 1862. See also Arthur B. Carter, *The Tarnished Cavalier: Major General Earl Van Dorn, C.S.A.*, 90–108; Peter Cozzens, *The Darkest Days of the War: The Battles of Iuka & Corinth*, 148, 231, 276, 280–306; Garland A. Haas, *To the Mountain of Fire and Beyond: The Fifty-third Indiana Regiment from Corinth to Glory*, 45–53; Catton, *Grant*, 265–346; Nickell, Grant's Lieutenants," 339–47; and Hubbell and Geary, *Northern Leaders*, 383–84.

77. Albert Castel, *General Sterling Price and the Civil War in the West*, 108–27; Robert G. Hartje, *Van Dorn: The Life and Times of a Confederate General*, 233–38; William M. Lamers, *The Edge of Glory: A Biography of General William S. Rosecrans*, 131–80; Cozzens, *Iuka & Corinth*, 311, 313; Anderson, *Southern Federals*, 109, 110. For further detail on the acrimonious dispute between Hurlbut and Rosecrans, and for Hurlbut's favorable opinion of James B. McPherson, another critic of Rosecrans, see John Y. Simon, ed., *The Personal Memoirs of Julia Dent Grant (Mrs. Ulysses S. Grant)*, 104–105, and Hurlbut to Ralph P. Buckland, June 23, 1881, in "Letter from Stephen Hurlbut, Belvidere, Ill., relating to Gen. James B. McPherson," Ohio Historical Center, Columbus, Ohio. "Very worst" remark in Katharine M. Jones, *Heroines of Dixie: Confederate Women Tell Their Story of the War*, 180–81. See also Barber, *Memoirs*, 69–70.

78. Alfred Holmes Bodman Diary, Mar. 15, 1863, Chicago Historical Society, Chicago, Ill. For a published version of this work, see Leo M. Kaiser, ed., "'In Sight of Vicksburg': Private Diary of a Northern War Correspondent," 202–21.

79. Nina B. Baker, *Cyclone in Calico: The Story of Mary Ann Bickerdyke*, 148–50, 226–27. For another sketch of Bickerdyke, see *National Tribune*, Aug. 14, 1884.

80. Dugan, *Fighting Fourth Division*, 185.

81. Bodman Diary, Mar. 15, 1863; Kaiser, "'In Sight of Vicksburg,'" 211. See also *OR,* 17, pt. 2: 297.

82. Thomas B. Jones, *Complete History of the 46th Regiment Illinois Volunteer Infantry,* 223–24. For Hurlbut's dealings with a 14th Illinois officer threatened with dismissal, see Haskell, "Diary of Camm," 894.

83. Alex VanWinkle, "Hell on the Hatchie," 632. See also *OR,* 17, pt. 1: 315; *St. Louis Missouri Democrat,* May 9, 1861, *Memphis Bulletin,* Sept. 10, 1862, and *Illinois State Journal,* Aug. 19, Sept. 30, 1863. Hurlbut himself styled the battle near Davis's Bridge as "Hell on the Hatchie." An officer of the 15th Illinois thereafter had the general's apt expression inscribed on the regiment's battle flag; Barber, *Memoirs,* 84, 85.

84. Fred A. Shannon, ed., *The Civil War Letters of Sergeant Onley Andrus,* 26, 52; *Belvidere Standard,* Nov. 25, 1862; *Cincinnati Daily Commercial,* Sept. 30, 1862; *Des Moines Daily State Register,* May 8, 1862; Mary E. Kellogg, comp., *Army Life of an Illinois Soldier, Including a Day-by-Day Record of Sherman's March to the Sea: Letters and Diary of Charles W. Wills,* 144. Reporting Hurlbut's transfer from the District of Jackson to Sherman's District of Memphis in mid-November 1862, a correspondent observed, "He is a decided loss to this wing of the Army where he is very popular"; *New York Times,* Nov. 30, 1862. See also *St. Louis Missouri Republican,* Oct. 15, 1862.

85. Hurlbut to Washburne, Nov. 10, 1862, Washburne Papers; *OR,* 17, pt. 2: 362; *St. Louis Missouri Republican,* June 16, 1863; Boatner, *Dictionary,* 420.

86. Hurlbut to Washburne, Dec. 6, 1862; *OR,* 17, pt. 2: 353, 508. A sharp dispute on March 12, 1862, between McClernand and Hurlbut over their respective seniority as brigadier general (and Hurlbut's authority to commandeer one of McClernand's troop transports shortly before its debarkation at Pittsburg Landing) probably contributed to Hurlbut's dislike and criticism of McClernand; Kiper, *Politician,* 96, and 1–154, 181–84, 207, 292, 297, 309–11. See also Hicken, "John A. McClernand," 1–199; Malone, *DAB,* 11: *Larned-MacCracken,* 587–88; and Boatner, *Dictionary,* 525.

87. Hurlbut to Sherman, Jan. 1, 1863, William T. Sherman Papers, 1820–1891, Manuscript Division, Library of Congress, Washington, D.C. See also Kiper, *Politician,* 154–55, 161; Hicken, "John A. McClernand," 219–51; Lewis, *Fighting Prophet,* 257–58; and Hubbell and Geary, *Northern Leaders,* 476.

88. Kiper, *Politician,* 161–79; *Memphis Bulletin,* Nov. 26, 1862.

CHAPTER 4: MILITARY RULER OF MEMPHIS

1. Gerald M. Capers, *The Biography of a River Town, Memphis: Its Heroic Age,* 135–61, 164; Joseph H. Parks, "A Confederate Trade Center under Federal Occupation: Memphis, 1862 to 1865," 285–303; Ernest W. Hooper, "Memphis, Tennessee: Federal Occupation and Reconstruction, 1862–1870," 1–28; Douglas W. Cupples, "Memphis Confederates: The Civil War and Its Aftermath," 6–27, 55–91.

2. "Augean stable" remark in Livermore, *My Story,* 502. See also 282–94, 476–546. "Charnel-house" and "dead-house" remarks in Mrs. A. H. (Jane) Hoge, *The Boys in Blue; Or Heroes of the "Rank and File,"* 125. See also 54, 62–63, 116–31, 181–97, 261–64; Linus P. Brockett and Mary C. Vaughan, *Woman's Work in the Civil War: A Record of*

Heroism, Patriotism and Patience, 174–77. See also Frank R. Freemon, *Gangrene and Glory: Medical Care during the American Civil War,* 51–60, 191, 198, 209–10; Stewart Brooks, *Civil War Medicine,* 41–49, 50–62, 106–12, 120. For Bickerdyke, Mary G. Holland, *Our Army Nurses: Stories from Women in the Civil War,* 2, 25–35, 161, 192; and for the Gayoso and "Small-Pox" hospitals, 30, 137, 138, 227, 258, 286. U.S. War Department, *The Medical and Surgical History of the War of the Rebellion (1861–1865),* vols. 4, 6, 7, 8, 9, 10, 11, 12, and passim; and Patricia M. LaPointe, "Military Hospitals in Memphis, 1861–1865," 325, 335–36, 337. For other comments on Fort Pickering and military hospitals, see *Illinois State Journal,* Feb. 27, July 20, 1863, *Cincinnati Daily Commercial,* Aug. 7, 1863, and *Memphis Bulletin,* Sept. 11, 1863.

3. Lyman B. Pierce, *History of the Second Iowa Cavalry: Containing a Detailed Account of Its Organization, Marches, and the Battles in Which It Has Participated; Also, a Complete Roster of Each Company,* 67. Another Union soldier, in a journal entry of January 13, 1863, gloomily lamented: "Whiskey O Whiskey! Drunk men staggered on all the streets. In every store. The saloons were full of *drunk men.* The men who had fought their way from Donelson to Corinth and who had met no enemy able to whip them now surrendered to Genl *Intoxication.*" The soldier wryly concluded, "The whiskey here seems to be very effective at short range"; Throne, *Civil War Diary,* 106, and see 107, 109–10. See also Barber, *Memoirs,* 74–75, 77; *Cincinnati Daily Times,* Jan. 31, 1863; and *Illinois State Journal,* Nov. 25, 1863, Feb. 8, 1864.

4. Carrol H. Quenzel, ed., "A Billy Yank's Impressions of the South," 101. Hurlbut himself had previously characterized Memphis as "Sodom" on the Mississippi. From a letter of Lt. David White to his family, Jan. 29, 1863, qtd. in Haas, *Fifty-third Indiana,* 67.

5. Livermore, *My Story,* 290; Hoge, *Boys in Blue,* 62–63, 261. See also Kennett, *Sherman,* 174; Karamanski, *Rally 'Round the Flag,* 27–28, 102–105, 117–20, 123, 132, 229, 242–44; Richard Wheeler, *The Siege of Vicksburg,* 6; Capers, *Memphis,* 132; Jonathan Daniels, *Prince of Carpetbaggers,* 65; William H. Russell, *My Diary North and South,* 160–61; and *St. Louis Missouri Republican,* Jan. 30, 31, Apr. 11, 1863. The Sanitary Commission was established on June 9, 1861, by Secretary of War Simon Cameron and approved by Lincoln as an auxiliary organization of the Union army's medical department.

6. *OR,* 17: 362; *Memphis Bulletin,* Nov. 26, 1862. For a general theoretical discussion of the intricate command structure at Memphis in 1862 and 1863, see Frank Freidel, "General Orders 100 and Military Government," 552–53; Frank Freidel, *Francis Lieber: Nineteenth-Century Liberal,* 317–41; Robert J. Futrell, "Federal Military Government in the South, 1861–1865," 187; and Boatner, *Dictionary,* 420.

7. *Memphis Bulletin,* Nov. 26, and Dec. 27, 1862.

8. *OR,* 17, pt. 2: 432–33, and 24, pt. 3: 35. As for Veatch's background and jurisdiction, see *Memphis Bulletin,* Jan. 13, May 13, June 19, 1863; Boatner, *Dictionary,* 420, 868–69; and Hubbell and Geary, *Northern Leaders,* 555–56.

9. *OR,* 24, pt. 3: 35, 291, 576. For background on and a photographic illustration of Binmore, see Sparks, *Lincoln-Douglas Debates,* 76, 80, 594; Holzer, *Debates,* 10–12; *Illinois State Journal,* Aug. 9, 1862; and the *St. Louis Missouri Republican,* Mar. 29, 1863. See also *Memphis Bulletin,* Nov. 27, 28, 1862, Apr. 3, 30, 1863; *Cincinnati Daily Commercial,* Aug. 16, Sept. 30, 1862, July 22, 1863; and *Daily Richmond Enquirer,* Jan. 1, 1863.

10. Affidavit of James L. Loop, Apr. 29, 1864, "Generals' Papers and Books," Stephen A. Hurlbut, File 159, RG 94, NA; Simon, *Papers of Grant*, 7: 360; and Boatner, *Dictionary*, 839.

11. Basler, *Collected Works*, 4: *1860–1861*, 487–88; Parks, "Confederate Trade Center," 285–303; *Memphis Bulletin*, Nov. 18, Dec. 2, 10, 1862, Jan. 3, 6, 1863; Kennett, *Sherman*, 175–78; Noel C. Fisher, "Prepare Them for My Coming: General William T. Sherman, Total War, and Pacification in West Tennessee," 75–86. See also *New York World*, June 21, 28, Aug. 9, 1862, and *Cincinnati Daily Commercial*, Aug. 5, 11, 12, 1862.

12. For a thorough treatment of Grant's controversial "Jew Order" of November 9, 1862, see *OR*, 17, pt. 1: 330; pt. 2: 424. Simon, *Papers of Grant*, 6: 283, 393–94; Stephen V. Ash, "Civil War Exodus: The Jews and Grant's General Orders No. 11," 505–23; John Y. Simon, "That Obnoxious Order," 12–17; Bertram W. Korn, *American Jewry and the Civil War*, 122–55; James A. Wax, "The Jews of Memphis: 1860–1865," 74–78; and Selma S. Lewis, *A Biblical People in the Bible Belt: The Jewish Community of Memphis, Tennessee, 1840s–1960s*, 37–43. See also Simpson, *Grant*, 163–65; Korn, *American Jewry*, 122–55; Wax, "Jews of Memphis," 88; Lewis, *Jewish Community*, 31–53; and *Indianapolis Daily State Sentinel*, Jan. 5, 1863.

13. Lewis, *Jewish Community*, 22, 27, 34–35, 47, 58–59; Maxwell Whiteman, ed., "Kronikals of the Times: Memphis, 1862, by Abraham Ephraim Frankland," 106, 111–13. Frankland and Hurlbut met after the war as Masons, though members of different lodges. But Frankland never forgave him, asserting that the general as "that great ruler" of Memphis "should have been hurled [to the devil] but was not"; ibid. See other items concerning Hurlbut and Memphis Jews in *Illinois State Register*, Jan. 10, 1864, and *St. Louis Missouri Republican*, Jan. 7, 8, 11, 1864.

14. Quoted (from a circa 1900 typescript copy of Meyer's autobiography, "My Life, Travels, and Adventures by Land and Sea," and housed in the American Jewish Archives) in Jacob R. Marcus, *Memoirs of American Jews, 1775–1865*, 330–31, 346–50.

15. Ibid., 346–50. However, not until December 1863 did Hurlbut promulgate General Orders No. 162, which banished Memphis merchants who sold articles of official military clothing to "improper persons" without permission from army headquarters; *Davenport Democrat and News*, Dec. 5, 1863. For a Confederate opinion of Hurlbut's questionable control of trade, see (under "Bribery at Memphis") *Richmond Whig*, Apr. 29, 1863. For the latter's role in confiscations of "smuggled goods," see *Memphis Bulletin*, Mar. 14, Apr. 27, 28, May 2, 28, 1863.

16. Simon, *Papers of Grant*, 10: *January 1–May 31, 1864*, 290–91, 15: *May 1–December 31, 1865*, 555–57. See also *Memphis Bulletin*, Apr. 19, 1864; *Davenport Democrat and News*, Dec. 18, 1863; *Cincinnati Daily Commercial*, Dec. 24, 1863; *Illinois State Journal*, Dec. 18, 1863; Cadwallader C. Washburn to Washburne, Apr. 23, 1864, Washburne Papers; Boatner, *Dictionary*, 420, 868–69, 892; and Hubbell and Geary, *Northern Leaders*, 570. For a similar incident illustrating the enforcement of Hurlbut's prohibition of illicit removal of gold bullion from Memphis, see Elizabeth A. Meriwether, *Recollections of Ninety-two Years, 1824–1916*, 138–43.

17. "A General officer" and succeeding remarks of Worthington to Lincoln, Apr. 12, 1864. See also Feb. 28, Mar. 1, 1863, Aug. 30, Sept. 1, 1864, Lincoln Papers (after Shiloh,

Worthington was court-martialed by Sherman on charges of incompetence and drunkenness on duty; Kennett, *Sherman,* 169–70); Basler, *Collected Works,* 7: 276n. "Disgusting drunkenness" and following remarks in *Cincinnati Daily Times,* Jan. 31, Feb. 13, 1863. See also *New York Tribune,* Jan. 24, Feb. 2, 4, 1863; *Chicago Times,* Feb. 12, 1863; *Memphis Daily Appeal,* Feb. 28, June 8, 1863; affidavit of Stephen A. Hurlbut, Apr. 29, 1864, "Generals' Papers and Books," Stephen A. Hurlbut, file no. 159, RG 94, NA; Bodman Diary, Feb. 28, 1863; and Kaiser, "'In Sight of Vicksburg,'" 202–21.

18. Reprinted in *Charleston Daily Courier,* Feb. 4, 1863, and (under the sarcastic heading "Great Men Will Differ") *Mobile Advertiser and Register,* Jan. 30, 1863. At the end of May 1863, Hurlbut continued to question the wisdom of Grant's plan to capture Vicksburg. Although Grant had won several "gallant battles" before commencing his investment of Vicksburg, Hurlbut feared that Confederate forces under Joseph E. Johnston would attack and destroy Grant's army. Hurlbut complained to Sherman, commander of the Fifteenth Corps of the Army of the Tennessee, that Grant had thereby produced "a great muddle & there is much reason to believe it will be singularly serious. It would be sad indeed if after these many battles our Western force should by sheer weight of numbers be pressed down at last." Hurlbut to Sherman, May 31, 1863, Schoff Civil War Collection, Letters and Documents, Manuscripts Division, William L. Clements Library, Univ. of Michigan, Ann Arbor, Mich.

19. *OR,* 17, pt. 2: 432–33, 461; 24, pt. 3: 38, 44–45. *Memphis Bulletin,* Jan. 13, 17, 18, 1863; *Illinois State Journal,* Jan. 17, 1863; *New York Tribune,* Jan. 24, 1863; Boatner, *Dictionary,* 368–69.

20. Simon, *Papers of Grant,* 6: 318; 7: *December 9, 1862–March 31, 1863,* 308n; *Memphis Bulletin,* Feb. 4, 1863; *Belvidere Standard,* Mar. 17, 1863; Cozzens, *Iuka & Corinth,* 34, 63–64, 72–75, 80, 82–83, 109, 131, 152–53, 155, 158, 198–202, 216–18, 220, 223–24, 227, 274, 277, 293–94, 301, 325–26; Boatner, *Dictionary,* 368–69, 420, 868–69; Hubbell and Geary, *Northern Leaders,* 555–56; Faust, *Encyclopedia,* 333.

21. Hamilton to Doolittle, Jan. 7, 30, 1863, James R. Doolittle Collection, State Historical Society of Wisconsin, Madison. Fearing, or else resenting, the influence of still another potential rival, Hamilton also attacked the reputation of Maj. Gen. Gordon Granger, a West Point graduate of 1845 and the former commander of the District of Central Kentucky. Granger had participated in the siege of Corinth and had gained the rank of major general of U.S. Volunteers, effective Sept. 17, 1862—the same date as Hurlbut's promotion. Hamilton wrote Doolittle that "Granger is not fit for a Major General" because "He drinks whiskey continually—is vulgar & obscene," Ibid.

22. Hamilton to Doolittle, Feb. 11, 1863, Doolittle Collection. See also Simon, *Papers of Grant,* 7: 308; *St. Louis Missouri Republican,* May 5, 1863; Edwin C. Bearss, *The Campaign for Vicksburg,* 1: *Vicksburg Is the Key,* 731–32; Boatner, *Dictionary,* 351–52, 368–69; Hubbell and Geary, *Northern Leaders,* 206–207, 231; and Faust, *Encyclopedia,* 319.

23. Livermore, *My Story,* 310–11. On Grant's drinking, see Holland, *Army Nurses,* 31, 109, 114, 137, 165–66, 227, 281; Wilson, *Rawlins,* 67–79; Smith, *Grant,* 16, 83, 85–89, 90–92, 96–97, 105, 142, 145, 172–73, 177, 205, 209, 231–32, 235–56, 262, 282, 300; McFeely, *Grant,* 50, 55, 74, 77, 87–88, 96–97, 109, 120, 132–135, 140, 147–48, 153, 283, 341, 351, 472–73; and Perret, *Ulysses S. Grant,* 87, 100, 202–208, 262–63. For other instances of

Hurlbut's drinking, see Brackett and Vaughan, *Woman's Work*, 174–77, and Annie T. Wittenmyer, *Under the Guns: A Woman's Reminiscences of The Civil War*, 106–14. For an assessment of Grant's intemperance on his capacity for command, see Lyle W. Dorsett, "The Problem of Ulysses S. Grant's Drinking during the Civil War," 37–48.

24. Simon, *Papers of Grant*, 8: *April 1–July 6, 1863*, 367; *Memphis Bulletin*, Dec. 16, 17, 19, 1862; *Cincinnati Daily Commercial*, Jan. 30, 1863; *New York Times*, Apr. 10, 1864; *St. Louis Missouri Republican*, Jan. 22, 1863. On Hurlbut, see William A. Veatch, *James Clifford Veatch: Scholar, Solicitor, Statesman, and Soldier*, passim.

25. Hurlbut to Washburne, Jan. 17, 1863, Lincoln Papers; *Belvidere Standard*, Jan. 13, 20, 1863; Basler, *Collected Works*, 6: *1862–1863*, 70. According to Frank R. Freemon, in *Gangrene and Glory* (231), "erysipelas" referred in earlier times to a swelling of a wound, with redness and heat, but is now known to be caused by a bacterial infection; the modern term would be "cellulitis." Medical authorities agree, however, that heavy drinkers are particularly susceptible; the characteristic facial inflammation closely resembles the symptoms associated with overindulgence.

26. *Belvidere Standard*, Jan. 27, Feb. 10, 1863 (see also Feb. 3, 1863); *Illinois State Journal*, Jan. 31, Feb. 2, 1863; *Chicago Times*, Feb. 12, 1863; *Illinois State Register*, Feb. 4, 24, Mar. 5, 14, 1863; *Quincy Herald*, Mar. 18, 1863; *Memphis Bulletin*, Feb. 4, 7, 1863.

27. *Chicago Times*, Dec. 6, 1862, Jan. 7, 12, 26, Feb. 2, 11, 1863. *OR*, 24, pt. 3: 50; *Memphis Bulletin*, Feb. 10, 12, 1863.

28. *Chicago Times*, Feb. 7, 1863. See also Benjamin P. Thomas, ed., *Three Years with Grant as Recalled by War Correspondent Sylvanus Cadwallader*, 56–57, 129–31. For detailed discussion of the Yates administration, see Nortrup, "Richard Yates," 235–332, and Yates II and Pickering, *Richard Yates*, 149–229.

29. *OR*, 24, pt. 3: 50; Simon, *Papers of Grant*, 7: 316–18; Thomas, *Three Years with Grant*, 56–57; *Memphis Bulletin*, Feb. 10, 1863; *Illinois State Journal*, Feb. 13, 14, 1863.

30. *Belvidere Standard*, Feb. 17, Mar. 3, 1863; *Chicago Tribune*, Feb. 12, 1863; *Illinois State Journal*, Feb. 14, 1863; *Chicago Times*, Feb. 12, 13, 14, 16, 19, Mar. 17, 1863; *Quincy Herald*, Feb. 23, Mar. 2, 1863; *Memphis Bulletin*, Mar. 21, 1863. The Democratic journal of Davenport, Iowa, gloated over Hurlbut's "Humiliating Back-Down" at Grant's hands, asserting that Hurlbut's order had sprung from a desire to "show a little vindictive spleen" toward the *Chicago Times*. See *Davenport Democrat and News*, Feb. 21, 25, 1863, and Hurlbut to Yates, Mar. 7, 1867, Yates Papers.

31. *Illinois State Register*, Feb. 24, Mar. 5, 14, 1863; *Illinois State Journal*, Feb. 14, 1863, and see also Mar. 13, 1863. The Democratic *Freeport Bulletin*, having previously criticized Hurlbut's suppression of the *Chicago Times*, subsequently charged him with defaulting on his subscription. Hurlbut had taken the *Bulletin* for nearly seven years and yet "during all this time that gentleman has never paid us one cent." The *Bulletin* tauntingly declared, "Pay up General, or we will willingly discontinue your paper, and thank you for the privilege"; *Freeport Bulletin*, Nov. 12, 1863.

32. For examples of Hurlbut's pronouncements proscribing cotton speculation and military profiteering in Memphis, see *OR*, 22, pt. 1: 230–31; 24, 3: 58–59, 92; *Memphis Bulletin*, Feb. 18, 1863; and *Memphis Daily Appeal*, Feb. 25, 1863. Besides Hurlbut's ineffectual control over illicit trading in cotton, his imposition of martial law, as imple-

mented by General Orders No. 65, antagonized prominent Memphis men. In June 1863 Judge John T. Swayne complained to Sherman, then near Vicksburg, about Hurlbut's demand that he swear loyalty to the U.S. government. Sherman refused to address Swayne's case but counseled Hurlbut to exercise greater restraint—while, however, punishing civilians convicted by a military court on charges of espionage, sedition, or treason. Sherman to Swayne, June 11, 1863, in Brooks D. Simpson and Jean V. Berlin, eds., *Sherman's Civil War: Selected Correspondence of William T. Sherman, 1860–1865*, 479–81.

33. Jones to Washburne, Jan. 6, Feb. 5, 15, 19, 20, Apr. 4, 6, May 20, 1863; James W. Kellogg to Washburne, Aug. 19, 1863; Washburn to Washburne, Jan. 28, 1863; and Augustus L. Chetlain to Washburne, Feb. 9, 1863, Washburne Papers. Wilson, *Rawlins*, 120; Jones, *Jones*, 29–33, 89; Lewis, *Captain Sam Grant*, 406; Hutchins, *Letters from Lloyd Lewis*, 22–24; Nickell, "Grant's Lieutenants," 352–59.

34. Dean to Washburne, Apr. 27, 1863, Washburne Papers. For another incident illustrating Hurlbut's sporadic and inconsistent enforcement of smuggling regulations, see William M. Cash and Lucy S. Howorth, eds., *My Dear Nellie: The Civil War Letters of William L. Nugent to Eleanor Smith Nugent*, 137. See also Basler, *Collected Works*, 7: *1863–1864*, 75, 275; George A. Williams to Thomas H. Harris, Apr. 3, 1864, Lincoln Papers; *St. Louis Missouri Republican*, May 5, 1863; and *Illinois State Journal*, Mar. 13, 1863.

35. For instance, see Basler, *Collected Works*, 6: 159–60. See also Parks, "Confederate Trade Center," 285–303.

36. Affidavits of C. C. Copeland, Apr. 20, 1864; Edward McCarty, Mar. 16, 1864;, James G. Parks, Apr. 15, 1864; James L. Loop, Apr. 29, 1864; and Stephen A. Hurlbut, Apr. 29, 1864; in "Generals' Papers and Books," Stephen A. Hurlbut File, RG 94, NA. Hirsch to Lincoln, Dec. 23, 1863, Lincoln Papers; Edward D. Townsend to Hirsch, July 19, 1864, in "Union Provost Marshal's File of Papers Relating to Individual Civilians" [hereafter Union Provost Marshal's File], NA Microfilm Publication M345, roll 129: Him–Hiz, War Department Collection of Confederate Records, RG 109, NA. James L. Loop died in Rockford, Ill., on Feb. 8, 1865, at the age of fifty. Loop received this (dubious) eulogy from the *Belvidere Standard*: "Mr. L. possessed a very genial, social disposition, and like too many of such temperaments, easily fell into the use of alcoholic stimulants, thereby impairing his usefulness and no doubt shortening his days. He was a man of brilliant powers of mind, and his own worst enemy." *Belvidere Standard*, Feb. 14, 1865.

37. *OR*, 32, pt. 3: 86–87. Stanton had earlier learned of the venality imputed to the Union military at Memphis. Lincoln himself endorsed a letter sent from John L. Scripps of Chicago, who had advised him that "corruption is openly and constantly charged upon the officers in that Department. The President should order a Court of Inquiry." Lincoln explained to Stanton that Scripps, whom he termed a "good man," had quoted Brig. Gen. Joseph D. Webster, "also a good man, and the *locus in quo* [place in which], as you know, is under Gen. Hurlbut." Basler, *Collected Works*, 7: 104. For specific allegations regarding Hurlbut's and Veatch's involvement in "sharp operations" (particularly Hurlbut's granting of special favors), see *Indianapolis State Sentinel*, Feb. 11, 1864.

38. Affidavits of Copeland, McCarty, Parks, Loop, and Hurlbut, "Generals' Papers and Books," Stephen A. Hurlbut, file no. 159, RG 94, NA.

39. Hurlbut to Trumbull, May 15, 1864, Trumbull Papers. Hurlbut had also denied "cotton fever" in a letter to Yates, but Yates had not defended him publicly; Hurlbut to Yates, Nov. 8, 1863, Yates Papers. See also *New York Times,* Jan. 25, 1864. Conversely, in November 1863 an anonymous contributor to the *Memphis Bulletin* accused prominent Treasury -Department agents of "incompetency, favoritism or fraud" and recommended that the War Department impose its direct and close supervision over all cotton trafficking. The writer declared, "Gen. Hurlbut is a wise, just, and honorable ruler" and whose "incorruptible" integrity would ensure his impartial regulation of cotton trading. The contributor asserted, "The military power is the only shield left for the people" (and the "ONLY PERMANENT REMEDY FOR THE EVILS EXISTING!")—which was indeed ironic, in view of the rapacious cotton ring that Hurlbut had secretly created earlier in 1863; *Memphis Bulletin,* Nov. 21, 22, 24, 1863. Hurlbut appeared before a military court of inquiry at Memphis on May 8, 1863, and furnished incriminating evidence against a few officers whom he had commanded earlier in West Tennessee in 1862 and 1863, but he refrained from implicating members of his staff. For his testimony, see *Memphis Bulletin,* May 29, 1863, and *St. Louis Missouri Republican,* May 26, 1863.

40. *OR,* 22–24, 26, 30–31, and passim; Cooling, *Fort Donelson's Legacy,* 217, 250–53, 265–67, 284, 286, 311–12, 336; Edwin C. Bearss, "The Great Railroad Raid," 147–60, 222–39; *New York World,* May 5, 1863; *New York Times,* Aug. 11, 24, 25, 1863; *Belvidere Standard,* Aug. 25, Sept. 15, 1863; *Illinois State Journal,* Aug. 24, 1863; Catton, *Grant,* 347–489. Hurlbut complained to Veatch that, "Grant is stripping me down very closely"; Hurlbut to Veatch, June 4, 1863 (and see July 24, 1863), Veatch Papers.

41. Washburn to Washburne, July 5, 1863, Washburne Papers. See also Hubbell and Geary, *Northern Leaders,* 570.

42. Hurlbut to Grant, July 7, 1863, "Generals' Papers and Books," Stephen A. Hurlbut, file no. 159, RG 94, NA; Simon, *Papers of Grant,* 9: *July 7–December 31, 1863,* 185–87; Hurlbut to Lincoln, July 10, 1863, Lincoln to Hurlbut, July 31, 1863, Lincoln Papers; Grant to Hurlbut, Aug. 14, 1863, qtd. in Hurlbut, *In the Midst of War,* 22. See also Basler, *Collected Works,* 7: 358–59; Michael Burlingame and John R. Turner Ettlinger, eds., *Inside Lincoln's White House: The Complete Civil War Diary of John Hay,* 68. *OR,* 52, pt. 1: 398–99; 24, pt. 3: 436–37, 566. *Memphis Bulletin,* Aug. 14, 1863. For Northern and Southern editorial opinions on Hurlbut's resignation, see *Belvidere Standard,* July 28, Aug. 25, 1863, and (concerning his "brutal rule") *Memphis Daily Appeal,* Aug. 21, 1863. The *Appeal* had moved to Atlanta from Jackson, Miss., on May 14, 1863.

43. Hurlbut to Lincoln, July 10, Aug. 11, 1863, Lincoln Papers. For reconstruction in Arkansas, see Carl H. Moneyhon, *The Impact of the Civil War and Reconstruction on Arkansas: Persistence in the Midst of Ruin,* 77, 87, 142–71.

44. Burlingame and Ettlinger, *Civil War Diary,* 68–69, 74–75.

45. Basler, *Collected Works,* 6: 358–59, 387–88; Hurlbut to Lincoln, Aug. 18, Sept. 8, 19, Nov. 10, Dec. 8, 1863, and Hurlbut to Samuel B. Walker, Aug. 10, 1863, Lincoln Papers; Hurlbut to Andrew Johnson, Feb. 21, Sept. 15, 1863, and Johnson to Hurlbut, Oct. 3, 1863, Andrew Johnson Papers, 1829–1891, Manuscript Division, Library of Congress, Washington, D.C. (microfilm copy, Kent State Univ. Library, Kent, Ohio); *OR,* 22, pt. 2: 330, 331–32, 482–84, 585–86, 677, 701; James W. Fertig, *The Secession and*

Reconstruction of Tennessee, 45–60; *New York Times,* Mar. 21, 1864; and Hubbell and Geary, *Northern Leaders,* 457–58.

46. *OR,* 30, pt. 3: 664; James H. Wilson, *Under the Old Flag: Recollections of Military Operations in the War for the Union, the Spanish War the Boxer Rebellion, Etc.,* 252–53; Hubbell and Geary, *Northern Leaders,* 595–96.

47. *New York Times,* Oct. 3, 1863, see also Mar. 22, 1864. Not until mid-April 1864, or shortly before Hurlbut's removal from command in West Tennessee, did the superintendent of military hospitals in Memphis appoint a health officer to clean up the streets to prevent "contagions and epidemics." The *Memphis Bulletin* declared, unlike negligent municipal officials, "The military authority cannot acquiesce in these Rip Van Winkle views; these snorings from Sleepy Hollow"; *Memphis Bulletin,* Apr. 14, 1864.

48. Affidavits of Loop and Hurlbut, "Generals' Papers and Books," Stephen A. Hurlbut, file no. 159, RG 94, NA; Simon, *Papers of Grant,* 7: 359–60. For more on Willard, see *Belvidere Standard,* Dec. 27, 1864, Oct. 16, 1866.

49. *Memphis Bulletin,* May 1, 3, 1863; *Cincinnati Daily Commercial,* May 4, 1863. See also *St. Louis Missouri Republican,* May 5, 9, Aug. 18, Sept. 15, 1863. Put differently, in April of 1863 Veatch had ordered the expulsion of "two boat loads of fallen humanity"; Barber, *Memoirs,* 105.

50. *New York Times,* Oct. 3, 1863. Hurlbut's lax enforcement of orders prohibiting prostitution manifested itself again in September 1863 when he arrested sixty men for dancing with "ladies of easy virtue" on Main Street. He sent "Sixty Gay and Festive 'Cusses'" to Irving Block for a night but did not incarcerate their companions; *Memphis Bulletin,* Sept. 12, 13, 1863. See also *Des Moines Daily State Register,* Dec. 1, 1863; *Cincinnati Daily Commercial,* Nov. 25, 1863. A St. Louis correspondent in Memphis asserted that Binmore had passed a certain harlot off as his wife and that the ladies of officers visited her; "The *denouement* was soon reached, and the explosion follows." Another reporter from St. Louis, however, afterward declared that Binmore (whom other officers despised for his "intolerable insolence" and "despotic acts") had successively introduced two harlots (including a fair-haired young woman whom he had lodged at the Gayoso) to other officers' wives. *St. Louis Missouri Republican,* Nov. 23, 1863, Jan. 8, 1864. See also Thomas, *Three Years with Grant,* 128–31. In August 1864 Harris assumed the concurrent duty of acting mayor of Memphis; he sought to assist Major General Washburn in devising a set of regulations to govern the newly and officially permitted prostitution in the city. *Medical and Surgical History,* 6: 895–96; Thomas P. Lowry, *The Story the Soldiers Wouldn't Tell: Sex in the Civil War,* 83–87.

51. *OR,* 32, pt. 2: 75; *St. Louis Missouri Republican,* Jan. 9, 11, Feb. 2, 1864; *Memphis Daily Appeal,* Feb. 12, 1864.

52. Mark Anthony D. Howe, ed., *Home Letters of General Sherman,* 281, 282–83. For an army correspondent's allusions to Hurlbut's renewed ambition for field command, see *St. Louis Missouri Republican,* July 21, 1863, and Feb. 2, 1864. See also *Memphis Bulletin,* Jan. 26, 1864; Simpson, *Grant,* 216–44; Bruce Catton, *Grant Takes Command,* 3–103; Lewis, *Fighting Prophet,* 332; Kennett, *Sherman,* 187–219; Hubbell and Geary, *Northern Leaders,* 208, 337, 476; and Boatner, *Dictionary,* 538.

53. *OR,* 32, pt. 1: 164–391; 32, pt. 2: 499. See also Richard M. McMurry, "Sherman's Meridian Campaign," 24–32.

54. "Reign" and "Hell-under-Hurlbut" remarks in a letter of Jan. 11, 1863, of Cpl. Wilford B. McDonald, included in his "War Journal and Notes" as qtd. in Haas, *Fifty-third Indiana*, 67; *Charleston Daily Courier*, Mar. 26, 1863; *Richmond Sentinel*, Mar. 24, 1863. See also *Memphis Daily Appeal*, Apr. 2, 7, 1863; Asher R. Eddy to Washburn, Sept. 13, 1864, Lincoln Papers; and Hubbell and Geary, *Northern Leaders*, 556.

55. *New York Times*, Oct. 3, 1863. See also *Cincinnati Daily Commercial*, June 18, 1863; *Richmond Daily Dispatch*, Nov. 28, 1863; and Cupples, "Memphis Confederates," 117–22, 139–44.

56. "Fine countenance" and succeeding remarks in *St. Louis Missouri Republican*, Jan. 9, 1864; "golden egg" and preceding remarks in *Mobile Advertiser and Register*, Nov. 21, 1863, as reprinted in *Richmond Daily Dispatch*, Nov. 28, 1863, and *Charleston Mercury*, Dec. 3, 1863; *Belvidere Standard*, July 7, Aug. 11, 1863; *Illinois State Journal*, Sept. 17, 1863.

57. John Hallum, *The Diary of an Old Lawyer, Or, Scenes behind the Curtain*, 278–89, 317–18; "black holes" remark in *Memphis Daily Appeal*, June 8, 1863. For further background on Williams, see *OR*, vols. 1, 10, 17, 24, and passim, and Simon, *Papers of Grant*, 6: 227, 228n, 230, 241, 244, 318, and 7: 59–60, 114n, 115n, 117n, 385n, 455n. In addition to being the chief provost marshal upon Hurlbut's Sixteenth Corps staff, Williams undertook concurrent duty as provost marshal of the District of Memphis in the fall of 1863; *Memphis Bulletin*, Oct. 14, 1863.

58. *Memphis Daily Appeal*, June 8, 1863. In 1895, Hallum again bitterly denounced Hurlbut, alleging that his "normal sensibilities were to a great extent obliterated by excessive drink" and that his insobriety had largely accounted for "the apparent ease with which his subalterns managed him." Hallum further charged Hurlbut's "favorites" with swaying his judgment against suspected speculators; "A ton of proofs after the most flagrant outrages" upon aggrieved merchants "was of no avail when presented to Gen. Hurlbut, if subalterns opposed. Whether he was deadened to all sense of justice by the vintage so freely supplied, or more costly influences was not known, because Moses [Capt. George A. Williams] always stood between him and the injured citizen"; Hallum, *Diary*, 278–89, 317–18. In 1902 Hallum, who continued to harbor his grudge, bluntly declared, "Hurlbut was a drunken sot. The author says this of his own knowledge." John Hallum, *Reminiscences of the Civil War*, 28. For Confederate views on Hurlbut and the military prisons at Memphis, see *Charleston Daily Courier*, Mar. 26, 1863; *Memphis Daily Appeal*, Apr. 2, 7, 1863; *Richmond Whig*, Sept. 21, 1863; and *Richmond Sentinel*, Mar. 24, 1863. For descriptions of conditions in Irving Block, see *Memphis Bulletin*, May 5, 7, 29, June 27, July 13, Aug. 19, Sept. 3, Nov. 22, 1863. See also Lonnie R. Speer, *Portals to Hell: Military Prisons of the Civil War*, 96, 327–28, 337, and Meriwether, *Recollections*, 82–83, 88, 136–37.

59. "Incendiarism" remark in *Charleston Mercury*, Dec. 8, 1862, and related comments, *Daily Richmond Enquirer*, Jan. 26, 1863; "mercantile business" in *Cincinnati Daily Commercial*, Feb. 5, 1864. See also *Memphis Bulletin*, Apr. 19, 1864; Hallum, *Diary*, 313; *Belvidere Standard*, Dec. 1, 1863; *Memphis Daily Appeal*, Dec. 11, 29, 1863, Feb. 6, 1864; Kennett, *Sherman*, 223; and *OR*, 31, pt. 3: 160–61.

60. Leroy P. Graf and Ralph W. Haskins, eds., *The Papers of Andrew Johnson*, 6: *1862–1864*, 325, 361–62, 373–74, 453, 533–36, 613, 625, 680–81, 758; 7: *1864–1865*, 29n,

194, 297. *Memphis Bulletin,* May 27, 30, Nov. 19, 1863, Mar. 1, 12, 16, Apr. 19, 1864. *Memphis Daily Appeal,* Mar. 16, 1864; *New York Times,* Apr. 18, 1864; *Cincinnati Daily Commercial,* July 22, Dec. 24, 1863. Even earlier, however, in May 1863, Hurlbut had issued an order requiring all male residents of Memphis not then serving in the Union army to register with the provost marshal's office and swear allegiance to the U.S. government. As the *St. Louis Missouri Republican* explained, "Gen. Hurlbut is an efficient officer, and no doubt means to have all who are disloyal marked so that he will know them." *St. Louis Missouri Republican,* May 30, 1863, and June 24, Aug. 8, 1863.

61. *Memphis Bulletin,* Mar. 3, 5, 6, 1864; Hallum, *Diary,* 313–18; Parks, "Confederate Trade Center," 308; William H. Hughes, "John Hallum, Lawyer and Historian," 261. Subsequently, McDonald outdid even Hurlbut when in 1875 he formed the notorious "Whiskey Ring" at St. Louis. A crony of Grant's after 1870, McDonald served a federal prison term for his misconduct in Missouri in 1875; Grant pardoned him in 1877, because of their friendship. See Hesseltine, *Grant,* 207–208, 216, 220–21, 380–88, 422.

62. *OR,* 32, pt. 3: 206. Hallum, a member of the Memphis bar, had practiced before the Civil Commission for the District of Memphis, a quasi-judicial body under martial law for the disposition of civil cases. See *Memphis Bulletin,* June 26, 1863, and Jan. 27, 1864; and pertinent legal documents and military orders in Union Provost Marshal's File, M345, roll 116: Halla–Hemo, RG 109, NA. Late in March 1864, Hurlbut arrested and tried in military court another Memphis lawyer for abetting contraband smugglers. He fined this lawyer a thousand dollars and imposed three years' imprisonment at the military prison at Alton, Ill. Hurlbut based his decision largely on accusations from a black informer, even though the man's allegations had been vigorously rebutted by "three good respectable citizens" of Memphis. The lawyer escaped from Memphis and fled to Richmond; See J. W. Sharp to Jefferson Davis, June 22, 1864, "Letters Received by the Confederate Secretary of War, 1861–1865," M437, roll 141: March to September 1864, RG 109, NA; and a dossier on J. W. Sharp, in Union Provost Marshal's File, M345, roll 242: Sew–Sha, RG 109, NA. For related incidents, see *St. Louis Missouri Republican,* June 27, 1863, and Jones, *Heroines of Dixie,* 272, 275. See also Speer, *Portals to Hell,* 67–70, 80–89, 134–35, 177–78, 222, 229, 303, 323.

63. Hallum to Hurlbut, Apr. 3, 10, 18, 1864, Union Provost Marshal's File, roll 116: Halla–Hemo, RG 109, NA.

64. Hallum to Washburn, May 12, 1864, ibid. See also Hallum, *Diary,* 320–21; Hughes, "John Hallum," 261–62; Cupples, "Memphis Confederates," 120–22; *Memphis Daily Appeal,* June 27, 1863; Graf and Haskins, *Papers of Johnson,* 7: 406; Boatner, *Dictionary,* 892; and Hubbell and Geary, *Northern Leaders,* 570.

65. *OR,* II, 6: 864; 7: 404–408, 920–22, 1049–50; 8: 997–1002. "My daily fare" and succeeding remarks in M. M. Quaife, ed., *Absalom Grimes: Confederate Mail Runner,* 148–59, 162, particularly 150–51, 157; *Memphis Bulletin,* May 5, 1863. For an earlier description of Irving Block prison, which one detractor termed "a miserable uncomfortable place" that urgently needed "wholesome reform," see *St. Louis Missouri Republican,* Sept. 18, 1863. The *Richmond Enquirer* indignantly reported that it was "a hell upon earth" where cruel guards allowed black inmates to torture Confederate prisoners (chiefly by ducking their heads in barrels of water); *Daily Richmond Enquirer,* Oct. 21, 1864.

66. Washburn to Washburne, Apr. 23, 1864, and Chetlain to Washburne, Apr. 30, 1864, Washburne Papers. *Memphis Bulletin,* Apr. 22, 1864. Curiously, in June 1863 a military correspondent in Memphis asserted that Washburn had been designated to supersede Hurlbut at Memphis; Hurlbut's enemies would receive this new intelligence with a "considerable satisfaction," and very prominent Secessionist" had assured him that even the "Union men" of Memphis would "rejoice" at Hurlbut's early departure. *St. Louis Missouri Republican,* June 6, 1863. For an analysis of Union military rule over Memphis, see Stephen V. Ash, *When the Yankees Came: Conflict and Chaos in the Occupied South, 1861–1865,* 16, 58, 63, 70, 73, 81, 84, 86, 108–118, 119, 122, 173, 182–83.

67. *New York Times,* Apr. 16, 1864. See also Apr. 17, 18, 19, 27, 1864. The Republican paper in Quincy, Ill., branded the carnage on the Mississippi "a blistering shame and disgrace to our army" and asserted, "There is a fearful dereliction of duty somewhere"; *Quincy Daily Whig and Republican,* Apr. 18, 1864. See also *St. Louis Missouri Republican,* Apr. 16, 1864; Richard L. Fuchs, *An Unerring Fire: The Massacre at Fort Pillow,* 11–186, particularly 50, 70, 85, 99, 101–102, 150–51; and Brian S. Wills, *A Battle from the Start: The Life of Nathan Bedford Forrest,* 179–96.

68. *OR,* 31, pt. 1: 602–15; 32, pt. 3: 12–14, 51, 67, 70–71, 75, 106–107, 112, 119, 169, 201, 214, 225, 382; 39, pt. 2: 8, 9–11, 13. Hurlbut to Lorenzo Thomas, Apr. 24, 25, 1864, Hurlbut to Halleck, May 21, 1864, "Letters Received by General Henry W. Halleck," Records of the Headquarters of the Army, RG 108, NA. See also Sherman to Grant, Apr. 2, 1864, and Sherman to Ellen Ewing Sherman (remarking, "Hurlbut is timid and there is no use in denying it"), Apr. 22, 1864, in Simpson and Berlin, *Sherman's Civil War,* 611, 626; John A. Wyeth, *That Devil Forrest: Life of General Nathan Bedford Forrest,* 250–343; *Memphis Bulletin,* Apr. 19, 1864; *New York Times,* Apr. 18, 22, 1864; *Illinois State Journal,* May 12, 1864; *Richmond Daily Dispatch,* Nov. 28, 1863; Simon, *Papers of Grant,* 10: 251, 272, 284–285, and see also 286, 290–91, 295–96, 336, 374; Boatner, *Dictionary,* 288–89; and Hubbell and Geary, *Northern Leaders,* 208, 476. On March 20 Hurlbut had returned briefly to Belvidere to attend to Sophronia, who had sustained injuries in a railroad car accident; *Illinois State Journal,* Mar. 18, 22, 1864, and *Belvidere Standard,* Mar. 22, 29, May 17, 31, 1864. Following his removal from command in mid-April 1864, Hurlbut demanded a court of inquiry to "prove or disprove" Sherman's charge of "marked timidity." Lincoln advised him not to press Grant and Sherman to convene such a hearing with their spring campaigns in Virginia and Georgia about to begin; Basler, *Collected Works,* 7: 327–28.

69. Graf and Haskins, *Papers of Johnson,* 6: 534–36, 681. On Dec. 25, 1864, in a letter to Johnson, Bingham accused Hurlbut of having conspired with Maj. Gen. Edward R. S. Canby, commander of the trans-Mississippi Division at New Orleans, to remove Washburn from his post at Memphis. Early in December the War Department had assigned Washburn to Vicksburg, and he returned to Memphis by early March 1865. Bingham informed Johnson, without offering proof, that it was "through the wicked machinations of Hurlbut with Gen. Canby at New Orleans," that Washburn had lost his Memphis command. Fearing that Hurlbut would return to Memphis for a second tour of duty, Bingham exclaimed: "God forbid that Hurlbut or any of *his friends,* should be longer allowed to tyrannise [*sic*] over the poor but true Union men of our much neglected portion of the State"; ibid., 7: 296–97, 352–54.

70. *Belvidere Standard,* May 3, 1864.

71. *OR,* 32, pt. 1: 592, 602, 612, 623; 39, pt. 1: 468–84; 39, pt. 2: 296; 41, pt. 2: 37; 53: 597. Basler, *Collected Works,* 7: 370; Burlingame and Ettlinger, *Civil War Diary,* 200, 349n. See also *Memphis Bulletin,* Apr. 7, Aug. 23, 24, 25, 26, 1864; *Cincinnati Daily Commercial,* Aug. 25, 31, 1864; *Richmond Daily Dispatch,* Nov. 28, 1863; "hang every man" and succeeding remarks in *Daily Richmond Enquirer,* Jan. 1, 1864. A Southern military historian, in reference to the Hurst affair and Sherman's removal of Hurlbut from command at Memphis, asserts, "Brutality to citizens and barbarity to prisoners called forth no protest; 'timidity' in the face of danger was the only sin"; James D. Porter, *Confederate Military History Extended Edition: A Library of Confederate States History, in Seventeen Volumes, Written by Distinguished Men of the South, and Edited by Gen. Clement A. Evans of Georgia,* vol. 10: *Tennessee,* 231–33.

72. Henry W. Dudley, *Autobiography of Henry Walbridge Dudley,* 93–94; Robert S. Henry, ed., *As They Saw Forrest: Some Recollections and Comments of Contemporaries,* 258–59; James Dinkins, "The Capture of Memphis by Gen. Nathan B. Forrest," 188–89; Wills, *Forrest,* 27–45, 239–46; Boatner, *Dictionary,* 118; and Hubbell and Geary, *Northern Leaders,* 83. The Confederates did capture Col. John McDonald, but he later escaped; *St. Louis Missouri Republican,* Aug. 25, 1864. James B. Bingham, editor of the *Memphis Bulletin,* also narrowly escaped seizure by Forrest's cavalry—under embarrassing circumstances derisively described by a Southern editor. Bingham hastily concealed himself "half naked" in a chimney at his boarding house, from which "he came out as he went in, a dirty Black Republican"; *Richmond Daily Dispatch,* Oct. 20, 1864.

73. *Cincinnati Daily Commercial,* July 22, 1863. See also, with respect to Hovey's Memphis service, the *Des Moines Daily State Register,* Aug. 1, 1862, and Hubbell and Geary, *Northern Leaders,* 261.

74. *OR,* 41, pt. 3: 16, 297, 316; pt. 4: 530. Faust, *Historical Encyclopedia,* 330; Boatner, *Dictionary,* 42, 118; and Hubbell and Geary, *Northern Leaders,* 25, 82–83.

CHAPTER 5: ARMY COMMANDER AT NEW ORLEANS

1. Charles L. Dufour, *The Night the War Was Lost,* 15–354; Chester G. Hearn, *The Capture of New Orleans 1862,* 1–268; Gerald M. Capers, *Occupied City: New Orleans under the Federals, 1862–1865,* 5–6, 121; Elizabeth J. Doyle, "Civilian Life in Occupied New Orleans, 1862–65," 1–2; Louis S. Gerteis, *From Contraband to Freedman: Federal Policy toward Southern Blacks, 1861–1865,* 101; Joseph G. Dawson III, *Army Generals and Reconstruction: Louisiana, 1862–1877,* 19, 21–22. "Gomorrah" remark in *Illinois State Journal,* Feb. 2, 1863.

2. Leonard V. Huber, *New Orleans: A Pictorial History,* 7, 53, 63, 78–80, 83–85, 111, 144, 167, 288, 323; James Parton, *General Butler in New Orleans: History of the Administration of the Department of the Gulf in the Year 1862,* 284–90; Benjamin F. Butler, *Butler's Book: Autobiography and Personal Reminiscences of Major-General Benjamin F. Butler,* 374, 375; Nash, *Stormy Petrel,* 148; Trefousse, *Ben Butler,* 107, 109; and Harrington, *Fighting Politician,* 126–27; *New Orleans Bee,* Sept. 25, 1864. See also *Belvidere Standard,* Oct. 4, 1864.

3. *OR,* 41, pt. 3: 16, 316, 630–31; pt. 4: 233–34, 530. *New York Times,* Nov. 9, 1864; Boatner, *Dictionary,* 420; Hubbell and Geary, *Northern Leaders,* 25, 75, 83; Basler, *Collected*

Works, 7: *1863–1864,* 457; Lincoln to Canby, July 25, 1864, Lincoln Papers. See also Chester G. Hearn, *When the Devil Came Down to Dixie: Ben Butler in New Orleans,* 40–224, particularly 70–84, 101–109, 130–32, 139–41, 143, 219–21.

4. Capers, *Occupied City,* 25–97, 120–36; Amos E. Simpson and Vaughan Baker, "Michael Hahn: Steady Patriot," 232–44; Peyton McCrary, *Abraham Lincoln and Reconstruction: The Louisiana Experiment,* 3–270; Joe G. Taylor, *Louisiana Reconstructed, 1863–1877,* 1–52; John D. Winters, *The Civil War in Louisiana,* 125–48; Henry C. Warmoth, *War, Politics and Reconstruction: Stormy Days in Louisiana,* 32–37; Butler, *Butler's Book,* 373–552; Nolan, *Damnedest Yankee,* 150–225; Trefousse, *Ben Butler,* 107–34; Nash, *Stormy Petrel,* 145–77; David M. Nellis, "The Damned Rascal: Benjamin F. Butler in New Orleans," 4–10; Hollandsworth, *Pretense of Glory,* 3–44, 84, 162–71, 206–10; Harrington, *Fighting Politician,* 144–550; Doyle, "Civilian Life," 29–187, 213–311; Hubbell and Geary, *Northern Leaders,* 25, 75–76, 178, 223–24; Boatner, *Dictionary,* 42, 109–10, 365; Faust, *Encyclopedia,* 330. For a sketch of Hahn's life and career, see *Cincinnati Daily Times,* Mar. 5, 1864.

5. Hahn to Hurlbut, Dec. 5, 1864, Lincoln Papers. See also Eric Foner, *Reconstruction: America's Unfinished Revolution, 1863–1877,* 45–50.

6. Keith Wilson, "Education as a Vehicle of Racial Control: Major General N. P. Banks in Louisiana, 1863–64," 161–70; "colored schools" remark in *St. Louis Missouri Republican,* Apr. 7, 1864.

7. Ronald E. Butchart, *Northern Schools, Southern Blacks, and Reconstruction: Freedmen's Education, 1862–1875,* 108, 127–29, 171, 178; on the AMA, 4–201 and passim. Robert C. Morris, *Reading, 'Riting, and Reconstruction: The Education of Freedmen in the South 1861–1870,* 14, 22–32, 43; Joe M. Richardson, *Christian Reconstruction: The American Missionary Association and Southern Blacks, 1861–1890,* 15–33, 271; Henry L. Swint, *The Northern Teacher in the South, 1862–1870,* 10–169.

8. Patricia Brady, "Trials and Tribulations: American Missionary Association Teachers and Black Education in Occupied New Orleans, 1863–1864," 5–20. See also Messner, *Free Labor,* 21–39, 54, 74; Hollandsworth, *Pretense of Glory,* 211–13; Dawson, *Army Generals,* 10, 14; and Gerteis, *Southern Blacks,* 101–15.

9. *OR,* 24, pt. 3: 149–50.

10. Simon, *Papers of Grant,* 7: 487–88. See also John Eaton, with Ethel O. Mason, *Grant, Lincoln and the Freedmen: Reminiscences of the Civil War with Special Reference to the Work for the Contrabands and Freedmen of the Mississippi Valley,* 5–32, 35–36, 54–55, 57–58, 66, 119, 124–25, 127, 192–93, 197, 199, 201–204, 210–11, 232; *Cincinnati Daily Times,* Jan. 31, Feb. 13, 1863; and *Cincinnati Daily Commercial,* Sept. 19, 1863; *New York Daily Tribune,* Feb. 4, 1863; *Davenport Democrat and News,* Mar. 31, 1863; "tilling the soil" remark in *St. Louis Missouri Republican,* Mar. 31, 1863; "Yankee" and succeeding comments in *Charleston Mercury,* Dec. 22, 1863; *Memphis Daily Appeal,* Oct. 28, 1863; Ira Berlin et al., eds., *Freedom: A Documentary History of Emancipation, 1861–1867,* ser. 1, vol. 3: *The Wartime Genesis of Free Labor: The Lower South,* 43, 630, 709–10, 736; Gerteis, *Southern Blacks,* 120–21; and Hubbell and Geary, *Northern Leaders,* 159–60.

11. *New York Times,* Nov. 26, 1864. See also Oct. 7, 24, 30, 1864, Jan. 13, 15, Feb. 2, 21, 1865. Applauding Hurlbut's strict enforcement of Banks's free black labor policy, a New York reporter remarked, "Gen. Hurlbut enters upon the work in his department with

great alacrity"; ibid., Oct. 7, 1864. Another correspondent in New Orleans asserted that Hurlbut exhibited "superior executive ability and indomitable energy" and "infuses new life into everything he touches, and secures the confidence and respect of both the citizen and soldier"; *St. Louis Missouri Republican,* Oct. 19, 1864. See also *Cincinnati Daily Times,* Feb. 18, 1865, and *Illinois State Journal,* Mar. 24, 1865. By early 1865, however, this optimistic view of Hurlbut's tenure had undergone modification. Although "Generals Canby and Hurlbut are universal favorites in their administration, although seldom seen, . . . General Banks is anxiously looked for"; *Memphis Bulletin,* Jan. 19, 1865.

12. *OR,* 48, pt. 1: 1146–48.

13. Jean-Charles Houzeau, *My Passage at the New Orleans Tribune: A Memoir of the Civil War Era,* 103–106; "colored Citizens" and other remarks in Ira Berlin et al., eds., *Free at Last: A Documentary History of Slavery, Freedom, and the Civil War,* 318–25; Berlin, *History of Emancipation,* 372–75, 568–71, 575, 577–81, 591–96, 875–86n; Messner, *Free Labor,* 21–39, 54, 74; Hollandsworth, *Pretense of Glory,* 92–95; Foner, *Reconstruction,* 54–57; John W. Blassingame, *Black New Orleans: 1860–1880,* 25–38, 50–56; Wilson, "Racial Control," 157–61.

14. Houzeau, *My Passage,* 2, 17, 23, 36–37, 73n.

15. Houzeau, *My Passage,* 103–106; *OR,* 48, pt. 1: 1146–48; Foner, *Reconstruction,* 62–66; Blassingame, *Black New Orleans,* 152–53, 170; Hubbell and Geary, *Northern Leaders,* 20–21.

16. *New York Daily Tribune,* Dec. 30, 1862. See also *New York Times,* Jan. 22, 26, 1865; *OR,* 26, pt. 1: 39, 262–64, and passim. See also U.S. War Department, *Supplement to the Official Records of the Union and Confederate Armies,* pt. 2: *Record of Events,* 23: 433–53.

17. Qtd. in Mark E. Neely, ed., "John Tauro to Abraham Lincoln, January 7, 1865: New Orleans under the 'Beast' and Banks," 1 (emphasis in the original). See also U.S. War Department, Adjutant General's Office, "Report of The Special Commission, September 23, 1865, Maj. Genl Wm. F. Smith, Jas. T. Brady, Esq., Lt. Col. Nicholas Bowen AAG, Judge Advocate," entry no. 737: 88–100, RG 94, NA [hereafter Smith-Brady Report]. For a condensed and published portion of this report, see *Report of Maj.–Gen. Wm. F. Smith and Hon. James T. Brady, on the Official Conduct of General S. A. Hurlbut, and Others, at New Orleans, April 12, 1865,* 3–23. See also *Cincinnati Daily Times,* Oct. 24, 1864; Dufour, *War Was Lost,* 243–44, 288, 302; Hearn, *New Orleans,* 142–45, 188, 243; and Hearn, *Ben Butler,* 78, 86, 177–78.

18. Basler, *Collected Works,* 7: 492; *New York Times,* Nov. 1, 1864; *Richmond Whig,* Oct. 21, 1864. See also Butler, *Butler's Book,* 429–37; and Nash, *Stormy Petrel,* 152–53. Perhaps imitating the severity of Butler toward William Mumford, Hurlbut threatened "the instant arrest of any one insulting the flag" of the United States, which he ordered draped conspicuously over the principal entrance to the Ladies Fair; *Cincinnati Daily Commercial,* Dec. 26, 1864; *Cincinnati Daily Times,* Dec. 26, 1864. See also *Richmond Daily Dispatch,* Nov. 24, 1864, and *Mobile Advertiser and Register,* Nov. 21, 1863.

19. Hurlbut to Hoyt, Oct. 23, 25, 1864, Lincoln to Hurlbut, Nov. 14, 1864, Lincoln Papers. See also Max L. Heyman Jr., *Prudent Soldier: A Biography of Major General E. R. S. Canby, 1817–1873: His Military Service in the Indian Campaigns, in the Mexican War, in California, New Mexico, Utah, and Oregon; in the Civil War in the Trans-Mississippi*

West, and as Military Governor in the Post-War South, 1–236; Donald S. Frazier, *Blood and Treasure: Confederate Empire in the Southwest,* 54–300 and passim; and Hubbell and Geary, *Northern Leaders,* 82–83.

20. Basler, *Collected Works,* 8: *1864–1865,* 107–108; *OR,* 41, pt. 4: 412–13. See also Canby to Hurlbut, Oct. 29, 1864, in U.S. War Department, Adjutant General's Office, "Department of the Gulf, Letters Received, Bureau of Civil Affairs, 1864–1865," vols. A–C, and D–I, RG 393, NA.

21. Hahn to Lincoln, Oct. 29, Nov. 11, 1864, Hahn to Robinson, Nov. 17, 1864, Lincoln Papers; Simpson and Baker, "Michael Hahn," 246–47; McCrary, *Abraham Lincoln,* 303–304; Doyle, "Civilian Life," 26–27. For Hurlbut's raid on the quarters of a suspected Confederate cotton dealer, William G. Betterton, and his investigation of Lincoln's podiatrist, see Charles M. Segal, "Isachar Zacharie: Lincoln's Chiropodist," 92–93, and Isidore S. Meyer, ed., "The American Jew in the Civil War, Catalog of the Exhibit of the Civil War Centennial Historical Commission," 377–78. See also "Letters from George S. Denison to Salmon P. Chase, May 15, 1862, to March 21, 1865," 353, 355–56, 360, 375, 390.

22. Pease and Randall, *Diary of Browning,* 1: *1850–1864,* 692; Hubbell and Geary, *Northern Leaders,* 63.

23. Basler, *Collected Works,* 8: 106–108; Lincoln to Hurlbut, Nov. 14, 1864, Lincoln Papers; *OR,* 41, pt. 4: 555–56; Donald, *Lincoln,* 485–88, 563. Noah Brooks, the Washington correspondent for the *Sacramento Daily Union* and a confidant of President Lincoln, by Nov. 25, 1864, learned that Banks aspired to the post of secretary of war, but Brooks believed that he instead really sought to be "sent back to New Orleans with full power over Canby, who is inimical to the new Constitution" of Louisiana; Michael Burlingame, ed., *Lincoln Observed: Civil War Dispatches of Noah Brooks,* 146. See also Hubbell and Geary, *Northern Leaders,* 57.

24. Basler, *Collected Works,* 8: 163–65. Hurlbut to Lincoln, Nov. 29, 1864, Canby to Lincoln, Dec. 2, 1864, Lincoln Papers. See also *St. Louis Missouri Republican,* Apr. 2, 1865.

25. Hurlbut to Hoyt, Nov. 26, 1864, Hoyt to Hurlbut, Nov. 28, 1864, Hahn to Hurlbut, Dec. 1, 5, 1864, Hahn to Lincoln, Dec. 9, 1864, Lincoln Papers. *OR,* 41, pt. 4: 735–38; Simpson and Baker, "Michael Hahn," 247–48. See also Hahn to Hurlbut, Dec. 5, 1864, in U.S. War Department, "Department of the Gulf, Letters Received," vols. F–M, RG 393, NA; and Hubbell and Geary, *Northern Leaders,* 224.

26. "Whole city" and succeeding remarks in *Illinois State Journal,* Mar. 24, 1865. See also *New Orleans Picayune,* Mar. 5, 17, 1865; *Belvidere Standard,* Mar. 28, 1865; *Cincinnati Daily Commercial,* Mar. 11, 17, 1865; Walter M. Lowrey, "The Political Career of James Madison Wells," 995–1024; Simpson and Baker, "Michael Hahn," 248–49; and Graf and Haskins, *Papers of Johnson,* 7: 648–50, 651–53. In late March 1865, Hurlbut informed Canby that high legislative and judicial officials within "this Civil Government & by the U.S. Dist. Judge" in occupied Louisiana had sent to President Lincoln "a strong Petition" demanding his prompt removal, for "improper and arbitrary interference with the Sovereign State and its officers, and contempt of their dignity." Hurlbut acknowledged the validity of the complaints lodged against him, defiantly declaring that he had rather "sinned in forbearance" by refraining from executing further intrusions; Hurlbut to Chris-

tian T. Christensen, Mar. 24, 1865, Clinton H. Haskell Collection, Manuscripts Division, William L. Clements Library, Univ. of Michigan, Ann Arbor, Michigan.

27. John S. Kendall, ed., "Christ Church and General Butler," 1241–57; Headquarters Department of the Gulf, Special Orders 339, Dec. 15, 1864, Lincoln Papers. See also Doyle, "Civilian Life," 106–107.

28. *New York Times,* Jan. 31, 1864. See also Feb. 19, 1864.

29. Wells to Hurlbut, Mar. 17, 1865, Hurlbut to Wells, Mar. 17, 1865, Johnson Papers; *New Orleans Picayune,* Mar. 19, 22, May 9, June 17, 1865; Capers, *Occupied City,* 159–60; McCrary, *Abraham Lincoln,* 308–16; Taylor, *Louisiana Reconstructed,* 53–73; Winters, *Civil War in Louisiana,* 405–406. Also Graf and Haskins, *Papers of Johnson,* 7: 647–48; 8: *May–August 1865,* 105n, 575, 576n.

30. Denison to Chase, Mar. 21, 1865, in "Letters from Denison to Chase," 362, 456–58. See also Denison to Hugh McCulloch, May 6, 1865, George S. Denison Papers, 1851–1866, Manuscript Division, Library of Congress, Washington, D.C. A reporter's impression was that Hurlbut's support of Wells (in the replacement of Hoyt by Kennedy) "has not been well received by the Union men" in New Orleans; *New York Times,* May 5, 1865.

31. Hurlbut to Lincoln, Mar. 15, 1865, Lincoln Papers. See also *New Orleans Picayune,* Oct. 20, 1864, Jan. 8, 1865; *New York Times,* Oct. 29, Nov. 6, 1864, Jan. 9, 15, 26, Feb. 21, Mar. 1, 1865; *Quincy Herald,* Jan. 16, 1865; *St. Louis Missouri Republican,* Nov. 1, 1864, Feb. 21, Mar. 1, 1865; Doyle, "Civilian Life," 135, 139, 292; and Futrell, "Federal Military Government," 191. For a perceptive examination of Union military rule in New Orleans, see Ash, *When the Yankees Came,* 14–17, 23–24, 60, 70, 77, 83–91, 114, 117, 121, 173, 176.

32. *Richmond Daily Dispatch,* Mar. 6, 1865.

33. Basler, *Collected Works,* 7: 457, 8: 163–64. For Lincoln's involvement with the problem of unauthorized cotton trading in the lower Mississippi Valley in 1864 and 1865, see Ludwell H. Johnson, "Northern Profit and Profiteers: The Cotton Rings of 1864–1865," 101–15.

34. Canby to Lincoln, Jan. 14, 1865, Lincoln Papers. See also Hollandsworth, *Pretense of Glory,* 157–61; Heyman, *Prudent Soldier,* 237–49; Ludwell H. Johnson, *Red River Campaign: Politics and Cotton in the Civil War,* 49–78, 252; Ludwell H. Johnson, "Contraband Trade during the Last Year of the Civil War," 637–40. *New York Times,* Oct. 23, Nov. 1, 6, 1864, Jan. 8, Mar. 26, 1865. *St. Louis Missouri Republican,* Jan. 22, Feb. 3, 1865.

35. Hurlbut to Lincoln, Sept. 26, 1864, Lincoln Papers.

36. *OR,* 41, pt. 3: 630–31; pt. 4: 245–46, 743–44, 964; 48, pt. 1: 941–42, 1003–1005. See also *New Orleans Picayune,* Oct. 2, Dec. 13, 1864, and *New Orleans Bee,* Dec. 13, 1864.

37. Smith-Brady Report, 88–100; J. Lothrop to Fessenden, Dec. 2, 1864, William P. Fessenden Papers, 1864–1868, William L. Clements Library, Univ. of Michigan, Ann Arbor; Stephen N. Siciliano, *Major General William Farrar Smith: Critic of Defeat and Engineer of Victory,* 400–402, 407.

38. James H. Wilson, *Life and Services of William Farrar Smith, Major General, United States Volunteers in the Civil War,* 1–121; Siciliano, *Smith,* 14–399. See also Edward G. Longacre, "'A Perfect Ishmaelite': General 'Baldy' Smith," 10–20; Smith to Robert Johnson, Jan. 9, 1865, Johnson Papers; Capers, *Occupied City,* 118–19; Hubbell and Geary, *Northern Leaders,* 491; and Faust, *Encyclopedia,* 699.

39. Brady to Lincoln, Feb. 15, 16, 1865, Lincoln Papers. For background on Brady's career, see Allan Nevins and Milton H. Thomas, eds., *The Diary of George Templeton Strong*, 2: *The Turbulent Fifties 1850–1859*, 313; 3: *The Civil War 1860–1865*, 29, 164, 482, 532. Also *OR*, II, 3: 43–44.

40. Smith-Brady Report, 100–10. See also Hurlbut to Canby, May 11, 1865, in "Generals' Papers and Books," Stephen A. Hurlbut, file no. 159, RG 94, NA; Siciliano, *Smith*, 402.

41. *New Orleans Bee,* Apr. 13, 1865; Hurlbut to Oglesby, May 21, 1865, Richard J. Oglesby Papers, 1824–1899, Illinois State Historical Library, Springfield. On April 19, 1865, following Hurlbut's arrest for alleged misconduct, Canby revoked these general orders. See Siciliano, *Smith*, 402; Smith-Brady Report, 283–86; and *OR*, 48, pt. 2: 61–62.

42. Smith-Brady Report, 110–15. See also *New Orleans Bee*, Apr. 4, 10, 13, 27, 1865; and Siciliano, *Smith*, 407.

43. Smith-Brady Report, 116–19; Siciliano, *Smith*, 407.

44. Ibid., 106, 120–24. According to the commission's report, Hurlbut's backdated instructions for Robinson indicated the general's belief that "huge cheating is expected. The profits are bound to be enormous. Watch these operators and especially [George S.] Denson [Denison].'" The commission also reported that Hurlbut had explained that "many people of large consequence are in the affair; that the General dislikes to put the Colonel on detective duty, but the affair is large," adding, "You want their confidence first; I need not tell you how to work the problem. This must be strictly confidential"; ibid., 124.

45. Smith-Brady Report, 123–26. See also *New Orleans Bee*, Apr. 4, 10, 13, 27, 1865; Siciliano, *Smith*, 399–409; and Hollandsworth, *Pretense of Glory*, 235.

46. Oates, *Lincoln*, 426–36; Catton, *Grant*, 104–492; Hurlbut to Oglesby, May 21, 1865, Oglesby Papers. Hurlbut had also helped to end hostilities in Texas by assisting Maj. Gen. Lewis Wallace negotiate a truce with Confederate forces in the Southwest in April 1865. See *OR*, 49, pt. 1: 601–602; 49, pt. 2: 37, 122, 457–63. Lewis Wallace, *Lew Wallace: An Autobiography*, 2: 836–39; and Robert L. Kerby, *Kirby Smith's Confederacy: The Trans-Mississippi South, 1863–1865*, 225, 228–29, 320, 400.

47. *OR*, 49, pt. 2: 156; *New Orleans Bee*, Apr. 24, 1865; Hollandsworth, *Pretense of Glory*, 217–22.

48. James Marten, "A Glimpse at Occupied New Orleans: The Diary of Thomas H. Duval of Texas, 1863–1865," 314; *New Orleans Picayune*, Apr. 23, 1865; *New Orleans Bee*, Apr. 22, 24, 1865; *Illinois State Journal*, May 13, 1865; *Lincolniana: In Memoriam*, 251–57. See also Donald, *Lincoln*, 594–99.

49. Hurlbut to Canby, May 11, 1865, Hurlbut to Halleck, Apr. 26, 1865, "Generals' Papers and Books," Stephen A. Hurlbut, file no. 159, RG 94, NA; Hurlbut to Oglesby, May 21, 1865, Oglesby Papers. See also Canby to Stanton, May 1, 1865, William R. Morrison Papers, 1858–1898, Illinois State Historical Library, Springfield; and Siciliano, *Smith*, 407–408. Following the war, Hurlbut once again sought profitable employment for Lawrence L. Crandall. In mid-February 1867 he procured the hiring of Crandall as an officer at the Illinois State Penitentiary in Chicago. Governor Oglesby, however, soon learned that Andrew Shuman, his trusted friend and adviser, had seen Crandall "hanging about the Prison" for several weeks awaiting the commencement of this post; "This man has been *drunk* since his arrival there. He is not the sort of man to have in

Prison as an officer, and I wish there was some way of getting rid of him." Actually, Oglesby had already decided to abolish the whole "lessee system" of prison management in Illinois—an action that, not incidentally, also removed Crandall from his official post; Shuman to Oglesby, Apr. 16, 1867, Oglesby Papers.

50. Simon, *Papers of Grant*, 15: 466–67; Siciliano, *Smith*, 403; Hurlbut to Johnson, May 14, 1865, Morrison Papers.

51. Hurlbut to Yates, May 15, 1865, Morrison Papers.

52. Hurlbut to Oglesby, May 15, 1865, Morrison Papers; Oglesby to Johnson, June 11, 1865, Johnson Papers; Graf and Haskins, *Papers of Johnson*, 8: 221.

53. Autograph MS., 1874, Morrison Papers. A Democratic congressman, Morrison apparently sought to build a dossier to use against Hurlbut, a Republican running for Congress in another race later in 1874. After the War Department finally released the Smith-Brady Report in January 1874, Morrison succeeded in obtaining statements and affidavits that documented the suspicious circumstances surrounding Hurlbut's departure from the army. Hurlbut's detractor expressed his opinion that "Hurlbut's defense consists solely in letters subsequently written by Rawlins & Stanton, stating that they had looked over the Smith-Brady report, & thought there was nothing in it!! and a letter written by himself in July following, from his home in Belvidere, demanding a court [-martial]. Hurlbut had been twice before that relieved from service & sent home, for drunkenness & general worthlessness. The first time from Missouri by [John C.] Frémont & the 2d from Memphis"; ibid. See also Edward D. Townsend to Canby, June 2, 1865, and an order from President Andrew Johnson honorably mustering Hurlbut out of the army, in "Generals' Papers and Books," Stephen A. Hurlbut File, RG 94, NA; Simon, *Papers of Grant*, 15: 466–67; Siciliano, *Smith*, 403–408; and Hubbell and Geary, *Northern Leaders*, 366.

54. *Illinois State Journal*, Mar. 24, 1865.

55. Ibid., June 7, 1865.

56. *New Orleans Picayune*, June 18, 1865; *OR*, 49, pt. 2: 985.

57. *Belvidere Standard*, July 4, 18, Aug. 22, 1865.

58. Ibid., Dec. 5, 12, 1865.

CHAPTER 6: THE PASSING OF A DIPLOMATIC PARTISAN

1. Carpenter, *History of Boone County*, 1: 2, and 2: 680–808; Moorhead, *Boone County*, 1–165; *Belvidere Illustrated*, 13–70; Sager, "Hurlbut," 68; *Belvidere Standard*, June 4, July 18, 26, Aug. 17, 1865.

2. *Belvidere Standard*, Aug. 17, Dec. 26, 1865, Jan. 16, 1866. See also "Circuit Court Record, Boone County," book 6, 1860–1866; book 7, 1866–1869; book 8, 1869–1879, BCCH. Also Jones, *Jones*, 1–19, 38–41.

3. *Belvidere Standard*, Sept. 17, 1867. Fuller had raised his "rather aristocratic" Gothic Revival-style mansion in the summer of 1853, at a cost of five thousand dollars; *Belvidere Standard*, Sept. 13, 1853. For notices of Sophronia Hurlbut's realty purchases in Belvidere during the war, see "Warranty Deeds, Book X, 1864, Boone County," 521–23, 568–69, BCCH.

4. From a file of letters and bills of estate in "Circuit Clerk Probate Record, Letters of Estate, Stephen Augustus Hurlbut," 1882, 1885, roll 130, no. 969, BCCH. See also Carpenter, *History of Boone County,* 759; and Moorhead, *Boone County,* 12. In 1877, an admiring observer declared: "Mr. H. is living quietly at his beautiful home in Belvidere, wearing with becoming modesty his well-earned laurels in both military and civil life"; *Past and Present of Boone County,* 354.

5. "Deed Record, Boone County," book 28, 568–70, book 30, 140, 636, and book 38, 237, BCCH. See also Carpenter, *History of Boone County,* 682. *Belvidere Standard,* Aug. 10, 1858 (on a branch road to Belvidere), Aug. 24, 28, 1866. Aug. 19, 1873. Also "Affidavit of Sophronia R. Hurlbut, June 3, 1882," in "Circuit Clerk Probate Record, Letters of Estate, Stephen Augustus Hurlbut," roll 130, no. 969, BCCH.

6. "Three hearty cheers" remark in *Belvidere Standard,* July 10, 1866, and see also June 26, July 3, 1866; Hurlbut to Stevens, Dec. 25, 1865, in Beverly W. Palmer and Holly B. Ochoa, eds., *The Selected Papers of Thaddeus Stevens,* 2: *April 1865–August 1868,* 58–59. See also Foner, *Reconstruction,* 176–227; and Hubbell and Geary, *Northern Leaders,* 506–507.

7. *Belvidere Standard,* July 3, 10, Aug. 14, Oct. 2, 23, 1866; *Chicago Tribune,* Oct. 9, 1866. See also Hans L. Trefousse, *Andrew Johnson: A Biography,* 214–352; Eric McKitrick, *Andrew Johnson and Reconstruction,* 142–52, 274–335; Jones, *"Black Jack,"* 275–86; Jones, *Stalwart Republican,* 1–2, 17–32; and Hubbell and Geary, *Northern Leaders,* 274–75, 314.

8. Robert B. Beath, *History of the Grand Army of the Republic,* 59, 63; Mary C. Logan, *Reminiscences of a Soldier's Wife: An Autobiography,* 216–17; *Illinois State Journal,* July 13, 1866; and Jones, *"Black Jack,"* 273–75.

9. Stuart McConnell, *Glorious Contentment: The Grand Army of the Republic, 1865–1900,* 25, 28, 243n; Mary A. Dearing, *Veterans in Politics: The Story of the G.A.R.,* 115–16, 128–33, 190; Beath, *Grand Army,* 67–69, 71–72, 77–79; Oglesby to Palmer, July 20, 1866, Oglesby Papers; *Belvidere Standard,* Dec. 25, 1866.

10. *Indianapolis Journal,* Nov. 21, 22, 1866.

11. Beath, *Grand Army,* 77–79; Dearing, *Veterans,* 128–33, 190; McConnell, *Glorious Contentment,* 25, 28, 243n; Jones, *Stalwart Republican,* 11–270 and passim; Faust, *Encyclopedia,* 317–18; *New York Tribune,* Jan. 18, 1868.

12. *Illinois State Journal,* July 13, 1866, Jan. 7, 1867; *Indianapolis Journal,* Nov. 21, 22, 1866. Hurlbut served on the Committee on Education and acted as chairman of the Committee on Railroads. *Belvidere Standard,* Dec. 12, 1865, June 26, July 3, 10, Aug. 14, Oct. 2, 23, 1866, Jan. 15, 22, 29, 1867; *New York Tribune,* Jan. 18, 1868.

13. *Belvidere Standard,* Oct. 2, 23, 1866, Jan. 15, 22, 29, 1867. *Illinois State Journal,* Jan. 7, Feb. 18, 1867; *Aurora Beacon,* Mar. 21, 1867; *Journal of the House of Representatives of the Twenty-fifth General Assembly of the State of Illinois, at Their Regular Session, Begun and Held at Springfield, January 7, 1867,* 404–405, 410–15; Moses, *Illinois, Historical and Statistical,* 2: 768–69; *Belvidere Standard,* Apr. 28, 1868.

14. Oglesby to Theophilus L. Dickey, Dec. 10, 1867, and Jan. 25, Feb. 3, 1868; Hurlbut to Oglesby, Feb. 2, 20, May 28, 1868, Oglesby to Hurlbut, Feb. 13, June 1, 1868; Palmer to Oglesby, June 25, 1869; all Oglesby Papers. U.S. Congress, House, *The Congressional Globe, Containing the Debates and Proceedings of the Second Session Fortieth Congress,* pt. 2: *1867–1868,* 1717, 1759; *New York Times,* June 21, 1869; Moses, *Illinois, Historical and*

Statistical, 2: 464–68; Ernest L. Bogart and Charles M. Thompson, *Illinois: The Industrial State, 1870–1893,* 307–308.

15. Hurlbut to Yates, Mar. 7, 1867, Yates Papers. See also Yates II and Pickering, *Richard Yates,* 267–78; Richard Yates II, *Serving the Republic: Richard Yates, Illinois Governor and Congressman, Son of Richard Yates, Civil War Governor, an Autobiography,* 1–22; Nortrup, "Richard Yates," 333–60.

16. Hurlbut to Oglesby, Feb. 2, 1868, Oglesby to Hurlbut, Feb. 13, 1868, Oglesby Papers; Northrup, "Richard Yates," 338, 354–56; and Yates II and Pickering, *Richard Yates,* 278–82.

17. Hurlbut to Logan, Feb. 6, 1868, John A. Logan Papers, 1826–1886, Manuscript Division, Library of Congress, Washington, D.C.; Hurlbut to Oglesby, Feb. 20, May 22, 1868; Oglesby to Hurlbut, June 1, 1868, including a file of endorsements; both in Oglesby Papers. Hurlbut to Washburne, Nov. 14, 19, 1868, Washburne Papers; Hurlbut to Palmer, Nov. 19, 1868, John M. Palmer Papers, 1839–1902, Illinois State Historical Library, Springfield; John M. Palmer, *Personal Recollections of John M. Palmer: The Story of an Earnest Life,* 280–312; Palmer, *Conscientious Turncoat,* 66–75, 191–98, 207–34; Jones, *"Black Jack,"* 264–86; Jones, *Stalwart Republican,* 17–32, 47; George F. Dawson, *Life and Services of Gen. John A. Logan as Soldier and Statesman,* passim; Church, *Republican Party,* 101–104; *Belvidere Standard,* May 12, 19, Dec. 22, 1868; Thomas J. McCormack, ed., *Memoirs of Gustave Koerner, 1809–1896, Life Sketches Written at the Suggestion of His Children,* 2: 479; Joseph Logsdon, *Horace White: Nineteenth Century Liberal,* 157–58; Hesseltine, *Grant,* 118–21, 123–33, 138, 140.

18. For a trenchant treatment of Grant's patronage policy, see Hesseltine, *Grant,* 145–56, 303–304; and Jones, *Jones,* 48–61, 71–73. The *New York Times,* criticizing the appointments of Washburne, Jones, and Hurlbut, asserted that (as friends of Grant) they owed their nominations entirely to the "spoils of party victory" and not to individual merit; *New York Times,* Apr. 24, 1869.

19. Grant, *Personal Memoirs,* 1: 194–99; Simpson, *Grant,* 54–56; Perret, *Grant,* 92–96; Smith, *Grant,* 78–79; Hesseltine, *Grant,* 13, 203; E. Taylor Parks, *Colombia and the United States, 1765–1934,* 347; James D. Richardson, *A Compilation of the Messages and Papers of the Presidents, 1789–1913,* 6: 3987.

20. Parks, *Colombia,* 194–215, 485–86. See also Claude M. Fuess, *The Life of Caleb Cushing,* 2: 301–302; Gerstle Mack, *The Land Divided: A History of the Panama Canal and Other Isthmian Canal Projects,* 166–67; Lawrence O. Ealy, *Yanqui Politics and the Isthmian Canal,* 33–34; Miles P. Duval, *Cadiz to Cathay: The Story of the Long Struggle for a Waterway across the American Isthmus,* 74–75; Charles S. Campbell, *The Transformation of American Relations, 1865–1900,* 61; John B. Moore, *A Digest of International Law as Embodied in Diplomatic Discussions, Treaties and Other International Agreements, International Awards, the Decisions of Municipal Courts, and the Writings of Jurists,* 3: 20–21; and *New York Times,* Apr. 23, 24, 1869.

21. Fish to Hurlbut, May 4, 1869, Hurlbut to Fish, May 6, June 24, July 2, Aug. 7, 1869, in U.S. State Department, "Despatches from U.S. Ministers to Colombia, 1820–1906, April 30, 1868–August 9, 1869," roll 27, RG 59, General Records of the Department of State, NA; Fish to Hurlbut, June 3, 25, Aug. 19, 24, Sept. 4, Oct. 25, 1869, in U.S. State

Department, "Diplomatic Instructions of the Department of State, 1801–1906, Colombia, May 29, 1861–June 18, 1875," roll 45, RG 59, NA; Hurlbut to Fish, Aug. 11, 18, 29, Sept. 11, 27, Nov. 16, 27, 29, 1869, in U.S. State Department, "Despatches from U.S. Ministers to Colombia, August 11, 1869–August 17, 1873," roll 28, RG 59, NA; Hurlbut to Fish, Nov. 16, 1869, Hamilton Fish Papers, 1808–1893, Manuscript Division, Library of Congress, Washington, D.C.; Mack, *Land Divided,* 166–67; Parks, *Colombia and the United States,* 347–48; *Belvidere Standard,* Jan. 4, 1870.

22. The complete text of the "Hurlbut Convention" is in U.S. Congress, Senate, *Executive Documents,* 46th Cong., 2d sess., 1879–1880, vol. 4, no. 112, 38–84; and in Hurlbut to Fish, Jan. 26, 1870, in "Despatches from U.S. Ministers to Colombia," roll 28, RG 59, NA. See also Moore, *International Law,* 3: 21–22; and Eduardo Lemaitve, *Panama y Su Separacion de Colombia,* 92–97.

23. Hurlbut to Fish, Feb. 1, March 1, 4, 12, 16, Apr. 3, 4, 5, 6, 7, 26, 29, May 6, 16, June 3, 5, 6, 10, 12, 16, 29, 30, July 13, 1870, Mar. 10, 1872; in "Despatches from U.S. Ministers to Colombia," roll 28, RG 59, NA. See also *Mompos (Colombia) la Palestra,* May 21, 1872; Hurlbut entries for Mar. 3, 26, Apr. 7, 29, May 3, 26, 1870, in "Letter Book, March 8, 1869–Oct. 24, 1870," Fish Papers; Hurlbut to Washburne, June 16, 1870, Washburne Papers; Moore, *International Law,* 3: 22; Richardson, *Messages and Papers,* 6: 4011; and Parks, *Colombia and the United States,* 350.

24. Denna F. Fleming, *The Treaty Veto of the American Senate,* 56–57. See also Royden J. Dangerfield, *In Defense of the Senate: A Study in Treaty Making,* 230; W. Stull Holt, *Treaties Defeated by the Senate: A Study of the Struggle between President and Senate over the Conduct of Foreign Relations,* 180–81; Joseph Smith, *Illusions of Conflict: Anglo-American Diplomacy toward Latin America, 1865–1896,* 35, 93–98; and Lemaitve, *Panama,* 96–97. Hurlbut also engaged in the negotiation of three other unsuccessful treaties with Colombia: a tariff agreement, on the extradition of fugitives, and on the modernization of Colombian ordnance at American arsenals; Hurlbut to Fish, Oct. 3, 14, 17, Nov. 9, 15, 17, 1870, Mar. 21, Apr. 23, 1871; in "Despatches from U.S. Ministers to Colombia," roll 28, RG 59, NA. Hurlbut entries for Oct. 29, Nov. 17, 1870, in "Letter Book," Fish Papers; Parks, *Colombia and the United States,* 247, 263, 350. See also Moore, *International Law,* 3: 22–23; Mack, *Land Divided,* 167; Duval, *Cadiz to Cathay,* 76; Campbell, *Transformation of American Relations,* 61; Ealy, *Isthmian Canal,* 34; and Allan Nevins, *Hamilton Fish: The Inner History of the Grant Administration,* 2: 912–14.

25. Hurlbut to Phillips, Sept. 25, 1871, Stephen A. Hurlbut Collection, Illinois State Historical Library, Springfield. David L. Phillips owned and edited the *Illinois State Journal* of Springfield from 1862 to 1866 but sold his interest in the paper to Hurlbut's wealthy Rockford supporter, William H. Bailhache, in March 1866; Franklin W. Scott, *Newspapers and Periodicals of Illinois, 1814–1879,* 132. See also *New York Times,* July 12, 13, 14, 1871; Hesseltine, *Grant,* 257–60, 271; McFeely, *Grant,* 239–457; and Perret, *Grant,* 380–446.

26. Hurlbut to Fish, Apr. 28, May 4, 25, June 2, Aug. 29, 1869, Aug. 5, 1871, Mar. 7, Apr. 17, 1872, in "Despatches from U.S. Ministers to Colombia," roll 28, RG 59, NA. Hurlbut to Fish, Nov. 16, 1869, Fish Papers; Fish to Hurlbut, June 21, 1871, in "Diplomatic Instructions of the Department of State," roll 45, RG 59, NA; U.S. State Department, *Diplomatic Correspondence and Foreign Relations of the United States, 1861–1899,*

10: *1871,* 230–31, 240–41, 11: *1872,* pt. 2: 138–39, 142–54, 154–58; *New York Times,* Nov. 23, 1873; *Mompos la Palestra,* May 20, June 5, Nov. 20, 1871; Moore, *International Law,* 6: 973–74. Nevins, *Hamilton Fish,* 1: 120, 176–200, 231–48; 2: 667–94. Parks, *Colombia and the United States,* 307; Thomas A. Bailey, *A Diplomatic History of the American People,* 380–81. Hurlbut's resignation from the diplomatic service apparently arose from his expectation of nomination as the Republican candidate from the Fourth Congressional District in 1872. For specific references, see Simon, *Papers of Grant,* vol. 23: *February 1–December 31, 1872,* 203n, 204n, 205n, 239n.

27. Church, *Republican Party,* 117, 137; *Belvidere Standard,* June 4, 11, 18, 1872; Sager, "Hurlbut," 71.

28. John G. Sproat, *"The Best Men": Liberal Reformers in the Gilded Age,* 4–10, 71–88, 279; Earle D. Ross, *The Liberal Republican Movement,* 21, 63, 86–105, 107; Hesseltine, *Grant,* 180–260, 269–79.

29. *Belvidere Standard,* July 2, 9, 1872. Horace White, editor of the *Chicago Tribune,* attributed Hurlbut's gaining the district nomination to Lathrop's refusal to bribe the De Kalb delegation. Apparently, Lathrop described to White his encounter with the De Kalb delegates, with the hope that, when his story appeared in the *Tribune,* the Republican State Central Committee in Chicago would deny Hurlbut the nomination. Although White refrained from accusing Hurlbut of bribing the De Kalb delegates, he characterized the circumstances surrounding his nomination as "offensive and disgusting"; *Chicago Tribune,* Sept. 24, 1872, July 21, 1874. See also *Chicago Journal,* July 18, 1872.

30. *Madison State Journal,* July 5, 6, 1872; *Madison Democrat,* July 5, 1872; *Chicago Tribune,* July 6, 1872; *Belvidere Standard,* July 16, 1872.

31. *Madison Democrat,* July 5, 1872; *Madison State Journal,* July 5, 6, 1872; *Chicago Tribune,* June 29, July 5, 6, 16, Sept. 24, 30, 1872; *Belvidere Standard,* July 30, Nov. 12, 1872; *Aurora Beacon,* Oct. 26, 1872, *New York Times,* Aug. 30, Sept. 11, 1872; Hurlbut to Mason Brayman, July 10, 1872, Brayman to Hurlbut, Sept. 23, 1872, William H. Bailhache–Mason Brayman Papers, 1820–1895, Illinois State Historical Library, Springfield. See also Church, *Republican Party,* 117; Hesseltine, *Grant,* 279–90; Ross, *Liberal Republican Movement,* 150–91; Glyndon G. VanDeusen, *Horace Greeley: Nineteenth-Century Crusader,* 407–408, 409–21; and Lusk, *Politics and Politicians,* 208, 232, 234.

32. *Washington Evening Star,* Dec. 13, 1873; U.S. Congress, House, *The Congressional Record, Containing the Debates and Proceedings of the First Session Forty-third Congress,* pt. 1, vol. 2: 6, 74, 205, 216, 656.

33. U.S. Congress, House, *The Congressional Record, First Session Forty-third Congress,* pt. 1, vol. 1: 846–48; pt. 2, vol. 2: 241–290, 1198–1201, 1964–68; pt. 3, vol. 2: 2142, 4144, 4393–94, 4520–21, 4620, 4626–27. Hurlbut to Brayman, Dec. 21, 1873, Bailhache-Brayman Papers; Hesseltine, *Grant,* 241, 278, 290, 313–14, 360–61. Referring to Hurlbut as a rising congressman, Speaker Blaine later remarked that "General Hurlbut" had "soon acquired a prominent position in the House" and just recognition as "a ready debater"; James G. Blaine, *Twenty Years of Congress: From Lincoln to Garfield, with a Review of the Events Which Led to the Political Revolution of 1860,* 2: 542; *New York Times,* Mar. 25, 1874; Malone and Johnson, *DAB,* 5: 579–80.

34. Stephen A. Hurlbut MS., "To the Voters of the Fourth Congressional District of Illinois," 1874, Chicago Historical Society; *Belvidere Standard,* Sept. 8, 22, Nov. 10,

1874. *Chicago Tribune,* Nov. 1, 1872, July 21, Sept. 11, Oct. 2, 13, 19, 28, Nov. 5, 9, 16, 1874. Church, *Republican Party,* 123; Lusk, *Politics and Politicians,* 243. For sketches of John F. Farnsworth, see Hubbell and Geary, *Northern Leaders,* 170–71, and Boatner, *Dictionary,* 275.

35. U.S. Congress, House, *The Congressional Record, Second Session Forty-third Congress,* pt. 1, vol. 3: 93. U.S. Congress, House, *The Congressional Record, Containing the Debates and Proceedings of the First Session Forty-fourth Congress,* pt. 1, vol. 4: 250, 251; pt. 2, vol. 1: 547–48; pt. 2, vol. 4: 1–8. U.S. Congress, House, "Vicksburg Troubles," HR Rept. 265, 43d Cong., 2d sess., 1874, 1–560; *New Orleans Times Picayune,* Dec. 19, 1874; *New York Times,* Feb. 28, 1875; *Washington Evening Star,* Dec. 24, 1875; *Belvidere Standard,* Sept. 5, 1876; Burke A. Hinsdale, ed., *The Works of James Abram Garfield,* 2: 376; Harry J. Brown and Frederick D. Williams, eds., *The Diary of James A. Garfield,* 3: *1875–1877,* 223; Allan Peskin, *Garfield: A Biography,* 299–300; Foner, *Reconstruction,* 228–601, particularly 454–59, 528, 530–31; James W. Garner, *Reconstruction in Mississippi,* 328–37; Blanche A. Ames, *Aldelbert Ames, 1835–1933: General, Senator, Governor,* 407–409; Richard A. McLemore, ed., *A History of Mississippi,* 1: 585.

36. U.S. Congress, House, "Testimony Taken by the Committee on Reform in the Civil Service in Relation to the Chicago Pension-Agency," HR Misc. Rept. no. 182, 44th Cong., 1st sess. (1876), 1–106; *Chicago Pension Agency,* 3–5; Jones, *Jones,* 40–41, 75–77. Grant to Jones, May 18, 19, 1870, Jan. 9, Dec. 12, 1871, Feb. 19, 1872, Aug. 13, 1876, all Ulysses S. Grant Papers, 1844–1922, Manuscript Division, Library of Congress, Washington, D.C. (microfilm copy, Kent State Univ., Kent, Ohio). Hesseltine, *Grant,* 98, 263–64, 295, 359, 365–66, 380–88; Simon, ed., *Julia Dent Grant,* 186, 189.

37. *Chicago Tribune,* May 4, 7, 1876. See also George Levy, *To Die in Chicago: Confederate Prisoners at Camp Douglas, 1862–1865,* 303, 135–280, and passim; and Speer, *Portals to Hell,* 181.

38. U.S. Congress, House, "Testimony Taken by the Committee on Reform in the Civil Service," 1–106, particularly 41–49; *Chicago Pension-Agency,* 3–7; *New York Times,* Jan. 12, Apr. 23, 1876; Grant to Jones, Aug. 13, 1876, Grant Papers; Jones, *Jones,* 40–41, 75–77; Jones to Grant, Aug. 16, 17, 1876, Washburne Papers; Green B. Raum to Logan, Jan. 7, 1877, Logan Papers. See also Mary C. Logan to Rutherford B. Hayes, May 11, 1879, Rutherford B. Hayes Papers, 1829–1897, Rutherford B. Hayes Presidential Library, Fremont, Ohio.

39. Brown and Williams, *Diary of Garfield,* 3: 279; *Chicago Times,* June 6, 1876; *Belvidere Standard,* July 4, 1876; Hesseltine, *Grant,* 398–406; David S. Muzzey, *James G. Blaine: A Political Idol of Other Days,* 205–20; Church, *Republican Party,* 126–27; Sager, "Hurlbut," 72–73. For Hurlbut's candid views on Blaine's political ambitions, see Hurlbut to Phillips, Sept. 25, 1871, Hurlbut Collection.

40. *Cincinnati Daily Commercial,* June 21, 1876; Hurlbut to Blaine, July 2, 1876, James G. Blaine Papers, 1859–1892, Manuscript Division, Library of Congress, Washington, D.C.

41. Lewis C. Weir to Hayes, July 17, 1876, Hayes Papers; U.S. Congress, House, *The Congressional Record, First Session Forty-fourth Congress,* pt. 3, vol. 4: 882–87; *Aurora Beacon,* July 22, 1876, qtd. in *Belvidere Standard,* Aug. 1, 1876. See also John Bigelow,

The Life of Samuel J. Tilden, 1: *1814–1876,* 305–306; and Alexander C. Flick, *Samuel Jones Tilden: A Study in Political Sagacity,* 192–230.

42. *Belvidere Standard,* Sept. 5, 12, Oct. 17, 24, Nov. 14, 1876; Smith to Hayes, Oct. 30, 1876, Hayes Papers. For a scholarly study of Smith, see Edgar L. Gray, "The Career of William Henry Smith, Politician-Journalist," and see Charles W. Marsh, *Recollections, 1837–1910,* 202–203. Marsh explained, retrospectively, "I had known Gen. Hurlbut many years but had never become closely acquainted with him. I was a member of the committee and was supporting Lathrop in the contest; so Hurlbut and I met in the committee room as political opponents, but he was always as friendly as if we were working together. He discussed the difficulties and disagreeable features of the situation fairly and frankly. He was the party most aggrieved yet he complained the least. We became very good friends and later did some political work together. He was of an open and generous nature. We maintained occasional correspondence until his death at Lima, Peru, where he was U.S. Minister. His last letter reached me a considerable time after the notice of his death"; ibid., 203–204. See also Lusk, *Politics and Politicians,* 253.

43. Flick, *Study in Political Sagacity,* 279–402; Bigelow, *Tilden,* 2: *1877–1887,* 9–103; Ari A. Hoogenboom, *Rutherford B. Hayes: Warrior and President,* 256–465; Hamilton J. Eckenrode, *Rutherford B. Hayes: Statesman of Reunion,* 174–205; Hurlbut to Fuller, Nov. 13(?), 1876, qtd. in Church, *Republican Party,* 128–29.

44. Brown and Williams, *Diary of Garfield,* 3: 392, 397, 420, 439; Peskin, *Garfield,* 405–11, 415–17; Hesseltine, *Grant,* 343–58, 414–15, 418–19; Warmoth, *Stormy Days,* 197–243; *New York Times,* Feb. 14, 1876; *Belvidere Standard,* Feb. 9, 1876; William Dennison to Hayes, Jan. 22, 1877, Hayes Papers; Eckenrode, *Hayes,* 206–38; Sidney I. Pomerantz, "Election of 1876," *History of American Presidential Elections,* 2: *1848–1896,* 1379–1435.

45. Hurlbut to Garfield, Mar. 28, June 24, 1877, James A. Garfield Papers, 1852–1881, Manuscript Division, Library of Congress, Washington, D.C. See also Peskin, *Garfield,* 420–22, 452–53, 483–84, 517.

46. Peskin, *Garfield,* 420–27; Hurlbut to Garfield, June 24, 1877, Garfield Papers. On June 17, 1877, Sherman informed Sheridan, "Hurlbut has special claims on me. I knew him as a law pupil of Mr. Pettigrew [James Louis Petigru] in Charleston in 1842, and he was one of the first to fall under my command in the War. He was at Shiloh, and afterwards was with me at Memphis, made a corps commander by the same order that appointed [George H.] Thomas, [James B.] McPherson and myself, and I saw his intelligence, manliness and patriotism throughout the war. Surely will I do anything and everything for him now. Please let Hurlbut know how I feel for him, for not alone in the Army was he our friend, but eminently so in Congress"; from "A Letter of Sherman to Sheridan," in Hurlbut, *In the Midst of War,* 23. Sherman wished to help Hurlbut because, when in Congress, Hurlbut had defended Sherman's keeping of a large staff and had championed funding for the U.S. Military Academy; U.S. Congress, House, *The Congressional Record, Containing the Debates and Proceedings of the First Session Forty-third Congress,* pt. 3, vol. 2: 4393–94; Kennett, *Sherman,* 310; Brown and Williams, *Diary of Garfield,* 3: *1875–1877,* 223; and Peskin, *Garfield,* 299–300.

47. Hurlbut to Oglesby, June 20, 1877, Oglesby Papers; Hurlbut to Garfield, June 24, 1877, Garfield Papers; Peskin, *Garfield,* 420–22, 425–26; Thomas M. Hope to Hayes,

May 6, 1877, Hayes Papers. See also Stanley P. Hirshon, *Farewell to the Bloody Shirt: Northern Republicans and the Southern Negro, 1877–1893,* 25–36; Charles R. Williams, ed., *Diary and Letters of Rutherford Birchard Hayes, Nineteenth President of the United States,* 3: *1865–1881,* 439; and Garfield to William M. Evarts, July 30, 1877, Garfield Papers. For a sketch of Hilliard, see Malone and Johnson, *DAB,* 9: 54–55.

48. Hurlbut to Ichabod M. Butler, Jan. 7, 1878, Hurlbut Collection; U.S. Department of Justice, "Attorney Rolls of the Supreme Court of the United States, 1790–1951," roll 3, "H" series, RG 267, NA; U.S. Department of Justice, "Dockets of the Supreme Court of the United States, 1791–1950," roll 22: "1875–1880," RG 267, NA.

49. Thomas N. Doutney, *Thomas N. Doutney: His Life-Struggle and Triumphs, Also a Vivid Pen-Picture of New York, Together with a History of the Work He Has Accomplished as a Temperance Reformer,* 452, 484, 521; Ernest H. Cherrington, ed., *Standard Encyclopedia of the Alcohol Problem,* 5: *Newton–Sims,* 2268–69; John A. Krout, *The Origins of Prohibition,* 262–96; D. Leigh Colvin, *Prohibition in the United States: A History of the Prohibition Party and of the Prohibition Movement,* 65–144. See also *The Cyclopedia of Temperance and Prohibition: A Reference Book of Facts, Statistics, and General Information on All Phases of the Drink Question, the Temperance Movement and the Prohibition Agitation,* 559–80.

50. *Belvidere Standard,* Feb. 26, May 21, July 2, 9, 16, Aug. 6, 10, 13, 20, Sept. 3, 10, Oct. 1, 15, 22, Nov. 12, 1878, Nov. 4, 1879; *Janesville Gazette,* Oct. 29, 30, 31, Nov. 1, 2, 5, 1879; Smith to Hayes, Aug. 20, 1878, Hayes Papers; Logan, *Reminiscences,* 388–89; McFeely, *Grant,* 451–52, 459, 466, 475–76, 478–79, 487. For a discussion of the protracted agitation against "Demon Rum," see Clifford S. Griffin, *Their Brothers' Keepers: Moral Stewardship in the United States, 1800–1865,* 3–321, particularly 100–103, 146–51, 222–33. See also Frank L. Byrne, *Prophet of Prohibition: Neal Dow and His Crusade;* Joseph C. Furnas, *The Life and Times of the Late Demon Rum,* 270–72; and Mary Earhart, *Frances Willard: From Prayers to Politics.*

51. Logan to Washburne, Apr. 4, 1880, Washburne Papers. See also Herbert J. Clancy, *The Presidential Election of 1880,* 31–36, 47–51, 83, 97; Gaillard Hunt, comp., *Israel, Elihu, and Cadwallader Washburn: A Chapter in American Biography,* 274; and Hesseltine, *Grant,* 431–36.

52. Spalding to Logan, Apr. 6, 1880, Logan Papers.

53. *Illinois State Journal,* May 19, 20, 1880; *Illinois State Register,* May 19, 21, 1880; *Belvidere Standard,* Jan. 6, Apr., 27, 1880; Church, *Republican Party,* 135–39; Marsh, *Recollections,* 225–27; Moses, *Illinois: Historical and Statistical,* 2: 862–63; Hubbell and Geary, *Northern Leaders,* 428. Actually, the unit rule had been used in Springfield in the five previous presidential elections (1860, 1864, 1868, 1872, and in 1876). However, Raum had contravened tradition and precedent by appointing a committee to select the Grant delegates instead of using a party caucus to choose them; Clancy, *Election of 1880,* 93.

54. Green B. Raum, *History of Illinois Republicanism Embracing a History of the Republican Party in the State to the Present Time,* 159. Although he criticized Hurlbut's convention ploy, Raum wrote that Hurlbut "was a man of marked ability, well known throughout the State, an experienced parliamentarian; his splendid military career and his eloquence as a public speaker gave him great influence. He, however, was quick of

temper, keenly sarcastic of his opponents, and wanting in that spirit of conciliation and compromise so essential to the success of political deliberations"; ibid. See also Church, *Republican Party,* 139; Lusk, *Politics and Politicians,* 362–71, 401–402, 425–26; Jones, *Stalwart Republican,* 127–40; and *Illinois State Journal,* May 22, 1880.

55. *Illinois State Journal,* May 22, 1880; *Illinois State Register,* May 22, 1880. See also Malone, *DAB,* 6: 363–65.

56. Hurlbut to Garfield, June 8, 9, 27, July 8, 1880, Garfield Papers; Logan to Hayes, Aug. 24, 1880, Hayes Papers; *Belvidere Standard,* June 29, July 6, Aug. 31, Oct. 12, 1880; Church, *Republican Party,* 140–41; Hesseltine, *Grant,* 437–39; Peskin, *Garfield,* 452–81; Glenn Tucker, *Hancock the Superb,* 268–72, 300–305. For Logan's support of Grant's third-term candidacy in Illinois, see Clancy, *Election of 1880,* 82–84, 93, 98. See also Leonard Dinnerstein, "Election of 1880," *History of American Presidential Elections,* 2: *1848–1896,* 1493–96, 1502–505.

57. Hurlbut to Garfield, Dec. 20, 1880, Jan. 11, 28, Feb. 24, 25, 1881; Garfield Papers. Hurlbut to Kiler K. Jones, Jan. 9, Feb. 8, 14, 1881, Hurlbut Folder, Chicago Historical Society, Chicago; *Belvidere Standard,* Jan. 11, Mar. 29, 1881; Peskin, *Garfield,* 320–22, 396–97, 506–10, 518–20; Dinnerstein, "Election of 1880," 1513–14; Richardson, *Messages and Papers,* 6: 4601.

58. Herbert Millington, *American Diplomacy and the War of the Pacific,* 9–81; William J. Dennis, *Tacna and Arica: An Account of the Chile-Peru Boundary Dispute and of the Arbitrations by the United States,* 26–141; Kenneth W. Crosby, "The Diplomacy of the United States in Relation to the War of the Pacific, 1879–1884," 1–139; William F. Beck, "A Comparison of British and United States Relations with Chile, 1879–1883: A Study in Diplomatic History," 6–26; Henry C. Evans, *Chile and Its Relations with the United States,* 100–107. For a Chilean account of the antecedents of the War of the Pacific, see Victor M. Maurtua, *The Question of the Pacific,* 19–91. See also Frederick B. Pike, *Chile and the United States, 1880–1962,* 54–55; and Campbell, *American Relations,* 93–94.

59. Alice F. Tyler, *The Foreign Policy of James G. Blaine,* 107–29, 165–74; Muzzey, *Blaine,* 246–48.

60. Samuel J. Martin, *"Kill-Cavalry," Sherman's Merchant of Terror: The Life of Union General Hugh Judson Kilpatrick,* 15–249. For further background on Kilpatrick, see G. Wayne King, "The Civil War Career of Hugh Judson Kilpatrick"; John L. S. Daley, "A General's Education: The Combat Leadership of Hugh Judson Kilpatrick"; Edward G. Longacre, "Judson Kilpatrick," 24–33; Hubbell and Geary, *Northern Leaders,* 286–87; Malone and Johnson, *DAB,* 10: 374–75; and *National Tribune,* Oct. 27, Nov. 3, 1887. For elaboration on Blaine's motivation in urging the Hurlbut and Kilpatrick appointments, see Crosby, "War of the Pacific," 139–40; Beck, "United States Relations with Chile," 37–40; Evans, *Chile,* 107; and *New York Times,* May 20, 1881. The *Chicago Tribune* asserted that Hurlbut had received Senate approval of his commission only with the acquiescence of Logan; "Hurlbut was poor, and needed the position and he would leave his case with the Senate without opposing him." *Chicago Tribune,* Feb. 3, 1882. See also *National Tribune,* Apr. 29, 1882.

61. Blaine to Hurlbut, June 15, 1881, in "Diplomatic Instructions of the Department of State, 1801–1906, Peru, July 7, 1863–June 23, 1883," roll 131, RG 59, NA; U.S. State

Department, *Foreign Relations, 1881,* 914–15, 920–21; Millington, *American Diplomacy,* 83–87; Dennis, *Tacna and Arica,* 143–47; Evans, *Chile,* 105–107, 110–11; Pike, *Chile and the United States,* 49–50; Crosby, "War of the Pacific," 140; Muzzey, *James G. Blaine,* 242–45; William Henry Hurlbert, *Meddling and Muddling: Mr. Blaine's Foreign Policy; Being a Review of His Nine Months' Tenure of the State Department; In a Letter to the Editor of the* New York Herald, 55–56.

62. Harriet S. Blaine Beale, *Letters of Mrs. James G. Blaine,* 1: 202–203, from a letter of George H. Hurlbut to the editor, *Belvidere Standard,* Sept. 6, 1881; *New York Times,* Aug. 28, 1881; *Cochabamba (Bolivia) el Heraldo,* Sept. 14, 1881; Dennis, *Tacna and Arica,* 147; Peskin, *Garfield,* 582–604; Alberto Tauro, "Francisco G. Calderon," *Diccionario o Enciclopedico del Peru,* 2: *G–P,* 19; Kilpatrick to John Sherman, Dec. 1, 1881, John Sherman Papers, 1846–1894, Manuscript Division, Library of Congress, Washington, D.C.; Blaine to Kilpatrick, June 15, 1881, in "Diplomatic Instructions of the Department of State," roll 131, RG 59, NA; U.S. State Department, *Foreign Relations Series, 1880–1881, Message from the President of the United States Transmitting Papers Relating to the War in South America, and Attempts to Bring About a Peace,* 157–59; Pike, *Chile and the United States,* 50–51; Evans, *Chile,* 107; Muzzey, *Blaine,* 213.

63. Hurlbut to Blaine, Aug. 10, 1881, in "Despatches from U.S. Ministers to Peru, 1826–1906, Apr. 16–Sept. 27, 1881," roll 36, RG 59, NA. See also U.S. State Department, *Foreign Relations, 1881,* 921–24, 925–26; and Tauro, "Nicholas de Pierola," *Diccionario o Enciclopedico,* 2: *G–P,* 540–42.

64. Hurlbut to Lynch, Aug. 25, 1881, Hurlbut to Blaine, Aug. 27, Sept. 13, 21, 1881, in "Despatches from U.S. Ministers to Peru," roll 36, RG 59, NA; U.S. State Department, *Foreign Relations, 1881,* 926–38; D. Patricio Lynch, *Memoira Que el Contra-Almirante D. Patricio Lynch, Jeneral en Jefe del Ejercito de Operaciones en el Norte del Peru presenta al Supremo Gobierno de Chile,* 11–92, 95–122, and a file of documents, LIII–LX; Juan A. Rodriguez, *Patricio Lynch: vicealmirante y general en jefe, Sintesis de la Guerra del Pacifico,* 1–191; Dennis, *Tacna and Arica,* 148–60; Maurtua, *Question of the Pacific,* 91–137; Millington, *American Diplomacy,* 88–89; Pike, *Chile and the United States,* 50–51; Evans, *Chile,* 109; *Cochabamba el Heraldo,* Oct. 14, 17, Dec. 20, 23, 1881; Hurlbut to Pierola, Sept. 4, 28, 1881, Pierola to Hurlbut, Sept. 16, 1881, "Despatches from U.S. Ministers to Peru," roll 36, RG 59, NA; Hurlbut to Blaine, Oct. 4, 1881, in "Despatches from U.S. Ministers to Peru, 1826–1906, Oct. 4, 1881–Aug. 30, 1882," roll 37, RG 59, NA.

65. Martinez to Blaine, Sept. 12, 1881, including Peruvian and Chilean newspaper clippings, in "Notes from Chilean Legation in U.S. to Dept. of State, 1831–1906, June 1, 1881–Dec. 31, 1886," roll 3, RG 59, NA.

66. *Cochabamba el Heraldo,* Dec. 28, 1881; *New York Tribune,* Oct. 21, 1881; *New York Times,* Oct. 24, 1881. Later, the *Times* declared that "diplomats who represent their country abroad cannot denude themselves of their official character and write letters of advice and reprimand to dignitaries. Minister Hurlbut's essay is likely to produce a great deal of mischief"; *New York Times,* Nov. 3, 1881. See also *The Nation: A Weekly Journal Devoted to Politics, Literature, Science, & Art* 33 (Oct. 27, 1881): 325.

67. Hurlbut to Kilpatrick, Aug. 5, 1881, Hurlbut to Blaine, Aug. 10, 27, Sept. 21, 1881, in "Despatches from U.S. Ministers to Peru," roll 36, RG 59, NA; Hurlbut to Blaine,

Oct. 4, 13, 26, 31, Nov. 9, 1881, in "Despatches from U.S. Ministers to Peru," roll 37, RG
59, NA; U.S. State Department, *Foreign Relations, 1881,* 923–24, 929–33, 935, 941–43,
946, 948; Kilpatrick to Sherman, Dec. 1, 1881, Sherman Papers; U.S. State Department,
Foreign Relations Series, 1880–1881, Message from the President, 160–64, 166–71. In a dispatch to Hurlbut on Sept. 30, 1881, Kilpatrick informed him: "I am very ill, and have
been for two months, I should not like to die here, and yet I may"; U.S. State Department, *Foreign Relations, 1881,* 942.

68. *New York Times,* Nov. 18, 27, Dec. 4, 1881, Jan. 7, 27, 28, Mar. 13, 1882; *New York
Tribune,* Nov. 18, 24, 28, Dec. 12, 1881. See also *The Nation* 33 (Nov. 24, 1881): 405. Also
Cochabamba el Heraldo, Nov. 4, 9, 20, 23, 26, 29, Dec. 6, 1881, Feb. 23, Mar. 5, 9, 1882.

69. Muzzey, *Blaine,* 211–14; Evans, *Chile,* 11–13, 115; Pike, *Chile and the United States,*
56–57; Campbell, *American Relations,* 96–100; Dennis, *Tacna and Arica,* 171; Martin,
Kilpatrick, 258–63; Peskin, *Garfield,* 605–607; "drunk" remark in dispatch of Martinez
to Chilean Ministry of Foreign Relations, Nov. 18, 1881, in "Legacion de Chile en los
EE. UU. de N. America, 1881," II, Archivos, Ministerio de la Relaciones Exteriores,
Lima, Peru, qtd. in Pike, *Chile and the United States,* 56 (the original document is in
Lima); Blaine to Hurlbut, Nov. 22, 1881, in "Diplomatic Instructions of the Depart-
ment of State," roll 131, RG 59, NA; U.S. State Department, *Foreign Relations, 1881,*
948–51, 955–57; *Cochabamba el Heraldo,* Mar. 5, 9, 1882; Millington, *American Diplo-
macy,* 91, 93–95; Samuel Ward to Blaine, Nov. 28(?), 1881, Blaine Papers; James G. Blaine,
Foreign Policy of the Garfield Administration: Peace Congress of the Two Americas, 1–8;
Walker Blaine to Mrs. James G. Blaine, Jan. 20, 1882, qtd. in Mary A. Dodge, *Biography
of James G. Blaine,* 553; Trescot to Frelinghuysen, Jan. 27, Feb. 3, 1882, in William Henry
Trescot Papers, 1822–1898, Manuscript Division, South Caroliniana Library, Univ. of
South Carolina, Columbia. See also Russell H. Bastert, "Diplomatic Reversal:
Frelinghuysen's Opposition to Blaine's Pan-American Policy in 1882," 654; and *National
Tribune,* Dec. 10, 1881.

70. Hurlbut to William Henry Hurlbert, Feb. 8, 22, Mar. 15, 1882, qtd. in *New York
World,* Apr. 3, 4, 1882; Justus D. Doenecke, *The Presidencies of James A. Garfield and
Chester A. Arthur,* 58–62, 127–32. See also Smith, *Anglo-American Diplomacy,* 35, 63, 67–
72; Millington, *American Diplomacy,* 123, 127, 128, 134, 135; Campbell, *American Relations,* 97–99; and Rodriguez, *Patricio Lynch,* 191–95.

71. Hurlbut to Logan, Dec. 21, 1881, Frelinghuysen to Logan, Jan. 21, 1882, Logan
Papers; J. M. Moore to William Hunter, Mar. 29, 1882. See also Moore to Hunter, Jan.
18, 23, Apr. 5, 17, May 27, June 7, 28, 1882, and Hurlbut to Fredrick B. Leiding, Jan. 16,
1882, in "Despatches From United States Consuls in Callao, 1854–1906," 10: January 6,
1879–June 28, 1882, M155, roll 10, RG 59, NA; Edward H. Talbott to Hurlbert, Apr. 1(?),
1882, qtd. in *New York World,* Apr. 4, 1882; George H. Hurlbut to Hurlbert, Apr. 5(?),
1882, qtd. in *New York World,* Apr. 22, 1882; *National Tribune,* Apr. 8, 29, 1882. For
Peruvian opinions of Hurlbut in the *Tribune,* see Jan. 21, 1882, May 27, Oct. 15, 1885.
See also Dennis, *Tacna and Arica,* 171–73; and Bastert, "Frelinghuysen," 653–54.

72. Fish to Davis, Apr. 3, 1882, Fish Papers. Fish suspected, however, that "Old
Mulligan Letters" Blaine would expurgate his official correspondence to avoid implicating himself in financial speculation in Peru and would resort to "mulliganizing" Trescot's

dispatches; ibid. For the full text of the House report on Blaine's foreign policy during the War of the Pacific, besides Hurlbut's ministerial actions, see U.S. Congress, House, "Chile-Peru Investigation," HR Rept. 1790, 47th Cong., 1st sess., vol. 6: I–XXVII, and 1–388, 1100–1106. See also Hurlbut to (Chairman of House Committee on Foreign Affairs) Charles G. Williams, Feb. 27, 1882, qtd. in *New York Times,* Apr. 1, 1882. See also Feb. 26, Mar. 17, 22, Apr. 6, 11, 14, 25, June 14, July 24, Aug. 2, 1882; and *New York Tribune,* June 14, Aug. 2, 1882.

73. Walker Blaine to Mrs. James G. Blaine, Apr. 9, 1882, qtd. in Dodge, *James G. Blaine,* 562. See also a letter of sympathy from the Peruvian legation to Chester A. Arthur, May 19, 1882, in "Notes from the Peruvian Legation in the U. S. to the Dept. of State, 1827–1906, May 24, 1880–April 12, 1897," roll 5, RG 59, NA.

74. *Belvidere Standard,* Apr. 4, 25, 30, May 2, 1882; *New York World,* Apr. 18, 1882; *National Tribune,* May 6, 1882. Appraisement bills, June 3, Sept. 22, 1882, Jan. 20, 1885, in "Circuit Clerk Probate Record, Letters of Estate, Stephen Augustus Hurlbut," 1882, 1885, BCCH. See also Talbott to Hurlbert, Apr. 1(?), 1882, qtd. in *New York World,* Apr. 4, 1882; U.S. Congress, House, *The Congressional Record, Containing the Debates and Proceedings of the First Session Forty-seventh Congress,* pt. 1, 13: 532, 4359, 5429, 6528, 6530, 6544, 6573; Hurlbut to Lauman, Oct. 25, 1918, Winfield Scott Folder; Sager, "Hurlbut," 79–80.

75. Dennis, *Tacna and Arica,* 174–94; Maurtua, *Question of the Pacific,* 137–63; U.S. Congress, House, "Chile-Peru Investigation," vol. 6: I–XXVII, and 1–388, 1100–1106. Hurlbut explained his intervention in Peruvian affairs in letters to the House Committee chairman and to William Henry Hurlbert, his brother and the editor of the *New York World.* Later, in a private letter to a friend, Hurlbut insisted, "My conversations with President Garfield and Mr. Blaine can not appear, but they were the real motive of my course"; Perry Belmont, *An American Democrat: The Recollections of Perry Belmont,* 232–33. See also 214–77 and passim. See also *National Tribune,* Mar. 25, Apr. 29, 1882.

BIBLIOGRAPHY

MANUSCRIPT COLLECTIONS

Appleton, Jesse. Papers. Bowdoin College Library. Brunswick, Maine.

Bailhache, William. Brayman, Mason. Papers. Illinois State Historical Library. Springfield, Illinois.

Blaine, James G. Papers. Library of Congress. Washington, D.C.

Bodman, Alfred H. Diary. Chicago Historical Society. Chicago, Illinois.

Browning, Orville H. Folder. Chicago Historical Society. Chicago, Illinois.

Davis, David. Papers. Chicago Historical Society. Chicago, Illinois.

Denison, George S. Papers. Library of Congress. Washington, D.C.

Doolittle, James R. Collection. State Historical Society of Wisconsin. Madison, Wisconsin.

Douglas, Stephen A. MSS. Univ. of Chicago Library. Chicago, Illinois.

Eastman, Zebina. Collection. Chicago Historical Society. Chicago, Illinois.

Fessenden, William P. Papers. Manuscripts Division. William L. Clements Library. Univ. of Michigan. Ann Arbor, Michigan.

Fish, Hamilton. Papers. Library of Congress. Washington, D.C.

Garfield, James A. Papers. Library of Congress. Washington, D.C.

Grant, Ulysses S. Papers. Library of Congress. Washington, D.C. Microfilm copy. Kent State Univ. Kent, Ohio.

Haskell, Clinton H. Collection. Manuscripts Division. William L. Clements Library. Univ. of Michigan. Ann Arbor, Michigan.

Hatch, Ozias M. Papers. Illinois State Historical Library. Springfield, Illinois.

Hayes, Rutherford B. Papers. Rutherford B. Hayes Presidential Library. Hayes Presidential Center. Fremont, Ohio.

Hurlbut/Hurlbert Family. Folder. South Carolina Historical Society. Charleston, South Carolina.

Hurlbut, Martin Luther, to Jedidiah Morse. March 11, 1812. South Caroliniana Library. Univ. of South Carolina. Columbia, South Carolina.

Hurlbut, Stephen A., to Ralph P. Buckland. June 23, 1881. Ohio Historical Center. Columbus, Ohio.

Hurlbut, Stephen A. Collection. Illinois State Historical Library. Springfield, Illinois.

———. Folder. Chicago Historical Society. Chicago, Illinois.

———. Folder. Stephenson County Historical Society Museum. Freeport, Illinois.

———. MS. "To the Voters of the Fourth Congressional District of Illinois." Chicago Historical Society. Chicago, Illinois.

Johnson, Andrew. Papers. Library of Congress. Washington, D.C. Microfilm copy. Kent
    State Univ. Kent, Ohio.
Johnston, William P. Papers. Mrs. Mason Barrett Collection. Howard-Tilton Memorial
    Library. Tulane Univ. New Orleans, Louisiana.
Lincoln, Abraham. Papers. Robert Todd Lincoln Collection. Library of Congress. Wash-
    ington, D.C. Microfilm copy. Kent State Univ. Kent, Ohio.
Logan, John A. Papers. Library of Congress. Washington, D.C.
Morrison, William R. Papers. Illinois State Historical Library. Springfield, Illinois.
Oglesby, Richard J. Papers. Illinois State Historical Library. Springfield, Illinois.
Palmer, John M. Papers. Illinois State Historical Library. Springfield, Illinois.
Petigru, James Louis. Letters. Library of Congress. Washington, D.C.
Pettigrew, J. Johnston. Papers. Department of Cultural Resources. Division of Archives
    and History. Raleigh, North Carolina.
Pugh, Isaac C. Letters. 41st Illinois File. Shiloh National Military Park. Shiloh, Tennessee.
Schoff Civil War Collection. Letters and Documents. Manuscripts Division. William
    L. Clements Library. Univ. of Michigan. Ann Arbor, Michigan.
Scott, Winfield. Folder. Chicago Historical Society. Chicago, Illinois.
Sherman, John. Papers. Library of Congress. Washington, D.C.
Sherman, William T. Papers. Library of Congress. Washington, D.C.
Smith, Caleb B. Papers. Library of Congress. Washington, D.C.
Trescot, William Henry. Papers. South Caroliniana Library. Univ. of South Carolina.
    Columbia, South Carolina.
Trumbull, Lyman. Papers. Library of Congress. Washington, D.C.
Veatch, James C. Papers. William Henry Smith Library. Indiana Historical Society.
    Indianapolis, Indiana.
Washburne, Elihu B. Papers. Library of Congress. Washington, D.C.
Webster, Daniel. Papers. Library of Congress. Washington, D.C.
Yates, Richard. Papers. Illinois State Historical Library. Springfield, Illinois.

ARCHIVAL RECORDS

Illinois. Boone County. "Circuit Clerk Probate Record, Letters of Estate, Stephen
    Augustus Hurlbut." 1882, 1885. Boone County Courthouse. Belvidere, Illinois.
————. Boone County. "Circuit Court and Mortgage Records." 1843–79. Boone County
    Courthouse. Belvidere, Illinois.
————. Boone County. "Warranty Deeds, Boone County." 1864–82. Boone County
    Courthouse. Belvidere, Illinois.
South Carolina. Charleston District. "Minutes of the Journals of the Board of Trustees,
    1791–1870." College of Charleston Library. Charleston, South Carolina.
————. Charleston District. "Typed Newspaper Articles on the College of Charleston
    and on Education in South Carolina Generally, 1798–1841." College of Charleston
    Library. Charleston, South Carolina.
————. Charleston District. "Mortgage, Bills of Sale, Court of Equity, and Miscella-
    neous Records, 1818–45." South Carolina Department of Archives and History. Co-
    lumbia, South Carolina.

U.S. Department of the Interior. Bureau of the Census. "Fifth Census of the United States. South Carolina, 1830." Population Schedules. Ward I. Volume 2. Microfilm copy. South Carolina Department of Archives and History. Columbia, South Carolina.

U.S. Department of Justice. "Attorney Rolls of the Supreme Court of the United States, 1790–1951." Microfilm copy. Roll 3: "H" series. Record Group [hereafter RG] 267. National Archives [hereafter NA]. Washington, D.C.

———. "Dockets of the Supreme Court of the United States, 1791–1950." Microfilm copy. Roll 22: "1875–1880." RG 267. NA. Washington, D.C.

U.S. State Department. "Despatches from United States Consuls in Callao, 1854–1906." Vol. 10: "January 6, 1879–June 28, 1882." Microfilm copy. Roll 10. RG 59. NA. Washington, D.C.

———. "Despatches from U.S. Ministers to Colombia, 1820–1906, April 30, 1868–August 9, 1869." Microfilm copy. Roll 27. RG 59. NA. Washington, D.C.

———. "Despatches from U.S. Ministers to Colombia, 1820–1906, Aug. 11, 1869–Aug. 17, 1873." Microfilm copy. Roll 28. RG 59. NA. Washington, D.C.

———. "Despatches from U.S. Ministers to Peru, 1826–1906, Apr. 16–Sept. 27, 1881." Microfilm copy. Roll 36. RG 59. NA. Washington, D.C.

———. "Despatches from U.S. Ministers to Peru, 1826–1906, Oct. 4, 1881–Aug. 30, 1882." Microfilm copy. Roll 37. RG 59. NA. Washington, D.C.

———. "Diplomatic Instructions of the Department of State, 1801–1906, Colombia, May 29, 1861–June 18, 1875." Microfilm copy. Roll 45. RG 59. NA. Washington, D.C.

———. "Diplomatic Instructions of the Department of State, 1801–1906, Peru, July 7, 1863–June 23, 1883." Microfilm copy. Roll 131. RG 59. NA. Washington, D.C.

———. "Notes from Chilean Legation in U.S. to Dept. of State, 1831–1906, June 1, 1881–Dec. 31, 1886." Microfilm copy. Roll 3. RG 59. NA. Washington, D.C.

———. "Notes from the Peruvian Legation in the U.S. to the Dept. of State, 1827–1906, May 24, 1880–April 12, 1897." Microfilm copy. Roll 5. RG 59. NA. Washington, D.C.

U.S. War Department. Adjutant General's Office. "Department of the Gulf, Letters Received, Bureau of Civil Affairs, 1864–1865." Vols. A–O. RG 393. NA. Washington, D.C.

———. Adjutant General's Office. "Generals' Papers and Books, John Pope File, 1861–1865." RG 94. NA. Washington, D.C.

———. Adjutant General's Office. "Generals' Papers and Books, Stephen A. Hurlbut, 1861–1865." File 159. RG 94. NA. Washington, D.C.

———. Adjutant General's Office. "Letters Received by General Henry W. Halleck." Records of the Headquarters of the Army. RG 108. NA. Washington, D.C.

———. Adjutant General's Office. "Report of the Special Commission, September 23, 1865, Maj. Genl Wm. F. Smith, Jas. T. Brady, Esq., Lt. Col. Nicholas Bowen AAG, Judge Advocate." Entry no. 737. RG 94. NA. Washington, D.C.

———. "Letters Received by the Confederate Secretary of War, 1861–1865." NA Microfilm Publication. M437, roll 141: March to September 1864. U.S. War Department Collection of Confederate Records. RG 109. NA. Washington, D.C.

———. "Union Provost Marshal's File of Papers Relating to Individual Citizens." NA Microfilm Publication. M345, roll 116: Halla–Hemo, roll 129: Him–Hiz, and roll 242: Sew–Sha. U.S. War Department Collection of Confederate Records. RG 109. NA. Washington, D.C.

GOVERNMENT DOCUMENTS

Illinois. House. *Journal of the House of Representatives of the Twenty-first General Assembly of the State of Illinois, at Their Regular Session, Begun and Held at Springfield, January 3, 1859.* Springfield: Bailhache and Baker, 1859.

———. *Journal of the House of Representatives of the Twenty-second General Assembly of the State of Illinois, at Their Regular Session, Begun and Held at Springfield, January 7, 1861.* Springfield: Bailhache and Baker, 1861.

———. *Journal of the House of Representatives of the Twenty-fifth General Assembly of the State of Illinois, at Their Regular Session, Begun and Held at Springfield, January 7, 1867.* Springfield: Baker, Bailhache., 1867.

U.S. Congress. *Congressional Globe, Containing the Debates and Proceedings of the Second Session Fortieth Congress.* Washington, D.C.: F. and J. Rives and George A. Bailey, 1868.

———. *Congressional Record, Containing the Debates and Proceedings of the First Session Forty-third Congress.* Washington, D.C.: F. and J. Rives and George A. Bailey, 1874.

———. *Congressional Record, Containing the Debates and Proceedings of the Second Session Forty-third Congress.* Washington, D.C.: F. and J. Rives and George A. Bailey, 1874.

———. *Congressional Record, Containing the Debates and Proceedings of the First Session Forty-fourth Congress.* Washington, D.C.: F. and J. Rives and George A. Bailey, 1874.

———. *Congressional Record, Containing the Debates and Proceedings of the First Session Forty-seventh Congress.* Washington, D.C.: F. and J. Rives and George A. Bailey, 1882.

———. House. "Chile-Peru Investigation." HR Rept. no. 1790. 47th Congress. 1st Session. Vol. 6. 1882.

———. House. "Testimony Taken by the Committee on Reform in the Civil Service in Relation to the Chicago Pension-Agency." HR Misc. Rept. no. 182. 44th Congress. 1st Session. 1876.

———. "Vicksburg Troubles." HR Rept. no. 265. 43d Congress. 2d Session. 1874.

U.S. Congress. Senate. Executive Documents. 46th Congress. 2d Session. 1879–80. Vol. 4. no. 112.

———. *Journal of the Executive Proceedings of the Senate of the United States of America, from December 6, 1858, to August 6, 1861, Inclusive.* Vol. 11. Washington, D.C.: U.S. Government Printing Office [hereafter GPO], 1887.

———. *Journal of the Executive Proceedings of the Senate of the United States of America, from December 1, 1862, to July 4, 1864, Inclusive.* Vol. 13. Washington, D.C.: GPO, 1887.

U.S. State Department. *Diplomatic Correspondence and Foreign Relations of the United States, 1861–1899.* 56 vols. and index. Washington, D.C.: GPO, 1861–1902. Reprint, New York: Kraus, 1965–1966.

———. *Foreign Relations Series, 1880–1881, Message from the President of the United States Transmitting Papers Relating to the War in South America, and Attempts to Bring About a Peace.* Washington, D.C.: GPO, 1882. Reprint, New York: Kraus, 1966.

U.S. War Department. Adjutant General's Office. *The War of the Rebellion: A Compilation of the Official Records of the Union and Confederate Armies.* 128 vols. and index. Washington, D.C.: GPO, 1880–1901.

————. *Supplement to the Official Records of the Union and Confederate Armies*. Pt. 2: Record of Events. Vol. 23. Transcribed from "Compiled Records Showing Service of Military Units." Microfilm Publication no. M594. RG 94. NA. 68 vols. Washington, D.C. Reprint, Wilmington, N.C.: Broadfoot, 1994–98.

————. Office of the Surgeon General. *The Medical and Surgical History of the War of the Rebellion, (1861–1865)*. 12 vols. and index in 3 vols. Washington, D.C.: GPO, 1870–83. Reprint, Wilmington, N.C.: Broadfoot, 1990–91.

BOOKS, ARTICLES, AND DISSERTATIONS

Adams, Jasper. *A Historical Sketch of the College of Charleston, South Carolina*. Charleston, S.C.: J. P. Stratton, 1836.

Ambrose, Stephen E. *Halleck: Lincoln's Chief of Staff*. Baton Rouge: Louisiana State Univ. Press, 1962.

Ames, Blanche A. *Adelbert Ames, 1835–1933: General, Senator, Governor*. London: McDonald, 1914. Reprint, New York: Argosy-Antiquarian, 1964.

Anders, Leslie. "'Farthest North': The Historian and the Battle of Athens." *Missouri Historical Review* 69 (Jan. 1975): 147–68.

————. *The Twenty-first Missouri: From Home Guard to Union Regiment*. Westport, Conn.: Greenwood, 1975.

Anderson, Charles C. *Fighting by Southern Federals*. New York: Neale, 1912.

Aptheker, Herbert. *American Negro Slave Revolts*. New York: Columbia Univ. Press, 1943. Reprint, New York: International, 1970.

Ash, Stephen V. "Civil War Exodus: The Jews and Grant's General Orders No. 11." *Historian* 44 (Aug. 1982): 505–23.

————. *When the Yankees Came: Conflict and Chaos in the Occupied South, 1861–1865*. Chapel Hill: Univ. of North Carolina Press, 1995.

Bailey, Thomas A. *A Diplomatic History of the American People*. New York: Meredith, 1964.

Baker, Nina B. *Cyclone in Calico: The Story of Mary Ann Bickerdyke*. Boston: Little, Brown, 1952.

Barber, Lucius W. *Army Memoirs of Lucius W. Barber, Company "D," 15th Illinois Volunteer Infantry, May 24, 1861, to Sept. 30, 1865*. Chicago: J. M. W. Jones, 1894. Reprint, n.p. [Alexandria, Va.]: Time-Life Books, 1984.

Basler, Roy P., ed. *Abraham Lincoln: His Speeches and Writings*. Preface by Carl Sandburg. Cleveland: World, 1946. Reprint, New York: Da Capo, 1990.

————. *The Collected Works of Abraham Lincoln*. 8 vols. and index. New Brunswick, N.J.: Rutgers Univ. Press, 1953–55.

Bastert, Russell H. "Diplomatic Reversal: Frelinghuysen's Opposition to Blaine's Pan-American Policy in 1882." *Mississippi Valley Historical Review* 42 (Mar. 1956): 653–71.

Baxter, Maurice G. *Henry Clay and the American System*. Lexington: Univ. Press of Kentucky, 1995.

————. *Orville H. Browning: Lincoln's Friend and Critic*. Bloomington: Indiana Univ. Press, 1957.

Beale, Harriet S. Blaine, ed. *Letters of Mrs. James G. Blaine.* Vol. 1. New York: Duffield, 1908.

Beardsley, Harry M. *Joseph Smith and His Mormon Empire.* Boston: Houghton and Mifflin, 1931.

Bearss, Edwin C. *The Campaign for Vicksburg.* Vol. 1: *Vicksburg Is the Key.* 3 vols. Dayton, Ohio: Morningside, 1985, 1986.

————. "The Great Railroad Raid." *Annals of Iowa* 40 (Fall and Winter 1969–70): 147–60, 222–39.

Beath, Robert B. *History of the Grand Army of the Republic.* Introduction by Lucius C. Fairchild. New York: Bryan, Taylor, 1888.

Beck, William F. "A Comparison of British and United States Relations with Chile, 1879–1883: A Study in Diplomatic History." Ph.D. diss., Univ. of Pittsburgh, 1942.

Bell, Michael E. "Regional Identity in the Antebellum South: How German Immigrants Became 'Good' Charlestonians." *South Carolina Historical Magazine* (Jan. 1999): 9–28.

Bellows, Barbara L. Benevolence among Slaveholders: Assisting the Poor in Charleston, 1670–1860. Baton Rouge: Louisiana State Univ. Press, 1993.

Belmont, Perry. *An American Democrat: The Recollections of Perry Belmont.* 2d ed. New York: Columbia Univ. Press, 1940, 1941.

Belvidere Illustrated: Historical, Descriptive and Biographical. Belvidere: Daily Republican, 1896.

Berlin, Ira, et al., eds. *Free at Last: A Documentary History of Slavery, Freedom, and the Civil War.* New York: New Press, 1992.

————. *Freedom: A Documentary History of Emancipation, 1861–1867. Ser. 1.* Vol. 3: *The Wartime Genesis of Free Labor: The Lower South.* 4 vols. Cambridge, U.K.: Cambridge Univ. Press, 1990.

Bigelow, John. *The Life of Samuel J. Tilden.* 2 vols. New York: Harper and Brothers, 1895.

Billings, John D. *Hardtack and Coffee, Or the Unwritten Story of Army Life.* Illustrated by Charles W. Reed. Boston: George M. Smith, 1887. Reprint, n.p. [Alexandria, Va.]: Time-Life Books, 1982.

Billington, Ray A. *The Protestant Crusade, 1800–1860: A Study of the Origins of American Nativism.* New York: Macmillan, 1938. Reprint, New York: Rinehart, 1952.

Blaine, James G. *Foreign Policy of the Garfield Administration: Peace Congress of the Two Americas.* Chicago: Chicago Weekly Magazine, Sept. 16, 1882. Reprint, Chicago: n.p., 1882.

————. *Twenty Years of Congress: From Lincoln to Garfield, with a Review of the Events Which Led to the Political Revolution of 1860.* Vol. 2. Norwich, Conn.: Henry Bill, 1884–86.

Blassingame, John W. *Black New Orleans: 1860–1880.* Chicago: Univ. of Chicago Press, 1973.

Boatner, Mark M., III. *The Civil War Dictionary.* New York: David McKay, 1959.

Bogart, Ernest L., and Charles M. Thompson. *Illinois: The Industrial State, 1870–1893.* Springfield: Illinois Centennial Commission, 1920.

Boyd, Julian P., and Robert J. Taylor, eds. *The Susquehanna Company Papers.* 11 vols. Wilkes-Barre, Pa.: Wyoming Historical and Geological Society, 1930. Reprint, Ithaca, N.Y.: Cornell Univ. Press, 1962–71.

Brady, Patricia. "Trials and Tribulations: American Missionary Association Teachers and Black Education in Occupied New Orleans, 1863–1864." *Louisiana History* 31 (Winter 1990): 5–20.

Brockett, Linus P., and Mary C. Vaughan. *Woman's Work in the Civil War: A Record of Heroism, Patriotism and Patience.* Introduction by Henry W. Bellows. Philadelphia: Zeigler, McCurdy, 1867.

Brooks, Arthur A. *The History of Unitarianism in the Southern Churches, Charleston, New Orleans, Louisville, Richmond.* Boston: American Unitarian Association, 1906.

Brooks, Stewart. *Civil War Medicine.* Springfield, Ill.: Charles C. Thomas, 1966.

Broome, John P. "How Gen. A. S. Johnston Died." *Confederate Veteran* 16 (Dec. 1908): 629.

Brown, Harry J., and Frederick D. Williams, eds. *The Diary of James A. Garfield.* Vol. 3. East Lansing: Michigan State Univ. Press, 1967–81.

Brownlee, Richard S. *Gray Ghosts of the Confederacy: Guerrilla Warfare in the West, 1861–1865.* Baton Rouge: Louisiana State Univ. Press, 1958.

Buell, Don Carlos. "Shiloh Reviewed." In *Battles and Leaders of the Civil War, Being for the Most Part Contributions By Union and Confederate Officers, Based upon "The Century War Series."* Vol. 1. Ed. Robert U. Johnson and Clarence C. Buel. New York: Century, 1884–88, 487–536. Reprint, with an introduction by Roy F. Nichols. 4 vols. New York: Thomas Yoseloff, 1956.

Burlingame, Michael, ed. *Lincoln Observed: Civil War Dispatches of Noah Brooks.* Baltimore: Johns Hopkins Univ. Press, 1998.

Burlingame, Michael, and John R. Turner Ettlinger, eds. *Inside Lincoln's White House: The Complete Civil War Diary of John Hay.* Carbondale: Southern Illinois Univ. Press, 1997.

Butchart, Ronald E. *Northern Schools, Southern Blacks, and Reconstruction: Freedmen's Education, 1862–1875.* Westport, Conn.: Greenwood, 1980.

Butler, Benjamin F. *Butler's Book: Autobiography and Personal Reminiscences of Major-General Benjamin F. Butler.* Boston: A. M. Thayer, 1892.

Byrne, Frank L. *Prophet of Prohibition: Neal Dow and His Crusade.* Madison: State Historical Society of Wisconsin, 1961.

Campbell, Charles S. *The Transformation of American Relations, 1865–1900.* New York: Harper and Row, 1976.

Capers, Gerald M. *John C. Calhoun, Opportunist: A Reappraisal.* Gainesville: Univ. of Florida Press, 1960.

———. *Occupied City: New Orleans under the Federals, 1862–1865.* Lexington: Univ. of Kentucky Press, 1965.

———. *Stephen A. Douglas: Defender of the Union.* Ed. Oscar Handlin. Boston: Little, Brown, 1959.

———. The *Biography of a River Town, Memphis: Its Heroic Age.* Chapel Hill: Univ. of North Carolina Press, 1939.

Carpenter, Richard V., ed. *Historical Encyclopedia of Illinois and History of Boone County.* Vol. 2. Chicago: Munsell, 1909.

Carson, James P. *Life, Letters and Speeches of James Louis Petigru, the Union Man of South Carolina.* Introduction by Gaillard Hunt. Washington, D.C.: W. H. Lowdermilk, 1920.

Carter, Arthur B. *The Tarnished Cavalier: Major General Earl Van Dorn, C.S.A.* Knoxville: Univ. of Tennessee Press, 1999.

Cash, William M., and Lucy S. Howorth, eds. *My Dear Nellie: The Civil War Letters of William L. Nugent to Eleanor Smith Nugent.* Jackson: Univ. Press of Mississippi, 1977.

Castel, Albert. "Fort Sumter: 1861." *Civil War Times Illustrated* 15 (Oct. 1976): 4–50.

———. *General Sterling Price and the Civil War in the West.* Baton Rouge: Louisiana State Univ. Press, 1968.

Catalogue of an Exhibition of Portraits by John Neagle. Philadelphia: Pennsylvania Academy of Fine Arts, 1925.

Catton, Bruce. *Grant Moves South.* Boston: Little, Brown, 1960.

———. *Grant Takes Command.* Boston: Little, Brown, 1969.

Cherrington, Ernest H., ed. *Standard Encyclopedia of the Alcohol Problem.* Vol. 5. Westerville, Ohio: American Issue, 1925–30.

Chicago Pension-Agency. *Sworn Statement of Joseph Russell Jones, Chicago, Illinois, July 3, 1876.* Chicago: Evening Journal Book and Job Printing House, 1876.

Church, Charles A. *History of Rockford and Winnebago County Illinois from the First Settlement in 1834 to the Civil War.* Rockford, Ill.: W. P. Lamb, 1900.

———. *History of the Republican Party in Illinois, 1854–1912, with a Review of the Aggressions of the Slave Power.* Rockford, Ill.: Wilson Brothers, 1912.

Clancy, Herbert J. *The Presidential Election of 1880.* Chicago: Loyola Univ. Press, 1958.

Clayton, John, comp. *The Illinois Fact Book and Historical Almanac, 1673–1968.* Carbondale: Southern Illinois Univ. Press, 1970.

Cole, Arthur C., ed. *The Constitutional Debates of 1847.* Springfield: Illinois State Historical Library, 1919.

———. *The Whig Party in the South.* Philadelphia: 1912. Reprint, Gloucester, Mass.: Peter Smith, 1962.

Colvin, D. Leigh. *Prohibition in the United States: A History of the Prohibition Party and of the Prohibition Movement.* New York: George H. Doran, 1926.

Cooling, Benjamin F. *Fort Donelson's Legacy: War and Society in Kentucky and Tennessee, 1862–1863.* Knoxville: Univ. of Tennessee Press, 1997.

———. *Forts Henry and Donelson: The Key to the Confederate Heartland.* Knoxville: Univ. of Tennessee Press, 1987.

Cooper, William J. *The South and the Politics of Slavery, 1828–1856.* Baton Rouge: Louisiana State Univ. Press, 1978.

Cory, Earl W. "The Unitarians and the Universalists of the Southeastern United States during the Nineteenth Century." Ph.D. diss., Univ. of Georgia, 1970.

Cozzens, Peter. *General John Pope: A Life for the Nation.* Urbana: Univ. of Illinois Press, 2000.

———. *The Darkest Days of the War: The Battles of Iuka and Corinth.* Chapel Hill: Univ. of North Carolina Press, 1997.

Cozzens, Peter, and Robert I. Girardi, eds. *The Military Memoirs of General John Pope.* Foreword by John Y. Simon. Chapel Hill: Univ. of North Carolina Press, 1998.

Crooker, Lucien B., et al. *The Story of the Fifty-fifth Regiment Illinois Volunteer Infantry in the Civil War, 1861–1865.* Pt. 1: *From Chicago to Arkansas Post, October, 1861, to January 1863.* Clinton, Mass.: W. J. Coulter, 1887.

Crosby, Kenneth W. "The Diplomacy of the United States in Relation to the War of the Pacific, 1879–1884." Ph.D. diss., George Washington Univ., 1949.

Cullom, Shelby M. *Fifty Years of Public Service: Personal Recollections of Shelby M. Cullom, Senior United States Senator from Illinois.* Chicago: A. C. McClurg, 1911.

Cupples, Douglas W. "Memphis Confederates: The Civil War and Its Aftermath." Ph.D. diss., Univ. of Memphis, 1995.

Current, Richard N. *Lincoln and the First Shot.* Philadelphia: J. B. Lippincott, 1963.

Daley, John L. S. "A General's Education: The Combat Leadership of Hugh Judson Kilpatrick." M.A. thesis, Kent State Univ., 1985.

Dangerfield, Royden J. *In Defense of the Senate: A Study in Treaty Making.* Introduction by Quincy Wright. Norman: Univ. of Oklahoma Press, 1933.

Daniel, Larry J. *Shiloh: The Battle That Changed the Civil War.* New York: Simon and Schuster, 1997.

Daniels, Jonathan. *Prince of Carpetbaggers.* Philadelphia: J. B. Lippincott, 1958.

Dawson, George F. *Life and Services of Gen. John A. Logan as Soldier and Statesman.* Chicago: Belford, Clarke, 1887.

Dawson, Joseph G., III. *Army Generals and Reconstruction: Louisiana, 1862–1877.* Baton Rouge: Louisiana State Univ. Press, 1982.

Dearing, Mary R. *Veterans in Politics: The Story of the G.A.R.* Baton Rouge: Louisiana State Univ. Press, 1952.

Dell, Christopher. *Lincoln and the War Democrats: The Grand Erosion of Conservative Tradition.* Rutherford, N.J.: Associated Univ. Presses, 1975.

Dennis, William J. *Tacna and Arica: An Account of the Chile-Peru Boundary Dispute and of the Arbitrations by the United States.* New Haven, Conn.: Yale Univ. Press, 1931. Reprint, New York: Archon, 1931.

Dinkins, James. "The Capture of Memphis by Gen. Nathan B. Forrest." *Southern Historical Society Papers* 36 (1908): 180–96.

Dinnerstein, Leonard. "Election of 1880." In *History of American Presidential Elections, 1789–1984.* Ed. Arthur M. Schlesinger, Jr. 5 vols. New York: Chelsea House, 1971, 1986.

Dodge, Mary A. *Biography of James G. Blaine.* Norwich, Conn.: Henry Bill, 1895.

Doenecke, Justus D. *The Presidencies of James A. Garfield and Chester A. Arthur.* Lawrence: Regents Press of Kansas, 1981.

Donald, David H. *Lincoln.* New York: Simon and Schuster, 1995.

Dorsett, Lyle W. "The Problem of Ulysses S. Grant's Drinking during the Civil War." *Hayes Historical Journal* 4 (Fall 1983): 37–48.

Doutney, Thomas N. *Thomas N. Doutney: His Life-Struggle and Triumphs, Also a Vivid Pen-Picture of New York, Together with a History of the Work He Has Accomplished as a Temperance Reformer.* Battle Creek, Mich.: W. M. C. Gage, 1893.

Doyle, Elizabeth J. "Civilian Life in Occupied New Orleans, 1862–65." Ph.D. diss., Louisiana State Univ., 1955.

Doyle, Julie A., John D. Smith, and Richard M. McMurry, eds. *This Wilderness of War: The Civil War Letters of George W. Squier, Hoosier Volunteer.* Foreword by Frank L. Byrne. Knoxville: Univ. of Tennessee Press, 1998.

Dudley, Henry W. *Autobiography of Henry Walbridge Dudley.* Menasha, Wisc.: George Banta, 1913.

Dufour, Charles L. *The Night the War Was Lost*. Garden City, N.Y.: Doubleday, 1960.

Dugan, James. *History of Hurlbut's Fighting Fourth Division: And Especially the Marches, Toils, Privations, Adventures, and Battles of the Fourteenth Illinois Infantry*. Cincinnati: E. Morgan, 1863.

Duval, Miles P. *Cadiz to Cathay: The Story of the Long Struggle for a Waterway across the American Isthmus*. Stanford, Calif.: Stanford Univ. Press, 1940.

Dwight, Timothy. *Travels in New England and New York*. Vol. 3. New Haven, Conn.: Timothy Dwight, 1821–22. Reprint, edited by Barbara M. Solomon and Patricia M. King. 4 vols. Cambridge, Mass.: Belknap Press of Harvard Univ. Press, 1969.

Ealy, Lawrence O. *Yanqui Politics and the Isthmian Canal*. Univ. Park: Pennsylvania State Univ. Press, 1971.

Earhart, Mary. *Frances Willard: From Prayers to Politics*. Chicago: Univ. of Chicago Press, 1944.

Easterby, James H. *A History of the College of Charleston, Founded 1770*. Charleston, S.C.: Scribner, 1935.

Eaton, Clement. *The Freedom-of-Thought Struggle in the Old South*. Durham, N.C.: Duke Univ. Press, 1940. Reprint, New York: Harper and Row, 1964.

Eaton, John, with Ethel O. Mason. *Grant, Lincoln and the Freedmen: Reminiscences of the Civil War with Special Reference to the Work for the Contrabands and Freedmen of the Mississippi Valley*. New York: Longmans, Green, 1907.

Eckenrode, Hamilton J. *Rutherford B. Hayes: Statesman of Reunion*. New York: Dodd, Mead, 1930.

Edwards, George N. *A History of the Independent or Congregational Church of Charleston, South Carolina, Commonly known as Circular Church*. Boston: Pilgrim, 1947.

Eisenhower, John S. D. *Agent of Destiny: The Life and Times of General Winfield Scott*. New York: Free Press, 1997.

Encyclopedia of Connecticut Biography: Genealogical, s.v. "Memorial, Representative Citizens." New York: American Historical Society, n.d.

Evans, Henry C. *Chile and Its Relations with the United States*. Durham, N.C.: Duke Univ. Press, 1927. Reprint, New York: Johnson, 1971.

Evans, John H. *Joseph Smith: An American Prophet*. New York: Macmillan, 1936.

Faust, Patricia L., ed. *Historical Times Illustrated Encyclopedia of the Civil War*. New York: Harper and Row, 1986.

Fellman, Michael. *Citizen Sherman: A Life of William Tecumseh Sherman*. New York: Random House, 1995.

———. *Inside War: The Guerrilla Conflict in Missouri during the American Civil War*. New York: Oxford Univ. Press, 1989.

Fertig, James W. *The Secession and Reconstruction of Tennessee*. Chicago: Univ. of Chicago Press, 1898.

Fisher, Noel C. "Prepare Them for My Coming: General William T. Sherman, Total War, and Pacification in West Tennessee." *Tennessee Historical Quarterly* 51 (Summer 1992): 75–86.

Fleming, Denna F. *The Treaty Veto of the American Senate*. New York: G. P. Putman's Sons, 1930.

Flick, Alexander C. *Samuel Jones Tilden: A Study in Political Sagacity.* New York: Dodd, Mead, 1939. Reprint, Port Washington, N.Y.: Kennikat, 1963.

———. *Reconstruction: America's Unfinished Revolution, 1863–1877.* New York: Harper and Row, 1988.

Frazier, Donald S. *Blood and Treasure: Confederate Empire in the Southwest.* College Station: Texas A&M Univ. Press, 1995.

Freehling, William W. *Prelude to Civil War: The Nullification Controversy in South Carolina, 1816–1836.* New York: Harper and Row, 1966.

———. The *Road to Disunion.* Vol. 1: *Secessionists at Bay, 1776–1854.* New York: Oxford Univ. Press, 1990.

Freemon, Frank R. *Gangrene and Glory: Medical Care during the American Civil War.* Madison, N.J.: Fairleigh Dickinson Univ. Press, 1998.

Freidel, Frank. *Francis Lieber: Nineteenth-Century Liberal.* Baton Rouge: Louisiana State Univ. Press, 1947.

———. "General Orders 100 and Military Government." *Mississippi Valley Historical Review* 32 (Mar. 1946): 541–56.

Fuchs, Richard L. *An Unerring Fire: The Massacre at Fort Pillow.* Rutherford, N.J.: Fairleigh Dickinson Univ. Press, 1994.

Fuess, Claude M. *The Life of Caleb Cushing.* Vol. 2. New York: Harcourt, Brace, 1923.

Furnas, Joseph C. *The Life and Times of the Late Demon Rum.* New York: G. P. Putman's Sons, 1965.

Futrell, Robert J. "Federal Military Government in the South, 1861–1865." *Military Affairs: Journal of the American Military Institute* 15 (Dec. 1951): 181–91.

Garner, James W. *Reconstruction in Mississippi.* New York: Macmillan, 1901. Reprint, Gloucester, Mass.: Peter Smith, 1964.

Geffen, Elizabeth M. "Philadelphia Unitarianism (1796–1861)." Ph.D. diss., Univ. of Pennsylvania, 1958.

Gerteis, Louis S. *From Contraband to Freedman: Federal Policy Toward Southern Blacks, 1861–1865.* Westport, Conn.: Greenwood, 1973.

Gienapp, William E. *The Origins of the Republican Party, 1852–1856.* New York: Oxford Univ. Press, 1987.

Gilman, Caroline. *Record of Inscriptions in the Cemetery and Building of the Unitarian, Formerly Denominated the Independent Church, Archdale Street, Charleston, S.C., from 1777 to 1860.* Charleston, S.C.: Walker, Evans, 1860.

Graf, Leroy P., and Ralph W. Haskins, et al., eds. *The Papers of Andrew Johnson.* 16 vols. Knoxville: Univ. of Tennessee Press, 1967–2000.

Grant, Ulysses S. *Personal Memoirs of U. S. Grant.* Vol. 1. New York: Charles L. Webster, 1885–86.

Gray, Edgar L. "The Career of William Henry Smith, Politician-Journalist." Ph.D. diss., Ohio State Univ., 1951.

Grayson, William J. *James Louis Petigru: A Biographical Sketch.* New York: Harper and Brothers, 1866.

Griffin, Clifford S. *Their Brothers' Keepers: Moral Stewardship in the United States, 1800–1865.* New Brunswick, N.J.: Rutgers Univ. Press, 1960.

Grosh, Aaron B. *The Odd Fellow's Manual: Illustrating the History, Principles, and Government of the Order, and the Instructions and Duties of Every Degree, Station, and Office.* Philadelphia: H. C. Peck and Theo. Bliss, 1853.

Gue, Benjamin F. *History of Iowa, from the Earliest Times to the Beginning of the Twentieth Century, Four Volumes.* Vol. 2: *The Civil War.* New York: Century History, 1903.

Haas, Garland A. *To the Mountain of Fire and Beyond: The Fifty-third Indiana Regiment from Corinth to Glory.* Carmel: Guild Press of Indiana, 1997.

Hagy, James W. *Directories for the City of Charleston, South Carolina for the Years 1830–31, 1835–36, 1836, 1837–38, and 1840–41.* Baltimore: Genealogical, 1997.

Hallum, John. *Reminiscences of the Civil War.* n.p.: 1902. Reprint, Little Rock, Ark: Tunnah and Pittard, 1903.

———. *The Diary of an Old Lawyer, Or, Scenes behind the Curtain.* Nashville, Tenn.: Southwestern, 1895.

Hamer, Philip M. "Great Britain, the United States, and the Negro Seamen Acts, 1822–1848." *Journal of Southern History* 1 (Feb.–Nov. 1935): 3–28.

Harrington, Fred H. *Fighting Politician: Major General N. P. Banks.* Philadelphia: Univ. of Pennsylvania Press, 1948.

Harris, J. O. "Recollections of an Army Surgeon." *Blue and Gray: The Patriotic American Magazine* 3 (Mar. 1894): 137–42.

Harris, N. Dwight. *The History of Negro Servitude in Illinois and of the Slavery Agitation in That State, 1719–1864.* Chicago: A. C. McClurg, 1904.

Hartje, Robert G. *Van Dorn: The Life and Times of a Confederate General.* Nashville, Tenn.: Vanderbilt Univ. Press, 1967.

Haskell, Fritz, ed. and comp. "Diary of Colonel William Camm, 1861 to 1865." *Journal of the Illinois State Historical Society* 18 (Jan. 1926): 793–969.

Hearn, Chester G. *The Capture of New Orleans 1862.* Baton Rouge: Louisiana State Univ. Press, 1995.

———. *When the Devil Came Down to Dixie: Ben Butler in New Orleans.* Baton Rouge: Louisiana State Univ. Press, 1997.

Henry, Robert S., ed. *As They Saw Forrest: Some Recollections and Comments of Contemporaries.* Jackson, Tenn.: McCowat-Mercer, 1956.

Hesseltine, William B. *The South in American History.* New York: Prentice Hall, 1937 (as *A History of the South*). Reprint, New York: Prentice Hall, 1943, 1947.

———. *Ulysses S. Grant: Politician.* New York: Dodd, Mead, 1935. Reprint, New York: Frederick Ungar, 1967.

Heyman, Max L., Jr. *Prudent Soldier: A Biography of Major General E. R. S. Canby, 1817–1873: His Military Service in the Indian Campaigns, in the Mexican War, in California, New Mexico, Utah, and Oregon; in the Civil War in the Trans-Mississippi West, and as Military Governor in the Post-War South.* Glendale, Calif.: Arthur H. Clark, 1959.

Hicken, Victor. "From Vandalia to Vicksburg: The Political and Military Career of John A. McClernand." Ph.D. diss., Univ. of Illinois, 1955.

———. *Illinois in the Civil War.* Urbana: Univ. of Illinois Press, 1966.

Higginbotham, R. Don. "The Martial Spirit in the Antebellum South: Some Further Speculations in a National Context." *Journal of Southern History* 58 (Feb. 1992): 3–26.

Hinman, R. R. *Catalogue of the Names of the First Puritan Settlers of the Colony of Connecticut, with the Time of Their Arrival in the Colony.* Hartford: E. Gleason, 1846.

Hinsdale, Burke A., ed. *The Works of James Abram Garfield.* Vol. 2. Boston: James R. Osgood, 1882–83.

Hirshon, Stanley P. *Farewell to the Bloody Shirt: Northern Republicans and the Southern Negro, 1877–1893.* Bloomington: Indiana Univ. Press, 1962.

Hoar, George F. *Autobiography of Seventy Years.* Vol. 1. New York: Charles Scribner's Sons, 1903.

Hoge, Mrs. A. H. (Jane). *The Boys in Blue: Or Heroes of the "Rank and File."* Introduction by Thomas M. Eddy. New York: E. B. Treat, 1867.

Holland, Mary G. *Our Army Nurses: Stories from Women in the Civil War.* Introduction by Daniel J. Hoisington. Roseville, Minn.: Edinborough, 1998.

Hollandsworth, James G., Jr. *Pretense of Glory: The Life of General Nathaniel P. Banks.* Baton Rouge: Louisiana State Univ. Press, 1998.

Holt, Michael F. *The Rise and Fall of the American Whig Party: Jacksonian Politics and the Onset of the Civil War.* New York: Oxford Univ. Press, 1999.

Holt, W. Stull. *Treaties Defeated by the Senate: A Study of the Struggle between President and Senate over the Conduct of Foreign Relations.* Baltimore: Johns Hopkins Univ. Press, 1933.

Holzer, Harold, ed. *The Lincoln-Douglas Debates: The First Complete, Unexpurgated Text.* New York: HarperCollins, 1993.

Hoogenboom, Ari A. *Rutherford B. Hayes: Warrior and President.* Lawrence: Univ. Press of Kansas, 1995.

Hooper, Ernest W. "Memphis, Tennessee: Federal Occupation and Reconstruction, 1862–1870." Ph.D. diss., Univ. of North Carolina, 1957.

Horner, Harlan H. "Lincoln Rebukes a Senator." *Journal of the Illinois State Historical Society* 44 (Summer 1951): 103–19.

Horner, Henry. "Grand Orators of Illinois: Eloquent Address Delivered at the 1924 Grand Lodge Meeting." *Masonic Chronicler* (Dec. 27, 1924): 16–18.

Houzeau, Jean-Charles. *My Passage at the New Orleans Tribune: A Memoir of the Civil War Era.* Edited and with an introduction by David C. Rankin. Translated by Gerard F. Denault. Baton Rouge: Louisiana State Univ. Press, 1984.

Howe, David W. *The Political Culture of the American Whigs.* Chicago: Univ. of Chicago Press, 1979.

Howe, Mark Anthony D., ed. *Home Letters of General Sherman.* New York: Charles Scribner's Sons, 1909.

Hubbell, John T., and James W. Geary, eds. *Biographical Dictionary of the Union: Northern Leaders of the Civil War.* Advisory ed. Jon L. Wakelyn. Westport, Conn.: Greenwood, 1995.

Huber, Leonard V. *New Orleans: A Pictorial History.* Foreword by Charles L. Dufour. New York: Crown, 1971.

Hughes, Nathaniel C., Jr. *The Battle of Belmont: Grant Strikes South.* Chapel Hill: Univ. of North Carolina Press, 1991.

Hughes, William H. "John Hallum, Lawyer and Historian." *Arkansas Historical Quarterly* 10 (Autumn 1951): 258–67.

Hunt, Gaillard, comp. *Israel, Elihu, and Cadwallader Washburn: A Chapter in American Biography.* New York: Macmillan, 1926.

Hurlbert, William H. *Meddling and Muddling: Mr. Blaine's Foreign Policy; Being a Review of His Nine Months' Tenure of the State Department; In a Letter to the Editor of the* New York Herald. New York: private printing, 1884.

Hurlbut, Henry H. *The Hurlbut Genealogy, Or Record of the Descendants of Thomas Hurlbut, of Saybrook and Wethersfield, Conn., Who Came to America as Early as the Year 1637.* Albany, N.Y.: Joel Munsell's Sons, 1888.

Hurlbut, Martin Luther. "Reply to the Charleston *Southern Intelligencer.*" *Unitarian Defendant* 1 (June 1822): 1–2.

Hurlbut, Stephen A. "Late Martin L. Hurlbut: With a Memoir of the Author." *Christian Examiner* 35 (Sept. 1843): 32–44.

———. *Oration Delivered at the Anniversary Celebration of the Independent Order of Odd Fellows, of the State of South-Carolina, January 1, 1842.* Charleston, S.C.: Grand Lodge, 1842.

Hurlbut, Stephen A., L. H. D. *Between Peace and War: A Report to Lincoln from Charleston, 1861. In the Midst of War: A Letter from Shiloh, 1862. Edited from the Manuscripts of Maj.-Gen. Stephen A. Hurlbut.* Charleston, S.C.: St. Albans Press, 1953.

Hutchins, Robert M., ed. *Letters from Lloyd Lewis, Showing Steps in the Research for his Biography of U. S. Grant.* Boston: Little, Brown, 1950.

Jenkins, Ida P., and Ruby H. Ellis, et al., comps. *Lineage Book, National Society of the Daughters of the American Colonists.* 32 vols. Washington, D.C.: Judd and Detweiller, 1929–97.

Jewey, Elizabeth H., ed. "Marriage and Death Notices from the *City Gazette* of Charleston, S.C." *South Carolina Historical and Genealogical Magazine* 44 (July 1943): 148–54.

Johannsen, Robert W. *Stephen A. Douglas.* New York: Oxford Univ. Press, 1973. Reprint, Urbana: Univ. of Illinois Press, 1997.

Johns, Jane M. *Personal Recollections of Early Decatur: Abraham Lincoln, Richard J. Oglesby, and the Civil War, 1849–1865.* Ed. Howard C. Schaub. Decatur, Ill.: Daughters of the American Revolution, 1912.

Johnson, Ludwell H. "Contraband Trade during the Last Year of the Civil War." *Mississippi Valley Historical Review* 49 (Mar. 1963): 635–52.

———. "Northern Profit and Profiteers: The Cotton Rings of 1864–1865." *Civil War History: A Journal of the Middle Period* 12 (June 1966): 101–15.

———. *Red River Campaign: Politics and Cotton in the Civil War.* Baltimore: Johns Hopkins Univ. Press, 1958.

Johnson, Thomas C. *The Life and Letters of Benjamin Morgan Palmer.* Nashville, Tenn.: Cumberland, 1906.

Johnson, Timothy D. *Winfield Scott: The Quest for Military Glory.* Lawrence: Univ. Press of Kansas, 1998.

Johnston, Wesley. "Mortality Schedule Remarks." *Illinois State Genealogical Society Quarterly* 9 (Mar. 1977): 47.

Johnston, William P. "Albert Sidney Johnston at Shiloh." In *Battles and Leaders of the Civil War, Being for the Most Part Contributions by Union and Confederate Officers,*

Based upon "The Century Series." Vol. 1. Ed. Robert U. Johnson and Clarence C. Buel. New York: Century, 1884–88.

Jones, George R. *Joseph Russell Jones.* Ed. Richard Penn Hartung. Chicago: George R. Jones, 1964.

Jones, James P. *"Black Jack": John A. Logan and Southern Illinois in the Civil War Era.* Tallahassee: Florida State Univ. Press, 1967.

———. *John A. Logan: Stalwart Republican from Illinois.* Tallahassee: Univ. Press of Florida, 1982.

Jones, Katharine M. *Heroines of Dixie: Confederate Women Tell Their Story of the War.* Indianapolis: Bobbs-Merrill, 1955.

Jones, Thomas B. *Complete History of the 46th Regiment Illinois Volunteer Infantry.* Freeport, Ill.: W. H. Wagner, 1907.

Jordan, Winthrop D. *White over Black: American Attitudes toward the Negro, 1550–1812.* Chapel Hill: Univ. of North Carolina Press, 1968.

Kaiser, Leo M., ed. "'In Sight of Vicksburg': Private Diary of a Northern War Correspondent." *Historical Bulletin* 24 (May 1956): 202–21.

Karamanski, Theodore J. *Rally 'Round the Flag: Chicago and the Civil War.* Chicago: Nelson-Hall, 1993.

Kellogg, Mary E., comp. *Army Life of an Illinois Soldier, Including a Day-by-Day Record of Sherman's March to the Sea: Letters and Diary of Charles W. Wills.* Foreword by John Y. Simon. Carbondale: Southern Illinois Univ. Press, 1996.

Kendall, John S., ed. "Christ Church and General Butler." *Louisiana Historical Quarterly* 4 (Oct. 1940): 1241–57.

Kennett, Lee. *Sherman: A Soldier's Life.* New York: HarperCollins, 2001.

Kerby, Robert L. *Kirby Smith's Confederacy: The Trans-Mississippi South, 1863–1865.* New York: Columbia Univ. Press, 1972.

King, Ameda R. "The Last Years of the Whig Party in Illinois: 1847 to 1856." In *Transactions of the Illinois State Historical Society for the Year 1925.* Vol. 32. Springfield: Board of Trustees of the Illinois State Historical Library, 1900–36, 1953. 108–54.

King, G. Wayne. "The Civil War Career of Hugh Judson Kilpatrick." Ph.D. diss., Univ. of South Carolina, 1969.

Kiper, Richard L. *Major General John Alexander McClernand: Politician in Uniform.* Kent, Ohio: Kent State Univ. Press, 1999.

Klein, Maury. *Days of Defiance: Sumter, Secession, and the Coming of the Civil War.* New York: Knopf, 1997.

Korn, Bertram W. *American Jewry and the Civil War.* Introduction by Allan Nevins. Philadelphia: Jewish Publication Society of America, 1951.

Krout, John A. The *Origins of Prohibition.* 2d ed. New York: Knopf, 1925. Reprint, New York: Russell and Russell, 1967.

Krug, Mark M. *Lyman Trumbull: Conservative Radical.* New York: A. S. Barnes, 1965.

Lamers, William M. *The Edge of Glory: A Biography of General William S. Rosecrans.* New York: Harcourt, Brace and World, 1961.

Lamon, Ward H. *Recollections of Abraham Lincoln, 1847–1865.* Ed. Dorothy Lamon. Chicago: A. C. McClurg, 1895.

LaPointe, Patricia M. "Military Hospitals in Memphis, 1861–1865." *Tennessee Historical Quarterly* 42 (Winter 1983): 325–42.

Leland, Charles G. *Memoirs, by Charles Godfrey Leland (Hans Breitman)*. New York: D. Appleton, 1893.

Lemaitve, Eduardo. *Panama y su separacion de Colombia*. Prologo por Abelardo Forero Benarides. Bogota: n.p., 1972.

"Letters from George S. Denison to Salmon P. Chase, May 15, 1862, to March 21, 1865." *Annual Report of the American Historical Association for the Year 1902, in Two Volumes* 2 (1902): 297–458.

Levy, George. *To Die in Chicago: Confederate Prisoners at Camp Douglas, 1862–1865*. Evanston, Ill.: Evanston Pub., 1994.

Lewis, Lloyd. *Captain Sam Grant*. Boston: Little, Brown, 1950.

———. *Sherman: Fighting Prophet*. New York: Harcourt, Brace and World, 1960.

Lewis, Selma S. *A Biblical People in the Bible Belt: The Jewish Community of Memphis, Tennessee, 1840s–1960s*. Macon, Ga.: Mercer Univ. Press, 1998.

Lincolniana: In Memoriam. Boston: William V. Spencer, 1865.

Litwack, Leon F. *North of Slavery: The Negro in the Free States, 1790–1860*. Chicago: Univ. of Chicago Press, 1961.

Livermore, Mary A. *My Story of the War: A Woman's Narrative of Four Years Personal Experience*. Hartford, Conn.: A. D. Worthington, 1890.

Lofton, John. *Insurrection in South Carolina: The Turbulent World of Denmark Vesey*. Yellow Springs, Ohio: Antioch, 1964.

Logan, Mary C. *Reminiscences of a Soldier's Wife: An Autobiography*. New York: Charles Scribner's Sons, 1913.

Logsdon, Joseph. *Horace White: Nineteenth Century Liberal*. Westport, Conn.: Greenwood, 1971.

Longacre, Edward G. "'A Perfect Ishmaelite': General 'Baldy' Smith." *Civil War Times Illustrated* 15 (Dec. 1976): 10–20.

———. "Judson Kilpatrick." *Civil War Times Illustrated* 10 (Apr. 1971): 24–33.

Lowrey, Walter M. "The Political Career of James Madison Wells." *Louisiana Historical Quarterly* 31 (July 1948): 995–1123.

Lowry, Thomas P. The *Story the Soldiers Wouldn't Tell: Sex in the Civil War*. Foreword by Robert K. Krick. Mechanicsburg, Pa.: Stackpole Books, 1994.

Ludlow, Daniel H., ed. *Encyclopedia of Mormonism: The History, Scripture, Doctrine, and Procedure of the Church of Jesus Christ of Latter-Day Saints*. 4 vols. New York: Macmillan, 1992.

Lusk, David W. *Politics and Politicians: A Succinct History of the Politics of Illinois from 1856 to 1884, With Anecdotes and Incidents, and Appendix from 1809 to 1856*. Springfield, Ill.: H. W. Rokker, 1884.

Lynch, D. Patricio. *Memoira Que el Contra-Almirante D. Patricio Lynch, Jeneral en Jefe del Ejercito de Operaciones en el Norte del Peru presenta al Supremo Gobierno de Chile*. Lima, Peru: n.p., 1882.

Mack, Gerstle. *The Land Divided: A History of the Panama Canal and Other Isthmian Projects*. New York: Knopf, 1944.

Malone, Dumas, and Allen Johnson, eds. *Dictionary of American Biography.* 20 vols. and index. New York: Charles Scribner's Sons, 1928–36.

Marcus, Jacob R. *Memoirs of American Jews, 1775–1865.* Vol. 2. New York: American Book–Stratford Press, 1955.

Marsh, Charles W. *Recollections, 1837–1910.* Chicago: Farm Implement News, 1910.

Marten, James. "A Glimpse at Occupied New Orleans: The Diary of Thomas H. Duval of Texas, 1863–1865." *Louisiana History* 30 (Summer 1989): 303–16.

Martin, Samuel J. *"Kill-Cavalry," Sherman's Merchant of Terror: The Life of Union General Hugh Judson Kilpatrick.* Madison, N.J.: Fairleigh Dickinson Univ. Press, 1996.

Mason, John. "A Brief History of the Pequot War; Especially of the memorable Taking of Their Fort at Mistick in Connecticut in 1637. Written by Captain John Mason, a principal Actor therein, as then chief Captain and Commander of Connecticut Forces." *Collections of the Massachusetts Historical Society.* 2d ser. Vol. 8. Introduction and notes by Thomas Prince. Boston: S. Kneeland and T. Green, 1736. Reprint, Boston: Massachusetts Historical Society, 1819. Reprint, New York: Johnson, 1968. 120–53.

Maurtua, Victor M. The *Question of the Pacific.* Santiago, Chile: n.p., 1882. Reprint, translated by George F. Lasher. Philadelphia: F. A. Pezet, 1901.

McConnell, Stuart. *Glorious Contentment: The Grand Army of the Republic, 1865–1900.* Chapel Hill: Univ. of North Carolina Press, 1992.

McCormack, Thomas J., ed. *Memoirs of Gustave Koerner, 1809–1896: Life Sketches Written at the Suggestion of His Children.* Vol. 2. Cedar Rapids, Iowa: Torch, 1909.

McCrary, Peyton. *Abraham Lincoln and Reconstruction: The Louisiana Experiment.* Princeton, N.J.: Princeton Univ. Press, 1978.

McDonough, James L. *Shiloh: In Hell before Night.* Knoxville: Univ. of Tennessee Press, 1977.

McFeely, William S. *Grant: A Biography.* New York: W. W. Norton, 1981.

M'Gillicudy, T. D. "General Grant's First Service in the War." *Confederate Veteran* 16 (Feb. 1908): 62.

McKitrick, Eric L. *Andrew Johnson and Reconstruction.* Chicago: Univ. of Chicago Press, 1960.

McLemore, Richard A., ed. *A History of Mississippi.* Vol. 1. Hattiesburg: Univ. and College Press of Mississippi, 1973.

McMurry, Richard M. "Sherman's Meridian Campaign." *Civil War Times Illustrated* 14 (May 1975): 24–32.

Meerse, David E. "Buchanan, the Patronage, and the Lecompton Constitution: A Case Study." *Civil War History: A Journal of the Middle Period* 41 (Dec. 1995): 291–312.

Meriwether, Colyer. *History of Higher Education in South Carolina, with a Sketch of the Free School System.* Washington, D.C.: GPO, 1889. Reprint, Spartanburg, S.C.: Reprint Company, 1972.

Meriwether, Elizabeth A. *Recollections of Ninety-two Years, 1824–1916.* Nashville: Tennessee Historical Commission, 1958.

Messner, William M. *Freedom and Ideology of Free Labor: Louisiana, 1862–1865.* Lafayette: Univ. of Southwestern Louisiana, 1978.

Meyer, Isidore S., ed. "The American Jew in the Civil War: Catalog of the Exhibit of the Civil War Centennial Historical Commission." *Publication of the American Jewish Historical Society* 50 (June 1961): 263–408.

Miller, Francis T., ed. *The Photographic History of the Civil War, in Ten Volumes*. Vol. 10. New York: Review of Reviews, 1912. Reprint, with an introduction by Henry S. Commager, New York: Thomas Yoseloff, 1957.

Millington, Herbert. *American Diplomacy and the War of the Pacific*. New York: Columbia Univ. Press, 1948.

Molloy, Robert. *Charleston: A Gracious Heritage*. New York: D. Appleton-Century, 1947.

Moneyhon, Carl H. *The Impact of the Civil War and Reconstruction on Arkansas: Persistence in the Midst of Ruin*. Baton Rouge: Louisiana State Univ. Press, 1994.

Moore, Frank, ed. *The Rebellion Record: A Diary of American Events*. 12 vols. and supplement. New York: G. P. Putman, 1862–65.

Moore, John B. *A Digest of International Law as Embodied in Diplomatic Discussions, Treaties and Other International Agreements, International Awards, the Decisions of Municipal Courts, and the Writings of Jurists*. Vol. 3. Washington, D.C.: GPO, 1906.

Moore, John H., ed. "The Abiel Abbot Journals: A Yankee Preacher in Charleston Society, 1818–1827." *South Carolina Historical Magazine* 68 (Apr. 1967): 51–73.

Moorhead, Virginia B., ed. *Boone County Then and Now, 1835–1976: A History in Words and Pictures by Her Sons and Daughters to Celebrate the Bicentennial of the Signing of the Declaration of Independence*. Belvidere: Boone County Centennial Commission, 1976.

Morgan, Forrest, ed. *Connecticut as a Colony and as a State, Or One of the Original Thirteen*. Vol. 1. Hartford: Society of Connecticut, 1904.

Morris, Robert C. *Reading, 'Riting, and Reconstruction: The Education of Freedmen in the South 1861–1870*. Chicago: Univ. of Chicago Press, 1981.

Morse, Jedidiah. *The American Universal Geography: Or a View of the Present State of All the Empires, Kingdoms, States and Republiks in the Known World, and of the United States in Particular. In Two Parts*. Pt. 1. Boston: J. T. Buckingham, 1805.

Moses, John. *Illinois: Historical and Statistical, Comprising the Essential Facts of Its Planting and Growth as a Province, County, Territory, and State*. 2 vols. Chicago: Fergus, 1889–92.

Most Worthy Grand Lodge of Charleston, South Carolina, First Public Procession of the Independent Order of Odd Fellows, of the State of South-Carolina, Saturday, January 1st, 1842. Charleston, S.C.: Burges and James, 1842.

Muzzey, David S. *James G. Blaine: A Political Idol of Other Days*. New York: Dodd, Mead, 1935.

Myers, Robert M., ed. *The Children of Pride: A True Story of Georgia and the Civil War*. New Haven, Conn.: Yale Univ. Press, 1972.

Nash, Howard P. *Stormy Petrel: The Life and Times of General Benjamin F. Butler, 1818–1893*. Rutherford, N.J.: Fairleigh Dickinson Univ. Press, 1969.

Neely, Mark E., ed. "John Tauro to Abraham Lincoln, January 7, 1865: New Orleans under the 'Beast' and Banks." *Lincoln Lore* 1624 (June 1973): 1–4.

———. "Lincoln's Springfield Friends: Friends of the Negro." *Lincoln Lore* 1899 (Sept. 1979): 1–3.

Neilson, James W. *Shelby M. Cullom: Prairie State Republican*. Urbana: Univ. of Illinois Press, 1962.

Nellis, David M. "The Damned Rascal: Benjamin F. Butler in New Orleans." *Civil War Times Illustrated* 12 (Oct. 1973): 4–10, 41–47.

Nelson, Russell K. "The Early Life and Congressional Career of Elihu B. Washburne." Ph.D. diss., Univ. of North Dakota, 1953.

Nevins, Allan. *Frémont: Pathmarker of the West.* Vol. 2: *Frémont in the Civil War.* New York: D. Appleton-Century, 1939. Reprint, New York: Frederick Ungar, 1961.

———. *Hamilton Fish: The Inner History of the Grant Administration.* Introduction by John B. Moore. 2 vols. New York: Dodd, Mead, 1937. Reprint, New York: Frederick Ungar, 1957, 1967.

———. *The War for the Union.* Vol. 1: *The Improvised War, 1861–1862.* New York: Charles Scribner's Sons, 1959.

Nevins, Allan, and Milton H. Thomas, eds. *The Diary of George Templeton Strong.* 4 vols. New York: Macmillan, 1952.

Nickell, Franklin D. "Grant's Lieutenants in the West, 1861–1863." Ph.D. diss., Univ. of New Mexico, 1972.

Nicolay, John G., and John Hay. *Abraham Lincoln: A History.* Vol. 3. New York: Century, 1890–1909.

Nolan, Dick. *Benjamin Franklin Butler: The Damnedest Yankee.* Novato, Calif.: Presidio, 1991.

Nortrup, Jack J. "Richard Yates: Civil War Governor of Illinois." Ph.D. diss., Univ. of Illinois, 1960.

Oaks, Dallin H., and Marvin S. Hill. *Carthage Conspiracy: The Trial of the Accused Assassins of Joseph Smith.* 1975. Urbana: Univ. of Illinois Press, 1979.

Oates, Stephen B. *With Malice toward None: The Life of Abraham Lincoln.* New York: Harper and Row, 1977.

O'Brien, Michael, and David Moltke-Hansen, eds. *Intellectual Life in Antebellum Charleston.* Knoxville: Univ. of Tennessee Press, 1986.

Oliphant, Mary C. Simms, et al., eds. *The Letters of William Gilmore Simms.* Introduction by Donald Davidson. Vol. 1. Columbia: Univ. of South Carolina Press, 1952–82.

Overdyke, William D. *The Know-Nothing Party in the South.* Baton Rouge: Louisiana State Univ. Press, 1950. Reprint, Gloucester, Mass.: Peter Smith, 1968.

Palmer, Beverly W., and Holly B. Ochoa, eds. *The Selected Papers of Thaddeus Stevens.* Vol. 2. Pittsburgh: Univ. of Pittsburgh Press, 1997–98.

Palmer, George T. *A Conscientious Turncoat: The Story of John M. Palmer, 1817–1900.* New Haven, Conn.: Yale Univ. Press, 1941.

Palmer, John M. *Personal Recollections of John M. Palmer: The Story of an Earnest Life.* Cincinnati: Robert Clarke, 1901.

Parks, E. Taylor. *Colombia and the United States, 1765–1934.* Durham, N.C.: Duke Univ. Press, 1935.

Parks, Joseph H. "A Confederate Trade Center under Federal Occupation: Memphis, 1862 to 1865." *Journal of Southern History* 7 (Sept. 1941): 285–314.

Parrish, William E. *Frank Blair: Lincoln's Conservative.* Columbia: Univ. of Missouri Press, 1998.

Parton, James. *General Butler in New Orleans: History of the Administration of the Department of the Gulf in the Year 1862.* 8th ed. New York: Mason Brothers, 1864.

Pease, Theodore C., ed. *Illinois Election Returns, 1818–1848.* Springfield: Illinois State Historical Library, 1923.

Pease, Theodore C., and James G. Randall, eds. *The Diary of Orville Hickman Browning.* Vol. 1. Springfield: Illinois State Historical Library, 1927, 1933.

Pease, William H., and Jane H. Pease. *James Louis Petigru: Southern Conservative, Southern Dissenter.* Athens: Univ. of Georgia Press, 1995.

Perret, Geoffrey. *Ulysses S. Grant: Soldier and President.* New York: Random House, 1997.

Peskin, Allan. *Garfield: A Biography.* Kent, Ohio: Kent State Univ. Press, 1978.

Pierce, Lyman B. *History of the Second Iowa Cavalry: Containing a Detailed Account of its Organization, Marches, and the Battles in Which It Has Participated; Also, a Complete Roster of Each Company.* Burlington, Iowa: Hawk-Eye Steam Book and Job Printing Establishment, 1865.

Pike, Frederick B. *Chile and the United States, 1880–1962.* Notre Dame: Univ. Press of Notre Dame, 1963.

Plummer, Mark A. *Lincoln's Rail-Splitter: Governor Richard J. Oglesby.* Urbana: Univ. of Illinois Press, 2001.

Pomerantz, Sidney I. "Election of 1876." In *History of American Presidential Elections, 1789–1984.* Ed. Arthur M. Schlesinger. 5 vols. New York: Chelsea House, 1971, 1986.

Pooley, William V. "The Settlement of Illinois from 1830 to 1850." *Bulletin of the Univ. of Wisconsin* 220 (May 1908): 1–595

Porter, James D. *Confederate Military History Extended Edition: A Library of Confederate States History, in Seventeen Volumes, Written by Distinguished Men of the South, and Edited by Gen. Clement A. Evans of Georgia.* Vol. 10: *Tennessee.* n.p: Confederate, 1899. Reprint, Wilmington, N.C.: Broadfoot, 1987–89.

Portrait and Biographical Album of McLean County, Ill. Chicago: Chapman Brothers, 1887.

Portrait and Biographical Album of Stephenson County, Ill., Containing Full Page Portraits and Biographical Sketches of Prominent and Representative Citizens of the County. Chicago: Chapman Brothers, 1888. Reprint, Mount Vernon, Ind.: Windmill, 1990.

Portrait and Biographical Record of Winnebago and Boone Counties, Illinois. Chicago: Biographical, 1892.

Potter, David M. *The Impending Crisis, 1848–1861.* Completed and edited by Don E. Fehrenbacher. New York: Harper and Row, 1976.

Proceedings of the Massachusetts Historical Society. 2d ser. Vol. 12. Boston: Massachusetts Historical Society, 1899. 1884–1903.

Quaife, M. M., ed. *Absalom Grimes: Confederate Mail Runner.* New Haven, Conn.: Yale Univ. Press, 1926.

Quenzel, Carrol H., ed. "A Billy Yank's Impressions of the South." *Tennessee Historical Quarterly* 12 (June 1953): 99–105.

Ramsay, David. *Ramsay's History of South Carolina, from Its First Settlement in 1670 to the Year 1808.* Vol. 2. Newberry, S.C.: W. J. Duffie, 1858.

Raum, Green B. *History of Illinois Republicanism Embracing a History of the Republican Party in the State to the Present Time.* Chicago: Rollins, 1900.

Record Book of Independent or Congregational Church, 1796–1824, Charleston County.
Columbia, S.C.: Works Progress Administration, 1940.

Rent Lists of Pews and Accounts, the Independent or Congregational Church, S.C., 1806–1820. Columbia, S.C.: Works Progress Administration, 1940.

Report of Maj.-Gen. Wm. F. Smith and Hon. James T. Brady, on the Official Conduct of General S. A. Hurlbut, and others, at New Orleans, April 12, 1865. Chicago: *Evening Journal* Book and Job Printing House, 1876.

Richardson, James D. *A Compilation of the Messages and Papers of the Presidents, 1789–1913.* Vol. 6. New York: Bureau of National Literature, 1897–1917.

Richardson, Joe M. *Christian Reconstruction: The American Missionary Association and Southern Blacks, 1861–1890.* Athens: Univ. of Georgia Press, 1986.

Riddle, Donald W. *Congressman Abraham Lincoln.* Urbana: Univ. of Illinois Press, 1957.

Robinson, David. *The Unitarians and the Universalists.* Westport, Conn.: Greenwood, 1985.

Rodriguez, Juan A. *Patricio Lynch: vicealmirante y general en jefe, Sintesis de la Guerra del Pacifico.* Santiago, Chile: Editorial Nascimento, 1967.

Rolle, Andrew F. *John Charles Frémont: Character as Destiny.* Norman: Univ. of Oklahoma Press, 1991.

Rosengarten, Theodore. *Tombee: Portrait of a Cotton Planter, with the Journal of Thomas B. Chaplin* (1822–1890). Edited and annotated with the assistance of Susan W. Walker. New York: William Morrow, 1986.

Ross, Earle D. *The Liberal Republican Movement.* Ithaca, N.Y.: Cornell Univ. Press, 1910. Reprint, with an introduction by John G. Sproat, Seattle: Univ. of Washington Press, 1970.

Ross, Theodore A. *Odd Fellowship: Its History and Manual.* Introduction by John H. White. New York: Hazen, 1889.

Rowland, Lawrence S., Alexander Moore, and George C. Rogers, Jr. *The History of Beaufort County, South Carolina.* Vol. 1. Columbia: Univ. of South Carolina Press, 1996.

Russell, William H. *My Diary North and South.* Edited and with an introduction by Fletcher Pratt. New York: Harper and Brothers, 1954.

Sager, Juliet G. "Stephen A. Hurlbut, 1815–1882." *Journal of the Illinois State Historical Society* 28 (July 1935): 53–80.

Savage, James. *A Genealogical Dictionary of the First Settlers of New England, Showing Three Generations of Those Who Came before May, 1692, on the Basis of the Farmer's Register.* Vol. 2. New York: 1860–62. Reprint, Baltimore: Genealogical, 1965.

Schutz, Wallace J., and Walter N. Trenerry. *Abandoned by Lincoln: A Military Biography of General John Pope.* Urbana: Univ. of Illinois Press, 1990.

Scott, Franklin W. *Newspapers and Periodicals of Illinois, 1814–1879.* Springfield: Illinois State Historical Library, 1910.

Sears, Stephen W., ed. *Mr. Dunn Browne's Experiences in the Army: The Civil War Letters of Samuel W. Fiske.* New York: Fordham Univ. Press, 1998.

Segal, Charles M. "Isachar Zacharie: Lincoln's Chiropodist." *Publication of the American Jewish Historical Society* 43 (Dec. 1953): 71–126.

Sellers, Charles G., Jr. "The Election of 1844." In *History of American Presidential Elections, 1789–1984.* Ed. Arthur M. Schlesinger, Jr. 5 vols. New York: Chelsea House, 1971, 1986.

Shannon, Fred A., ed. *The Civil War Letters of Sergeant Onley Andrus.* Urbana: Univ. of Illinois Press, 1947.

Sherman, William T. *Memoirs of Gen. W. T. Sherman, Written by Himself.* Vol. 1. New York: Charles L. Webster, 1891.

Siciliano, Stephen N. *Major General William Farrar Smith: Critic of Defeat and Engineer of Victory.* Ph.D. diss., College of William and Mary, 1984. Ann Arbor, Mich.: Univ. Microfilms International, 1991.

Simon, John Y. "From Galena to Appomattox: Grant and Washburne." *Journal of the Illinois State Historical Society* 58 (Summer 1965): 165–89.

———. "That Obnoxious Order." *Civil War Times Illustrated* 23 (Oct. 1984): 12–17.

———. ed. *The Papers of Ulysses S. Grant.* 26 vols. to date. Carbondale: Southern Illinois Univ. Press, 1967–.

———. ed. *The Personal Memoirs of Julia Dent Grant [Mrs. Ulysses S. Grant].* n.p.: 1886–94. Reprint, New York: G. P. Putman's Sons, 1975.

Simpson, Amos E., and Vaughan Baker. "Michael Hahn: Steady Patriot." *Louisiana History* 13 (Summer 1972): 229–52.

Simpson, Brooks D., and Jean V. Berlin, eds. *Sherman's Civil War: Selected Correspondence of William T. Sherman, 1860–1865.* Chapel Hill: Univ. of North Carolina Press, 1999.

Simpson, Brooks D. *Ulysses S. Grant: Triumph over Adversity, 1822–1865.* New York: Houghton Mifflin, 2000.

Smart, James G., ed. *A Radical View: The "Agate" Dispatches of Whitelaw Reid, 1861–1865.* Vol. 1. Memphis, Tenn.: Memphis State Univ. Press, 1976.

Smith, Jean E. *Grant.* New York: Simon and Schuster, 2001.

Smith, Joseph. *Illusions of Conflict: Anglo-American Diplomacy Toward Latin America, 1865–1896.* Pittsburgh: Univ. of Pittsburgh Press, 1979.

Sparks, Edwin E., ed. *Collections of the Illinois State Historical Library.* Vol. 3: *Lincoln Series* in 3 vols., Vol. 1: *The Lincoln-Douglas Debates of 1858.* Springfield: Illinois State Historical Library, 1908.

Speer, Lonnie R. *Portals to Hell: Military Prisons of the Civil War.* Mechanicsburg, Pa.: Stackpole, 1997.

Sproat, John G. *"The Best Men": Liberal Reformers in the Gilded Age.* New York: Oxford Univ. Press, 1968.

Steenrod, Robert L., comp. *Boone County, Illinois: Marriage Records, 1838–1860.* Madison: State Historical Society of Wisconsin at Madison, 1960.

Stern, Philip Van D. *Prologue to Sumter: The Beginnings of the Civil War from the John Brown Raid to the Surrender of Fort Sumter.* Bloomington: Indiana Univ. Press, 1961.

Stillwell, Leander. "In the Ranks at Shiloh." *Journal of the Illinois State Historical Society* 15 (Apr.–July 1922): 460–76.

———. *The Story of a Common Soldier of Army Life in the Civil War, 1861–1865.* 2d ed. Kansas City, Mo.: Franklin Hudson, 1920. Reprint, n.p. [Alexandria, Va.]: Time-Life Books, 1983.

Stoney, Samuel G., ed. "The Autobiography of William John Grayson." *South Carolina Historical and Genealogical Magazine* 48 (July 1947): 125–33; and 49 (July 1948): 163–69.

Stuart, Addison A. *Iowa Colonels and Regiments: Being a History of Iowa Regiments in the War of the Rebellion; And Containing a Description of the Battles in Which They Have Fought.* Des Moines, Iowa.: Mills, 1865.

Swint, Henry L. *The Northern Teacher in the South, 1862–1870.* New York: Octagon, 1967.

Sword, W. Wiley. *Shiloh: Bloody April.* New York: William Morrow, 1974. Reprint, Dayton, Ohio: Morningside, 1983.

———. "The Battle of Shiloh." *Civil War Times Illustrated* 17 (May 1978): 4–50.

Tauro, Alberto. *Diccionario Enciclopedico del Peru.* Vol. 2. Lima, Peru: Editorial Mejia Baca, 1966.

Taylor, Joe G. *Louisiana Reconstructed, 1863–1877.* Baton Rouge: Louisiana State Univ. Press, 1974.

The Cyclopedia of Temperance and Prohibition: A Reference Book of Facts, Statistics, and General Information on All Phases of the Drink Question, the Temperance Movement and the Prohibition Agitation. New York: Funk and Wagnalls, 1891.

The Past and Present of Boone County, Illinois. Chicago: H. F. Kett, 1877.

The Rules of the South Carolina Society Established at Charlestown in the Said Province, September, 1737, Originally Incorporated, May 1, 1751. Reprint. Charleston: South Carolina Society, 1937.

Thomas, Benjamin P. *Abraham Lincoln: A Biography.* 9th ed. New York: Knopf, 1952. Reprint, New York: Knopf, 1967.

Thomas, Benjamin P., ed., *Three Years with Grant as Recalled by War Correspondent Sylvanus Cadwallader.* New York: Knopf, 1955.

Thomas, Richard J. "Caleb Blood Smith: Whig Orator and Politician: Lincoln's Secretary of Interior." Ph.D. diss., Indiana Univ., 1969.

Thompson, Seymour D. *Recollections with the Third Iowa Regiment.* Cincinnati: private printing, 1864.

Throne, Mildred, ed. *The Civil War Diary of Cyrus F. Boyd, Fifteenth Iowa Infantry 1861–1863.* Iowa City: State Historical Society of Iowa, 1953, 1976. Reprint, with a new introduction by E. B. Long, Millwood, N.Y.: Kraus, 1977.

Trefousse, Hans L. *Andrew Johnson: A Biography.* New York: Norton, 1989.

———. *Ben Butler: The South Called Him Beast!* New York: Twayne, 1957.

Trumbull, J. Hammond, and Charles J. Hoadly, eds. *The Public Records of the Colony of Connecticut, Prior to the Union with New Haven Colony, May, 1665.* 15 vols. Hartford, Conn.: Brown and Parsons, 1850–90. Reprint, New York: Ams, 1968.

Tucker, Glenn. *Hancock the Superb.* New York: Bobbs-Merrill, 1960.

Turkoly-Joczik, Robert L. "Frémont and the Western Department." *Missouri Historical Review* 82 (July 1988): 363–85.

Tyler, Alice F. *The Foreign Policy of James G. Blaine.* Minneapolis: Univ. Press of Minnesota, 1927. Reprint, Hamden, Conn.: Archon, 1965.

Van Deusen, Glyndon G. *Horace Greeley: Nineteenth-Century Crusader.* Washington, D.C.: American Historical Assn., 1953. Reprint, Philadelphia: Univ. of Pennsylvania Press, 1967.

————. *The Life of Henry Clay.* Boston: Little, Brown, 1937.

Vanwinkle, Alex. "Hell on the Hatchie." *Confederate Veteran* 16 (Dec. 1908): 632.

Veatch, William A. *James Clifford Veatch: Scholar, Solicitor, Statesman and Soldier.* Redmond, Ore.: private printing by W. A. Veatch, 1980.

Verlie, Emil J., ed. *Illinois Constitutions.* Springfield: Trustees of the Illinois State Historical Library, 1919.

Villard, Henry. *Memoirs of Henry Villard: Journalist and Financier, 1835–1900.* Vol. 1. Boston: Houghton, Mifflin, 1904.

Wade, Richard C. *Slavery in the Cities: The South 1820–1860.* New York: Oxford Univ. Press, 1964.

Wallace, Isabel. *Life and Letters of General W. H. L. Wallace.* Chicago: R. R. Donnelley, 1909.

Wallace, Lewis. *Lew Wallace: An Autobiography.* Vol. 2. New York: Harper and Brothers, 1906. Reprint, New York: Garrett, 1969.

Warmoth, Henry C. *War, Politics and Reconstruction: Stormy Days in Louisiana.* New York: Macmillan, 1930.

Warner, Ezra J. *Generals in Blue: Lives of the Union Commanders.* Baton Rouge: Louisiana State Univ. Press, 1964.

Wax, James A. "The Jews of Memphis: 1860–1865." *West Tennessee Historical Society Papers* 3 (1949): 39–89.

Way, William. *History of the New England Society of Charlestown, South Carolina for One Hundred Years, 1819–1919.* Introduction by Joseph W. Barnwell. Charleston, S.C.: New England Society, 1920.

Weber, Jesse P., ed. "Dedication of a Tablet Marking the Site at Decatur, Illinois, of the Old Wigwam in Which the Illinois State Republican Convention of 1860 Was Held." *Journal of the Illinois State Historical Society* 8 (Apr. 1915): 150–53.

Wheeler, Richard. *The Siege of Vicksburg.* New York: Thomas Y. Crowell, 1978.

White, Horace. *The Life of Lyman Trumbull.* Boston: Houghton Mifflin, 1913.

Whiteman, Maxwell, ed. "Kronikals of the Times: Memphis, 1862, by Abraham Ephraim Frankland." *American Jewish Archives* 9 (Oct. 1957): 83–125.

Who Was Who in America: Historical Volume (1607–1896). 11 vols. and indexes. Chicago: A. N. Marquis, 1963.

Williams, Charles R., ed. *Diary and Letters of Rutherford Birchard Hayes, Nineteenth President of the United States.* Vol. 3. Columbus: Ohio State Archaeological and Historical Society, 1924.

Wills, Brian S. *A Battle from the Start: The Life of Nathan Bedford Forrest.* New York: HarperCollins, 1992.

Wilson, James H. *Life and Services of William Farrar Smith, Major General, United States Volunteers in the Civil War.* Wilmington, Del.: John M. Rogers, 1904.

————. *The Life of John A. Rawlins, Lawyer, Assistant Adjutant-General, Chief of Staff, Major General of Volunteers, and Secretary of War.* New York: Neale, 1916.

————. *Under the Old Flag: Recollections of Military Operations in the War for the Union, the Spanish War the Boxer Rebellion, Etc.* Vol. 1. New York: D. Appleton, 1912.

Wilson, Keith. "Education as a Vehicle of Racial Control: Major General N. P. Banks in Louisiana, 1863–64." *Journal of Negro Education* 50 (Spring 1981): 156–70.

Winters, John D. *The Civil War in Louisiana.* Baton Rouge: Louisiana State Univ. Press, 1963.

Wittenmyer, Annie T. *Under the Guns: A Woman's Reminiscences of the Civil War.* Introduction by Julia Dent Grant. Boston: E. B. Stillings, 1895.

Wright, Conrad. *The Beginnings of Unitarianism in America.* 1955. Hamden, Conn.: Archon Books, 1976.

Wright, John S. "The Background and Formation of the Republican Party in Illinois, 1846–1860." Ph.D. diss., Univ. of Chicago, 1946.

Wyeth, John A. *That Devil Forrest: Life of General Nathan Bedford Forrest.* New York: Harper and Brothers, 1959.

Yates, Richard, II. *Serving the Republic: Richard Yates, Illinois Governor and Congressman, Son of Richard Yates, Civil War Governor, an Autobiography.* Ed. John H. Krenkel. Danville, Ill.: Interstate, 1968.

Yates, Richard, II, and Catherine Y. Pickering. *Richard Yates: Civil War Governor.* Ed. John H. Krenkel. Danville, Ill.: Interstate, 1966.

NEWSPAPERS AND PERIODICALS

Aurora Beacon, 1867, 1872

Baltimore Sun, 1844

Belvidere Republican, 1848

Belvidere Standard, 1851–68, 1870, 1872–74, 1876–82

Charleston Daily Courier, 1814–17, 1823, 1837–38, 1840–45, 1861, 1863

Charleston Mercury, 1840–45, 1861–63

Chicago Democrat, 1849

Chicago Evening Journal, 1848, 1861, 1872

Chicago Times, 1861, 1863, 1876

Chicago Tribune, 1861, 1863, 1866, 1872, 1874, 1876, 1882

Cincinnati Daily Commercial, 1861–65, 1876

Cincinnati Daily Enquirer, 1861

Cincinnati Daily Times, 1861, 1863–65

Cochabamba El Heraldo, 1881–82

Davenport Democrat and News, 1861, 1863

Des Moines Daily State Register, 1862–63

Dubuque Herald, 1861

Freeport Bulletin, 1858, 1860–63

Galena Weekly Northwestern Gazette, 1848, 1861

Illinois State Journal, 1848, 1850, 1852, 1858–67, 1880

Illinois State Register, 1861–63, 1865, 1880

Indianapolis Daily Journal, 1862, 1866

Indianapolis Daily State Sentinel, 1863–64

Janesville Gazette, 1879

Madison Democrat, 1872

Madison State Journal, 1872

Memphis Daily Appeal, 1861–64

Memphis Daily Bulletin, 1862–65
Mobile Advertiser and Register, 1863
Mompos La Palestra, 1871–72
New Orleans Bee, 1864–65
New Orleans (Times) Picayune, 1864–65, 1874
New York Herald, 1861
New York Times, 1861–65, 1869, 1871–76, 1881–82
New York Tribune, 1861–63, 1868, 1881–82
New York World, 1861–63, 1882
Philadelphia Inquirer and National Gazette, 1843
Quincy Daily Whig and Republican, 1861–62, 1864
Quincy Herald, 1861–63, 1865
Richmond Daily Dispatch, 1863–65
Richmond Enquirer, 1863–64
Richmond Sentinel, 1863
Richmond Whig, 1863–64
Rockford Republican, 1856, 1858, 1860–62
Sangamo Journal, 1847
St. Louis Missouri Democrat, 1861
St. Louis Missouri Republican, 1861–1865
The National Tribune, 1881–82, 1884–87
*The Nation: A Weekly Journal Devoted to Politics,
Literature, Science, and Art,* 1881
Washington Evening Star, 1861, 1873, 1875.

INDEX